Sugar and Slavery, Family and Race

Johns Hopkins Studies in Atlantic History and Culture

EDITED AND TRANSLATED BY
Elborg Forster and
Robert Forster

Sugar and Slavery,

 THE JOHNS HOPKINS UNIVERSITY PRESS
Baltimore and London

Family and Race

The Letters and Diary of Pierre Dessalles,
Planter in Martinique, 1808–1856

05 04 03 02 01 00 99 98 97 96   5 4 3 2 1

The Johns Hopkins University Press
2715 North Charles Street
Baltimore, Maryland 21218-4319
The Johns Hopkins Press Ltd., London

Library of Congress Cataloging-in-Publication Data will be found
at the end of this book.
A catalog record for this book is available from the British Library.

ISBN 0-8018-5153-X
ISBN 0-8018-5154-8 (pbk.)

Illustration, title page: Sugar plantation in the French Caribbean. *Encyclopédie, ou Dictionnaire universel des arts & des sciences, Recueil des Planches*, vol. 1, *Sucrerie* (1772), pl. 1, *Vue d'une habitation*. Detail: (1) Master's dwelling and its outbuildings; (2) some of the slave huts form one or two streets, depending on their number and location; (3) part of the meadow or pasture; (4) border or thick hedge separating the meadow from the cane fields; (5) part of the fields planted in sugar cane on slopes and on flat land; (6) water mill; (7) sugar building, with chimney and hangar for the furnaces; (8) gutter to bring water from the canal to the mill wheel; (9) runoff for the water from the mill; (10) one of the shacks for storing trash cane (i.e., crushed cane); (11) curing house or main storehouse to keep sugar after it is put in molds to let surplus syrup drip out and to clay it; (12) oven to dry sugar loaves; (13) high ground interspersed with plantings of manioc, banana groves, and provisioning grounds; (14) *morne*, which is what mountains that seem to stand by themselves are called in the Antilles.

Contents

Sugar and Slavery, Family and Race

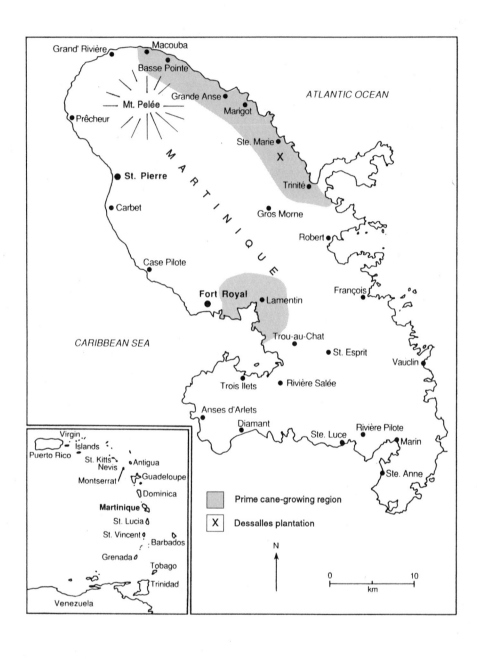

Grand' Rivière

Macouba

Basse Pointe

Grande Anse

Mt. Pelée

Marigot

Prêcheur

Ste. Marie

X

St. Pierre

Trinité

Carbet

Gros Morne

ATLANTIC OCEAN

M A R T I N I Q U E

Robert

Case Pilote

François

Fort Royal

Lamentin

Trou-au-Chat

CARIBBEAN SEA

St. Esprit

Vauclin

Rivière Salée

Trois Ilets

Anses d'Arlets

Diamant

Ste. Luce

Rivière Pilote

Marin

Ste. Anne

Virgin

Islands

Puerto Rico

St. Kitts

Nevis

Antigua

Montserrat

Guadeloupe

Dominica

Martinique

St. Lucia

St. Vincent

Barbados

Grenada

Tobago

Trinidad

Venezuela

Prime cane-growing region

X   Dessalles plantation

N

0   10
            km

Introduction
"Paternalism" in a Slave Society

> One pays a high price for fortune if it brings distress to the soul.
> Pierre Dessalles, 1825

Pierre Dieudonné Dessalles, Martinique planter, left a voluminous Journal for the period 1808 to 1857. An abbreviated version of the diary, supplemented by a series of letters, was published by Henri de Frémont (a descendant of Pierre Dessalles) and Léo Elisabeth between 1984 and 1988.[1] This volume presents a condensed and translated version of that publication.

Fortunately for the historian, Pierre Dessalles was a reflective and opinionated person. He did not limit himself to describing daily tasks, counting and consigning hogsheads of sugar, negotiating with factors and creditors, or disciplining a labor force of 200, though these were time-consuming operations, essential to the business operation of a sugar plantation. Dessalles interspersed his daily economic concerns with comments on the society around him—the slaves, the people of color, the white Creoles, the future of the colony, his own goals and family obligations, and what standards, moral and utilitarian, a white planter should uphold in this beautiful, bountiful, yet fragile island whose relations with France were slowly changing.

More broadly than Thomas Chaplin, the slave-owner from Sea-Island, Geor-

---

1. Henri de Frémont and Léo Elisabeth, ed., *Pierre Dessalles (1785–1857). La Vie d'un colon à la Martinique au XIXe siècle*, 4 vols (Courbevoie: private printing, 1984–88), hereafter cited as HF and LE.

gia, before the Civil War, or Thomas Thistlewood, the English landowner in Jamaica in the late eighteenth century,[2] Pierre Dessalles reflected on his island society, permitting the historian to reconstruct one man's attempt to cope with a world whose moorings were shifting. However formidable the challenges from the outside, Pierre Dessalles's values and goals were of a piece and cohered. With some minor adjustments at the time of slave emancipation in 1848, they lasted his entire lifetime. What were these values, and how did he apply them to his tropical island?

Eugene Genovese applies the term *paternalism* to slave society in the American South. In *Roll Jordan, Roll* he writes that "Southern paternalism, like every other paternalism, had little to do with Ole Massa's ostensible benevolence, kindness, and good cheer. It grew out of the necessity to discipline and morally justify a system of exploitation. It did encourage kindness and affection, but it simultaneously encouraged cruelty and hatred."[3]

Was Pierre Dessalles a paternalist, even an unconscious one, whose behavior reflected a belief in patriarchal authority (*patronage* was his word) founded on a strict social hierarchy prescribing deference and obedience from below and a "firm but just" protection from above? If so, what were the interlocking elements of his brand of paternalism? How was it adapted to slave society in Martinique? How did Dessalles's values confront and absorb the growing pressures for slave emancipation and full civil equality for the people of color? Did his paternalistic world survive the shock of the Revolution of 1848? Is Pierre Dessalles the authentic ancestor of the "Békés" of late-twentieth-century Martinique, the white planter elite whose code of behavior recalls, not the nineteenth-century French bourgeoisie, but an even earlier landed aristocracy?[4]

2. Theodore Rosengarten, *Tombee: Portrait of a Cotton Planter with the Journal of Thomas B. Chaplin, 1822–1890* (New York: Morrow, 1986) and Douglas Hall, ed., *In Miserable Slavery: Thomas Thistlewood in Jamaica, 1750–86* (Basingstoke: Macmillan, 1989). The original Thistlewood manuscript represents more than 10,000 pages and will surely yield more than Dessalles's journal. We eagerly await Philip Morgan's study based on the entire diary.

3. Eugene D. Genovese, *Roll Jordan, Roll: The World the Slaves Made* (New York: Vintage, 1976), 4. "Paternalism defined the involuntary labor of the slaves as a legitimate return to their masters for protection and direction" (5).

4. "Under no condition is the *mulâtre* permitted to enter the intimate family circle of the Béké as an associational equal. He is not included among the guests of private parties when female Békés are present." Marian Slater, *The Caribbean Family: Legitimacy in Martinique* (New York: St. Martin's, 1977), 62.

Politics, Religion, Family, Home

Consider political loyalties first. On January 21 of each year until his death in 1857, Pierre made an entry in his diary commemorating the execution of Louis XVI, usually commenting that this tragic event marked the beginning of a series of political and social disasters for France and the world. If only the violent *secte révolutionnaire* could be uprooted, the old world, especially the colonial world, would return to normal. Legitimist to the end, Dessalles lost his office as magistrate at the colonial Court in Fort-Royal because he refused to register an edict legislated by the new Orleanist regime in 1830 ordering the permanent exile of the Bourbon pretender. For Dessalles, Louis-Philippe was always the "usurper," and his officials and agents were men without independent fortune and therefore without honor in public affairs. In short, Dessalles accepted the stereotype evoked by Tocqueville and Daumier.

Dessalles associated this lack of honor with the new colonial policy of the July Monarchy toward slavery. A government that began to enforce the abolition of the slave trade and attempted to monitor the planters' treatment of the slave work force was one that lacked both respect for the "sacred right" of private property and the perspicacity to foresee how such interference would undermine the whole colonial system. More than unlawful and unwise, such policies were as illegitimate as the regime itself. Only in December 1848 did Dessalles suspend his hopes for a second Bourbon restoration when he accepted Louis Bonaparte as the man of order and, three years later, as the authority needed to bury that "dirty Republic." For Republicanism was also of a piece. In Dessalles's mind, class and race were closely associated. The Lamartines and Schoelchers would overthrow the distinctions of both class and race. The misdeeds of the "reds" of the June Days in Paris presaged the racial slaughter to come in Martinique. Dessalles was always a defender of political authority; although he would have preferred a monarchy with hallowed historic roots, it was most important to him that the government be firm and consistent. It was the same for the management or command of the slave gangs. A manager or an overseer must be just but firm and never vacillate between harshness and leniency.

Royalist in a counterrevolutionary French tradition of which he was proud, Dessalles was also a planter and a notable at a distance of 1,800 leagues from the mother country. Monarchical authority need not, should not, imply centralization. How could those "Europeans" inside and outside of the central government understand the peculiar conditions of the sugar colonies? Not only the *secte philosophique* and those well-intentioned but naive deputies such as Broglie and Tocqueville but, even more insidious, the agents of the central administration in Martinique were undermining the security and prosperity of the colony. Encouraged by "English agents," the contagion from Saint-Domingue was further abetted by the governor and the imported judicial apparatus. In 1833, when Paris granted full civil rights to people of color, giving them access to judicial redress, Dessalles considered this policy a threat to the tripartite racial system of the colonies. In 1841, the government addressed slavery itself by attempting to enforce regulations regarding the religious instruction, education, and punishment of the slaves and instituting government inspection of the plantations. Here was a direct abrogation of planter "rights." [5]

To make the negro think about all these ideas for improvement is to expose the colonists to the most baneful disorders. M. de Moges [the governor] contradicts himself: opening the ports and permitting the export of our sugar is an attempt to rekindle the spirit of the colonists who had for so long carried the burden of the injustice the metropolis had heaped on them; to touch the internal system designed to regulate the work and discipline of individual plantations is to promote revolt and compromise the livelihood of the Whites. Ameliorating conditions on one plantation but not on another will say to the negroes of the latter, "Go and obtain by force what your masters will not give you voluntarily" [4 July 1839].

Fortunately for him, as an influential notable solicited by the governor, Dessalles belonged to a network of planters whose views carried considerable weight with a governor and a civil service subject to recall to France. Dessalles recorded the personality and ideas of each key administrator even more thoroughly than they recorded his in the reports on local notables. In such a small white society, it was inevitable that many of the officials were related to the planters, often by marriage. All the planters on the Comité Agricole knew how to use a good dinner at Fort Royal or under the banana trees and bougainvilleas of their plantations to bring the governor around to their way of thinking. Civil rights, after all, did not give the free people of color access to the dinner table, even the governor's. Distant though the planters were from the "machinations" of the Parisian and foreign abolitionists, they kept abreast of the debates in the Chambers and were in close contact with their lobby in the *métropole*. Dessalles relied not only on the *Courrier de la Martinique*, but even more on the contents of letters of relatives in France which, in un-French manner, the planters shared with each other. Benefitting from the hesitancy of the July Monarchy to enforce

5. Dale W. Tomich, *Slavery in the Circuit of Sugar: Martinique and the World Economy, 1830–1848* (Baltimore: Johns Hopkins University Press, 1990), 58–59.

its principles and the relative indifference of the French public to slavery on some tiny islands, the informal political power of white planters like Dessalles was not inconsiderable.

Dessalles was also a *Catholique pratiquant* in the full force of the French phrase. His mother and his wife were both fervent Catholics, the former donating money to various church orders and the latter ascribing many family problems to the will of God. Although he found both tendencies excessive, Pierre Dessalles attended mass regularly, usually with his wife and daughters at Fort-Royal, partook of the sacraments, and prayed before the cross in his plantation home. He described the day he believed he was dying with all the baroque drama of a Sicilian deathbed scene, complete with relics on his chest and his hands raised to heaven.[6]

Dessalles also believed that those outside the Catholic Church were either barbarians or without honor. There were degrees of barbarism, of course. Education and proper manners (*les convenances*) might compensate for lack of religion to a degree, but the example of the people of color and most white Creoles convinced him that all three qualities — education, proper behavior, religion — were of a piece and usually absent in the colonial setting. As for the slaves, the *nègres* or "*ces gens-là*," he was quite certain that they were congenitally, racially incapable of moral behavior; they had no sense of transcendence, and there was little hope that baptism, catechism, or communion could convert even black children. "Little hope," yet there was some. Dessalles's favorite slave, Nicaise, seemed to have sincerely converted to Catholicism. He not only took the sacraments regularly, he was also devoted, obedient, and hard working — for Dessalles, all signs of a wholesome religious influence. Just before his death, Nicaise did everything right. He summoned the white doctor, the priest, and the notary and chased the African herbalist from his cabin. In short, Dessalles felt that Nicaise had become a civilized human being far from the dancing and drums of his ancestors, signs of "African barbarism."

In fact, Dessalles thought some of the sacraments were beneficial to the slaves and to the smooth operation of the plantation. Marriage, for example, was to be encouraged because it was thought to stabilize sexual relationships, reduce friction in the slave quarters, and, above all, increase birth rates, more necessary than ever after the slave trade ended for the French colonies in 1830. Some sacraments, such as last rites and a proper Christian burial, could be

---

6. 11 July 1845. Dessalles seems to have been pleased to have all his children on their knees before him. He recovered by nightfall and dispensed with confession.

religion = disciplinary arsenal [handwritten annotation]

withheld as a punishment to a "troublesome subject" (*mauvais sujet*) and an example to the work force. On one occasion when Dessalles had forbidden a Christian burial to one of his slaves, her family and the entire work gang came to beg him to reconsider, and he pardoned the miscreant. He also conducted daily prayer assemblies on the plantation, but this was essentially a time to gather the slaves together to make work assignments and announce punishments. On balance, Dessalles found the sacraments useful as part of a disciplinary arsenal rather than as a means to foster a sincere conversion to his own version of religious truth. Even so, unlike his counterparts in Saint-Domingue a half-century earlier, Dessalles was at least willing to expose the slaves to Christianity and even allow a priest to come on the plantation, though not without hesitation. Of course, he prayed for his slaves during mass. On New Year's Day 1839, when he was in France, he wrote, "I have asked God for his blessing to my family and my country [Martinique]. I included all my negroes" [1 January 1839].

Dessalles's relations with the Church establishment in Martinique were very ambivalent. He admired the somewhat misplaced zeal of the new apostolic prefect when he preached to and catechized the slaves in the area of Dessalles's plantation for six days, but he was not amused when one of the new priests began to chastise white individuals in the local government from the parish pulpit. He applauded when this priest was hauled before the municipal council and denounced for his indiscretions. Moreover, he felt that the clergy should be particularly selective in granting communion to the freedmen. Dessalles registered his disgust with the new apostolic prefect in 1823 with habitual directness:

This prefect . . . has acted with so much zeal that he has committed some grave errors. The kinds of people who inhabit the colonies are not like those in France; and so the prefect, before implementing his intentions and before taking steps to restore morality, which has been entirely forgotten by the people of color, should have thought about the interests of the colonial system. He should have . . . let himself be convinced that the established order must be preserved if slavery and the respect that free people of color owe the whites are to be maintained [4 July 1823].

In the end, it appears that Dessalles saw more than one role for Catholicism in Martinique. It was a source of self-discipline and even moral superiority for himself, solace for his womenfolk (though charities should not be excessive), and a disciplinary control for the slaves. But religion should be used sparingly for people of color, for it could enhance their respectability and encourage pretension, the two qualities Dessalles detested in "that rabble." Only after 1848 did Dessalles place more faith in the positive effects of religion on people of color. The revolution in France and slave emancipation in Martinique had forced him to make a reassessment of his allies and enemies. But by 1853, when the dust had settled, Dessalles had changed little in his own religious convictions or in his view of what sort of religion was appropriate for other classes of people in the islands.

In his letters to his mother in the 1820s, Dessalles claimed that the only reason he would live in this "accursed island" was his need to provide a fortune for his numerous progeny. No doubt Dessalles exaggerated the physical dangers of the island to convince his mother not to return to Martinique to supervise the family plantation. He had enough interference from family as it was. Yet there is no doubt about his dedication to the family's financial security and his constant anxiety about leaving his mother, wife, and six children in misery.

The Dessalles were originally a Breton family, which accounts for their fervent Catholicism and their fecundity. They probably emigrated to Martinique in the mid seventeenth century, becoming sugar planters and serving as magistrates (*conseillers*) in the High Court (Conseil Souverain) of the island. Pierre François Régis Dessalles (1755–1808), father of Pierre François Dieudonné, was an author and diarist in his own right. One of eleven children, he gave up his claim to the family plantation. Nevertheless, in 1783 he had sufficient resources or credit of his own to buy two nearby plantations. A year later, Dessalles *père* married an Albi de Gissac from Guadeloupe. They had six children, all of whom were born in Martinique except Pierre Dieudonné. Pierre was educated in France at the end of the Revolution and returned to Martinique in 1808 at his father's death to manage the family plantations. In the same year, honoring the deathbed wish of his father, Dessalles *fils* married into the Bence family, Creoles and close neighbors on the island since the 1760s. Pierre and Anna de Bence had six children—two sons, Adrien and Henri, and four daughters, Louise, Calixte, Antoinette, and Emilie.

Given this brief genealogical profile, we may wonder whether Pierre Dieudonné saw himself primarily as a Creole—a Franco-American—or as a metropolitan Frenchman whose residence in Martinique was only temporary, though long, and was undertaken to provide the means to establish himself, his wife, and his children in France. There is no doubt that Dessalles regarded the base of the family fortune to be in Martinique and that the properties in France were financially expendable. When money was short, he urged his mother to sell the recently acquired château near Bergerac and live in Bordeaux, and he advised his wife and two single daughters to join their eldest son and two married daughters in Martinique. They did so, but his wife, Anna, and his daughters Antoinette and Emilie hated Martinique and returned to France after a short stay. Adrien, Louise, Calixte, and Emilie all returned permanently to France after their father's death; Henri never lived in Martinique at all. As for Pierre himself, despite his constant lamentations about the dangers, boredom, vulgarity, and imminent end of the colony, his diary charts a slow evolution toward creolization, even at the price of separating himself from half of his family in France.

The creolization of Pierre Dessalles was a piecemeal, half-conscious process. For years he looked forward to returning to France to establish his two younger daughters and also to enjoy the *douceur* of an early retirement. His visit to France in 1844 made him aware of how much Martinique meant to him. Paris was very expensive, 22,000 francs a year! It was uncomfortable in winter, and there was a great deal of rain. Paris was a mecca of luxury shops and conspicuous consumption that constantly reminded him that he could not provide the *éclat* his women (*ces dames*) desired. More irritating, Paris was materialistic and artificial. Dessalles described the vulgar materialism of parvenu families of the July Monarchy in words that recall Balzac. As for their social manners, the affectation of Parisians repelled him.

One can only shrug one's shoulders and pity these simpleminded people for being enslaved, as it were, to the conventions of society. With their constant mincing they are play-acting all the time. Not relaxed in the slightest. They seem to be ashamed of getting old and consider it humiliating not to hold on to the ridiculous outward forms of high society to the last grimace. The fact is that in true high society, people are more natural and easygoing [9 January 1845].

Perhaps the incontestable naturalness and easygoing ways of creole society were not without their virtues. Somehow the colorful weddings of the people of color did not look quite so ridiculous from afar, or the all-night dancing of the black slaves quite so rowdy. Perhaps even Dessalles's former image of his planter neighbor, Pierre Cardin, "surrounded by mulatto women and his bastards," might now appear less vulgar to him. He came to feel that the proprieties should not smother all spontaneity in human relations.

There was something else that daily life in France revealed to Pierre Dessalles. His family in France—his wife, Anna, her father, Bence, and his children, Antoinette, Emilie, Adrien, and Henri—did not respect him. The women constantly pressed him for money to spend at the shops in the Palais Royal and pushed him to make contacts with prospective suitors for Antoinette and Emilie. But his candidates never seemed to suit "the ladies." His greatest disappointments, however, were Adrien and Henri. As if their republican politics, their supercilious literary tastes, and their religious skepticism were not bad enough, they flaunted their social pretensions expressly to humiliate their father, who could not afford too many frills. The night Adrien and Henri insisted that the only way to attend the Odéon Theater was to sit in "the first loge in white gloves and polished shoes" because of the "poor quality of the company" in the orchestra was too much for Dessalles *père*. "I am more bourgeois than these Messieurs, my sons. The orchestra is good enough for me. I have given up on the Odéon" [22 April 1845].

After countless incidents of this kind with his family, Dessalles would sigh, "Ha! how I miss my plantation in Martinique!" or "Ha! Where is La Nouvelle Cité? How I would love to be there!" The name of the plantation has a utopian ring, a resonance that may have increased Dessalles's nostalgia for his *pays* [27 January 1845; 4 November 1844]. In any event, as relations with "the ladies" deteriorated, Dessalles's idealization of Martinique grew apace:

Why did we come to Paris, for God's sake? To eat badly and suffer privations of every kind? In Martinique I could at least distract myself with the work of my plantation. I enjoyed the freshness of my trees, and I varied my food. Dessert is one of the things I always liked most, and there I had fresh fruit all year long, fresh compotes every day, and cream custard at every meal. Here it's those miserable almonds every day, which don't do the stomach any good. But I must keep all this to myself. From my daughters not a single sign of concern [9 February 1844].

Family tensions reached their climax a few years later after his wife's death in 1846 and Dessalles's return to Martinique. In addition to the problems caused by emancipation and the decline in sugar production, the children in France pressed for their share in the property. Henri, now a magistrate in a provincial tribunal, was especially coldhearted about his interests. Adrien, the eldest, had taken over management of the Nouvelle Cité in 1849, and Pierre finally agreed to sell the sugar plantation to his children for a pension of 3,000 francs. He spent his last years in his second, more modest plantation-house, La Caféière, overlooking the Atlantic. In the autumn of 1854, he went to Fort-de-France to attend the wedding of Calixte's daughter, the last of the family in Martinique. "The marriage contract was read at three in the afternoon. . . . After the ceremony we went to the plantation [of Calixte] where propriety and a subdued gaiety presided over this family celebration" [26 October 1854]. Soon thereafter, the widowed Calixte joined all her siblings in France, but Pierre Dessalles decided to remain independent and live where he was "at home" [6 April 1856]. He was only visiting France when he died there in March 1857.

The Sugar Plantation: "La Nouvelle Cité"

The Haitian Revolution (1791–1804) had dealt a heavy blow to French sugar cane production. In 1791 the French colonies alone produced 102,000 metric tons of sugar, 40 percent of world production. By the end of the Napoleonic Wars and after the rapid rise of Brazilian and Cuban production, the four remaining French sugar colonies (Martinique, Guadeloupe, Guiana, and Bourbon) produced barely 40,000 tons, or 11 percent of world production. Yet in the 1820s a favorable world market revived French sugar production, and by 1840 the colonies were producing 85,000 tons, or 13 percent of world production, equal to Brazil's share. In the 1840s about 30,000 tons of this total were produced in Martinique alone, all by slave labor.[7]

Martinique, as Dale Tomich tells us, had many advantages for sugar production. Soil, climate, topography, access to rivers, and steady winds were all especially favorable to production on the windward (northeast) side of the island on the coast from Macouba to Robert. Here along this 20-mile coast of contiguous cane fields were 100 of Martinique's 500 sugar plantations.[8] Compare the average holdings, number of slaves, and sugar production of the plantations in this northeast coastal corridor with the average for all plantations on the island, as shown in the table. It is immediately apparent that the 100 plantations in the northeast were 50 percent larger, had 25 to 50 percent more slaves, and produced about 50 percent more sugar than the average of the island's 500 plantations.

The sugar plantation of Pierre Dessalles was near Sainte-Marie in the middle of this fertile corridor. Although he planted only 120 acres in cane (half ratoons), Dessalles worked 159 slaves (1828) and produced an average of 150 tons of raw sugar yearly. In short, Dessalles's sugar plantation ranked among the most productive in Martinique, among the top sixty producing between 150 and 300 tons annually in 1839.[9] It would appear from this comparative perspective that this amount was attained by employing more slaves per acre rather than by planting more cane, although Dessalles commented in his diary that he produced his 300 hogsheads with a minimum labor force. To be sure, after 1830, replacements were more difficult to come by.[10]

---

7. Tomich, *Slavery*, 15, 103, 104.

8. Id., 102. This geographical concentration remained remarkably stable from 1820 to 1847.

9. Id., 100.

10. Barry Higman estimates that the optimal size of a Jamaican plantation before emancipation was 200 acres of cane worked by 200 slaves and producing 200 tons of sugar. The estimate has a seductive symmetry.

Average Holdings, Production, and Slave Labor, 1820–1847*

	1820	1832	1837	1842	1847
Land in sugar (acres)					
Northeast	145.2	145.2	142.1	127.7	130.1
Total	112.6	103.9	99.4	86.4	95.0
Slaves per sugar plantation					
Northeast	104.7	121.7	90.3	100.4	96.2
Total	89.0	70.2	63.5	74.4	81.2
Sugar produced (metric tons)					
Northeast	96.5	91.2	113.4	96.8	90.8
Total	75.6	64.1	59.6	64.9	64.4

*This is an abridgement of Dale W. Tomich's table (Tomich, *Slavery*, 104). We are assuming that "Land in sugar" designates the area in sugar cane and not the total area of the plantation, which normally included provision grounds, pasture, and waste land.

Was Dessalles an entrepreneurial planter? Not if that means employing new methods of sugarmaking and attempting to raise productivity by technical innovation. He responded to the market by shifting back and forth between the production of unrefined and semirefined sugar, but he was not willing to invest in new equipment such as horizontal cylinders, steam engines, or plows or to experiment with new refining processes. Observing a M. Guignaud, "educated in France," attempting to produce whiter sugar on the basis of some knowledge of chemistry, Dessalles commented that the young planter's expenses had not been compensated by the results obtained. He added with a certain pride, "I have not made any changes in my old method; I am waiting. I will make changes only after experience has proven that they offer substantial benefits" [10 December 1842].

Were managerial changes possible? Could the labor force be made more productive? These issues were highlighted when Dessalles's eldest son assumed temporary management of the plantation in 1837. Full of youthful optimism, Adrien claimed he could increase returns. His father was less sure.

If he could consistently produce 300 hogsheads and preserve the negroes, I would be very happy. But he will want to prove that he is cleverer than I am, and so he will plant a great deal, force everything, and in the end the net revenue will be less, and the resources for the future will be destroyed. I can hear his excuse now: "One cannot," he will tell me, "make money without losing oxen and mules, and even some negroes. I will reply that . . . given the difficult circumstances the colonies are in, it would be better to make less revenue and conserve resources" [12 August 1837].

"Resources" meant primarily labor, slave labor. Over thirty years, Dessalles employed many plantation managers, often the sons of other planters, young men making their way up on the island. All of them fell short in some way.

Octave Lalanne was constantly in the slave quarters, causing sexual disorder; Jules Cardin was inconsistent in his treatment of the slaves, too severe one day, too lenient the next; M. de Gaalon was both a libertine and a despot, always promising to increase returns and blaming the slaves for his failure to do so. As for Adrien as manager, he performed as his father feared. Inspecting the plantation on his return from France, Dessalles found Adrien in the cane fields with the slaves. "To my distress I observed that he had given them only 18 minutes off for lunch. This is not enough time, and the negroes must be upset about it. One must be fair with these people and give them the rest stipulated in the ordinances" [9 August 1837].

Dessalles liked to see himself as a paternal planter, and it pleased him when it was reported that the slaves wanted him, rather than his manager, to run the slave gangs. To be sure, he complained about the cost of providing three meals a day to over 200 individuals, but at least he did give them three meals. He was encouraged by the production of foodstuffs (*vivres*) on his newly planted plantation, La Caféière. "This coffee plantation, covered with provisions, will bring more life to our sugar mill." The 27 newly purchased slaves assigned "up there" [to the Caféière] were "superb," with a number of pregnancies already reported [13 September 1823; 5 April 1825]. Dessalles rejected his manager's proposal that some of the land in manioc, yams, and bananas be converted to cane. He also supplemented the slave diet with imported codfish. In later years, when he was very short of money, he would sometimes give his slaves half-days off in lieu of food, presumably to give them time to work on their garden patches. All in all, however, Dessalles appears to have provided his 200 slaves with an adequate, if monotonous, diet.

What of their general health? An outside inspector of the plantation in 1828 reported that there were no sick slaves and that Dr. Mouleng did not need to stop by [21 March 1828]. However, by the 1840s Dessalles worried about the diminution of the principal work gang. In September 1841 his head nurse (*hospitalière*) died, and he had to take care of the sick slaves himself. His entries in October were discouraging: "We have had ten deaths in eight months. If this goes on any longer, I soon will have no negroes left to work my land" [29 October 1841]. Even before the effective abolition of the slave trade in 1830, Dessalles said he needed about ten new slaves each year to keep up the work force. Unless he was attempting to enlarge operations—and this was unlikely, given his caution about innovation—this would represent a high net loss of about 5 percent of the slaves per annum.

Dessalles gives no numbers about birth rates, but he was disturbed that there were so few births on the sugar plantation. Abortions bothered him especially.

Jean-Pierre [a slave] . . . told me that every year we had eight, ten, twelve, and fourteen pregnancies, but that the negresses got rid of their fruits and that it was known throughout the work gang that Marie-Jeanne had very recently destroyed her child. And indeed, she was believed to be pregnant; she had an enormous belly, which one morning was gone, to everyone's great astonishment [15 September 1824].

Dessalles was equally shocked by suicides. While not as regular as abortions, suicide by a slave could be dramatic. Césaire, a driver on the plantation, had been very quiet when he was flogged twice in one day, 15 and 30 lashes respectively, by the manager, M. Chignac. Shortly after, Césaire climbed to the top of the mill wheel and shouted down to the assembled slaves: "Bonjour to all of you. Tell M. Chignac bonjour, and tell him that he won't be able to beat Césaire any more." With that, he threw himself into the wheel and was killed instantly.

Dessalles had been told earlier by a deputation of slaves that M. Chignac was worse than the devil and that "despair" pervaded the work force. Dessalles was more inclined to ascribe Césaire's suicide to the death of a negress he loved. In any case, he said "to dismiss Chignac would be to show weakness," even though he must eventually go [26 July 1823]. Six weeks later Raymond, accused of poisoning livestock, jumped from a breadfruit tree and also died instantly [13 September 1823].

Dessalles observed that Chignac was learning to take better care of the slaves: "He often visits the [plantation] hospital" [13 September 1823]. Nevertheless, the following spring, two newly purchased blacks hanged themselves. Dessalles reacted to the depression among the slaves by delivering a harangue which he claimed restored their "good spirits" [26 May 1824]. There were also the more mundane cases of death by eating earth, which Dessalles again ascribed to a kind of racial perversion, or even hostility to the planter class, rather than to an intestinal illness such as hookworm. Until near the end of his life, Pierre Dessalles did not seem to grasp what "despair" meant to a slave. In 1842 he discovered a boat beached off Sainte-Marie containing the bodies of two negresses and a child. What had happened to the others, including "my mulatto Tapté"? "They wanted to flee to a neighboring colony" was his only comment [25 January 1842].

With the effective end of the French slave trade in 1830, sugar planters had to rely on natural increase and the redistribution of the labor supply on the island. Although granting freedom to individual slaves was encouraged by the new government in Paris, annual manumissions fell after 1834 to fewer than 1,000 in a total slave population of 80,000 in 1833, 73,000 in 1847.[11] It is not surprising then that Dessalles rarely mentions a manumission.

11. Tomich, *Slavery*, 83.

Old slaves were the most likely candidates. Dessalles's own nanny, Prax-cède was freed [11 August 1843], as was the "old negress" who had cared for his children, but only on condition that she return to Martinique so that she would not have to be maintained "at huge cost" in France [22 February 1841]. Saint-Just was a troublesome slave. Dessalles had freed his mother and his younger brother, while his older brother, the mulatto Dieudonné, had died a house servant in Bergerac. But he believed that Saint-Just, a literate artisan, had too much influence over the other slaves and could be dangerous. Freedom was not in store for him. "I want him to deserve my kindness by submission to my orders and zeal in doing his duty" [27 December 1839]. Submission, however, was never forthcoming. Young Calixte asked to be freed, basing his claim on the fact that he had "touched" French soil. Dessalles refused, claim-ing that this new law had become operative after Calixte returned from France. Honoré, on the other hand, might be freed because he had been exposed to dangerous influences in Paris and should stay there. However, Dessalles asked Honoré to purchase his freedom for 6,600 francs, a very high price even for a house slave [4 July 1823].[12] All of these examples suggest reluctance to free any slaves, but especially productive field workers. Dessalles thought of himself as a generous master. He fed and cared for his slaves when they were ill and even baptized and married them, but manumission was not a conspicuous part of his paternal creed.

Although over the long run Dessalles appears to have preferred nonviolent methods of discipline, the whip, the chain and iron collar, the bar, and the dark prison cell (cachot) were always available. There was something casual about the way Dessalles referred to Jean-Pierre as "in the cachot for the last two weeks" [15 September 1824]. Physical punishment was especially prevalent during the outbreak of cattle deaths in the summer of 1824. When Ludovic Littée, Des-salles's neighbor, lost 30 oxen in a few weeks, Dessalles joined other devastated planters in interrogating the slaves and punishing them for the "contagion." Even though cattle disease, "épizootiques," had long been known in France, the white owners considered poison the only possible explanation, and they cut apart oxen, cows, and mules in search of evidence of a poison plot. They usually found what they were looking for. That summer Dessalles employed punishments ranging from the prescribed "29 lashes" (sometimes as many as 75) for his mule and cattle guards to the deprivation of "free time" on week-ends, evenings, and mealtimes. He also prohibited the entire slave force from

12. It seems remarkable that Honoré had been able to accumulate such a large sum. Occurring before the end of the slave trade, this case may reflect a new policy, namely, to sell less useful slaves at a high price and purchase new ones.

leaving the plantation at any time. As the plague abated, Dessalles told his slaves that they had paid for the lost livestock in extra work time: four and one-half Saturdays, four Sundays, and other hours, all recorded as meticulously as on a factory timecard [22 July 1824]. The manipulation of "free time" provides an interesting insight into planter-slave notions of work time.[13]

The whip remained, however, both a physical reality to his slaves and a symbol of authority for Dessalles. In January 1844, when Dessalles needed a new manager, he hired a young yet seasoned administrator who promised to increase sugar production from 300 to 350 hogsheads per annum. M. de Gaalon demanded that the slaves work in shifts day and night during the harvest, even Sundays. By February he was complaining that the slaves were not working hard enough and that the driver was negligent. Recaptured runaways like Césaire were flogged 29 times at prayer time as an example to the others. But the sluggishness of the labor force persisted. Dessalles remarked that M. de Gaalon talked too much and acted too little: "He reasons with them, but that is a language the negro does not understand. The whip alone can make him work; that is the cruel truth. It is the only means that has ever done me any good" [22 March 1844].

When Valentin cut the driver's whip in two with his machete, he was given the iron collar as well as 29 lashes. "Quite uppity, that young one," commented his master [15 April 1842]. Even more serious was rebelliousness in the black driver himself. During one cane harvest, when criticized for his leniency by Dessalles, the driver replied that he had his own way of working the slaves and that "he was not in the habit of killing people." Dessalles waited until noon to punish such "insolence."

At noon I had three stakes driven into the ground and had him tied to them; he was given fifty lashes. . . . Yet he persisted in saying that he would continue to act as before. So I had him put into an iron collar.

I called for my head mule driver, Charles, a young negro [originally] from Guinée, and made him the driver for the work gang. I then replaced Charles with Victor, another newly purchased young negro. All these changes will improve matters, I am convinced, because *I, the master,* have made them [1 February 1840].

Dessalles harbored a curious illusion about the whip. Or should we label it "denial?" In France in 1838 he resented a remark about "negro music." His provincial host taunted, "But the music of the negro is the whip." Dessalles replied with indignation:

13. "Time became a kind of currency, and a complex system of time-accounting emerged." See Tomich, *Slavery,* 254, and chapter 6 *passim.*

"Monsieur, . . . the whip is practically unknown in the colonies. It is used on horses and insolent individuals, and the most unfortunate negro in our colonies is still more fortunate than the most fortunate of your peasants." No doubt he [Dessalles's interlocutor] sensed how stupid he had been. . . . What prejudices there are against the colonists! [10 August 1838].

Dessalles employed quite another tone two years later in a long letter to the Governor of Martinique. One passage read: "the negro race is so uncivilizable, so lazy, that it would be completely impossible to obtain the least work from them without the fear of some punishment. If we deprive the master of the ability to repress by himself the daily faults of the negro, which he does only in the last extremity, it will bring insubordination and disorder" [15 May 1840].

A blend of racism and paternalism pervaded Dessalles's thinking about his slaves, his people, his *gens*. In his pessimistic moments they infuriated him by "their thievery and their grimacing." In 1844, after a suspected household theft, Dessalles fantasized about a specious golden age: "Twenty years ago [1820s], such things did not happen; one slept with the doors open, and everything that belonged to the masters was religiously respected. Ever since the ideas of philanthropy have come to corrupt our negroes, they go in for every kind of brigandage and soon, alas, our very lives will no longer be safe" [11 January 1842].

Without the contagion of "philanthropy," religion would presumably have inculcated respect for the master's property. Perhaps, Dessalles thought, it was still a good idea to give the slaves Good Friday to worship the Cross in Sainte-Marie [25 March 1842]. But alas, religion would not create the will to work. Did not the negroes feign illness? Did they not work at a minimal pace? Did they not hide in the quarters and the cane fields? "They are devoured by idleness" was Dessalles's phrase to characterize this presumed contagion. Moreover, it puzzled him that even an outwardly zealous slave seemed to harbor resentments: "Honoré is still full of zeal . . . but it is devilishly difficult to know what is in the bottom of the bag" [7 June 1825]. At one point Pierre Dessalles almost innocently expressed his inconceivable self-delusion about the nature of slavery in speaking about the purchase of a group of slaves: "I propose to pay the sum in six installments and to begin only in September 1839. I did not find his assessment exaggerated, but I cannot buy the cat in the bag: I must at least see them and *find out whether they want to serve me*" [7 September 1837; italics added].

What would the "ideal slave" be for Pierre Dessalles? Hard-working, personally spartan, obedient to the manager, and devoted to the master. All slaves would be baptized, go to mass, marry, form sexually stable families, and raise children. They would celebrate the four Christian holidays (Christmas, Easter, Assumption, and All Saints' Day), remember their master's name day, and salute him on their way to the fields. They would spend their free time working their gardens and marketing any surplus they might produce, though permission to go to town would always have to be carefully regulated. They should never be permitted to go to France or to visit neighboring islands. They should not be exposed to books, pamphlets, or newspapers beyond the catechism. The master would see that they received medical care. They should be allowed to sing and dance on the weekends, though not beyond midnight. Such an existence should encourage the above virtues, increase the labor force, maintain physical and mental health, and provide outlets for the "natural gaiety" and emotional exuberance of the slaves. In short, they would be happy workhouse children, contented Oliver Twists. In this fantasy world, what better name for a plantation than "La Nouvelle Cité!"

Outstanding Slaves, White Creoles, People of Color

Dessalles had his favorites among the slaves, individuals who somehow escaped his racial stereotypes and who were capable of becoming civilized, as he understood the word. Nicaise was his lifelong manservant and had won his master's confidence sufficiently to accompany him to France for one year in 1838–39 and for three years in 1844–47. Dessalles called Nicaise *mon petit nègre* and Nicaise called him *Monsieur*, but the exact nature of the relationship is never spelled out. Dessalles insisted that Nicaise was one of his servants. However, emotional scenes over minor matters, usually taking place in intimate settings, are suggestive of one of two equally unavowable relationships: Nicaise was either Dessalles's sexual companion or his son. Dessalles often ate with Nicaise, even in public; in France he defended him against racial slurs and let him roam about Paris without supervision except an occasional sermon. He eventually gave him his freedom, but kept him in his service. Nicaise went to mass, married, baptized his children, cared for Dessalles in sickness and in health, lent him money, and eventually helped with the transition to free labor on the plantation in the year of slave emancipation. His death in 1850 was deeply felt by Dessalles for years afterward. Madame Dessalles was uncharacteristically perceptive when she accused her husband of loving his house servants more than his own children.

Saint-Just was not a favored slave, but he was a personage to be reckoned with because he was a literate mulatto and suspect for this reason alone. Saint-

Just was also a skilled mason with a workshop and apprentices on the plantation. His common-law wife sold tafia under his supervision. He raised sheep and worked land in tobacco and manioc. To Dessalles, Saint-Just was ambitious and "speculated in everything." These commercial activities could degenerate into abuses if he were not watched. Dessalles suspected him of stealing plantation materials for his own commercial use [27 December 1839]. On the other hand, Saint-Just was indispensable for making repairs on the plantation, and he always displayed verbal deference to Dessalles. He was clever enough to ask to be sold and be refused, thus strengthening his position. To his master's distress, he was also a procurer of young negresses for Dessalles's son, Adrien; this gave him a certain leverage, despite Pierre Dessalles's threats to put him in the iron collar for such "dirty business" [8 July 1837]. During the crisis of 1848 in Martinique, Saint-Just became a foreman of the "Association" temporarily established on the Dessalles plantation. It was his frequentation of the free people of color and his lack of humility for which Dessalles reproached him most. Saint-Just reminds one of Chicken George in Alex Haley's *Roots*, a survivor with spirit.

And then there was the crafty mulatto Saturnin, also born as Dessalles's slave, the son of the house slave Trop, nephew of the rebellious Saint-Just and the even more rebellious Saint-Fort whom Dessalles had freed and exiled to Guadeloupe. Saturnin obtained his freedom when he was purchased by his grandmother, who subsequently manumitted him. Like his kinsmen, Saturnin was something of a rebel, an artisan, entrepreneur, and wheeler-dealer. He too went to Guadeloupe when he lost Dessalles's favor because of "bad talk" during the Revolution of 1848 and his efforts to teach black children to read. After the death of Nicaise, he returned to Martinique—possibly summoned by Dessalles's daughter, Mme de Valmenier—where he obtained Pierre Dessalles's forgiveness and moved in with him.

The French editors, without providing any details, assume that he was Dessalles's son, and there are many signs that this was indeed the case.[14] But Pierre Dessalles steadfastly upheld the fiction that Saturnin was his trusted servant. When Saturnin married, his wife, "Mme Saturnin," his mother-in-law, Mme Cognet, his children, Théodorine and Théodore (their names the Greek version of the French Dieudonné), and even his mistress, Cécé, lived with him, ostensibly as his household staff. This obviously hypocritical arrangement soon led to friction, especially with the spirited Mme Saturnin, who was given to

14. Vol. 4, p.193. "Mme de Valmenier [Calixte Dessalles, the author's daughter] at this point seems to feel very strongly that no one will take better care of her father than a half-brother of color."

telling him "a thousand impertinences," such as "We are living in a different age. You do not have the right to lord it over anybody" [10 April 1855]. This would not do, of course, and Mme Saturnin was thrown out, forgiven, thrown out again, forgiven again and again. The reason was that Dessalles did not want to part with Saturnin's children, whom he loved with the special affection that only a grandfather can feel. Unloved and even denied respect by his legitimate children and grandchildren, Pierre Dessalles in his old age found some solace and comfort in a family that he never acknowledged as his own. The only white person in his household, he did not feel that he was "wallowing in dirty linen," as he characterized the way of life of his son Adrien or other white planters who "surrounded themselves with mulatto women and their bastard children."

Pierre Dessalles professed to abhor the sexual passions, especially those between men and women of different races. He associated all people of color with *libertinage* and bastardy. For him, they were the living consequence of sexual disorder or what he termed *caraïbisme*. More, the people of color extended this self-indulgence to all corners of their lives, earning a reputation for laziness, cunning, and perfidy. The Creole whites who frequented, indeed spawned, "the yellows" were contaminated by these same traits, though to a lesser degree.

Pierre Dessalles used similar language to describe the households of his white planter neighbors Louisie Burot, Pierre Cardin, Mayor Caffié, and Alexandre Thébault:

Went to visit M. Louisie Burot, whom we found surrounded by his mulatto women and his bastards. In this colony, wine is a proud master. Since the death of one of his bastard sons, good old Burot has not left his place. He vaunts his [son's] good qualities; to hear him talk, the man was without faults. Yet there is proof that he was a rabid enemy of the whites, one of his class who most ardently wished for their ruin. . . . From . . . Burot's, I went to Pierre Cardin's; he is a good man, but also surrounded by mulattoes. His bastards live pell-mell with his legitimate children. Truly, such neglect of the proprieties is found only in Martinique. It makes me shudder [30 November 1837].

Such behavior was not unrelated, in Dessalles's mind, to the undistinguished social background of so many white Creoles. M. Caffié, for example, was without education, had poor manners, and displayed a tiresome *politesse*. He was made mayor of Sainte-Marie by the government because he was liked by the lower class. "We were not born to live closely to each other. He never stops calling me, '*mon cher*'. . . . What shocked me most were the little mulattoes, his bastards, who ran around our tables and annoyed us by their familarity" [22 October 1842]. Madame Littée was an "uncultivated Creole," jingling with cheap jewelry, "surrounded by free mulatto women who were brazen enough to sit down next to my wife and my daughters" [31 January 1842].

Surely the greatest shock to Dessalles's doctrine of racial distance and his rule that whites of proper breeding must never admit to "sexual disorder" was the behavior of his eldest son, Adrien. Already in 1837 Adrien had defied his father's formal interdiction and slept indiscriminately with the black house servants. Adrien was even worse than plantation managers like de Gaalon, who at least carried on their dirty affairs in their own quarters or in the cane fields. Adrien and his cousin, Eugène, used Nicaise and Saint-Just as pimps and paraded their sexual prowess almost in Pierre's presence. Adrien's open dalliance with the mulatto girl Victorine was bad enough, but he made Virginie, another mulatto, his permanent mistress and had four children by her. She slept on the plantation, ate in the salon, and brought her daughter — "whom Adrien believes to be his" — from Sainte-Marie [16, 17, 20 August 1837; 18 October 1837].

After ten years' absence, Adrien returned to Martinique in 1848 and reclaimed his children of color, quatroons in the color hierarchy described by Moreau de Saint-Méry. From Dessalles's comments, one would never guess that Palmire, now a girl of fourteen, was his granddaughter. For him she was always "the bastard girl" or "that girl":

The colored girl Palmire — supposedly Adrien's daughter — seems nice enough, but quite insignificant. My son spoils her to the point of making himself ridiculous. . . . During my absence [in France], he permitted himself to make her dine at the table with the Lalanne ladies, which has greatly upset me. I only keep her in my household because I consider her a member of my domestic staff and would not have her as my equal. One must be kind to these people, but one must keep them at a distance. To act differently would be immoral. My poor son has no idea of the proprieties; if this were his home he would wallow in dirty linen [9 February 1849].

The word *propriety* pervades Dessalles's attitude toward miscegenation. The great transgression was not the sexual act with a person of color, but the admission that such an act has taken place. Adrien was not to be forgiven for "parading around with his bastard girl" rather than treating her as just another servant. Here Pierre Dessalles came perilously close to Molière's Tartuffe:

Le scandale du monde est ce qui fait l'offense
Et ce n'est pas pêcher que pêcher en silence.

For Pierre Dessalles, the worst aspect of his son's "deviance" was the delegitimation of his family name. In 1849 Adrien told his father that during a patriotic banquet, the mulatto politician Bissette had called Palmire Mlle Dessalles. Dessalles was furious: "I explained to him that I had legitimate children and that I would never allow anyone to usurp their name" [27 October

1849]. Legitimacy and racial purity were inseparable. It was not carelessness of language when Dessalles referred to the Orleans branch of the royal family as "this infamous race" [20 October 1837]. In the political sense, they too were illegitimate.

Sometimes wealth might mitigate the absolute condemnation of such improper Creole white behavior for Dessalles, though not for his wife, Anna. Pierre Cardin's effort to negotiate a marriage between his protegé, Léopold Camouilly, and Antoinette Dessalles came to naught because of Anna. Dessalles admitted that the young man's birth was not equal to his, but that since no one of "our class" had appeared in the three years Antoinette had been in Martinique, perhaps the indiscretions of the suitor's father (presumably the existence of some illegitimate offspring) should not be exaggerated. After all, young Camouilly was worth 500,000 francs [25 November 1843].

Were there any people of color whom Dessalles could respect? Théotiste Fortier, "a mulatto bastard daughter" of M. Fortier, gained his respect on two counts. First, she left a fortune of more than one million francs. Second, she was "singularly attached to the Whites, particularly to her father's family." She left 900,000 francs to her three daughters of color and 300,000 to each of her father's four children, presumably her white half-brothers and half-sisters. "She will be missed by everyone in the colony." Théotiste passed muster [28 October 1839]. M. Pory Papy was another. "One praises this mulatto, the first of his class to be a barrister (*avocat*) in this country" [1 December 1837]. Dessalles changed his mind, however, in 1848 when Pory Papy became mayor of Saint-Pierre and campaigned for national representative with the promise of providing land for the new freedmen [23 July 1848].

When Adolphe Perrinon, a French-educated artillery officer, first arrived in Martinique as government commissioner in charge of transforming slave labor into free labor in the wake of the Revolution of 1848, Dessalles was impressed with his insistence on discipline and hard work on the part of the ex-slaves. "With one voice, everyone praises the noble heart of M. Perrinon. When I find good breeding and noble sentiments in a man, whatever his color, I like to honor him" [6 June 1848]. By 20 August of the same year, however, Perrinon became a partisan of the free men of color, and Pierre Dessalles reappraised his opinion. He now called Perrinon "nothing but a communist mulatto."

Dessalles did not consider the literacy and skills of the people of color positive achievements in themselves. It depended on how they were used. Even Saturnin, despite his privileged position, had to be watched. When he kept Dessalles informed by letter about de Gaalon's management of the plantation while he was in France, that was good use of his writing skills. But giving reading lessons and circulating newspapers in the slave cabins was something else [4 August 1848]. In a long letter to the new Director of Interior in December 1848, Dessalles described the people of color as "men who consider the cultivation of cane a dishonor because it was so closely linked to slavery [who] do not today set a good example by working together with the new freedmen. . . . Instead they prefer either to wallow in the most pernicious idleness or else to go from plantation to plantation in order to foment trouble and disorder." The education of the ex-slaves, he asserted, must be centered on religion and not left in the hands of unauthorized individuals such as Saturnin [17 December 1848; appendix B to chapter 9]. It is not surprising that the people of color fought for state-sponsored education in the years ahead.[15]

Pierre Dessalles was convinced all along that the free people of color were not content to be the intermediary class and wanted to take over Martinique from the whites. His attitude had not changed since April 1825 when, in a letter to his mother, he referred to the free mulattoes as "our most cruel enemies" [15 April 1825]. The rapid increase in the number of free people of color from under 11,000 in 1826 to over 36,000 in 1848, while the white population remained stationary at 9,500, did little to allay Dessalles's apprehension, not to say paranoia, about this group.[16]

Crisis and Resolution

Authority was a fundamental requirement of society for Pierre Dessalles. He believed that legitimate authority had four guarantors—monarchy, church, *patronage*, and a code of conduct. The Bourbon Monarchy, the Catholic Church, and the Roman paterfamilias were the best models. *Patronage* extended beyond the immediate family, however. In Dessalles's world it embraced 200 plantation slaves, "his people." His code of conduct prescribed a racial hierarchy maintained by a strict etiquette of daily behavior, especially between whites and people of color. It also prescribed traditional Catholic family discipline in

15. See Louis Abénon's chapter on the history of Martinique after 1870 in Pierre Pluchon et al., *Histoire des Antilles et de la Guyane* (Toulouse: Privat, 1984), 421 and *passim*.

16. For the changing population of Martinique in the early nineteenth century, see Léo Elisabeth, "The French Antilles" in David W. Cohen and Jack P. Greene, ed., *Neither Slave Nor Free: The Freedmen of African Descent in the Slave Societies of the New World* (Baltimore: Johns Hopkins University Press, 1972), 151–52. The proportion of the people of color in the total population of Martinique rose from 10 to 32% between 1826 and 1848. The slave population declined from 80,000 to 70,000 in these same years, though it still represented 60% of the population just before emancipation in 1848.

which sexual restraint was central, a spartan demand perhaps more honored in the breach than the observance.

All four of these guarantors of authority had been under attack for a half-century or more. It all went back to January 21, 1793 when Louis XVI was guillotined. The erosion of these bulwarks was brought home to Dessalles one October day in 1837 when Adrien and his friends were talking under a tropical sky at the Nouvelle Cité:

> I am witnessing some curious conversations: the posturing of today's young people *stinks to high heaven.* . . . Eugène plays the scholar to settle the most difficult questions of literature. Nothing is beautiful unless it comes from the pen of Victor Hugo, Eugène Sue, etc.; it is just too funny. . . . When it comes to politics, it's even worse; legitimacy is a hollow dream, the republic will prevail. . . . As for religious principles, these gentlemen have worked them out to suit their convenience: Jesus Christ is a prodigious *man*; to kill oneself when one is unhappy is a perfectly simple and natural thing. Seducing two sisters in the same family, running away with another man's wife—all of this is considered very nice. What distresses me is that my son . . . shares and defends their errors [4 October 1837].

One need only add Adrien's views about managing the field slaves and all of his father's authorities—political, religious, moral, and patriarchal—are represented and rejected.

No wonder Dessalles's journal has a Cassandra-like quality. For forty years, this increasingly crotchety planter predicted the coming catastrophe of slave emancipation and the end of the colonies. Yet when emancipation finally came, it was a far cry from the Haitian Revolution. To be sure, the whip cracked for the last time on the slave's back and a planter had to rely on the manipulation of sharecrop contracts to get the "workers" to cut cane and make sugar. But other forms of property were only briefly threatened, advocates of land redistribution were labeled "communists," and even the ex-slaves' cabins and garden plots were guaranteed as planter property that could be leased to the new freedmen.

For Dessalles, the greatest change was the new political role of the people of color. He was shocked, of course, by election campaigning with black freedmen carrying premarked ballots and by men of color becoming local mayors. Fourteen of the 21 new deputies to the National Assembly were people of color [24 December 1848]. Although the election of Louis Napoléon as President was a reassuring assertion of authority, Dessalles would have to live with the Pory Papys and the Cyrille Bissettes, mulatto politicians.

There are hints in his journal that Dessalles might come to terms with the people of color. In 1838, as he left for France, he dined next to a young mulatto on shipboard. He made an observation totally out of character, and one that he would not repeat often: "In the interest of the colonies, we must wish that prejudice will end. A well-bred man of proper manners cannot, of course, live and eat with an unprincipled and unmannerly mulatto, but education must do away with distinctions, and a man, whatever his color, must be included in all social relations if his manners warrant it" [30 March 1838].

Thinking of his younger son, Henri, Dessalles commented on the better pay and opportunities for promotion in the colonial magistracy. He would be repelled, he wrote, by the fact that a child of his would have to sit next to a man of color, but he noticed that his colleagues were able to make this sacrifice for their sons' careers. "Such prejudices disappear every day. I know it. Our children will not have the same repugnance as we do" [13 September 1845].[17]

More decisive than these signs of wavering was the experience of 1848. Dessalles was surely brought up short when Saturnin's mulatto wife replied to her former master, "We are living in a different age. You do not have the right to lord it over anybody" [10 April 1855]. This was strong stuff and Dessalles's vulgar reaction ("told her to go and have herself f——") showed that she had struck home.

But it was listening to Cyrille Bissette that did the trick. Bissette was a prominent mulatto abolitionist who had made a reputation in France as a publicist and orator for the cause.[18] In 1849 he arrived in Martinique in triumph, at least among the slaves and people of color. Adrien knew Bissette in France and persuaded his father to receive him on the plantation. Bissette made several speeches during his electoral campaign that greatly surprised and pleased Dessalles. The banquet for 40 settings under a tent at the Nouvelle Cité was an occasion for racial reconciliation. Bissette praised Dessalles as a "historic name in this country" and addressed Adrien with the unbelievable words, "My friend, your race will save this country!" Dessalles replied with the toast, "The flag you have adopted [the tricolor] guarantees you the sympathies of all honorable people in this country." His diary entry confessed that it would be unjust not to accord a certain merit to this Christian man [28 April 1849].

At still another patriotic banquet, Bissette's address won Dessalles's unqualified praise. The mulatto leader chastised the black freedmen in attendance for eating with a certain abandon.

17. Dessalles was in France when he wrote these words.
18. See Seymour Drescher, "British Way, French Way: Opinion Building and Revolution in the Second French Slave Emancipation," *American Historical Review* 96 (June 1991), 720–21 and *passim*. See also Drescher, "The Ending of the Slave Trade and the Evolution of European Scientific Racism," *Social Science History* 14 (1990), 415–50.

What are you doing, my friends? You behave like cannibals, like savages! The more I try to raise you up, the more you lower yourselves. You make me ashamed. Am I not a negro like you? Then do as I do, imitate the Whites! They alone will civilize you. Do not imitate the mulattoes. What use is the drum? Don't you see what the Whites use for their dances? Like them, use the violin. Then my daughters and I will come to your dances [4 December 1849].

Cyrille Bissette had returned to Martinique in April 1849 after an exile of 25 years in France. It appears that this long exile from his native island as well as the suppression of the Paris workers in the "June Days" of 1848 made Bissette a man of order by 1849. Bissette proclaimed that slave emancipation had ended all cause for racial tension and that the past should be forgotten. An accommodation between the white notables and at least a part of the *anciens libres de couleur* had been made. In the island election of June 1849 Bissette and Pécoul, moderates, won overwhelmingly over Schoelcher and Pory Papy, labelled *montagnards* by the *Courrier de la Martinique*. The Party of Order had won. The Second Empire was not far behind. Victor Schoelcher fought on the barricades in Paris against the *coup d'état* of Louis Napoléon and was exiled from France in 1852. Cyrille Bissette retired from island politics in 1851 and died in Paris in 1858.[19]

The Prince of Salinas in Lampedusa's novel *The Leopard* reflected that the old guard must change a little so that everything will remain the same. This did not mean that the Sicilian grandee liked these changes or minimized them. Piedmontese officials and soldiers in the streets of Palermo in 1860 were surely as distasteful to him as mulatto politicians and mayors were to Pierre Dessalles in Martinique in 1850. Yet if the newcomers were like Cyrille Bissette, the transition to a society of free labor need not be catastrophic. As the new freedmen put away their drums and trooped off to the cane fields, the aging Dessalles must have regarded the flag waving over the governor's mansion at Fort-de-France with a certain relief. It was not the fleur-de-lys, to be sure, but it was not the flag of Henri Christophe either.

19. Jean Bonniol et al., ed., *L'Historial Antillais* (Fort-de-France: Société Dajani, 1981), 4: 83–85, 457, 459–60.

PART I

Letters

CHAPTER ONE

1808-1821

[Martinique experienced the first five years of the French Revolution (1789–94) before the British attacked and occupied the island. The British landed just before the news of slave emancipation, passed by the Convention (4 February 1794), reached Fort-de-France, and they held the island from 1794 to 1802, when Britain and France signed the Peace of Amiens. However, war between the two major powers resumed a year later, and in 1809 Britain again occupied the French island and remained there until the end of the Napoleonic wars in 1815.

Hence, Martinique was under British occupation for 14 years. During this time, the French planters marketed their sugar through London and continued their daily existence under a British military government that maintained slavery. Unlike Guadeloupe and especially Saint-Domingue (Haiti), Martinique did not know emancipation until 1848.]

No. 1

To Pierre Nicholas Bence de Sainte-Catherine,
acting chief judge, at his estate at Lamentin

Sainte-Marie, 2 February 1808

Monsieur,
How can I thank you for the many marks of sympathy you have so kindly shown us in our misfortune. Our wounds are still open and will not close for a

long time to come.[1] Our loss is dreadful and irreparable. We take comfort in the thought that it was felt by the entire colony and especially by persons for whom he had great affection. You, Monsieur, were among their number, and we cannot doubt your attachment to him, for you have proved it over and over again. It would be a great satisfaction for me to occupy one day the place occupied by my father and my grandfather. More than ever, I desire to join that eminently honorable corps and I shall make every effort to attain that goal.[2] I dare hope, Monsieur, that you will be kind enough to afford me your advice and transfer your friendship from the father to the son. My mother sends her regards, asking you kindly to present them to Madame Bence and Mesdemoiselles your daughters. Please convey to them my respectful greetings as well.

With every expression of attachment and esteem, I remain, Monsieur,

your humble and obedient servant

P. Dessalles

No. 2

To M. de Bence

Saint-Pierre, 4 March 1808

M. de Geoffroy[3] related to me his conversation with you a few days ago at Fort-Royal. Its outcome is highly satisfying to me, and I consider myself extremely fortunate to meet with your approval. I am sorry to have lacked the strength to speak to you myself, but M. de Geoffroy, our kinsman and friend, knows how I think and that I have always wished to become allied with your family. He will have told you, much less timidly than I would have been able to do, that my happiness now depends upon you, Monsieur, upon Madame Bence, and upon Mademoiselle Anna.[4]

1. The author's father, Pierre François Régis Dessalles, had died on 27 January 1808, barely 53 years old, after a painful illness, probably cancer of the liver [HF and LE].

2. The Dessalles family had already furnished two generations of magistrates to the highest tribunal of Martinique; there had even been the unprecedented and never repeated case of a father and two sons serving at the same time in 1780. Pierre Dessalles, who was not a lawyer and did not have a law degree, should not have been appointed to this court. However, there were already three magistrates in the same situation. This letter seems to hint at his future appointment [HF and LE].

3. César de Geoffroy, family friend. On 18 January 1813 he was to sign the baptismal certificate of Louise, the author's third child, as a witness. At the time, he was identified as "46 years old, residing at Fort-Royal" [HF and LE].

4. In +Adrien Dessalles and Henri de Frémont's *Histoire et généalogie de la famille Dessalles ou Des Salles, Martinique et France (1650–1974)* (private printing, 1974), we read, "On several occasions, Pierre spoke to his father of various plans of alliance, for he was already thinking of a number of young women of the island, but *in all his life, Régis [his father] refused his son only one*

I must therefore no longer put off soliciting from you and Madame permission to pay my court to Mademoiselle your daughter. Today I myself ask you to accord me that favor, and, if I am fortunate enough to please Mademoiselle Anna and to obtain her hand, I shall do everything in my power to make her happy. I shall be so anxious to prove my gratitude to you that I shall certainly not fail to make every effort in this direction. . . .

I must tell you that my father was most unhappy that he died too soon to see the successful outcome of a project that occupied all his thoughts toward the end of his life. I shall be gratified in every way, Monsieur, to become a member of your family, where I expect to find all kinds of pleasures and satisfactions. What comfort it will be to me to think that my choice was that of my respectable father; I shall always cherish his memory and, although I was not fortunate enough to have him with me for as long as I would have wished, I will act all my life as if he were present. . . .

My mother asks me to present to you, Monsieur, as well as to Madame Bence and to your young ladies, her affectionate greetings. In such a moment as this, she needed to learn that you agreed to carry out a project that she had been pursuing in her heart for so long. She has told me of her great joy, and I can assure you that she will be as pleased as I will be when the moment of my happiness arrives. The day that will bring the fulfillment of my wishes seems rather remote to me; but if you wish to put it off, I have no right to quibble. I fully understand, Monsieur, the anxieties of a father as tender as yourself. Between now and then, I shall attempt to make myself better known to you, and I dare flatter myself that far from losing your esteem, I shall gain more. I hope that Mademoiselle Anna will be able to convince herself that my entire life will be spent in working for her happiness. It will be my sweetest pleasure to achieve it, and I do not doubt for a moment that I shall succeed.

Business will retain me for a few more days in this town, but I will be sure to arrive at Fort-Royal when the court begins its session.

Nos. 3–6

To M. and Mme Bence

[More expressions of pride at the prospect of marrying into the Bence family, also hints that the sixteen-year-old future bride is not enthusiastic.]

---

thing, and that was the choice of a wife" [154, italics in the original]. Pierre, obedient son that he was, promised not to marry anyone but Anna de Bence. The young woman's name was really Marie Magdeleine Calixte, but her family called her Annah. Pierre sometimes forgets to add the "h," hence his spelling of the name is inconsistent.

No. 7

To Madame Bence

Sainte-Marie, 16 August 1808

You will easily understand the pleasure I felt upon receiving your letter and that of Mademoiselle Annah. You only seconded my wishes when you left her free to think for herself and to write what no doubt her heart dictated. Could you doubt, Madame, my feelings for your charming daughter, and do you not see me already determined to ensure her happiness? Would I be willing to marry her if I did not love her? Who could force me to do so? I am not afraid to repeat all of this to you, Madame, and as a mother you must be as pleased to hear it as I am pleased to say it.

I am very fond of Mademoiselle Annah, and it is because I truly love her that I would wish to see her act a little more naturally with me. Should she not, when I speak to her of my love and when I ask her about her feelings for me, give me a simple answer? I confess that in my last conversation with her I had to summon all the patience of which I am capable in order not to let her see how displeased I was. You will witness, Madame, the gentleness with which I will always treat Mademoiselle Annah, but after all it is easy to understand that I should appear to be cold toward her. How could it be otherwise, despite my feelings for her when, after more than an hour of speaking to her, I am unable to obtain the tiniest little avowal? You can believe me when I say that it has pained me more than once that I was unable to act differently and that it was only the fear of annoying Mlle Annah that has always held me back. How it pleases me to open my heart to you! It almost seems to compensate me a little for the deprivation of being so far from you. When will I be able to cease speaking to you in this ceremonial tone and give free rein to the tenderness I feel for you?

Madame, this word seems harsh in view of my hope of being soon counted among your children. Please believe that it will be most important to me to keep your friendship and your benevolence and to prove to you that it will be easy for me to bring about everything I am saying here, if only Mlle Annah shares these feelings with me. I enclose another letter for her, hoping that you will give it to her and join me in urging her to mitigate her timidity, which really does not befit her relationship with me. All I ask of Mlle Annah is natural behavior and frankness; how, at the point we have reached, can she fear to tell me what she thinks? I have fully confided in you, Madame, and you know best what should be done now. I am ready to follow your advice and to give you every proof of my sincere attachment. . . .

No. 8

To Madame Bence

No date

Madame,

I arrived at Saint-Pierre about an hour ago. I am feeling perfectly happy today, what more can I ask? My heart is content: I shall never forget the day I had yesterday; it made three months of suffering vanish into thin air. How sweet it is not to have to doubt the feelings of one's beloved any longer. This joy is now mine, and I feel more than ever that Annah's affection was necessary to my happiness. . . .

I do not need to repeat here, Madame, all the things I have already said to you. As long as you are convinced of the sincerity of my feelings, you will never doubt that I will always endeavor to prove to you that I am worthy of your trust. . . .

[On 5 October 1808, an imperial decree declared Pierre Dessalles worthy of being admitted as associate judge (*conseiller assesseur*) to the High Court of Martinique. On the next day, the marriage took place in the parish church of Fort de France. The groom, Pierre François Marie Dieudonné, was twenty-three years old; the bride, Marie Magdeleine Calixte Bence (called Annah) was sixteen. The witnesses were men of considerable local prestige. For Pierre Dessalles, they were Admiral Villaret de Joyeuse, Grand Aigle of the Légion d'honneur, captain-general of Martinique and its dependencies, and M. Pierre Clément Laussat, member of the Légion d'honneur, colonial prefect of Martinique and its dependencies. Witnesses for Calixte (Annah) Bence were M. Charles Georges Cacqueray de Valmenier, imperial attorney general (*procureur général*) serving at the island's court of appeals, and M. Pierre François Xavier Lucy de Fossarieu, chevalier de Saint Louis, commissioner in charge of the parish of Marigot. The contract provided the bride with an annual income of 7,500 livres, with the capital to be paid at the end of the war with Great Britain. The couple's first child, Pierre (called Adrien), was born a year later, on 3 October 1809.]

No. 9   1811

To M. Bence, c/o M. de Leyritz,[5] Pacco [Paca] Street, Baltimore, Maryland (U.S.A.)

Martinique, 6 August 1811

5. Michel de Leyritz, also a planter in Martinique, was Nicholas de Bence's brother-in-law.

My dear Father-in-Law,

. . . Since your departure, our position has become worse and worse. Our sugar has no value at all, tafia[6] is selling poorly, and the syrups, which are still doing reasonably well, are barely enough to provide for our daily needs. We have a very hard time getting the rations for our negroes. Salt meats are cheap enough, but since they are only sold for cash, it becomes impossible for planters to obtain them. Those merchants who are still willing to provide these items to their suppliers [of sugar] charge a hundred percent more for them. Thus, however we go about it, we are rushing headlong to our ruin. All of this inspires sad reflections in the father of a family, and I must confess that I do not foresee anything that would allow us to hope for a better future. The news from Europe is not good for the colonies. M. de Grenonville[7] has arrived. He said that he had the opportunity of speaking to the minister, who told him that the government, aware of the conduct of the High Court, was most satisfied with this corps. . . .

No. 10[8]

To M. Bence

Lamentin, 4 October 1811

Yesterday we were at table at M. de Valmenier's when Narcisse[9] came to bring a big package containing several letters from you. I was happy to find that one of them was for me and thank you for thinking of me at a time when your affairs, your American relatives, and a country new to you must keep you very busy indeed.[10] . . .

In the colony an event has occurred that at first had everyone badly frightened, but which now occupies only the Court of Appeals. Some mulattoes and free and slave negroes had no doubt conceived hopes of founding at Martinique a second Haitian empire.[11] They had planned to set fire to all four corners of

6. Tafia is a liquor made from the by-products of sugar production. It was less costly than rum, which is derived from molasses.

7. Jean-Marie Duval de Grenonville, future president of the royal tribunal and gentleman of the king's bedchamber in 1819; deputy of Martinique in 1830 [HF and LE].

8. This very long letter was written over several days. Since one often had to wait days or weeks for the departure of the next boat, this was a common practice.

9. A house slave of the Bence family at their residence in Fort-de-France [HF and LE].

10. Apparently, Dessalles used the word "American" to apply only to the United States.

11. Allusion to Henri Christophe, who had recently proclaimed himself emperor of Haiti. Born the son of a freedman in Grenada about 1757, he took part in the American War of Independence. He subsequently became maître d'hotel at the best inn of Cap Haitien, an officer under Toussaint

Saint-Pierre during the night of 18–19 September, seize all guns and knives to be found in the stores, sound a fire alarm, and massacre all the whites indiscriminately—women, children, old men, everyone. From there, they would have moved into the countryside and, shortly after the inhabitants of Saint-Pierre, all the rest of us would have been killed. That was their plan, but could it have succeeded? It seems highly unlikely; in any case, it is much better that the plot was discovered and nipped in the bud, so that these wicked scoundrels did not have to tussle with our militia and the few soldiers we have left. A domestic servant of Pitault,[12] whom these scoundrels had wanted to corrupt, told his master about the plot. Pitault informed the royal solicitor-general, who in turn instructed the General,[13] who thereupon immediately went to Saint-Pierre.

The leaders of this conspiracy, seeing that their plot was discovered, lost their heads. Some went to neighboring plantations to try to win over the work gangs, while the others, in groups of five or six, took up positions above the Garou plantation. The latter were pursued, caught, and thrown into jail. When the ringleaders failed to succeed in their project, they fanned out all over the colony, but it was not long before they were discovered and subjected to the same fate as the others. The behavior of the work gangs was perfect. Many arrests were made, but many people were released. The High Court was called into extraordinary session in view of setting up a commission, composed of two of its members and the solicitor-general, to initiate the proceedings against these criminals. Perinelle[14] and la Motte were appointed; they went to Saint-Pierre ten days ago.

Yesterday the Court met at Fort-Royal to hear the commission's report on its work and to deliberate on what to do with these rogues. A new order of His Excellency has summoned us to Saint-Pierre for the 7th of this month. The General wants to handle this affair with as much publicity as possible, and

Louverture, generalissimo under Dessalines, elected president of Haiti, and finally president for life before proclaiming himself emperor of the northern part of the island under the name of Henri I in 1811.

An excellent administrator, Christophe left two extraordinary architectural monuments: the sumptuous palace of Sans-Souci (partly destroyed by the earthquake of 1842) and the formidable citadel of La Ferrière.

Following the stroke he suffered in August 1820 and abandoned by his guard, he realized he had become the helpless toy of his enemies. He shot himself through the head in October [HF and LE].

12. Relative of Pierre Dessalles.

13. Probably the English general Major General Charles Wale. Acting governor-general of Martinique, Wale had been appointed to this position in April 1812 following the British victory [HF and LE].

14. Distinguished Creole magistrate and distant relative of Dessalles.

he is right. A striking example will buy us a few more years of tranquillity —
if indeed it is possible to enjoy tranquillity in this country. So we will go to
Saint-Pierre on Monday. I find these journeys terribly disruptive, but in circumstances like these it would not do to show a lack of zeal. Annah was hoping
that I would be with her for her lying-in, but if she does not hurry, I might well
be the last of the family to make the acquaintance of a little human being who
from birth will share all my tenderness with my beloved Adrien. . . .

> [The rest of this letter provides a striking example of plans for "birth control by
> separation," which may have been a fairly common practice in the French Carib-
> bean colonies. In Pierre Dessalles's case, however, one senses rather too much
> enthusiasm for shipping off his wife and children. The birth control did not work
> very well, since the Dessalles eventually had six children, but the subsequent his-
> tory of their marriage, as revealed in Dessalles's diary, paints a picture of almost
> complete incompatibility of the spouses.]

Today, when I talked with Annah about her mother's departure for [North]
America, I urged her to accompany her mother and to spend three or four
years with you in America. She did not hesitate to show me that such a separation would pain her greatly. I was pleased, of course, at this little proof of her
affection, but because my love for my wife only aims at what is best for her and
her happiness as well as for the happiness of my children, I believe and have
reason to believe that they would be much better off in America than here,
even separated from me. In three years of marriage, my wife will have had two
children. You know how languid she was after her first confinement, and I hope
she will be more fortunate this time, but then who can guarantee this? She
might suffer the same discomforts and, in this case, her health would further
deteriorate. And yet this would not prevent her from becoming pregnant again
in the next 18 months, and so it would go on and on, and in the end she might
become so ill that she would be an invalid for the rest of her life. This would be
a great sorrow to me.

These, my dear Father-in-Law, are the worries that gnaw at me, things about
which I do not like to think. My wife is young, and so am I. What, then, is a
separation of three or four years? Nothing, surely, and by now we must know
each other so well that we never have to fear any changes in our mutual feelings.
As for my children, would they not be a hundred times happier and would they
not be much healthier in America? In four years, when Annah would come to
rejoin me, she could leave Adrien with you, since by then he would be almost
old enough to begin his education. Given my certainty that you, as well as
Madame Bence, would take excellent care of him, I would be blameworthy if
I thought only of my own happiness in having him with me and neglected the
chance of providing him with good health and a solid education.

The colonies are coming to an end, and you know the extent of my fortune and my expectations. I must not give up either until it is no longer possible to do otherwise. I am determined not to leave Martinique until I have invested enough money in France to maintain myself there along with my family. I must save from the shipwreck all that I possibly can. Beginning in 1814, the year when I start paying my mother's annuity, I shall send to France as much as I can and will do so every year until I have accumulated a sum large enough to buy a landed estate in France. If at that time your means permit you to begin paying Annah's dowry, I hope you will not enforce the clause of the contract under which the payments do not have to start until one year after the conclusion of a peace that we might never see. If you were to insist on that clause, my intentions would be cruelly thwarted, but I am concerned with your daughter's happiness, and so I feel that you are bound to help me carry out a project that will ensure that happiness forever. Let me repeat, my dear Father-in-Law, that I am too well aware of your tenderness for your children ever to conceive the idea that you would miss an opportunity to contribute to their happiness. As long as Annah would be in America, I would assign to her the income of her dowry, which you would promise to pay to her. Since she would have no other expenses but her own upkeep and that of her children, I assume that she would have more than enough, according to what you wrote to Madame Bence about what it costs Madame de Leyritz to run her household.

The next step is to persuade Anna to follow her mother. I know that she will invoke her duty and that she will tell me that she cannot make up her mind to separate from me. But none of this weighs very heavily; when I see that it would be very advantageous to her health and that of her children to send her on this journey, I gladly accept the separation and ask you to please help me persuade her.

America must really be a very monotonous country for you to realize this so soon, for one usually sees a country one visits for the first time as much more beautiful than it is. It took me no more than three months to become completely disgusted with it and to decide never to live there. France is the only country where I ardently wish to live; according to what M. de Grenonville tells us, one should not despair of some day enjoying there the greatest tranquillity. He says that wealthy people who are not involved in government are perfectly content. My hope is that some day all of us will be reunited there. . . .

Saint-Pierre, 9 October [1811]

I left Annah on Sunday and have not had any news from Le Bochet [the Bence plantation] since that day, which proves that everything is well there and that my dear Annah has not yet given birth. I have been here since Monday, and it is only today that I find a moment to write to you. Monday, from eight o'clock in the morning until half-past four in the afternoon, we were occupied with reading the procedure. Yesterday the guilty parties were interrogated and definitively judged. Today our decision will be submitted to the governor and, as soon as he has approved it, the executions will be carried out. Sixteen mulattoes or negroes, most of them free, are condemned to be hanged. Three mulattoes or negroes, among them Léveillé, a goldsmith at Fort-Royal, will be imprisoned for one year, at the end of which time they will be expelled from the colony or imprisoned for the rest of their lives. I could give you a great many details, but aside from the fact that I do not have the time to do so, they might only bore you.

In view of the evidence produced at the trial and the crimes committed by these scoundrels, new tortures with which to punish them should be invented. I can swear to you that our consciences are perfectly secure from any remorse. Molière, the leader of these rogues, unfortunately, was not captured; he destroyed himself right after the plot was discovered. The things we would have learned from him! I expect that a few of the conspirators will be done in by several of the leaders. There are still many guilty individuals in this colony, and they will be found out sooner or later. But goodness me, we are lucky that all of this was discovered, for this affair could have become very serious.

[A continuation of this letter, written on 12 October, reports the birth of a baby boy, Charles. This child lived for only a year.]

I am still sick at heart from my stay at Saint-Pierre, and will long remember this event. Everything is perfectly quiet, and the most reassuring fact for us is that the slaves were not at all involved in this whole plot. Some were forced to go along with the party of free people, but their number is very small and does not grow any larger. Some revelations were made, especially by a free mulatto from Saint-Domingue, who said that he had been on the staff of Christophe for six and a half years and that he had come to this colony with the intention of provoking an uprising of the mulattoes and negroes against the whites. He also claimed that he had left at Curaçao a group of comrades who would have come over here at the first signal. You can imagine that the most stringent precautions will be taken. I shall very carefully keep you informed of all of this, my dear Father-in-Law, but we will not, I hope, have to worry for a long time to come. — What does frighten me is the current philanthropy. — Our decision has been printed and I am enclosing a copy. . . .

No. 11   1812

To M. Bence

Lamentin, 12 January 1812

. . . Since my last letter, it seems that our misery is abating, for we now have hopes of selling our sugar. Letters received from various merchants in London indicate that, in that market, sugar will soon be worth a great deal of money and, indeed, that some of it is already being sold at fairly good prices. There is talk of granting licenses and allowing the exchange of our products for wine.[15] Messrs. Thélasson who, owing to their way of thinking and writing, were hitherto considered enemies of the colonies, seem today to have a very different opinion of our colonial fortunes. Their last letters would indeed be apt to inspire us with great hopes; but do they really know more than anyone else? There is no doubt that we are experiencing an improvement, since raw sugar is now sold at 36 livres and 40l 10s, and coffee, which earlier did not even fetch 2s 6d, is now worth 10 and 12s 2.[16]

But before we rejoice at this small improvement, we had better wait. We have been deceived so often.—Syrup is selling very poorly, but we owe this decline to the Americans, who no longer come here. Tafia sells fairly well. Cod, beef, butter, and the other necessities of life are excessively dear. There you have, in a few sentences, the position of our poor colony. Planters who owe two-thirds of the worth of their properties will never get out from under, those who owe only one-third may be able to liquidate their debts, and those who do not owe anything will live well and stay in business. It would, of course, be desirable if we could invest elsewhere, either in America or in France, what Louis Teissier used to call a nest egg, but how can we manage it in these difficult circumstances? In any event, I am planning to send a sum of 5 to 6,000 gourdes [25–30,000 francs][17] to America by 1813. I am more than ever determined never to settle on that continent; but if one has children and the prospect of increasing one's family, it is good to have money in many places.

It appears that Madame Bence is not thinking of joining you this year, but I am holding to my intention of giving her Annah and her children. Our fat little Adrien continues to enjoy vigorous health and is becoming more promising every day. His little brother has had a continuous fever for the last eight days

15. Napoleon was granting "licenses" to English sugar merchants to circumvent the continental blockade and enter the European market. France apparently needed cane sugar.
16. These prices are quoted in the French currency of livres, sols, and deniers, despite the English occupation [HF and LE].
17. A gourde or piastre was worth about five gold francs [HF and LE].

and has put us through some trying moments. The doctor is very reassuring; as long as he is with us, we do not see anything alarming in the dear child's state, but as soon as he leaves our anxiety redoubles. If one coolly thinks about it, one realizes that he is not in danger, but getting close and seeing his pale little face and his air of suffering, how can one help feeling pained? I hope that before I finish this letter I can tell you that he is completely well. . . .

A great blow has fallen upon your unhappy children! The dear child of whom I spoke to you on the 12th and whom I thought saved, was taken from us at half past three. My poor Annah is in a terrible state! And how the physician Desvaux must reproach himself! Arthur will give you all the details; I do not have the strength to do so. Adrien is left to us, and he will help us bear our grief. The sight of your poor wife breaks my heart. Great God, what a spectacle it is, your weeping family. . . .

No. 12

To M. Bence

Fort-Royal, 20 March 1812

Have you received my last letter, my dear Father-in-Law? I told you about a very sad event, the death of my poor little Charles. It is more than two months now that this unfortunate child is gone; Annah, who was at first in the deepest despondency and is still greatly afflicted, nonetheless seems to be less sad now. However, I am not satisfied with her health, and I think it is necessary for her to travel to America. I have done my utmost to persuade her to follow Madame Bence, but I think I have preached in the desert and have made up my mind not to say any more about it. She wants me to go with her; while it might be easy for me in my position to leave the colony, would it be right to think only of myself? My mother would be left alone, since she has no one else to take care of her business. I told this to Annah, and I repeat it every day. As long as I have not placed elsewhere enough resources to make me forget Martinique, I shall stay here. Traveling is ruinously expensive, and if one has decided to make a journey, one must at least see to it that its outcome is useful.

[Here follows a discussion of the possibility of both Pierre Dessalles and his wife spending some time in London, but Anna rejects this plan out of hand.]

Our position is still the same, we are more poverty-stricken than ever, and our sugar is without value. By now, you have no doubt heard about the arrests that have been made here. A M. Fauvel—a mulatto, I am told—has admitted to forming a conspiracy to seize the person of the General[18] and to declare the independence of Martinique. He incriminated several individuals, who have been arrested. The General himself interrogated them, and all of this was done in the greatest secrecy. The fact is that we do not even know what the conspirators were planning to do or that there was indeed a conspiracy, for it is generally felt that such a project could be conceived only by a fool or a madman. Nonetheless, how can one decide what is happening here if one sees the General expelling well-known people from the colony, all of them planters and heads of families? I would just as soon like to believe that these gentlemen are guilty, as the General's handling of this matter indicates. MM. Catalogne and Montrose are leaving for London, and MM. Masseracas and Fontanes for the United States. This, my dear Father-in-Law, is all I know about this affair. I shall here permit myself only one observation, namely, that if such a plan really did exist, the punishment is very light, for the colony would have been lost forever. . . .

[At this point there is a three-year gap in Pierre Dessalles's correspondence. Here are some of the relevant events of this period: On 6 December, Pierre and Anna's third child, Louise, was born. On 2 July 1814 Anna's brother Arthur Bence de Sainte-Catherine married Pierre's young sister Mérotte. The Bourbon monarchy was restored in France, and Martinique was returned to France by the Peace of Paris (1815). On 1 August 1814, Pierre Dessalles was decorated with the *Fleur de Lys*, and, on 9 December, he was confirmed in his position of magistrate at the High Court of Martinique. Madame Bence de Sainte-Catherine, Pierre's mother-in-law, died on 30 January 1815. The family's fourth child, Calixte, was born on 24 March 1815.

That summer, Pierre took his young family to the United States. Having first visited a number of cities on the East Coast, they planned to stay in New York for an extended period; but when their aunt Madame de Leyritz decided to return to France, Anna and the children went with her. Pierre returned to Martinique by himself. This was the separation for which he had worked for so long. No word of hostility can be found in Pierre's correspondence or diary (at least not yet), and long separations for the sake of the wife's and children's health do not seem to have been altogether uncommon in France's Caribbean colonies. Still, advocating a young couple's separation, presumably as a means of birth control, does not strike us as a sign of a companionable marriage.

The separation did not last long, for Pierre joined his family in Bordeaux in January 1816, and his wife was pregnant again by August. After a harsh winter in Paris, Pierre visited his cousins in the Dordogne. He was seduced by the handsome country château of Lespinassat, two kilometers south of Bergerac, and bought it. Here he installed his wife and children, along with her father and sister. His daughter Antoinette was born at Lespinassat in April 1817. After major

18. The British commander, Lieutenant Charles Wale; Martinique was under British occupation from 1794 to 1802 and again from 1809 to 1815.

improvements, the Dessalles family lived at the château for the next ten years, spending the winter season in Bordeaux. Pierre was absent much of the time, traveling back and forth to Martinique, a major and expensive undertaking, to manage his sugar plantation. He did, however, see enough of his wife to beget two more children, Emilie, born in April 1820, and Henri, born in May 1821.

In December 1821, Pierre reported on the state of his plantation to his brother-in-law Arthur Bence, also a landowner and a magistrate at the High Court.]

No. 17   1821

To Arthur Bence at his estate at Lamentin

Sainte-Marie, 20 December 1821

. . . Things are going reasonably well here, although they are far from what they used to be. A bit of charlatanry is needed in every occupation. M. Gruet [the long-time manager of the Dessalles property] did not tell Papin [the manager of another plantation] what is really going on here (but this is just between us).

Since the death of my father 14 years ago, we have 52 fewer negro slaves, and more than 60 of those that we bought since then are no longer alive. Since our labor force is no longer the same, we also have to give up some handsome revenues. The low price of sugar is the hardest blow of all. If I did not owe money to MM. Durant, and if my brother did not have a legal claim to the sums I must pay him in France, we would be doing fairly well, but how can I meet all these obligations? One must place all of this in the hands of Providence and not think too much about all the bad things that can happen.

In January, M. Gruet will hand over the reins of the plantation to me; he is tired out and has convinced himself that a journey to France will rejuvenate him. My mother too has made up her mind to leave in May. She will not spend any more money in France than she spends in Martinique, and she will enjoy herself more.

CHAPTER TWO

1822-1823

[From now on, virtually all of Pierre Dessalles's published letters are to his mother, who left Martinique for France in the spring of 1822. Letters to other recipients will be identified as such. Madame Dessalles seems to have been the co-owner of the plantation. She therefore understood its workings and particularly the interactions between the slaves, the managers, and the owners. Pierre felt that he had to justify his every move and discussed every detail of his management in his letters to her, thereby providing a rare glimpse into the manner in which interpersonal relations were played out on a plantation.]

No. 19

20 April 1822

It is eight days ago now, my dear Maman, that you sailed for France. . . . When I returned to the plantation, I wept bitterly for a time, and then I went back to our affairs. I found everything in good order, and all continues to go well. We are making sugar, although the cane does not yield as much as we expected. We still have a large number of negroes in the hospital, but not one of them is seriously ill. Israël is very much better. . . .

I had 300 molds of sugar clayed.[1] I shall send them to you along with the

---

1. In order to "clay" the raw sugar, a certain kind of white earth or clay was placed on the sugar in the molds and then doused with water [HF and LE]. See also Dale Tomich, *Slavery in the Circuit*

sugar that is already in the drying house. If my experiment with the earth bleaching turns out well, we shall continue doing it; if not, we will go back to our old method. If you see Madame Montard, tell her that her son [a newly hired *économe*, that is, an accountant or assistant manager on the Dessalles plantation] is full of eagerness and good will. I find it necessary to temper his severity. One notices that Europeans, who cry out so loudly against the barbarity of the colonial planters, are usually much harsher than the Creoles themselves. This is because they do not know the infernal race whom we have to guide. . . .

No. 21

15 July 1822

. . . I am back from Fort-Royal and Saint-Pierre. I had expected to stay longer in these two towns, but then I needed to be by myself. Everything is going beautifully at the plantation, the negroes are behaving well, and I have every reason to believe that our revenue will be assured with 7 to 8,000 molds [about 200 tons] of sugar. Since you are interested in every small detail, I do not hesitate to give them to you. I am going to marry five couples: Germain and Laurance, Saint-Cyr and Marie-Barnabé, Jean-Pierre and Jeanne-Rose (who has just given birth to two children), Edouard-Bibianne and Adrienne, and Lafortune and Monique. I am giving them advantages that will turn to our benefit and reestablish morality. To my mind, this is the only way to ward off evil and bad intentions. The future will tell if I am mistaken. The new negroes are doing well; nine of them have already been launched in their work, which they perform with great zeal. As you can imagine, I am treating them very leniently. Since you left I have only lost old Agnès. I have acquired six mules, which have cost me 1,100 francs . . . Quite a bargain![2] Expenses this year will be a little high, because of the new negroes, but I hope that, beginning in July 1823, I will be able to reduce them considerably.

Slaves from other places and free mulattoes are not to come to the plantation. Strict orders have been given to this effect. Fortunée[3] is at this moment at

---

of Sugar: Martinique and the World Economy, 1830–1848 (Baltimore: Johns Hopkins University Press, 1990), 182–83.

2. Said sarcastically [HF and LE].

3. Fortunée was a house slave of the Dessalles family. Devoted to her masters, she had prevented a fire at the plantation when there was serious unrest in 1792. Her sons Dieudonné and Saint-Fort went to France with Dessalles and his family in 1816. Dieudonné died at Lespinassat, while Saint-Fort eventually went to Guadeloupe, where he lived in 1848 when emancipation was declared [HF and LE]. See also diary entry of 27 November 1843.

Zozo's under the care of a healer, who gives her hopes of being cured, although the doctors have declared that it cannot be.

The weather has been so unfavorable that we will have planted only 22 carrés [69 acres];[4] we will take good care of the offshoots.[5] This year's harvest will make at least 9,000 molds. But we must face the fact that, in the future, our land and our labor force will not allow us to expect such good revenues. I believe, however, that we will obtain the same results if we are able to cut down on our expenses. I will make serious efforts to do so. . . .

I must tell you that I ordered Anne[6] off the plantation, but she cried and entreated me so much that I decided to buy her. Only under these conditions will I keep her on the place. She is in the house and will replace Scholastique, whom I will put in charge of the chickens,[7] since Man Zabeth can no longer do anything. The approach to the house and the garden are well kept. They are taken care of by Toing, and I am pleased with him. Chignac [head stewart of the plantation, born in Périgord] is well; he no longer annoys me quite so much and seems to understand that it is in his interest to please me. I shall keep him as long as I can, but I would not feel too badly if he left today. I am convinced that elsewhere this man would do very poorly. "Some shine in the second rank but are not seen at all in the first." Montard [the new assistant manager] will some day be very valuable to us; his activity and his zeal are unbelievable. I am delighted with them. If M. Carié does not come to see me, I have decided to put Montard in charge of this great machine when I go to France. . . .

No. 22

24 July 1822

Madame Dupuy [Dessalles's commission agent], who only charged a 5 percent commission on the sugar I would send to France, has just written to me to make it quite clear that she will not continue to advance you 36,000 francs per year. She tells me that she has so informed you. Do not worry about this new development; I shall get around it, and I hope that we will do even better. Since one has to be a little diplomatic in social relations, I answered Madame Dupuy just as she would have wanted; since I need her to advance the funds

---

4. In Martinique a *carré* measured 1.30 hectares [HF and LE] or 3.12 acres.

5. The "big canes" were those that grew the first year; the first, second, third, and later "offshoots" were those that grew in subsequent years.

6. Anne was a slave from another plantation, but she lived with one of the Dessalles's male slaves [HF and LE].

7. A job for aged and infirm slaves [HF and LE].

for the new negroes, I will handle her with kid gloves. But once I am out of
her clutches, she will have seen the last of me. For the moment, I will send
Mme Dupuy only the sugar needed for our obligations within the colony. I will
send MM. Durant no more than 80 *milliers* [80,000 pounds or 40 tons] every
year, for I believe that it would be best to send some sugar to all the seaports.
I will figure out how to go about this. You know my connections in le Havre;
I think the house of Forsans is solid. It is, after all, a branch of the Salle and
L'Hôtelier firms of Bordeaux. At Nantes, I have my good friend Gouin, who
is the very picture of probity. At Rouen, there is M. Bouchon, whose praises
are sung by Perinelle. Until I make my shipments, you can ask MM. Charles
and Olivier Durant to pay your annuity and that of my wife. But do not say
anything about my intention of sending sugar to other firms than theirs. Please
write how much you received from L'Hôtelier so that I can settle my accounts
with Madame Dupuy at the end of the year. Aside from that, I can tell you that
poor Mme Dupuy is going to lose all her good suppliers, for she is niggardly,
suspicious, and threatening. Her son, a kindly but inexperienced young man,
is the head of the firm. . . .

No. 23

11 August 1822

[Dessalles worries about meeting all his obligations, especially to his brother
Charles, who, he suggests, should be given only what is left when all other expenses have been met. Charles, a military attaché at the Bourbon court, constantly hounded his brother for his share of the plantation income.]

The Lamentin district (*quartier*) is ablaze right now; poison is causing horrendous ravages. Lassalle and Borck have suffered heavy losses. The [governor]
general[8] has decided to reinstate the special tribunal, but the wrong people are
on it, and it is feared that more harm than good will be done. God preserve
us from this scourge. I myself have neither white tongues[9] nor stomachaches[10]
among my people. The work gang is recovering very rapidly; Madame Champ[11]
cannot get over the beauty of the negro children and the healthy look of the
adults. Montard is doing well; he is becoming less harsh and severe. The con-

8. General Donzelot, governor of Martinique, 1816–25 [HF and LE].
9. A "white tongue" is a sign of severe anemia [HF and LE].
10. The "stomachache," which went hand in hand with progressive debility, primarily struck
people newly arrived from Africa. The illness was akin to sleeping sickness [HF and LE].
11. Mme de Champfleury, an old family friend who over the years spent a fair amount of time
at the Nouvelle Cité.

spiracy against Chignac is stronger than ever. If this man were less dull and less stubborn, it might be possible for me to keep him, but he is hopelessly stupid. Nonetheless, I will fire him only if I absolutely have to.

No. 24

8 September 1822

... The royal prosecutor at Saint-Pierre[12] continues his old tricks. The kind of individuals the government sends us makes it clear that it is not interested in the colonies. Today all the negroes arrested for poisoning declare that they harmed their masters only because these masters did not want to give the slaves three free days a week, as M. de la Mardelle[13] had proposed. Since protection of its colonies is not among France's concerns, the generous thing would be to let the colonists devise the means to protect themselves against the evils that threaten them. . . .

No. 25

Sainte-Marie, 18 October 1822, 8 o'clock in the morning

For the last five days, my dear Maman, we have been living in a state of great anxiety. During the night of October 12–13, thirty slaves who were working on the Canal du Carbet revolted, attacked several plantations, and barbarously murdered seven whites. Two died under their blows, and five are severely injured. The criminals then fled; they have given themselves colonels, and their watchword is Liberty. Colonel Barré with troops of the line and the militia is in pursuit. They are hiding in the woods, and it is to be feared that the core group will get larger. The royal prosecutor at Saint-Pierre writes to Survillié that nine of them have been arrested. Their plans are known now. They were first to pounce on Saint-Pierre, massacre everybody there, and then fan out into the countryside. They were counting heavily on the work gangs, who on this occasion maintained a dangerous neutrality.

We must face the fact, my good Mother, that this country is sinking fast. . . . In God's name, do not talk to me about coming back here. You would not believe how terrible it makes me feel to think that you still have the idea of returning to Martinique in three years. The government wants to do us in, and

12. In 1822 this was Dumas de Champvallier [HF and LE].
13. Baron de la Mardelle had been sent in 1808 by the justice department to elaborate a new judicial code for the colonies [HF and LE].

we have ample proof of it, for if it wanted to protect us, the colonies would recover. What is needed would be to be firm in dealing with a certain class and, in particular, never to permit a mulatto to return to the island once he had left it. Communications with Saint-Domingue take place every day. The apathy of the governor and his entourage is positively dreadful. One is almost tempted to think that they laugh at our troubles. What a government![14]

I receive the order to report to Fort-Royal on the 22nd; the High Court has been called into extraordinary session. Sixteen of the perpetrators have been arrested and will no doubt be judged immediately. I also assume that the governor will institute security measures and that he will wish to consult us. You can imagine that we will not miss this opportunity to speak to him with all the vigor that is called for. If Martinique is lost, General Donzelot will be given another governorship, but what about us, and what will become of our poor children? I repeat again, my dear Maman, do not ever think about returning to Martinique, whatever the state of your health.[15] It is better to die in one's bed than to run the risk of being massacred. I do not believe that this country will perish right away, but it seems impossible to me that it can last for long. . . . I am full of courage, and the reason that keeps me in Martinique would give me courage if ever I came to lack it. You must believe that I will always do what is needed to protect your interests and mine. I shall take risks only to the extent my duty and honor demand it. . . . I know that my life can be useful to you, to my wife, and to my children, and therefore consider it valuable. Everything is in excellent order on the plantation. If I am to believe some of the negroes, I can count on all of them. It is worth a great deal that they voice such good intentions, but I have little faith that good can come from such an evil race. Montard is as brave as Caesar. Chignac is more cowardly than should be allowed, and our interests mean very little to him. He worries only about his own money box. I am having the place thoroughly patrolled. . . .

14. Contrary to what the colonials thought—and Dessalles represents their views very well here—the government cared very much. The governors of Martinique and Guadeloupe had jointly hired an agent at Saint-Eustache, asking him to "watch the activities of the rebels of Saint-Domingue" and the insurgents of the Spanish colonies on the continent. See David Geggus, "The Slaves and Coloreds of Martinique during the Age of the French and Haitian Revolutions: Three Moments of Resistance" (forthcoming in Robert Paquette, ed., *The Lesser Antilles in the Age of European Expansion*, Gainesville: University of Florida Press).

15. Dessalles's mother wants to return to Martinique for the sake of her health; his wife must leave it for the same reason. Pierre seems anxious to keep both of them away. His entreaties to his mother not to return are a constant feature of his letters to her, although we have not included them here every time.

[In the course of October, almost all of the "rogues" were caught, and Dessalles felt somewhat reassured. Still, he repeatedly urged his mother to stay in France: "Make plans as to how to save money, carry them out, and pass them on to my wife." Also, "You will see a great deal of my Adrien; give him advice on how to be economical, for nothing is more pernicious than to bring up children with the idea that they are rich."]

No. 26

30 December 1822

. . . I have written a long letter to my wife, which she will send to you. You will see that at this moment I am occupied with restoring not the coffee plantation but a plantation for growing provisions. I already have two carrés [6 acres] planted in bananas, cabbage, and yams. In three months, I will have a cabin put up so I will be able to supervise the work myself. For a moment, I had hoped that M. François Sage would sell me 20 negroes. In that case, the new establishment could have been made into something important, but since M. Julien, to whom he was going to sell his land, did not keep his word to him, the affair did not go through. So I will have to do step by step what I would have done in one fell swoop. I have just bought three pretty young negroes at 2,200 livres each. From the sugar mill, I will take Montout, Louis de Saint-Jean, and Caco. All three of them were bought at Saint-Pierre, and they keep running away (*marrons*). To them I will add several house slaves, who can work the four carrés [12 acres] of land I am having cleared. From time to time, I will rent some negroes. With patience and organization one can achieve everything.

This establishment will be a great help to the sugar mill and will produce more food than we can consume. My plan is that, when I leave Martinique, the annual expenses for the plantation will be no more than 50,000 livres a year. . . . In the month of January, I will work on a statement of expenses for the plantation and will send you a summary of the number of negroes and animals we have. The year's end has been a cruel time for us; in the space of six weeks, I have lost two adult negroes, Lapin and Philoge, and two children. This does not diminish the number of workers, but I am far from saying, as some people do, that this just means fewer mouths to feed. Whatever shape he may be in, a negro is always doing something and must be replaced if he is gone. . . .

Montard was happy about your note to him. I am still pleased with him; he is full of zeal but still a bit rash. Chignac practices a despotic manner that I am constantly obliged to tone down. I do not think I will keep him much longer, which annoys me because he is really a competent agriculturalist. But I could not possibly entrust my property to him if I were to leave the colony. I must know the man with whom I leave the plantation, and so I must not lose any time hiring him. I don't have anyone in mind.

I must inform you of the death of poor M. Pierret [former manager of the sugar mill]. Despite his conduct, I am sorry to hear it. He would still be alive if he had not left the plantation. This has given pause to Montard who, I am sure, will never go in for debauchery.

1823

[The first letter of 1823 contains Pierre Dessalles's reaction to the famous "Affaire Bissette," which the French editors describe in the following terms (1:225):

The men of color of Fort-de-France had been accused of distributing a subversive pamphlet, thereby preparing a general slave uprising on the island. Accused of being the ringleaders were Volny, Fabien, and Bissette; the latter possibly was the son of a bastard of Joseph Tascher de la Pagerie, father of Empress Joséphine. The three were condemned to the galleys for life, but Pierre Dessalles and three other magistrates voted for the death penalty. When the decision was overturned by the Court of Appeals in France, the case was retried before the High Court of Guadeloupe, which brought a sentence of deportation. Bissette was deported to France and soon pardoned by the king. At the time, France experienced intense agitation in favor of the emancipation of the slaves, who idolized Bissette from afar. Bissette advocated gradual liberation and called for calm, while others wanted immediate and total liberation. After the promulgation of the government decree of 27 April 1848 (the so-called "Schoelcher law") providing for emancipation, Bissette was to return triumphantly to Martinique in early 1849. He encountered Pierre Dessalles at Sainte-Marie on 28 April, and [on this occasion] the two men forgave each other.

Pierre Dessalles's diary describes this meeting, and subsequent ones, in considerable detail (see chapter 10).]

No. 27

Fort-Royal, 6 January 1823

In the first moments of a terrible event, my dear Maman, I wrote all about it to Annah, but these letters were for you as much as for her. Things are calming down, and our tranquillity, which fortunately was not disturbed, is becoming more secure. We have come out of a dreadful crisis, and we owe God great gratitude. Today the government must make its position perfectly clear and no longer give hopes to a class that will never pass up an opportunity to revolt.

The conspiracy was serious; all the whites were to be massacred, and we must face the fact that this country is a volcano that will be ignited by the slightest spark. Renounce it forever, my good Mother; go to join my family, where all of you must live with the utmost economy. Above all, do not expect your revenues from Martinique to be as considerable as they were in the past. The land no longer yields as much, our labor force is smaller, and the price of sugar has fallen dramatically. I am here, our interests are the same, and I shall carefully watch them. You owe me your complete trust.

Honoré[16] has arrived. Many people were astonished by his manners, his looks, his pretension, and his language. He is a good fellow, but I would give a great deal not to have had him return to Martinique. I am thinking about him a lot. I have already given him several useful lessons, and he listens to me. I shall attach him to my personal service, and as soon as I find a favorable opportunity to get him out of this country I will seize it.[17] It has been decided that no more manumissions are to be authorized. . . .

No. 29

Sainte-Marie, 26 March 1823

. . . Since my last letters I have suffered some misfortunes on the plantation. Sacriste hanged himself, and I lost Baron, Elie, and poor little Délie, whom I miss very much. I was with this child when she breathed her last. She was attached to her masters and would have grown up to be a good subject. Otherwise, the plantation is in very good condition and, with the exception of Vieux-Corps and Roger, two pitiful subjects, there is no one in the hospital whose life is in danger. I sent Fortunée and some other negroes to take the waters,[18] and this has done them good. Our canes do not yield anything; this is a problem for everyone, and we owe it to the rain and the tornado of 1822. Our harvest this year will not be impressive; I barely expect 7,000 molds. Because of the scarcity and the high price of foodstuffs, our expenses will be fairly high, though no higher than in 1822; moreover, these expenses will include the establishment of our provisioning grounds. . . .

The news of the war[19] has been most detrimental to us here. The price of

16. Honoré was one of the Dessalles's slaves who had been a domestic in the family's château in France.

17. Dessalles soon changed his mind about this, and Honoré became his most trusted servant. He eventually became the overseer of all operations at the coffee plantation, the Caféière.

18. Probably the waters of Carbet [HF and LE].

19. The war with Spain. The French expedition to Madrid, authorized by Metternich's Congress system, was intended to repress the Spanish revolution. The "war" was brief.

sugar has fallen and that of foodstuffs has doubled. Since I have no money, I was unable to lay in food. The Good Lord will come to my aid, and with His help I will manage. Above all, my dear Maman, do not fret. If this war should prevent me from sending money, you can join my family. There you will be happy, and you will not need so much money. The High Court has just given me a long and difficult task. It is planning to rewrite the entire law code of Martinique[20] and two of the volumes have been assigned to me. Since I will need advice for this work, I am going to Fort-Royal and Saint-Pierre, where I will stay for some time. So I am not lacking work; fortunately, I have a good head and good health. . . .

No. 30

Sainte-Marie, 30 April 1823

[This letter begins with elaborate explanations as to why Dessalles was unable to ship a certain quantity of sugar to his mother, who fears that she will run out of money. Apparently, she had berated her son for his failure to act in a timely manner. He tries to calm her down and points out that, "in the colonies, one is not in a position to do what one wishes. The elements and political events interfere when one least expects them, and one is often forced to give up all of one's calculations." Actually, he has made a substantial shipment of sugar.]

. . . Madame Dupuy informs me that the *Zelina* has arrived at Bordeaux. I am very glad, for this shipment will bring good money. We have not yet decided to which port we will send the 25 hogsheads of raw sugar, but I think it will be to Nantes, as a consignment to M. de Laville. I must warn you that I will assign 6,000 francs of the proceeds to Chignac in partial payment of his salary for 1822 and 1823. I give him 6,600 livres a year and have no intention of raising his wages, which I consider sufficient. He has bought a small property in France, and I had promised that these 6,000 francs would be paid to his father. One must keep one's word. Once this letter of exchange is paid, you will receive the rest of the proceeds of this sugar.

[Here follow more lamentations about poor sugar prices and bad weather and more exhortations to his mother to stay in France.]

From what you tell me about Honoré, I expect to see him arrive here [at the Nouvelle Cité] in July. Do not forget to send me the government paper showing that you had permission to take him [to France] with you; I will need this paper to recover your bond. If you are not pleased with Antoinette, all I can say is that she is a good-for-nothing wench, for it would be in her own interest to

20. This project does not seem to have come to fruition [HF and LE].

serve you well. If one can avoid it, one is better off not taking people of color to France, for especially in the provinces one can find young girls one can train to one's liking. . . .

No. 33

Sainte-Marie, 4 July 1823

. . . I wish I could tell you that I am pleased with my work gang, but quite the contrary is true. I always have between 30 and 40 negroes in the hospital. Twelve have died since January, and several others are threatening to die. This is not normal, but I keep up my courage, although I am often quite dejected. What a terrible occupation I am engaged in! Yet I have to do it, the interest of my children demands it. Chignac knows about growing things, that's all. Montard is full of zeal, and that's all. So you see that I do not have the help I should have and that I have to involve myself in everything, foresee everything, figure out everything. . . .

I have just made an excellent purchase for our hospital. Since Martonne is falling apart, I tried to find someone to replace her. I did not see any capable negress, so I decided to buy a knowledgeable and active mulatto woman of appropriate age. She is very attentive to her work, and I am delighted with her. So here is one most important matter taken care of; Martonne hardly does anything anymore.

Fortunée has returned from taking the waters. Her stay in that place cost me a good bit. She says that she is cured, but I think her illness is incurable. Trop [21] behaves well, one never hears her, and she carries out her duties exactly. Praxcède says that she is pregnant, but her pregnancy does not show yet. As long as she is promiscuous anyway, I would at least like her to have many children, who would some day make good slaves (*sujets*) for us. Praxcède always behaves well; she is running everything in the house and especially in my room; she is eager and faithful. Edouard is the best negro one has ever seen, and Célicour will follow in his footsteps. Trépoli is growing up; he will be promiscuous, he is already doing some of this stuff! Héloise is very good, and I am also content with Anne and Aline. Foiry is a good negro, and Jean-Baptiste is a bit lazy, but I am patient. Madeleine is doing very well; I will take her to the Caféière [coffee plantation], where she will sell tafia; her daughter will stay with her. I can tell you that the Caféière [22] is almost finished. . . .

21. Trop, a house slave, became the mother of a very important person in Dessalles's life, Saturnin. See diary entries after 1850.
22. La Caféière was situated above the main plantation, Nouvelle Cité. Thanks to the trade

Let me tell you the latest about our priests and their foolishness. Dear Abbé Pierron is still the same; he will never change. He has been treated pretty badly by the apostolic prefect. This prefect, whom I had always gladly supported and defended—and whom I still support and defend today strictly for the sake of his office and our religion—has acted with so much zeal that he has committed some grave errors. The kinds of people who inhabit the colonies are not like those in France; and so the prefect, before implementing his intentions and before taking steps to restore morality, which has been entirely forgotten by the people of color, should have thought about the interests of the colonial system. He should have consulted and visited people and let himself be convinced that the established order must be preserved if slavery and the respect that free people of color owe the whites are to be maintained. He [the prefect] did not ask anybody's advice; he rushed forward without realizing, I believe, that he was carried away by his zeal until rather too late. Abbé Brizard, a vain and ambitious man, seized hold of the prefect's mind, praised his ideas, helped carry them out, and was rewarded by being appointed deputy prefect. Abbé Pierron stoically put up with all of this and earned much admiration. I confess that for six months I avoided going to the monastery,[23] so that I would not be called upon to divulge my opinion. I am on good terms with the prefect and with all the priests, but I know what I know.

Now here is what Abbé Brizard did: he gave communion to six free men of color at François, all of them rich. These same individuals were also confirmed. But a week later, the provost's court went to François to examine a rash of poisonings. The six men were compromised, convicted of poisoning, and by now must have been beheaded. The horror of it! Such ease in bestowing trust and giving out the sacraments right and left is dangerous; these gentlemen of the clergy should be a little more circumspect. Immorality in this dreadful country has been pushed entirely too far. At Saint-Pierre, some unfortunate newborns who had been abandoned there were found, still palpitating, under the gibbet. The people of color and the negroes have no belief in the truth of religion; they are thinking about one thing only, and that is the destruction of the whites and the overthrow of the government.

All this is just between us, for it is in our interest to propagate notions contrary to what I just said. But how fortunate you are to be in France! Stay there, my dear Maman, and forget Martinique, except to lament that your property

---

winds, the climate there was "delightful." Dessalles had a small house built in a clearing, where he intermittently lived until 1856 [HF and LE].

23. No doubt the old Dominican monastery, which served as the prefect's residence [HF and LE].

is there. Congratulations on the departure of Antoinette; she is a good-for-nothing who would eventually have caused you all kinds of troubles. Paris is a dangerous city for all our slaves. I would be very glad if Honoré had not returned to Martinique. I won't need him on the plantation; if he wants to give you 6,600 livres for his body [i.e., his liberty], accept. I found out from a letter he wrote to Praxcède that Edouard, the concierge of the court, owes him 4,000 livres. You can see that he has a nice little business going. As for Saint-Jean, I am not at all surprised at what you tell me about him. If our friend Gruet [former manager of the plantation] returns to Martinique, be sure you make him understand that he must prevent Saint-Jean from setting foot on our plantation. I no longer allow any slaves from the outside on the place, nor any free blacks. All these communications are dangerous. . . .

No. 34

26 July 1823

The convoy that left on the 15th brings you a letter from me, my dear Maman, in which I give you all the details that might be of interest to you. They were not as satisfactory as I would have wished them to be, but I did have to tell you the truth. Our negroes continue to torment me. The conspiracy to get rid of Chignac continues, and I see myself forced to dismiss him, which pains and upsets me very much. What I am telling you here must stay between us, and our domestics at Lespinassat must not find out about it. Remember that the correspondence between them and our people here is almost incredibly active and that they keep each other informed of everything.[24] Being very displeased with the work gang, I made it clear that I am outraged by their behavior. On the eve of my name day, I indicated that I would not accept the good wishes of any negro. I went up to the Caféière, and they seemed to be upset by my refusal to see them. I gave them to understand that nothing would please me more than to continue to show them my interest, but that they would have to prove worthy of it by sustained good behavior. They soberly listened to everything I said, and it was clear to me that they had made up their minds.

I have just spent a whole week at the Caféière. Several delegations came to see me, led by our most notable subjects. I received all their statements with the proper attentiveness. "Discouragement," they told me, "is at its height,

---

24. Unlike their counterparts in the United States, all of the Dessalles's house slaves were literate. This seems to be considered normal by Dessalles and his mother; they are only surprised by the activity of this correspondence.

your negroes are giving in to despair, nothing amuses them, they no longer get dressed, and when they think of M. Chignac, the hospital fills up, and they let themselves die." "Monsieur," Césaire told me, "give us the devil, if you can, but do not keep M. Chignac. You do not have poison on your place, and discouragement is the only cause of all your trouble."

All this took place on the 13th; on the 15th, Chignac came to me, wild-eyed and as pale as a dead man. I was resting on my bed and very calmly asked him what he had to tell me. "A misfortune," he replied, "Césaire has killed himself by throwing himself down from the top of the mill wheel." Remaining perfectly calm, I asked him the details of this event; here they are, as given to me by him. They were making sugar. That morning, M. Chignac noticed that the canal was not properly closed up, summoned Césaire, who was in charge of this operation, and had fifteen lashes given to him. At noon, M. Chignac, thinking that Césaire was drunk, had another 30 lashes administered. This negro was in despair but received the chastisements without a murmur. A half-hour later, Chignac was startled when he heard all the negroes in and around the buildings cry, "*Césaire tué corps li*" [Césaire has killed himself]. He immediately went to the place where the body lay and found it in the most horrible condition. He questioned the negroes, and Marie-Luce told him that when she saw Césaire on top of the mill wheel and asked him what he was doing there, he replied, "Hello, all of you, say hello to M. Chignac, and tell him that he won't find Césaire to beat him again," and that he then threw himself down. Having heard Chignac's account without flinching, I told him to return to the plantation without delay. I did not feel I should go myself and kept a profound silence. Actually, everything was in good order, and the work gang did not show any kind of sorrow about this event.

I do not know whether I told you that, since last January, Césaire was no longer the driver of the work gang. In December, he had come to ask me to relieve him of his command, saying he was not well and did not feel talented enough to be driver. Feeling that this was true, I accepted his resignation. I told him, however, that I would call on him to replace Jean whenever Jean was sick and that, in any case, not having been displeased with him, I would employ him in the woods or in the sugar buildings.[25] Since January, this Césaire has been accused by several negroes of having given them poison. When Aglaé died — she was a newly arrived young negress whom he wanted for his wife, although she preferred Bouriqué — I almost arrested him, convinced that she was the victim of her preference for another man. What held me back was the fear of

25. That is to say, not in the cane fields.

committing an injustice. You can see, my dear Maman, from what Césaire told me on the 13th, that he was determined to do something violent. The work gang attributes his deed only to despair and to Chignac's injustice.

I am in a dreadful position, and I feel it very keenly, but I also feel that it is very important for me to show strength of character and composure. Not to worry, I shall play my role to the very end. To dismiss Chignac would be to show weakness, yet he cannot stay with me much longer. He himself will eventually ask to be let go; that is what I am working on. Unfortunately, this Chignac is a brute, but I confess that he suited me very well in other respects. He is a talented agriculturalist, and I must say that he is absolutely honest. I would therefore not have dreamed of getting rid of him, but as the head of a family charged with your trust, I must do everything I can to protect your fortune and that of my needy children.

This year's harvest is zero, that is to say, it will amount to at most 650 molds, but this is a fate that has befallen the entire colony. We owe it to the heavy rains of 1822 and the tornado of 19 December. The plantation is looking beautiful right now. If nothing thwarts our hopes, we will produce 8,000 molds in 1824.

Heaven, which seems to give me special protection, has just given me a splendid bargain, and I can only praise its decrees. I was able to buy 27 negroes, both adults and children, and all of them Creoles, on very easy terms. They will cost me 59,400 livres, and I will pay 5 percent interest for four years, and thereafter the capital sum in two installments. Of these 27 negroes, 18 are already working; they are at the Caféière, and they are content. Later, I will put them to work at the sugar mill where they will help out the slaves working there. This affair seemed particularly good to me because I can foresee a combination of concrete advantages for the future. It will provide homegrown food for all the negroes, a labor force to maintain the revenues of the sugar mill, as well as a certain quantity of coffee which, when sold in France, will always fetch better prices than the shipments of sugar.

The Caféière is coming along nicely; we have just dug 1,500 yams and picked 8 barrels of maize. Our bananas will not bear until 1824, but I think that then we will have an abundance. Madame Champ prefers the Caféière to the sugar plantation, and it is certain that the air is better there. I have hired a young man for the Caféière. I pay him 800 livres for the first year, and he seems to be very hard-working. So that Montard can more closely supervise the work and the comings and goings of the plantation, I have relieved him of his responsibilities for the household and the hospital and have brought in a M. Joyau.[26]

26. A surgeon, or at any rate a practitioner of surgery [HF and LE].

He is 58 years old and knows about illnesses and how to treat them. His age makes me believe that his experience will substitute for the knowledge of a real physician. . . .

Some good individuals can be found among our slaves, but many are bad. I am pleased with the house slaves; they are all well. Edouard is worth his weight in gold, and I can assure you that he would be nursed in my room if he were ever seriously ill. I am satisfied with Fortunée and her children.

[Here follows a long lament about his persecution by Madame Dupuy, his commission merchant, "that wicked and tiresome woman" who can't seem to sell his sugar, about his work load, about life in the colonies in general, and about his martyrdom in the service of his family.]

No. 35

Caféière, 13 September 1823

. . . Things have been going better in the last month, but one must never shout victory, for the race of men we must command is diabolical and treacherous. I already told you about the death of Césaire and the arrest of Romuald. Romuald, who was kept in the top of the curing house, asked for me one day. I went to see him, and he confessed to having committed great crimes, but he never wanted to admit that poison was among the means he had used. I asked him about the work gang, and he named Césaire, Raymond, and Eulalie as the only ones who had caused us to suffer losses. Césaire was already dead, and he knew it. Raymond was dying even as we were speaking, and only Eulalie was still at liberty. This Raymond met an end very similar to that of Césaire, for he threw himself from the top of one of the breadfruit trees in the provisioning ground and died on the spot. Romuald told me positively that Eulalie[27] had sworn that no black baby would ever come to anything as long as she was on the plantation. Two days after she said that, I lost Vitaline's little girl and Hélène's, the prettiest little negro children we had on the place, and they died of very strange illnesses. Romuald died after he had received confession. I did my duty by him. Now I must deal with Eulalie; my poor heart has not yet found the strength to drag her from her children's arms. This criminal woman is astonishingly calm. Five months pregnant, she made her belly disappear. She is living with Abraham, a handsome new negro, whom you may remember.

The hatred against Chignac seems to have died down since I decided to make him head overseer, for this was the only thing I could do. In thinking

27. She seems to have been the plantation's midwife [HF and LE].

about it, I realized that to dismiss him outright would be to yield to the will of people who might well become even more demanding and might even go in for revolt if they noticed the slightest weakness on my part. Chignac, I repeat, is an excellent planter; he knows our plantation like the back of his hand and combines a number of valuable qualities. He may lose some of his minor faults, and now that he is in charge of everything, he may make more of an effort to get along with the negroes. I already notice that he handles them very carefully. He often visits the hospital. I have given him quarters upstairs in Montard's room and moved Montard to the sugar buildings. In the first few days, Chignac was very embarrassed; to eat at table was an ordeal for him, but by now he has almost become a man of proper manners. His trust in me is well established, but it was no small undertaking to bring him to this point. . . .

On Monday I shall go to Saint-Pierre to make purchases of food and other items urgently needed on the plantation. I am also planning to see Madame Dupuy, with whose suspiciousness and avarice I am thoroughly fed up. I will be extremely happy when we no longer owe her anything, and I will drop her without giving it another thought.[28]

I received the mail packets from Lespinassat. How sad it is to be so far from such a promising family! Heaven will recompense me for all these hardships. I know, my dear Maman, that this sacrifice will go on for a long time. In 1825 I will come to embrace my wife and children, but it will be for such a short time that it would be better if I could avoid this journey. Proprietors must no longer leave their interests, and there is another consideration as well. I have already been a magistrate for fifteen years; in six years, I will be entitled to a government office or pension. The father of a family must not neglect anything. I shall never ask my wife to join me here; this country is uninhabitable, and the way of life of the planters does not square with our own, which you will have come to appreciate. There is not a single person at Saint-Pierre with whom my wife could keep company. All the women there are silly and stuck-up. And you know what the men are. If it were not for Madame de Champfleury, I would live all alone. Once she has moved to Saint-Pierre, I will lead the kind of life that suits me. Once a month I will pay a half-hour visit to everyone in the district. I want to remain on decent terms with everybody. Lassalle and Mme Le Vassor treat me very well but I know where the limits are. I will soon start my enormous work on the code. General Donzelot also treats me well and writes me letters full of compliments, but when it comes to giving a favorable response to a just

---

28. The letter of 17 November 1823 indicates that Dessalles owed Mme Dupuy 122,000 livres, which he hoped to pay off by 1825. He was too optimistic.

request, I don't hear from him. People are all alike, and one should use them in moderation. Let's have few friends, that is the best way to have true ones. . . .

An accursed epidemic, called Spanish War or vapor, has mown down a prodigious number of negroes, and many whites have also fallen victim to it. It went through our work gang, and we were fortunate enough not to lose anyone, although several were at death's door.

No. 37

At the Caféière, 10 December 1823

. . . Now that you have decided to return to the colony, tell me only, my dear Maman, whether I shall expect you here, or whether you will wait for me in France. I came to the Caféière a few days ago. I like it here and expect this establishment to be extremely useful to us in the future and provide much-needed resources for the sugar plantation. Our foodstuffs are growing well, and the coffee looks good. . . .

As I told you, Louison and Eloïse [slaves] were married, as were Sainte-Rose and Sophie. Lucain came to tell me that he wishes to marry Batilde. I have the satisfaction of seeing that morality has come to our plantation. The negroes are doing better, I am generally more satisfied with them, but I am not shouting victory. I just lost Jeanne-Rose, a mother of four children, who was married last year. I had all the last rites administered to her in order to distinguish her from all the others. This is a loss for us; she died of that accursed vapor. . . . I am not pleased that you gave Honoré his body;[29] you will be sorry. I will wait before I make such a gift to Dieudonné. Did I tell you that Honoré had lent 4,000 livres to Edouard, the concierge of the court? Trop gave birth nine days ago to a boy, whom I have not yet seen.[30] Praxcède tells me that he is the son of a mulatto by the name of Favo, a bastard of Julien. . . . Trepoli is well; he does not leave me for a moment, and he is my personal servant. I am still very pleased with our poor Edouard. . . .

29. That is, his freedom. Dessalles seems to object to the fact that his mother *gave* this slave his freedom, since he would have been able to *buy* it.

30. This child may be Saturnin, who became an important figure in Dessalles's life in 1850.

1824–1833

No. 38

To his mother

Sainte-Marie, 12 March 1824

. . . I wrote you a few lines from Saint-Pierre and sent them by the frigate that carried all our mulatto insurgents to France.[1] I am sending you the newspaper containing the minutes of the session of the High Court on the occasion of the inauguration of the new solicitor-general.[2] You can judge from his address that he will be fairly ineffectual. We can wish for only one thing, namely, that he will be just, but I am afraid I can tell you that he comes armed with unfortunate preconceived notions he will not easily shed. We understand that Paris has decided to appoint paid members to the colonial High Court.[3] We for-

1. These "mulatto insurgents" were exiled to Senegal. Cf. *L'Affaire des déportés de la Martinique, 1823–1824* (Paris: Constant, July 1824), in–8⁰, Bibl. Nat. Paris, LK¹2 155A [HF and LE].

2. His name was Girard, and he was the first solicitor-general who was not a Creole [HF and LE].

3. This would have integrated the colonial courts into the system of courts of appeal in the metropolis. As previously mentioned, Dessalles expected to receive a government pension in six years; however, he only took it beginning 19 September 1832, when the regulation referred to here was revoked.

mally reject this plan; while we are most willing to continue serving, we want to do so under the same rules. They can change our robes, the name by which we are called, and all our prerogatives, we don't care, but we cannot willingly give up the only right that compensates us for our labor, that of dispensing justice, free of charge, to our fellow citizens. We expect this change to happen and are resigned to it, although we are certain that it will be bad for the colony. The colonists themselves will soon lament this new order of things; indeed, they are already beginning to give us the credit we deserve, and many are expressing their fears.

I have the satisfaction of telling you that I am infinitely more pleased with the negroes, but they vary so much that I do not dare shout victory. Still, there is a definite improvement, and that means a lot. Montard and Chignac are doing very well indeed; they are both equally valuable, but the former will be extremely useful to us some day, for he will combine the knowledge of a consummate planter with all his other assets, integrity, zeal, sure principles, and sufficient means to represent the landowners. In addition, he is a man of great honor and severity.

Your house slaves are behaving well; the little negro will soon be a big negro and follow in the footsteps of his father, with whom I am ever more satisfied. Célicour is a good fellow, although I lately have had reason to be displeased with him. Would you believe that, for a whole month, he was shameless enough to continue cooking for me, even though he was covered with venereal sores? M. Chignac noticed it, and you can imagine how worried I am. I never think of it without shuddering. The things one is exposed to in this dreadful country! . . .

As for the apostolic prefect,[4] he will be leaving for France in two months, and all the colonists wish he would stay there. His religious ideas simply do not fit in with the colonial system. . . . He used the arrival of the new solicitor-general [M. Girard] to preach some very inappropriate sermons that will do nothing to diminish the preconceived notions of M. Girard. All these things give rise to sad and distressing thoughts, and it is painful to see that the metropolis does not take a more favorable stance. Everything it does seems to promote the ruin of the colonies.

Everyone who sees our coffee plantation is astonished. Two years from now, it will be a promising place from every point of view. I am sending you some notes that will inform you about everything. The manager I had there suddenly quit, saying that he no longer wanted to be under Chignac's orders. It is a miserable thing to have a Creole as manager, and it is a risk I will never take again.

---

4. Abbé Carraud [HF and LE].

[The rest of the letter reports on Dessalles's social life in the district. It consists mostly of gambling parties, which assumed a frenzied quality during the visit to the district of two outsiders, MM. de Pompignan and de Lassichère. Dessalles tells his mother in confidence that he has won 15,000 livres recently and 5,300 livres in the course of the past year. He does not, of course, say anything about his losses. A passion for gambling was to remain an intermittent problem throughout his life.]

No. 39

29 April 1824

[Sudden escalation of the financial crisis, due to the action of Durant Brothers, merchants in Bordeaux, to whom the plantation owes a great deal of money and who now demand to be given a lien on the Lespinassat property.]

We must reassure MM. Durant by making a serious effort to pay them back and improve our fortune. I hear people talking about mine, and it is therefore most important that I be helped by my wife and that we henceforth practice the strictest economy. Whatever you decide to do for yourself, my wife must come and join me, I absolutely insist. She will leave Louise and Calixte in France in the care of a good teacher and will entrust them to you; as for Adrien, he will wait at Juilly until we decide what to do with him. . . . If you decide to return to Martinique . . . we will ask M. Bence to receive our two daughters and their teacher at his home and pay him room and board at a rate he will decide. . . . I am asking my wife to go to Bordeaux herself. She must negotiate with MM. Durant with that noble self-assurance that always comes with a righteous heart.

You are talking to me, my dear Maman, of religion, confession, and death. You know me; my principles are unchanged. If I should die suddenly, I will not be able to confess, but if my reason is adequate to know my state, I will fulfill all my religious duties. God knows my heart and recognizes my sentiments, and I therefore have the greatest confidence in his mercy, but I am not yet called to follow — as you are fortunate enough to do — all the rules of a religion I love, admire, and respect. I am too preoccupied with the fortune of my children, for I must make sure that they will not be left in poverty. . . .

No. 40

Caféière, 26 May 1824

I have just shipped off 25 hogsheads of raw sugar, my dear Maman, that will be loaded onto the *Valdor* and consigned to MM. Charles and Olivier Durant. This makes 80 thousand pounds since January. Between now and October, I will ship them another 50 thousand pounds and, by the end of the year, 20 or 25 more. That is the best I can do, given the obligations I have here. Keep in mind that I have to run and maintain a large property where there is no natural increase whatsoever and for which I have to purchase a certain quantity of negroes every year. If you were here with me, you would be forced to agree that everything is in good condition and that nothing has been neglected. I have no control over events, to which one must resign oneself without becoming discouraged. Once MM. Durant are paid off, we will have 200,000 pounds [100 tons] of raw sugar at our disposal, and I think that will be enough for our expenses, so we must just be patient.

I am expecting my wife; her return to me is absolutely necessary, for it will prove to the world our will to cut all our expenses and our strong determination to honor all our obligations. Arthur is fairly exact in paying me what he owes me.[5] On 31 December, I will assign his 16,000 livres payment to Madame Dupuy. We can no longer make clayed sugar (*sucre terré*), because it no longer sells at Saint-Pierre, but I have made four hogsheads of raw sugar, a superb batch. If it sells well, we will continue; one can earn one-fifth above cost. Syrup can no longer be bartered; it is worth barely 18 sols, and right now it is difficult to find anyone paying even 5 francs for tafia. I assure you it takes some fierce thriftiness to get along.

Two of our new [i.e., African-born] negroes have hanged themselves while I was at the session of the court.[6] They were the oldest, those whom M. Gruet had bought from the Spoutourne plantation. Nobody had done anything to them; they were having a perfectly gay and amiable time [*sic*]. Things are none the worse for it on the plantation. The negroes were very sad about this event, but I harangued them and they recovered their good spirits. I do not have one of them sick in the hospital. Since one cannot hope to be ever tranquil in this business we are in, I just decided to put up with it. You see these things from afar, my dear Maman, and therefore cannot judge them properly. And you are still thinking of returning to this accursed country, where I would not stay another 24 hours if my children's interests did not keep me here. As soon as MM. Durant are paid off, I shall send my wife back to France. If I cannot go with her, I am determined to sacrifice my person for the good of all my family. . . .

[Letters no. 41 and 42 again explain the plantation's difficult financial situation to Madame Dessalles *mère*, pointing out, however, that practically all planters are

5. Arthur Bence, Dessalles's brother-in-law, is paying off his sister's dowry.
6. That makes four suicides in two years!

in the same predicament. There is a first indication that Dessalles's oldest son, Adrien, is not doing well at school in France and wants to go into the military rather than take over the plantation in Martinique. There was to be no end of trouble with Adrien.]

No. 43

Sainte-Marie, 4 July 1824

. . . The July session [of the court] opens tomorrow, but I will not be there. And here is the reason: all the planters of our district are experiencing the dreadful ravages of poison. Madame Littée has already lost 30 oxen or mules. Lassalle is losing livestock, and so is Madame Ferdinand. The river separates me from their plantations. I am in deadly fear and feel that it would be imprudent to leave the place. Everything is going perfectly well here, nothing has suffered, the negroes are content and show me their affection; Praxcède's marriage[7] took place on the eve of my name day [Saints Peter and Paul], and I had given the work gang a holiday. It all came off in good order and with high spirits. My principal slaves reassure me. Our prosperity [!!] seems to astonish people, and there are signs of jealousy. I go out very seldom, and am extremely cautious—never a word that might offend anybody. Wickedness is at its height in this country; one must constantly guard against malice. . . .

5 July 1824

I had no sooner written these words, my dear Maman, when I saw M. Chignac coming in with M. Trachet.[8] A draft ox was found dead in our upper prairie [*savane*]. We immediately went there; the ox was opened, and we found all the signs of a natural death. The spirited animal had overstrained itself at the plow. You cannot imagine our negroes' joy at this discovery. I was dumbfounded by what our good people expressed; tears welled up, and I stepped aside to shed them.[9] In the present circumstances, such an event was bound to make me tremble. I thought I would die when they came to tell me. Always firm, I am able to keep my composure on such occasions. . . .

---

7. She married Honoré, who had accompanied Madame Dessalles to France and been given his liberty. Honoré became the paid manager of the Caféière, and Praxcède was in charge of the house and garden there.

8. Trachet seems to have been one of the assistant overseers of the sugar mill [HF and LE].

9. Dessalles's naiveté boggles the mind. The slaves knew perfectly well that severe retribution was in store for them if their master thought they were poisoning his livestock. Their fears were amply fulfilled, as the next few letters show.

I have bought six young mule drivers for the sugar mill and two young negro girls for the Caféière. Slaves are horrendously expensive, but one must budget the annual purchase of ten negroes in the expenses of the sugar mill. Without that, we cannot possibly continue our business. There are no births, and, although there may be some in the future, we have not had any in a long time, and yet we must produce income. . . .

No. 44

12–13 July 1824

[Recapitulation of the state of Dessalles's livestock. On July 13, the first mule was "found" to have died of poison.]

Last night at prayer I announced that I would be forced to imitate the severity of my neighbors. All the negroes gave me to understand that the trouble came from the outside; in order to take away all excuses, I canceled the distribution of tafia. I wrote to my neighbors to inform them of this and to tell them that I would no longer permit the negroes to take a shortcut through the cane-trash shacks [*cases à bagasses*]. Montard, whom I stationed at Sainte-Isle [a section of the plantation], and Durieu, at the lower part of the prairie, turned back all comers. I have established severe punishments for all outside negroes found on the plantation and for those of ours who receive outsiders in their cabins. All of this will perhaps produce a good effect. I have not slept for three days. I am full of determination, though rather tired. . . .

16 July 1824

. . . I continue my narration. . . . On the 14th at eleven o'clock in the morning . . . I sent for the government's veterinary practitioner who was in the district. He came, and when we opened the cadaver [of a mule], all the undeniable proofs of poisoning were found. The most severely affected part was the stomach. . . . I had it put into tafia and sent it to the [governor-]general, along with word that I would come to see him the next day. That night, I had 40 lashes administered to the head mule driver. I warned the plowmen, carters, prairie guards, and the head mule driver that each of them would receive the same punishment every time an animal died. I told the assembled work gang that starting this week they would get neither Saturday nor Sunday off, that all the negroes, without exception, would receive food but would return to their cabins only to sleep, and that things would not return to normal until they had paid me for the poisoned animals with their work. I exhorted them to patience and obedience. They are all submissive, upset, and full of zeal, and I would find it impossible to point to one guilty individual, but it is necessary to show firmness. This must be the right way to go about it if our misfortune is perpetrated by one of our slaves. If it comes from the outside, our negroes will be particularly watchful and avoid all contact. The general has been informed of all these measures, and I also told him that I would not do anything without writing to him first. . . . All of this must remain strictly secret. Only our family must know about these events. You do understand that the merchants in France would stop advancing us money, thinking that all is lost. . . .

22 July 1824

. . . The first arrests have been made. Three negroes were arrested at the Union.[10] The head mule driver of that plantation has accused Eusèbe, the guardian of our prairie; I had him arrested. Very important confessions have been obtained from the negroes of the Union. Eusèbe has not yet talked, but I think he will be easy to move. It is proven that there was a plot involving all the head carters and head mule drivers. Eusèbe must have accomplices here. . . . Once the oxen were destroyed, they would have started in on the negroes. . . . Thanks to my firmness and the severe measures I have taken, I have stopped our losses. If nothing more happens to us, we will barely notice this event. We will have gotten off more lightly than most, although this episode has added to our expenses for food. Do you realize that it is no small matter having to provide three meals a day to more than 200 individuals? All the punishments will cease on the ninth of next month, when I will have taken four and a half Saturdays, four Sundays, all noon breaks, and some evenings. I will announce to them that the poisoned animals have been paid for and that they can start over, but at the same time I will warn them that in the future I will take even more severe measures. . . .

24 July 1824

Everything continues to go well, but Eusèbe does not want to say anything. I will be sorry to lose this negro; he always worked very hard. I had to arrest him in the interest of the community. Since he was denounced everywhere, it would have been impolitic to let him remain at liberty. . . . Poor Madame de

10. Neighboring plantation owned by Mme Le Vassor [HF and LE].

Champfleury would be here with me if it were not for these events, but I felt that I should ask her not to come. One can't enjoy guests if one has to punish and adopt stringent precautions. . . .

[An exchange of letters concerning a different matter between Pierre Dessalles and one of his neighbors, M. de Lassalle, indicates that there were people in the colony who attributed the increased mortality of mules and oxen to an epidemic. Lassalle allegedly threatened to horsewhip anyone who talked to him of an epidemic!]

No. 47

To his mother

28 July 1824

On the evening of the 24th, they brought me a sick mule; by the 25th at three in the afternoon, it was dead. Such a thing had never happened before. Supposing that Eusèbe is guilty, he is not alone, that much is evident. The head carter of the Union plantation had run away, but he was caught and I confronted him with Eusèbe. He maintained that Eusèbe is a poisoner and had helped him poison the oxen at the Union. Eusèbe quite simply said he was lying. I do not know yet how the district will react. The punishments continue. None of the work gang sleeps in the cabins; I have had the top floor of the curing house arranged for this purpose. After the evening get-together [*veillée*],[11] all the negroes go up there, and the men are separated from the women. I think that they will dislike this existence so much that I will get some confessions. . . .

Here is a rather bizarre story about Bibiane. On Monday, 5 July, she said that Laprade had lost two oxen, whom she identified, and yet these two oxen only died the following Friday. I had this witch arrested, and she admitted that she had indeed foretold the death of the two oxen. Questioned as to how she could foresee such an extraordinary event, she said that she had heard about it from two persons who had passed by, whom she did not know. Impossible to budge her from this position.[12] I am telling you a lot of details, one stranger than the next. Mme Littée has had 46 heads of livestock poisoned. Six of her negroes are under arrest. She should lock up her entire work gang. This has ruined the poor woman. . . .

11. The term *veillée* suggests evening communal activities among slaves similar to those practiced in peasant communities in Europe. Apparently Dessalles permitted this kind of slave interaction. To be sure, he used some of this "free time" for his "prayer meetings." On these occasions he not only admonished his slaves to work harder but also had physical punishment administered.

12. Bibiane committed suicide shortly thereafter [HF and LE].

[By the end of July, a provost's court (*cour prévotale*) has come to the district to judge those accused of the crime of poisoning.[13] Dessalles anticipates that Eusèbe will be condemned to death and that his execution "might put an end to the evil." Meanwhile, Anna Dessalles has decided not to return to Martinique; while this was not good from a financial point of view, Pierre was clearly relieved.]

12 August 1824

This morning when I woke up, I was informed that an ox was found dead in the pen; we are in despair about it. . . . From a distance of 1,800 leagues, you cannot imagine what we feel. Such a thing has never been seen before, and there is something behind all this that would be useful to know. The free mulattoes certainly play a role in all of this. . . .

No. 49

15 September 1824

. . . Since my return from the tribunal, I have learned things that make me shudder. Jean-Pierre, having been confined in the *cachot*[14] for the last two weeks, asked to speak to me. I had him brought to my room, and here is what he declared to me. When M. Gruet took over the administration of the plantation, the work gang, who may have been pushed to work a little harder, plotted to rise up and assassinate M. Gruet, whom they would have buried in the very workroom where the negroes worked. Victor, Grand Joseph, Jean, Moïse, Raymond, Césaire, etc. were the leaders of the conspiracy. One day, M. Gruet, going out into the fields as usual, noticed a general unrest just as these criminals were about to execute their diabolical plan. He returned to the house, and 30 negroes ran away. They were brought back by M. de Séguin, and Jean received 100 lashes.

Jean-Pierre added a great many details that would be too long to relate to you here. In addition, he told me that every year we had eight, ten, twelve, and fourteen pregnancies, but that the negresses got rid of their fruits and that it was known throughout the work gang that Marie-Jeanne had very recently destroyed her child. And indeed, she was believed to be pregnant; she had

13. On this "Tribunal for the Repression of the Crime of Poisoning," cf. Archives Nationales, Section Outre-mer, fonds Martinique, carton 52, dossier 430 [HF and LE].

14. The *cachot* was a small hut with thick walls, a flattened entrance, and one very narrow window. First built at Saint-Domingue at the end of the eighteenth century to confine slaves who had committed serious crimes, they became increasingly prevalent in Martinique and Guadeloupe in the early nineteenth century [HF and LE].

an enormous belly, which one morning was gone, to everyone's great astonishment.[15] Jean-Pierre also added that Jean had done in a prodigious quantity of negroes in the first three years of M. Gruet's administration, when he put poison into the canal three times daily. He also assured me that my father's illness was due exclusively to poison. How dreadful to have to live among all these criminals! I am impassive and have ordered more *cachots* to be built and chains to be kept in readiness. All the known poisoners have been warned that, if I lose one man or one animal to poison, I will clap chains on two of them for the rest of their lives, but make sure that they will work hard just the same. This has been very successful on the plantations of the Lamentin district. I expect it to be so here.

29 September 1824

... Everything is going very well, order has been restored, there are no more signs of poison, but our discipline is severe. My *cachot* is being built, but my guys will remain at liberty as long as there is no trouble. I have chains only on Jean-Pierre, Léon, Barthélémy, and José. If this goes no further, as I have every reason to believe, the effects on our 1825 harvest will be minimal. We are very lucky, for our neighbors have suffered all manner of setbacks. . . .

I often hear from Madame de Champfleury, who is sorry that she could not spend the winter season in the country. But while all these scenes of horror were going on, one needed to be alone. I still do not know what happened to Fabien; he has either drowned or run away. Please make sure that the letters from Saint-Fort and Dieudonné[16] are sent to me and go through my hands. I am very sorry indeed that I passed the last ones on without first reading them. . . .

No. 53

Caféière, 6 December 1824

... Three weeks after the deaths of Chignac's mare and my little horse, I was informed that our best mule had died after two hours of horrible suffering. I had it opened, and when the same cause [i.e., poisoning] was found, I immediately had Jean and Lucain arrested, just as I had said I would, and had them put in leg irons. I was at the Caféière at the time and felt that I should stay

15. According to the French editors, this is one of the rare testimonies to the practice of abortion among slaves.

16. Two house slaves whom Madame Dessalles had taken with her to France. Note again that they are literate, as are those to whom the letters are addressed.

there in order to show the negroes that my mind was made up and that they had nothing to hope for. On the 24th, I went down to the sugar mill, because I expected the visit of Morando, Nina, and Laure.[17] On the 25th . . . I hear noise outside my room; I go to the door; imagine my astonishment to see before me, on their knees, not only all the negroes in chains, but the entire work gang. I ask what they want, and Jean is the first spokesman, asking me to release them. . . . My first question is, under what conditions? Monsieur, he replies, you will no longer have any losses on your place, the ravage of poison will stop. I forgave everything, the rogues were set free, but eight of them will be held responsible. At the first sign of trouble, they will be retaken and put into irons for the remainder of their days. This, then, my dear Maman, is the tragic end of my miseries. Have I made the right decision? The future will tell. I do hope that this is the end of all these scenes of horror and that we will never see them again. Jean is a great monster, and it appears that he and Marie Barnabé are the most guilty. Some day, I will tell you all the gory details.

Chignac's departure has now become indispensable, for all our misfortunes were caused by the slaves' hatred for him. I did not want to yield to my negroes by dismissing him, but today this will not be considered a sign of weakness, and so I no longer hesitate. By 1 January, he will no longer be on the plantation; this will be a loss for us, but I do not expect our revenues to suffer. Montard is very capable — he may already be one of the great agriculturalists of this country — and he is extremely sensitive. . . . In all, we have lost twelve mules, ten draft oxen, and three cows or heifers, plus Bibiane killed herself and Roc hanged himself. . . .

Honoré is very useful to me; he is a good fellow and well seconded by Praxcède. Saint-Fort seems indeed to be a fierce rogue. I have not passed on his last letters to his mother and his sister [Fortunée and Trop], for they were full of ideas contrary to good order. If you are displeased with him, do not hesitate to send him back to me; I will have him sold in a neighboring colony. The letter from Dieudonné was written in a proper style. When I am with you, we will have to decide *en famille* about a course for the future. . . .

Population increase at the sugar plantation is zero, so that we must figure into our expenses the purchase of eight negroes every year. At the Caféière, we have had four births this year, and these children are superb.

As soon as all the coffee bushes are planted so that we only have to maintain them, the negroes of the Caféière will work at the sugar mill four mornings a week. I am planning to establish at the Caféière a stable, where I will keep

17. White friends.

twelve mules, which will produce manure; every morning, four mule drivers of the Caféière will go down to the sugar mill with their mules and come back to sleep at the Caféière. . . .

I am telling you, my dear Maman, it will henceforth be impossible for me to go away from here. I will have to sacrifice my own tastes, and I will do it because the future of my family demands it, but I will never consent to live isolated in this manner and without a single member of my family. My present fate is too hard, and one must love one's children as I do in order to bear it. You know that I am a little bit rigid in my temperament and especially in my principles. I am the constant target of the poisoned darts of jealousy and calumny, but I would not care a fig if I were near my loved ones. I cannot be the friend of the human race; my path is mapped out and I shall follow it, and I do so not as a matter of pride or vanity, but because it is my duty. . . .

No. 54   1825

Sainte-Marie, 22 January 1825

On the first of the year, the negroes poisoned one of my oxen as a New Year's present, but Montard acted as if it had died a natural death. On the day of my arrival from La Grand' Anse . . . they poisoned a second one, and I found chains on all the rogues who had been taken out of them on 25 September last. Since then, everything is going well; the hospital is empty, and Camille, whom I had given up for lost, is recovering and gives reason for hope. You must not become discouraged, my dear Maman; Montard still exercises the greatest severity, and he will succeed, I am certain of it. The plantation is in magnificent condition, and we will bring in big revenues. All it takes is order and thrift. They will get tired of doing evil, and we will have a few more years of tranquillity.

[Nonetheless, Dessalles indicates that "poisonings" are beginning to recur on neighboring plantations.]

No. 55

1 February 1825

. . . The fact that no ships arrive is very disruptive to business, for Saint-Pierre is full of sugar that can't be sold. I have paid off all my accounts at La Trinité, where I no longer owe a single sol, and I have a six months' supply of codfish. I am awaiting the statements of Roignau and Mme Dupuy to draw up my account, which I will send to you. . . . I am making sugar right now; the canes yield very well, and the income will be handsome, although I was forced to buy a few negroes, for whom I have to pay. Do you realize that those who are in chains are our most valuable subjects? . . .

No. 56

Sainte-Marie, 18 February 1825

["Poisonings" in the district continue.]

. . . It is generally believed this time that the poison comes from the free people of color, who are giving evil advice to the slaves. These rogues are looking for vengeance, and they stop at nothing. At this moment, many arrests are being made at Robert, and more than twenty free mulattoes have been compromised or arrested. Lassalle is experiencing the same horrors on his plantation at Lamentin. It was no doubt a plot, and everything seems to point to perfidious plans, but we have nothing to fear.

No. 57

Sainte-Marie, 27 February 1825

. . . Since 1 February, we have lost three draft oxen, a little calf, and a small heifer. Mme Lépine has lost a cow that was in our prairie. Moïse, who was in chains, threw himself into the big vat just as it came to the boil. He was pulled out and died 24 hours later. He confessed to things that make your hair stand on end. Jean is dead; I believe that he communicated with somebody during the night and that they smuggled in some poison with which he killed himself. This is the general outline of what happened, I spare you the details. . . . The losses continue. All the plantations are in the same situation, and it is believed that the free mulattoes incite the slaves. . . .

No. 60

Sainte-Marie, 15 April 1825

. . . Let us talk of MM. Durant.[18] You are upset, you say, that MM. Salles *fils* and Thieubert refused to pay off our debt to them, because it would be

---

18. Recall that they were the merchants in Bordeaux who, having advanced the Dessalles plantation considerable capital, are asking for more security.

very bad for us if the state of our affairs became known. I do not share these fears of yours at all. I have never tried to hide the true state of our affairs and have never deviated from my candor. At the time, I only asked you not to let the poisonings become known, because any talk of poison would have caused the Europeans, who have only a very imperfect understanding of our colonies, to imagine that everything was lost, everything was desperate. But in fact the position of our colony is far from being so bad. With patience, diligence, order, and thrift, we will put everything back together, and things will return to a state of prosperity. But that presupposes the government's will to preserve the colonies, and to give them a little better protection than in the past. . . .

If it could be done, I would give up all my claims in Martinique tomorrow for 150,000 francs. It is not that I have given up on our fortune; I would do it for the sole purpose of getting away from the horrors I have recently experienced and in order to spare my unfortunate children such experiences. One pays a high price for fortune when it brings distress to the soul. M. Bence, who has lived through this, will understand me better than anyone. . . .

[As for M. Lalanne] I showed him my teeth on two occasions and just recently made a scene apropos of the two church pews he permitted himself to reduce in size without asking anybody, the reason being that he wanted to give pews to four mulattoes, our most cruel enemies. When I spoke to him about it, he . . . said he had nothing to do with this. . . .

No. 61

Sainte-Marie, 10 May 1825

. . . I will stay an extra 24 hours at Fort-Royal in order to attend the special session of the High Court held at the government building. On the agenda is the decision concerning three ships accused of having engaged in the slave trade. This has caused me some painful thoughts about the future of the colonies. General Donzelot is vigorously pursuing the slave ship owners. Our greatest enemies are some persons in the administration, even though these people owe their fortunes to the colonies. The apostolic prefect has left. May he never come back, for he has done a great deal of harm to this country. There is talk of establishing a bishopric of Martinique. If that ever happened, it would be the last straw for us.

No. 62

Sainte-Marie, 26 May 1825

... Above all, my good Mother, give up the thought of Martinique. You could no longer live here, for in the countryside you would be in constant terror, it is no longer possible to doubt it. The free people of color are the single driving force behind everything we are experiencing. Our slaves, who in the past had no use whatsoever for them, are now hand in glove with them. At every execution decreed by the provost court, we see free men of color executed, along with a lot of unclaimed recaptured runaways (*épaves*), an extremely dangerous class of people that is increasing in an alarming manner. The government cannot be bothered with devising vigorous means to prevent this. Indeed, on some major issues, it seems to side with the people of color, whose vanity is flattered by this attitude and who have become more insolent than ever, now that powerful voices have spoken in their favor. . . .

All our misfortunes have come and always will come exclusively from Fortunée's cabin. Her dear little lastborn [Saint-Fort], to whom you gave his liberty, is a criminal. He often comes to see his mother, and how can I prevent him? I give this servant woman all kinds of things, purely to keep her happy. Eugène, Trop, and Saint-Just[19] are doing their duty conscientiously, but full of vanity and pride. What a dreadful brood! Honoré is still showing a great deal of zeal, which I believe is more sincere. Manumissions are no longer authorized since the affair of the mulattoes;[20] otherwise, he [Honoré] would already have his.[21] . . .

No. 63

Sainte-Marie, 7 June 1825

[Increasingly desperate appeal to his mother to stay in France.]

... The Caféière is coming along beautifully. Our negro children there are magnificent; we already have four pregnancies there, and only one down here. Honoré is still full of zeal; I am pleased with him, but it is devilishly difficult to know what is in the bottom of the bag. What a dog's life one leads in the colonies!

19. Fortunée's other grownup children.
20. This "affair of the mulattoes" must refer to the unsuccessful uprising of mulattoes, free men of color, and slaves reported by Dessalles in a letter of 4 October 1811 or to the "Bissette Affair" of 1822.
21. This must mean that private manumissions were no longer recognized by the government, for on 10 December 1823, Pierre Dessalles had commented on the fact that his mother had "given his body" to Honoré.

No. 69

Sainte-Marie, 22 August 1825

... The news of the independence of Saint-Domingue[22] has been devastating to the entire white population of these colonies. It is an iniquitous act of the government that we owe to M. Villèle. To be sure, strong measures to safeguard the society of Martinique and Guadeloupe will have been stipulated, but will they stand up to the contagion? We will fall into a true slump. This is an honest warning, and we must heed it and make our bundle now. From now on, we must therefore live even more thriftily, if at all possible. ...

No. 72   1826

Sainte-Marie, 5 January 1826

... The news I have today of the district of Sainte-Marie is not good. The poison has not been entirely stopped at our place; from time to time, we still lose an animal or a negro, and one of our oxen or mules is always sick. Otherwise, everything is going well. But what is terribly upsetting is to see entire families of whites disappear. M. de Sainte-Julie, his wife, his daughter, his sister, his brother, and his son died within the space of seven weeks. The last two were opened, and a firm diagnosis of poison was made. It is very frightening. These good people are genuinely mourned; they were kind to their slaves, indulgent toward the free people of color, and generally loved by all their compatriots. No one yet understands anything about these multiple crimes, whose perpetrators will no doubt soon be known and punished. This is an example that happened before my very eyes, but I could cite you a hundred others. I hope, my dear Maman, that you have lost all desire of ever reappearing in a country whose inhabitants are surrounded by the most dreadful hazards. Every family must have its victim, and I devote myself to the interest of all; some day, it will be the turn of one of my children to so devote himself. ...

[Early in 1826, Pierre Dessalles went to France. He stayed there a little more than a year, during which time he sold Lespinassat and provisionally installed his family at Bordeaux near his father-in-law, M. Bence, and his sister-in-law,

22. Saint-Domingue (Santo Domingo) had just been given its independence by Charles X against payment of an indemnity of 150 million francs to be distributed among the former landowners.

Cécilie Bence. In October 1827, he returned to Martinique, bringing with him his eighteen-year-old son Adrien and the young slave Agricole. According to the French editors (1:200, n. 30), Agricole soon became an agitator for the abolition of slavery. In 1834, he was arrested as a ringleader of the uprising at La Grand' Anse and sent to the penal colony of Brest, where he eventually died.]

No. 73   1827

Sainte-Marie, 27 December 1827

Agricole is behaving very badly; I have refused to see him. He talks a lot about how people of color are treated in France. He constantly shows off a certificate [of good behavior] you have given him and about which I did not know, so that I look like a liar when I say that his behavior has not been good.

[Adrien, who had not done well in school, was now to learn the *métier* of a planter. Clearly, he was designated as the next "victim" to be sacrificed to the family's fortune. On the way to the Nouvelle Cité plantation, father and son visited many notables of the island and were well received wherever they went.[23] Adrien was struck by how *old* all of his father's associates were.

Dessalles's relations with his mother suffered considerable strain when she gave her brother-in-law, M. Dessalles de Boismarcel, proxy to act in her behalf and asked her son to share his management decisions with him. In letter No. 75 of 18 September 1828, Pierre vigorously protests against this interference, trying to prove that, given the many persons who have access to the plantation's books, he could not possibly cheat his mother, even if he wanted to. He then proceeds to describe to her the terrible state of his health ("I do not wish my wife and my children to be informed of what I am suffering at present, for they would think me sicker than I may actually be"). The empathetic observer cannot help but feel that he is punishing his mother. There is also a hint of other troubles to come: "Adrien embraces you with all his heart, his health is excellent, and he loves this country. He spends two-thirds of his day taking care of horses. . . ."

In addition, it was troublesome that Montard, the manager of the Nouvelle Cité, had resigned. A letter from Dessalles de Boismarcel to Madame Dessalles reveals the background of this resignation and confirms the impression conveyed by Pierre Dessalles's letters, and even more strongly by his subsequent diary, that he was woefully clumsy in all his human relations. In the case of Montard, Dessalles blamed his manager for his own mistakes.]

23. Adrien Dessalles, cited in +Adrien Dessalles and Henri de Frémont, *Histoire et généalogie de la famille Dessalles ou Des Salles, Martinique et France (1650–1974)* (private printing, 1974).

No. 77   1828

Dessalles de Boismarcel to Madame Dessalles, his
sister-in-law

25 November 1828

You asked me to correspond with you, and I will be glad to comply with your
wish, provided, as you yourself requested, that my letters not be communicated
to anyone, least of all to [Pierre] Dessalles.[24]

I put off writing to you because I did not want to worry you about an acci-
dent of M. Montard, who was bitten by a rabid dog. . . . The time when the
crisis would have occurred has passed; the danger is over, but Dessalles will
lose Montard. This young man is very touchy, and Dessalles is not sufficiently
sensitive to his feelings; otherwise, I am convinced that Montard would listen
to him as a son listens to his father, indeed, more than Adrien listens to him.

How sorry I feel for Adrien, whom I love with all my heart and who could
assume in society an honorable position worthy of his family. He has given himself over to all the passions of youth and to all the suggestions of the young men
of his age who, in this day and age, will only seek to take advantage of him. Poor
Adrien! I have pleaded his cause before I even knew him. I pleaded it to his
father when I advised against bringing him here. Dessalles is already punished
for it and, I am afraid, will be punished even more in the future. Adrien has
excellent natural gifts, but neither his father nor, I assume, his mother have
been able to develop his good qualities. We no longer live in the age that has
just ended; young people who believe they are smarter and more learned than
we are need different restraints than those that held us back. We need not bow
to their decisions, but we must treat them considerately and especially never
criticize them in public. This offends their pride and makes them bristle.

Your plantation is doing well so far, but I am afraid that the cartage for the
building of the new sugar mill is causing the mules and oxen to lose too much
weight. I must tell you that this is one of the reasons Montard gave me to justify
his decision to leave Dessalles. He was afraid that Dessalles would blame him
when what he had warned against came to pass. Let us hope that it will not
come to pass. . . .

I have heard from Dessalles. . . . He is very glad about Montard's departure,
according to what he writes to me in confidence, but he does not remember
how difficult Montard's task was, what with the new and poor quality negroes

---

24. It was not uncommon for absentee plantation owners to solicit information on their own
agents, even their own relatives, from several sources.

he had bought and left dying, both at the sugar mill and the Caféière. Although Montard was unable to please him, Dessalles does not impugn his zeal or his loyalty. However, I continue to believe that Dessalles will succeed.

[On 25 February 1829, Pierre Dessalles received his commission as captain in the colonial militia. In 1831 his wife Anna arrived in Martinique, accompanied by her second daughter, Calixte (15 years old), and her third daughter, Antoinette (13). She left her two youngest children, Emilie and Henri, in France under the care of their eldest sister Louise (18). Dessalles's diary, which forms the bulk of this book, will show that the presence of "the ladies" greatly complicated his already complicated life in the colonies. "The ladies," especially his wife, detested Martinique, suffered from its climate, and spent too much money on clothes, pianos, and knickknacks of all kinds that had to be sent from France. In February 1833, Calixte married her remote cousin Georges de Cacqueray-Valmenier, a sugar planter of excellent family background but of rather limited financial means, who lived near Fort-Royal. A year later, the eldest daughter, Louise, became engaged to a civil servant, Marie-Louis Cléret, *"receveur de l'enregistrement et conservateur des hypothèques"* at Fort-Royal. Two daughters were thus to be established in Martinique, but their mother returned to France after three years. In a desperate effort to save money, Dessalles called her to Martinique in 1840, but this stay as well did not last more than four years.

Here is one of Dessalles's letters to his brother Charles in France. A former member of Louis XVIII's Household Guard, Charles had ceded his co-ownership of the plantation to Pierre against a regular share of its income. In addition to a keen interest in perfecting his command of the English language, Charles cultivated a passion for hunting. For him, Martinique was strictly a source of income. Pierre's laments about the situation of the colonists should not be taken at face value, since he wanted to make it clear that the money he owed Charles was not easy to come by.]

No. 79　　　　1832

To his brother Charles in France

Sainte-Marie, 7 January 1832

. . . I have experienced a great many vexations in the last year. Fortunately, I am in very good health; another person might have broken down under the accumulation of vexations I have had to bear: M. Gruet has deeply offended me . . . then there are the Littées who treat me very badly, the Ballains with whom I have broken off all relations, the Survilliées who accuse me of having instigated the proceedings against Lagarigue and of having used my influence to have him imprisoned. . . .

None of these things would bother me very much, *mon cher ami*, if I saw a more secure future for the colonies, but I do see them threatened from every side, and events are becoming so dark that it will soon no longer be safe to live here. M. Dupotet [the governor] has just recently compromised our tranquillity by one of those blunders to which he is naturally prone. You know that Bissette[25] has asked the Chambers [of the parliament in Paris] to free the slaves. The governor thought that the free men of color of Martinique who had elected him [Bissette] would be quite willing to protest such a demand, especially at a time when officers' epaulets[26] had just been bestowed on some ten or twelve of them. The governor therefore approached the most prominent men of color of Fort-Royal, all of them friends and relations of Bissette, and they all refused to sign the protest. One of them declared that, far from protesting the action of Bissette, to whom they owed all the concessions they had obtained, he was willing to sacrifice the slaves he owned and indeed his last sou to avenge all the humiliations he had been made to suffer. They no longer hide their aims today; if the government is serious about preserving the colonies, it is woefully misinformed about the intentions of this infamous class, whose fondest dream is the destruction of the whites. The slaves found out about the governor's *démarche* and about the response of the men of color. Now they are making up songs about it and say that the whites are opposed to their emancipation, while the men of color insistently demand it. The negro's mindset has drastically changed; it is not hard to see why that should be, but today it is very difficult to lead him.

So this, *mon cher*, is our situation; you can see that it is far from pleasant. What will become of me and my large family if we have to give up everything? If only I had 20,000 francs outside of this country, I could use this sum to establish myself somehow; but is it not horrendous to have only poverty to look forward to? I suppose the colonies will hold out for another six, eight, or ten years and that, by then, I will have paid you your fortune and saved it for you, although this will not change my situation. . . .

No. 82

To his brother Charles

Fort-Royal, 28 July 1832

. . . In a few moments I will probably cease to be attorney-general; M. Dupotet [the governor] has received the law banishing Charles X and his family

25. For Bissette's background and the so-called Bissette Affair, see chapter 2, letter No. 27 (6 January 1823).

26. It had just been decided that free men of color could become officers in the colonial militia [HF and LE].

from the territory of France and her colonies.[27] He asked me to countersign the order to promulgate this law, but since hitherto such orders were never countersigned by the attorney-general, I felt it my duty to point out to the governor that the law does not stipulate anywhere that orders to promulgate a law must be countersigned by the head of an administration. I did not want to do this for a law of which my conscience does not approve; to make an exception in this circumstance would have brought disgrace upon my family. To attach my name to such an iniquitous act would have been a disgrace. I am convinced that my mother, you, and all our friends and relations will approve of my conduct in this matter. I have sworn loyalty to the government of Louis-Philippe, and I will remain loyal. It is known that my opinions are not subversive, but I must respect the misfortune of the princes I have honored in the past. My opinions have never varied, and to my last breath I shall wish, in the interest of France, for the principle of legitimacy to triumph.

[As he had expected, Dessalles was relieved of his functions as attorney-general and removed from his seat on the High Court (HF and LE). He was proud, however, to have "left public affairs by an honorable door."]

No. 86

To his brother Charles

Sainte-Marie, 17 October 1832

I was very pleased indeed, my dear Charles, to hear of your marriage to Mlle de Calbiac. I very well remember seeing her at Lespinassat almost six years ago; from all the good things my wife and my daughters say about her, it is certain that you have done very well. You cannot fail to be happy since your mate is of your own choosing and taste.[28] . . .

No. 87

To his brother-in-law Arthur Bence, Bordeaux

No date, but stamped "Bordeaux, 1 December 1832"

. . . From your letter to Annah, I see that you are much worried about [your son] Olivier's education. Boarding schools today are so bad that one can be almost certain not to find all the desirable features in the school one chooses.

27. This was the law of 10 April 1832 [HF and LE].
28. Does one detect a wistful note here? Dessalles had married Anna Bence because this was his father's dying wish.

But since you are right there, you can immediately rectify the situation. Henri [Dessalles's younger son] is still too young to be sent to a *collège*; as for the choice of a boarding school, Annah does not seem to be ready for a decision until she can personally look into it. I do not intend to interfere and would therefore ask you to follow all her instructions with regard to this child. Thank you very much, my dear Arthur, for all your kind endeavors on his behalf.

The colony is fairly quiet at this moment, but we were quite worried about Saint-Pierre. It appears that the slaves, prodded by the free people and the *patronés*, were again planning to set fire to the town and the surrounding countryside. It was even said that the bakers, or rather their apprentices, had been enlisted and that the bread was to be poisoned. The most stringent measures were taken, and things have now returned to their accustomed order.

It is rather difficult to make plans for the future, particularly when that future is so greatly threatened; yet I still cherish the hope of being able to accompany my wife to France in 1835. This will largely depend on Adrien, for we can entrust our fortune to him only if we can be sure that it is safe in his hands. There is nothing wrong with his heart, but he is still very young and very spirited. I would therefore not wish to leave him until I have married him off, yet it is very hard to encounter suitable matches these days. . . .

No. 88   1833

To his brother Charles

Sainte-Marie, 24 February 1833

. . . Our last harvest yielded 340 hogsheads of sugar from the two properties [Nouvelle Cité and the Caféière]. I was able to pay off only 12,000 francs of debts, not counting what I gave you and my mother, and I took only 5,000 francs for my expenses and those of my children. I do not know how things will go this year, what with the law that is threatening us.[29] We will produce about

---

29. After the Revolution of 1830, there was a distinct change in French public policy toward slavery and the people of color. In November 1831 the French signed the first mutual search agreement with the British, permitting the British to inspect French vessels suspected of transporting slaves to the West Indies in violation of the Treaty of Vienna (1815), which had abolished the slave trade. Then in 1833, full civil rights were granted to the free men of color. As for slavery itself, the French legislature passed a number of measures to prepare the way for general emancipation, beginning with outlawing the branding and mutilation of slaves in 1833. Heated debates on the modalities of emancipation continued throughout the 1830s and 1840s. It was the cumulative effect of these various measures that prompted planters like Dessalles to regard the central government in Paris as a "threat" to their economic prosperity, as indeed it was.

the same revenue; the expenses of the plantation come to 33,000 francs, and I no longer have the income from my office.[30] Our losses [of slaves?] are still going on, but more slowly. I can assure you that my affairs are a devil of a headache for me.

No. 89   1834

To his brother Charles

Sainte-Marie, 8 March 1834

. . . By now, you will have heard about the uprising at La Grand' Anse.[31] It surely would have spread to Sainte-Marie if it had not been nipped in the bud. I have sent all the details to Cécilie [sister-in-law], who can pass them on to you. Agricole was one of the leaders; he is in jail. Calm has been restored everywhere, but we can expect more such episodes, unless the recall of M. Dupotet [the governor], who is to be replaced by M. Algan [an admiral], can change the spreading ferment. The High Court has been in session since the first of the month, but I do not want to take part and only went to the election because I wanted to make it clear that henceforth I wish to live a strictly private and domestic life. I need to concentrate on the future of my large family. I will thank God if I have enough time both to pay off my obligations and to invest the modest sum of 50,000 francs in France. Then at least I will not face stark poverty with all its attendant horrors. . . .

My uncle Boismarcel conducted himself in the most courageous manner during all the troubles at Grand' Anse. He did not leave his plantation, and these scoundrels did not dare harm him in the slightest, despite the entreaties of Agricole who wanted them to set fire close to his house. . . .

---

30. See above, letter No. 82 (28 July 1832).

31. Instigated by the people of color, this uprising did not have the support of the slaves. The plot was widespread, but it soon came to grief at Trinité. At Grand' Anse, the planters had gathered at the Coeli plantation to put down the insurrection. Dessalles de Boismarcel and his wife, who lived at Grand' Anse, did not follow their neighbors' example and stayed on their plantation, where they were disarmed by the insurgents. One of the ringleaders was Agricole, the young slave Dessalles had brought back from France. Agricole was eventually arrested and sent to the penal colony of Brest, where he died [HF and LE].

Pierre Dessalles, 1816 (painting by Lacoma). Collection Henri de Frémont. Reproduced with kind permission.

Anna de Bence de Sainte Catherine, wife of Pierre Dessalles, 1818 (miniature). Collection Henri de Frémont. Reproduced with kind permission.

Pierre Dessalles and his family, 1821 (miniature). Owned by Gérard Cléret de Langavant. Reproduced with kind permission.

Pécoul and Bissette, deputies of Martinique. Fragments of a silk scarf (E. Hayot collection), published in *Les Gens de couleur libres du Fort-Royal* (E. Hayot, 1971). Reproduced with kind permission.

Slave quarters on a Martinique plantation. Sketch by Marie Chomereau-Lamotte. Reproduced with kind permission.

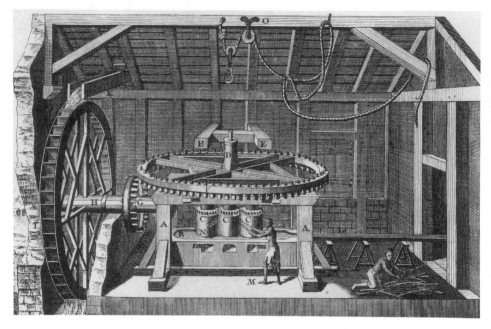

Sugar mill. *Encyclopédie, ou Dictionnaire universel des arts & des sciences, Recueil des Planches*, vol. 1, *Sucrerie* (1772), pl. 2, *Moulin mû par une chute d'eau.*

PART II

Diary

CHAPTER FOUR

1837

[From now on, Pierre Dessalles's existence is reflected in his diary rather than in letters. Historians debate the relative credibility of personal letters, diaries, or journals. Much depends on the intent of the author and on what is omitted or emphasized in the text. Dessalles's letters were evidently intended to persuade his mother in France that the family plantation was in good hands and to convey an atmosphere of racial distrust and hostility that would discourage Madame Dessalles from returning to Martinique. His intent in the diary is less clear. He made almost daily entries, usually recording specific events. Overall, the text, though laden with self-justification and self-pity, is not consciously contrived. Yet the author is sometimes cryptic — "I am not saying here everything I fear or everything I think" or "I told my son the secret reasons for this" — suggesting that he was holding back. Indeed, at one point, he records a delicate conversation on a separate sheet of paper.

Whatever the purpose of Dessalles's diary, its content is both reflective and descriptive. There are passages that he would not have wanted to be circulated. Although there is evidence that some friends and relatives knew he was keeping a diary, we doubt that it was intended for publication as were his father's and son's "histories." Dessalles's outpourings appear to mix apologia with aggressive hostility, stoic fortitude with Cassandra-like foreboding — but for his eyes alone.

There is a three-year gap between the end of the extant letters and the beginning of the extant diary, although the French editors surmise that Dessalles started his diary earlier than 1837. Here is an excerpt of their introduction:

We have left Pierre Dessalles at Sainte-Marie (Martinique) in March 1834. His wife Anna had been with him since 1830, as were their children Adrien (25) and Antoinette (17). Their daughter Calixte had married her distant relative Georges de Cacqueray-Valmenier in 1833 and had just had her first child, a little Louise, who was not to survive. This young couple lived at La Rivière Monsieur, the Cacqueray plantation outside Fort-de-France.

The Dessalles' two youngest children, Emilie (14) and Henri (13), had stayed in France under the care of their sister Louise (22).

But Anna did not like the colonies. She did not feel at ease; she was uncomfortable with slavery and anxious to return to "civilization." Shortly after her husband's last [published] letter of 3 August 1834, she therefore sailed for France, leaving on the island not only her husband but also her son Adrien and her happily married daughter Calixte.

At Bordeaux she rejoined her father, M. Bence de Sainte-Catherine. In order to accommodate her and her family, M. Bence had enlarged his house, which became one of the city's finest townhouses. It was here that the family celebrated the betrothal and marriage of the Dessalles' daughter Louise to Marie-Louis Cléret, *receveur de l'enregistrement et conservateur des hypothèques* at Fort-de-France. This young couple returned to Martinique in 1836.

At Sainte-Marie, Pierre Dessalles — having lived alone on his plantation for about a year, surrounded only by his slaves — seems somewhat troubled and depressed. His former manager, M. Michaud, who had kept him company and with whom he was on good terms, had become exhausted and sick and had tried to find some rest at the Caféière, which he was trying to rehabilitate. He had been replaced at the main plantation, La Nouvelle Cité, by young Oscar Lalanne, the son of an old friend who served as military commander of the parish.

Pierre Dessalles often went out or received company, but his circle of friends remained small and often bored him. Some of his neighbors were unpleasant, indeed downright hostile. There was deadly enmity — for reasons that are still not entirely clear — between Dessalles and the Ballain family, as well as M. de Lagarigue.

As for his extended family, he was in contact with only a few of its members, those who lived close by, separated from him only by the "river of Sainte-Marie" . . . at the Union plantation. Formerly belonging to the Dessalles family, this plantation had been inherited by Mme Ferdinand Le Vassor de Bonneterre, née Emilie Dessalles. . . . Emilie had left Martinique and lived in France. Her immense fortune was entrusted to a manager, and Pierre Dessalles, having reluctantly agreed to act as her legal representative, was supposed to monitor his activities. Emilie's two sons, Alexandre (25) and Louis (21), living by themselves and left to their own devices, frequently — too frequently! — visited their uncle. Sometimes Ajax de Ferbeaux, husband of Pierre Dessalles's niece Eglé Le Vassor . . . also visited.

And finally, there was Nicaise, who never left Pierre Dessalles's side, slept in his room, and clearly was more than a simple domestic servant to him. Referring to him as "*mon petit nègre*," Dessalles was inordinately attached to Nicaise. One wonders about the nature of his relationship with this young man of color, about 20 years old at the time, whose birth record we were unable to find, and whose bloodline is not clear to us.

Dessalles wrote an entry in his diary virtually every day. For the sake of simplicity, no indication is made in the following of deleted entries.]

Sainte-Marie, 1 January 1837

What a dreadful day I have spent! In tears when I woke up, thinking of my children and my wife, and again in tears when I went to bed. My existence is dreadful, I can hardly bear it. My negroes wore me out with insipid and insincere wishes; I harangued them, and they promised to behave well.

My young negro Nicaise asked me to let the people do some square dancing, and I consented. The same fiddlers who serenaded me returned at two o'clock; at six it was all over. Many negroes from other places took part in this little party, which came off in the best order.

This evening I had news from my children. They are in good health, thanks be to God! It seems that my letter made them cry, for I had told them how painful my isolation is to me.

Catala, Pierre Cardin, and Ludovic Littée sent their good wishes. I sent some candy to the Lalanne ladies and to Mme Catala.

3 January 1837

I finished the two patches at Jardin-Madame [a provision ground]; the weather was superb. I am hoeing Fond-Burot and the canes of the hospital grounds.[1] Catala came to see me this morning, and I went with him to Pierre Cardin's, where we had dinner. MM. Lesage and Louisie Burot were there. Tomorrow I am to spend the day at Catala's. I am sorry that I accepted, for it is always an ordeal for me to leave home.

4 January 1837

The weather was lovely. This morning they did hoeing in the hospital grounds and this afternoon digging in the prairie.

What a fatiguing day! At half-past seven I rode off, stopped by at Lesage's and Amelin Littée's, and arrived at Catala's at noon. Almost all the guests were

---

1. When Dessalles says "I," he presumably means that he was supervising the operation in person.

already there. The dinner was well presented, good, and convivial. Later we played *écarté*; I won 110 francs. It was excessively hot, and these mourning clothes are heavy and warm.[2] . . . I was home before nightfall.[3] . . .

6 January 1837

Still the same weather and the same work. I finished manuring the cane of the Bois-Lezard section. Today my negroes have pulled down several bunches of bananas from my provisioning ground. I shall be forced to resume the punishments!

This evening my young negro Nicaise was asked to come to the main road to meet a young negress belonging to M. de Survillié.[4] It appears that she would be glad to live with him, but can't quite make up her mind. If she does not decide by Wednesday, we can forget it. . . .

Madame Magloire, who supplies my bread and earns a lot of money from me, has sent me a terribly bad Twelfth-Night cake. The woman is really very greedy. This Magloire family, once devoted to the whites, no longer has any use for them, now that all these concessions have been made to the free people of color. Behind the polite behavior of Chéry, the oldest of the sons, there is pride and ambition. If it had not been for me, he would have been driven out of the colony in 1823.

7 January 1837

. . . My young negro Nicaise did not behave today as he did in the last few days. When the horn was sounded,[5] he was in the negro cabins. I wish he had a better understanding of his status. Since I treat him kindly, he should sense that he no longer ought to be so familiar with the negroes. I do not mean that he should be haughty with them, but I wish he were more careful about his body and his cleanliness. After all, he sleeps in my room and should not rub himself against everything. I would be very happy if I could instill delicate tastes in him and make him lose those that come with the sad state of slavery. I will not

2. No concession to living in the tropics: a proper gentleman wore a black wool suit for a year when he was in mourning. Dessalles's mother had died the previous year [HF and LE].

3. In Martinique, night falls between 6:30 and 6:45 P.M. year round [HF and LE].

4. Lagarigue de Survilliers. This negress was a slave, but not necessarily very dark skinned. The fact that Dessalles did not object to these negotiations in view of a concubinage indicates that he considered it respectable. It can therefore be assumed that the young woman was a domestic servant, rather than a field hand [HF and LE].

5. At the Nouvelle Cité the work day was punctuated by the sound of a horn rather than a bell [HF and LE].

spare any pains to achieve that. I do not wish him to serve anyone after me, and I wish him to be happy. However, if he wanted to attach himself to one of my children, I would be delighted because I am sure that there he would find the same care and the same kindness.

10 January 1837

. . . I was already in bed when someone came to tell me that the young negro Philibert had been stabbed by bayonet in his left side and that Valentin, another young negro, is the author of the crime.[6] I immediately had him arrested, then sent for the physician La Peyre and had the injured youth taken to the hospital.[7] . . . This Valentin is a lazy fellow who never works and who eats earth[8] in order to get out of work, whereas Philibert is conscientious about his work and behaves beautifully. The cries of his mother and his sister brought tears to my eyes. The things one has to put up with on a plantation! I am not sure how I will handle this situation; the judicial system is very slow in deciding, and its procedures are burdensome.

11 January 1837

Last night the doctor was not at home; he came only at noon today to see my young negro. He does not think the wound is fatal. I sent Octave [Lalanne, his steward at the Nouvelle Cité] to his father in order to find out what I am to do with this assassin.[9] He writes that I must punish him but not hand him over to the law. Accordingly, I have had him whipped. I also put a collar around his neck and will keep him in the work gang [*grand atelier*] for the rest of his life. . . .

[Dessalles continues to take an active and what can only be called prurient interest in Nicaise's sex life.]

13 January 1837

. . . I am irritated by the pouting of the young mulatto woman Adée, whom my young negro Nicaise had chosen to be his mistress. But I think he will

---

6. Philibert survived; he is mentioned as a member of the work gang in 1848. Valentin, who called himself Arcade after emancipation, was born around 1821 and thus was about 16 years old at the time of this incident [HF and LE].
7. The "hospital" was on the grounds of the plantation.
8. "Eating earth" may well be a symptom of an intestinal disease such as hookworm.
9. Dessalles seems to have bought, or perhaps even rented, Valentin from Lalanne.

abandon the idea; if not, I can no longer be bothered with him. I don't know if this is a matter of stupidity or affectation [on her part], but the fact is that I have never seen such grimacing. A vestal virgin would not have made more of a fuss. The devil take her! She is at least twenty-five years old and has roasted plenty of broomsticks.

14 January 1837

. . . This evening my little negro made Adée come to him; she was pretty nice about it, though she still made faces. This fatigues and annoys me.

I received the newspapers, where I read [the governor] M. de Mackau's speech at the opening of the new session of the Colonial Council.[10] Still the same phrases and the same perfidiousness covered up with fine promises. It seems that taxes are insufficient to cover expenses and that the coffers are empty. They are going to take us for our last sou and leave us only our eyes to weep with. The members of the Colonial Council are much to blame; without being rigid in their conduct, they should forcefully reject the attempts on the sacred rights they are called upon to defend. Their fear and their hesitancy are doing more harm than they think.

15 January 1837

. . . This evening the servant girl Adée came to Nicaise. She was so sullen that I sent her home to her mother. Seeing that this made my young negro unhappy, I made her come back, but then she was even more sullen! I do believe that this time Nicaise himself felt like sending her away. But since they seem to love each other, I will try to put up with her a little longer. She promises to correct her behavior, and Nicaise promises me that he will abandon her if she does not change. I find all this quite unnerving.

I am taking too strong an interest in my young servant, and that is a consequence of my loneliness. I need to have someone near me whom I love and who loves me. My wife, my children . . . how much you are to blame for leaving me alone!

10. The Colonial Council was created to replace the general Council, or High Court, by the "organic law," also called the *Colonial Charter of 24 April 1833*. Its 30 members were elected to five-year terms by voters possessing the requisite property qualifications. The Colonial Council was abolished after the Revolution of 1848. Playing an advisory role in financial matters, the council could issue provisional but immediately effective decrees. Its meetings were held at Fort-Royal [HF and LE].

17 January 1837

... While I was riding through town, I was stopped by the mulatto woman Laquiote, who asked me to lend her some plates and pots for the meal she is to give on the occasion of the marriage of her son Montard, that insolent mulatto who is so hostile to the whites. I was all the more astonished that she would approach me because I have reason to be dissatisfied with that family which, at the time of Bagour's death, stole silver and many other items.[11] A horrible race, these people of color: proud and insolent in prosperity, they will, if they think it necessary, resort to the vilest marks [of deference] to obtain help, which they then promptly forget.

19 January 1837

Last night, M. de Survillié's young negress sent word to Nicaise that she had decided to live with him and that she wished to know his feelings about this. Nicaise went to see one of his friends, a slave of M. de Survillié, asking him to tell the girl that she must come to talk to me today and that I was willing to see her. I will not oppose this relationship if it can be carried out in a respectable manner and if my mulatto girl Adée does not become more amiable. I would of course prefer that my young negro give to one of our slave women what he would otherwise give to someone else's slave [that is, a child]. . . .

21 January 1837

It is nineteen years today that Louis XVI, the best of kings, that most humane man, was led to the scaffold by the ferocity of his people. What a crime! Consequently, France has not known tranquillity since that atrocity was perpetrated, and constantly changes governments. She is searching in vain for something that can take the place of the paternal authority of her ancient kings.[12]

[On 30 January, Dessalles received word that his brother Charles had arrived in Fort-Royal. He did not stay with Pierre's children and did not seem to be plan-

11. Some years earlier, a mulatto by the name of Bagour had asked Dessalles to act as his testamentary executor. It seems that Dessalles, hard pressed by the deteriorating state of his own affairs, did not keep the funds belonging to the Bagour succession properly separated from his own and dipped into them to pay off his most urgent debts [HF and LE]. Accusing the "insolent mulatto" Montard of theft on that occasion thus seems somewhat hypocritical.

12. Until the diary ends in 1856, a statement deploring the death of Louis XVI appears without fail each January 21. We will not reproduce it every time.

ning a long stay. Pierre's feelings were hurt: "He shows no interest at all in my family." He was also worried, knowing that his brother expected to receive 20,000 francs from him. "This kind of money is hard to come by these days!"]

1 February 1837

. . . My brother arrived this evening after sundown. Never have I seen a colder approach; the conversation dragged. He retired to his room before supper. What a dreadful thought it is to me that business interests might someday destroy the sweet and precious union that now exists among my children!

3 February 1837

. . . My brother and I talked business. I laid out the true situation to him and told him that I would do everything he saw fit. I believe that my frankness and my loyalty were appreciated, but egoism is the basic trait of Charles's character.

[The next entry shows that Dessalles is completely captivated by the prevailing racial stereotypes in sexual matters.]

4 February 1837

. . . I dined at the Limbé plantation with the Le Vassor heirs; they made their negroes dance. I noticed that the house slaves stood aside. These unfortunates miss my aunt [their previous owner] very much, and with reason. Alexandre had taken six servant girls under his protection and had promised to buy them. He slept with all six of them. It seems that two of them became his favorites and that they were clever enough to exercise a great deal of power over their master's mind. There has been loose talk and even infidelity on the part of several of these women; in short, he lost control of the situation, and the favorites did so well for themselves that they had beatings administered to the other girls who only rarely enjoyed Alexandre's favors. This poor young fellow is of a feeble temperament; barely able to satisfy one woman, what made him think that he could entertain six! His brother Louis helped him out, but alas! this was small comfort to strapping young women accustomed to the vigor of broad-shouldered domestics endowed by nature with enormous instruments! The conduct of these young men, of whom I am very fond and in whose well-being I am extremely interested, is very unseemly and may even jeopardize their establishment. What guarantee can they offer the fathers of marriageable daughters?

My brother talked to me about his business interests. He wants 20,000 francs and will not budge from that. He does not realize how difficult it is to find money. We will have to go to see M. Victor Reynal at Saint-Pierre; if he is willing to make this advance, Charles will give him powers of attorney to receive what I owe Charles.

7 February 1837

[Dessalles permits his work gang a joyous celebration to mark the completion of a major cutting operation.]

One particular circumstance prevented me from taking part in my negroes' joy. Here are the facts: My young negro Nicaise, of whom I am as fond as if he were my child, to whom I give unlimited marks of confidence, has shown me the blackest ingratitude. When I decided to treat this young slave as a part of myself, I explained to him that he would have to give up the disgraceful habits of his class, their lying, stealing, and cheating. He seemed to understand me and promised me by all that he held most sacred in the world that he would tell me everything and deposit in my breast even his most secret thoughts. I was counting on this promise and therefore did not hesitate to entrust to him my keys and my money; indeed, I often spoke to him about the particular heartaches my affairs and my family might cause me.

On the 29th of last month, my negroes had a dance, and I had given Nicaise six francs to pay the fiddlers. That night before going to bed, I asked him if he had paid off the players and if they were content, and he said he had paid them. I believed him. But this afternoon I learned from Octave Lalanne that this money had been stolen from Nicaise and that he had hidden this fact from me, telling me instead that the fiddlers had been paid. My whole being was seized with indignation, and I went to see Nicaise, berating him in the strongest terms. He persisted in his lie. I threatened to confound him, and still he persisted. In the end, my reasoning defeated him and he became deeply dejected. I told him to leave my room, but he refused to go. At that moment, I made up my mind not to keep him there any longer, but then my heart remembered the past; my affection for him was still very much alive, and I forgave him. I talked with him until ten o'clock, making him feel the enormity of his transgression. I made him sleep far from me; again he protested his devotion. I told him that I would give him back my full confidence only after I had punished and tested him for two months.

8 February 1837

My young negro seems repentant; I have treated him severely, and I feel sorry for him. It is possible that his sin was more a matter of ignorance than anything else. I am angry at myself for having this weakness for him.

9 February 1837

. . . Just as I was going to bed, my young negro threw himself at my feet and asked my forgiveness, assuring me that he would never commit such a fault again. One must be indulgent with young people, so I have excused everything and he has returned to my good graces.

18 February 1837

My young negro is of an elegance that has caused a lot of attention. People are surprised that I give him so many pretty things. He is a bit of a spend-thrift and loves dissolute parties, so I always tremble that he will catch a nasty disease. He assures me that he is not after women, but can I count on that?[13]

[Dessalles spends 13–20 February at Fort-Royal and Saint-Pierre, trying to find the 20,000 francs for his brother, going to the theater and to dinner at the homes of local notables, and generally having a miserable time away from his plantation.]

21 February 1837

The first thing I did upon awakening was to visit my hospital and to question my supervisors [*économes*]. I do not have many sick. The work was slow in my absence; the dry conditions have stopped everything and will be very bad for the harvest of 1838. Octave Lalanne almost never comes to the house anymore. Completely taken over by a brazen *capresse*,[14] he treats her with an indulgence that makes one shudder. This little hussy cheats on him, but he thinks that she is one of the virtues. Nicaise tells me that he has kissed her and just about came to the point of enjoying her. During my absence Octave kept this girl in my quarters. All this can lead to disorder, and I do not like it one bit. And though Octave lives with this *capresse*, he also goes after my young negresses. If jealousy takes hold in this place, I will suffer its consequences. I must put a

13. In this passage the sexual ambiguity of Dessalles's relation to Nicaise almost ceases to be ambiguous.

14. A *capre* is the offspring of a mulatto and a black person. In Caribbean societies, degrees of racial mixing were very carefully calibrated.

stop to this state of affairs. What a bad idea I had when I hired this young man! Now I don't know how to get rid of him. . . .

3 March 1837

. . . Ferbeaux [an acquaintance and fishing companion] told me that Madame Ballain [member of a family with whom Dessalles was *brouillé*, and it was to get worse!] always talks about me and constantly worries about my *libertinage* [Nicaise?]. I defy anyone to find a more decent person than me. This woman is just enraged that she can no longer come to my house as she used to do. Her husband too is an old gossip, and their children are storytellers and slanderers.

[After another trip to the city, Dessalles returns to his plantation on 17 March.]

17 March 1837

Having left Fort-Royal at 6:10 A.M., I arrived on my plantation at 11:06, having stopped at Catala's for a half-hour. My people received me in stunned dismay; I saw sadness in all eyes and did not need to be told: I immediately guessed that my negress Adée had died.[15] I sent for Octave, who did not come right away. He told me that this excellent young slave was buried yesterday and that the doctor had recognized the signs of smallpox. I have not enough tears to shed for this young woman; she was punctual about her duties and never had to be punished. My soul is sick about it. . . . I did not have the courage to go to see my work gang, for I would not have found my young negress there.[16] . . . Such sorrow in the first moments would have taken away all my courage.

18 March 1837

First thing in the morning, I went to visit my hospital. I was not satisfied with the condition of a young negress by the name of Augustine, who has been wasting away for a long time. The doctor told me that she suffers from an irritation of the stomach. She is therefore given tranquilizers; to follow her illness more closely, I am keeping her in my house.

Nicaise, who has talked to Adée's brother, has it from him that his sister was not properly cared for. The doctor saw her only at the beginning of her

15. This was not the Adée with whom Nicaise was living; Dessalles had had word of her illness while he was away.

16. At about this time, Dessalles begins to make excessive use of the possessive pronoun "my": my work gang, my young slave, my hospital. At one point he even refers to "my staircase."

illness; although he was called several times, he did not come back until she was dead. These medical gentlemen are expensive and demanding and appallingly casual about their duties. Lalanne should have written to him or sent for another physician. If I had been at home, I might have saved my young negress. I feel great sorrow.

Octave Lalanne has told me that during my absence Adée's relatives spread the word that she had died from poison; this is another source of trouble for me. It seems that the children of several families were fighting; some of the negroes intervened to separate them, and there were sharp words and threats instead of blows. Adée was involved in this fight, and apparently Sophie and Humilité told her that her arrogant behavior would cost her her life. Chance determined that she would die, and the talk was caused by despair. Tomorrow I shall silence these rumors: the doctor recognized smallpox, so there can be no doubt about the cause of death.

The weather is magnificent. The cane I am cutting at Fonds-Riz is beautiful, though not as thick as it should be.

19 March 1837

Weather still very beautiful. This morning I gathered together the negroes who supposedly spread rumors about Adée's death. I listened to them. One of them was the young negro Elie, who was in love with the deceased. Despair and sorrow made all of them talk; but Adée's mother, pain written all over her face, told me that she had never suspected anyone of having caused her daughter's death and that God alone had decided her fate. I tried to restore peace and calm and announced that if I heard any more talk of poison I would severely punish those who revived such suspicions.[17]

A landowner's lot in the colonies is unfortunate indeed. The negro is naturally hateful and wicked, superstitious and unprincipled; he never hesitates to take vengeance and will use any means to do so.[18] Only the utmost justice in dealing with them can avoid great misfortunes.

---

17. Naive words indeed from one who during the epizootic (cattle epidemic) of 1823–24 was utterly convinced that his livestock had been poisoned and had his slaves punished mercilessly for committing these supposed crimes. How could he now expect his own or a physician's word to keep his slaves from believing that poisoning was rampant?

18. This sounds as if Dessalles himself believed that the girl was poisoned!

Maundy Thursday 1837

. . . Octave tells me that we are out of empty hogsheads, so I had to write to M. Simoneau to order some and meanwhile had to shut down my mill. Oh this young man! His lack of foresight upsets all my calculations! I really had to control myself. . . . I would have fired him long ago if he were not my friend's son. . . .

Good Friday 1837

. . . I again had reason to bemoan Octave Lalanne's negligence. My buildings are not taken care of, and he absolutely does not foresee anything, ever! The cylinder of one of the rollers slipped down five inches, but that did not bother him! I decided to write to the mechanic Godard, who will probably not break his neck to get here. So I will again be forced to shut down my mill. All these breakdowns are horribly disturbing to me. Octave's familiar manner with certain subjects really upsets me. The foreman of the refinery, for instance, instead of telling him in words that the mill wheel had broken one of its teeth, tapped him on the leg and winked his eye at him in a manner that I found revolting. All of this is particularly distressing to me because I am interested in this young man's future and because he also has some fine qualities.

28 March 1837

Same weather [dry and "too beautiful"]. My sugar is awful. My cane is old, and so the juice [*vesou*] cannot be very good. This morning and afternoon I planted in the Corbière section. My negroes worked well.

My brother and I have come to an understanding about our affairs.[19] I made a concession concerning the house in the town of Madeleine[20] and the income he was supposed to pay me under the terms of an agreement drawn up by Arthur Bence. Henceforth, I will only have to pay my brother 25,000 francs a year. In 1848 I will no longer owe him anything. I can't wait to see that day!

19. A private act (*acte sous seing privé*), drawn up in duplicate in the town of Sainte-Marie, stated that M. Charles Dessalles cedes to his brother M. Pierre Dessalles all his rights to two sugar plantations located at Sainte-Marie for the price of 140,000 francs, which M. Pierre Dessalles promises to pay in twenty installments, the first nineteen in the amount of 7,500 francs and the twentieth, of 1,500 francs. Every unpaid installment is to produce interest at the rate of 4% per annum. This act was duly registered with the courts and the public mortgage office [HF and LE].

20. A suburb of Bergerac (Dordogne), where Pierre and Charles owned a house they had inherited from their mother [HF and LE].

Louis Cléret [his son-in-law] is very helpful to me in all these matters, and I deeply appreciate his making the trip to be with me in this circumstance. . . .

30 March 1837

The pivot of one of my rollers came off, and we had to stop the mill. So many mishaps! What will become of the cane stacked by the entrance of the mill? I am the one who has to deal with all these calamities, which are caused by Octave's negligence. I have now made up my mind to write to Lalanne [Octave's father] to tell him that I am no longer able to keep Octave with me; this young man is simply too negligent, and his dissolute way of life has made him forget his duty.

31 March 1837

The rain has finally come, and there is enough to give our land a good soaking.

All the arrangements with my brother have been signed; I can finally relax. He left me at eleven o'clock and did not seem the least bit moved. He leaves me to take care of all the difficulties. May he be happy!

Lalanne sent me a very friendly reply; he wants his son to come home and approves of my decision. So Octave will leave me. That is a big load off my chest.

1 April 1837

It has rained a lot; our plantings needed it. I received a letter from Lalanne; he hopes that Octave's leaving me will not alter the sentiments that tie us to one another. I answered him that only death will break these ties.

[In early April both daughters, Mme de Valmenier and Mme Cléret, came to visit their father at the Nouvelle Cité. They stayed until the middle of May.]

12 April 1837

I cut cane and planted in the prairie. Weather fine and excessively hot, which means that it will rain. At noon they came to tell me that a tortoise we had bought yesterday [presumably for making into soup] had died and that my negro Jean-Baptiste was missing. I sent to Trinité for another tortoise. As for Jean-Baptiste's disappearance, I can't understand it; this negro was happy, and he lacked nothing. He has been keeping house for us since I brought him from Guadeloupe in 1813. He never ceased to do his duty with zeal, and there was only one occasion when I had to have him whipped; a gourmand by nature, he would sometimes steal food to eat. I often scolded him, but closed my eyes to this character flaw, the only one I knew him to have. He did not drink, he did not chase women, and he never left the house. This negro had no peer for taking care of the silver and the porcelain. I assume he will not be gone long.

My children are well; my granddaughters make me very happy and provide wonderful entertainment. When I am in my cane fields, I hurry home as soon as I can to caress them.

15 April 1837

I finished my sugarmaking. The weather was most favorable. My negroes had the afternoon off.

M. Constant Ernoult had my negro Jean-Baptiste arrested, and I had him brought back. Just as he was about to be punished [i.e., whipped], my daughters asked me to spare him, and he went back to his work. . . .

16 April 1837

. . . I received a letter from M. Auguste Bonnet, who now refuses to pay me more than 225 francs per barrel of sugar. He also sent me a memorandum in favor of the colonies to the King of the French by Charles Dupin.[21] I read it with pleasure; it is strongly reasoned and perfectly true. But I do not like certain concessions that run counter to sane ideas and probability: to hope that religion will civilize the negro is to believe in miracles, and we no longer live in times when certain stories put men to sleep. Religion is admirable; it alone can create true social relations, but it will never be understood by a class of people who will always be part animal. The head of our [local] church, M. Castelli, will be flattered by the praise he receives in the memorandum, but I don't think he deserves it, although at this moment we have no serious complaints about the clergy of Martinique.

18 April 1837

. . . I sent for Dr. La Peyre to see several negroes who are quite ill. I also asked him to examine the negress Zabeth, who has been saying for fifteen months that she is pregnant and who has not done any work in all this time. He told

---

21. A deputy in the parliament, Charles Dupin was immortalized in a caricature by Daumier. See Oliver Larkin, *Honoré Daumier, Man of his Time* (Boston: Beacon Press, 1968), 24.

me there was no sign of a pregnancy and that, if she were indeed pregnant—which he did not believe—it could at most be two or three months. Not being sure, I did not think I should have her whipped. I had an iron collar put on her and sent her to work in the field.

[More intimate details about Nicaise, whose temperament is such that he has relations with a young negress from another plantation in addition to Adée, with whom he lives conjugally. Dessalles closes his eyes to this, because he knows "how one is tormented at his age" and because he simply cannot get along without Nicaise.]

4 May 1837, Ascension Day

It is a holiday, which does not suit me at all. I had a response from MM. Fontenau [merchants in Bordeaux], and it was what I expected. Their refusal to give me money is very troubling, but it will be good for me in the long run, for one can never do well with them. They are veritable Jews.

The house slaves danced to the sound of the drum until prayer time.

9 May 1837

Weather too beautiful, burning sun. This morning I cut cane in the Fond-Saint-Isle section; the plants are young, but I cannot wait for them to mature, for the creditors are at my heels. . . .

13 May 1837

. . . This evening, I was told by M. Michaud [manager at the Caféière] that he had it from my brother that Octave had told him that, when I sent him negroes who had to be chastised, he used to close his eyes when the driver whipped them and that most of the time he sent them back without carrying out my orders. I did not know about this, but the indocility of my negroes made me suspect that Octave's carelessness was the cause of all our problems.[22]

15 May 1837

. . . Catala [a fellow planter in the area] talked to me about Octave Lalanne. It seems that this young man complains bitterly about me. He claims that I spied on him and that, jealous of my negresses, I did not want him to have a

---

22. Within their own circles, planters seemed to rely heavily on third- and fourth-hand information.

single one of them. Poor young man! This kind of talk shows me that he is a Creole without breeding! M. Octave says he reserves the right to express his dissatisfaction to me in person; but he will never dare forget himself in my presence, nor would I advise him to do so.

7 June 1837

Lots of rain. I planted in the third section of Jardin-Madame. My messenger returned from Saint-Pierre: there is still talk of emancipation, and the government would like to avoid paying compensation. For slaves twelve years old, one would receive 50 francs a year until they reached the age of twenty-five; for slaves between twenty-one and twenty-five, one would receive 25 francs. Thereafter, they would be definitively free, and general emancipation would be proclaimed in 65 years. What an absurdity! It is hard to understand that, in an age that calls itself Enlightened, such projects are being hatched. Let us hope that they will never be put into practice!

25 June 1837

... A letter from Adrien informs me that he will soon return to Martinique with a kinsman who bears my surname [Eugène Dessalles] whom he met at a spa and with whom he has become friends. This young man wrote me a charming letter; he is coming to the colony in order to see whether he can engage in some lucrative speculations. I hope that my son will not come to regret this encounter some day, for I am not lucky; whenever I do someone a good turn, he is sure to become ungrateful and hostile to me. . . .

M. Simoneau came to see me in my cane to talk to me about what I owe him. I promised to think of him when my next batch of sugar is ready.

2 July 1837

Today is the municipal *fête* of Gros-Morne. Throngs of people from all districts [23] are pouring into town. The women save their money all year long to buy fancy clothes for this occasion; they skimp and deny their children the most necessary things in order to show off luxuries that would make those who do not know them believe that they belong to the country's wealthiest families.

The females [*le Sexe*] of Gros-Morne are superb, and the parish, once so far

---

23. *Quartiers*, translated as districts, was the word for the many outlying settlements or hamlets that constituted the parishes or communities of the island. The pattern of Martinique's settlement was extremely dispersed [HF and LE].

removed from civilization, is now well governed. Its birthrate is excellent, and the planters get along very well with each other. Some years ago I rarely missed this fête, but nowadays I hate to leave home.

For three days I had guests and found some distraction from my troubles. But yesterday I returned to my regular preoccupations, which remain poignant and painful. I shall find peace only in the grave and will spend my life working to maintain a plantation that my children may lose at any moment, thanks to the malevolent intention of the French government.

Lalanne talked to me about the system of municipal government that is to be established here. It will be impossible to make it take hold, for there is not enough personnel. We went all through the planters of the district, and there is not one who would be capable of running such a system. The [free] men of color are more capable than certain whites. In this country, people think they can do anything; vanity prompts them to apply for and accept public offices, but how do they carry them out? It is pitiful! Wealthy, capable planters work hard only if the government compensates them with prestige for certain sacrifices and especially for completely unpaid functions. In our day and age, the man who does the right thing is vilified and envied. The result? The result is that only the rabble is in power. Hence the general unease, the malaise that hampers everything and deprives us of all security. Whenever attempts are made to place men without fortune and independence into high positions, it will turn out that such calculations are based on faulty reasoning. The old magistracy, composed of men from the highest rank of society by birth and capacity, was admirable.[24] Today's magistracy no doubt includes men of merit, but as a whole, can it be compared to the former group? In this respect the colonies were badly treated by the mother country, for the men sent from France are invariably obscure intriguemongers who hate the colony from which they make their living.

5 July 1837

Yesterday I was already in bed when I heard the noise of horses. I got up and it was my son [Adrien]. I joyfully embraced him. I spent some time alone with him in my room; the details he gave me about his mother were crushing. It appears that my wife's health is entirely destroyed and that there is reason to be extremely concerned. My existence would be broken if I lost my wife. My son

---

24. Dessalles lived with a nostalgic view of the past and regretted the demise of the solemn sessions of the High Court of Martinique, whose members served without pay. The members of this court, like Dessalles and his father, were deeply attached to what they considered a prerogative that guaranteed their independence [HF and LE].

also told me that MM. Durant [the commission merchants in Bordeaux] had refused to provide any help to my wife, who was in extremely straitened circumstances, and that M. Bence and his son, furious at this conduct, are no longer doing business with them. Indeed, the older M. Bence ordered M. Durant out of his house.

After this brief conversation with my son, which my heart will always remember with sadness, I composed myself and went downstairs to my salon to greet our kinsman [Eugène Dessalles], the young man who had travelled with Adrien.

The negroes were eager to present their dutiful greetings to my son. Adrien received the visit of Saint-Just, a dangerous mulatto who has given me a great deal of trouble.[25]

I am delighted with the kinsman who followed Adrien here; he is smart and clever, expresses himself with ease, and has excellent manners. I think he will be appreciated here. He and my son have told me about his family, which is very large and enjoys great respect and an enormous fortune. His uncle Jean Dessalles has an income of 50,000 francs. He has a son who has suddenly fallen in love with my daughter Antoinette; this is a marriage we cannot afford to pass up. The uncle wishes me to come to France to negotiate the matter; I would love to make the journey, but the state of my affairs will probably prevent me from going. Shortage of money is a dreadful thing.

6 July 1837

. . . I am more and more pleased with our new kinsman. He is well versed in literature, vivacious and possessed of very pleasing manners. His political opinions, though, are bad: he is a republican. We do not think alike.[26]

[The joy at Adrien's arrival very quickly comes to an end. Two days later, Dessalles begins complaining about the company his son keeps; he expresses his concern that Adrien has clearly been sent to the island by his mother to take over the plantation, a task for which his father considers him morally, temperamentally, and intellectually unfit. The first scene between father and son—precipitated by Adrien's insistence that slave girls must be permitted to come to his room in the main house—takes place the next day. Dessalles buries himself in work even more than usual in the subsequent weeks.]

25. Adrien's future relations with his father are ominously foreshadowed here; a major source of friction was to be Adrien's liberal attitude in racial matters, both personally and politically.
26. Trouble ahead here too!

23 July 1837

I had Lalanne and Pierre Cardin for dinner. They left early because Lalanne had to prepare himself for an unpleasant errand tomorrow; he must go to meet the governor, who will apparently spend a week in our district. He wants to ensure the loyalty of the mayors who are to take the place of the deputy commanders in our district; Louis Littée and Castet have been designated. It is really quite odd: the most important functions will end up being occupied by the local *incapacités*. The government is doing its best to disgust the rich and the capable. I doubt that it will be possible to find respectable people in the north part of the island who want these positions. . . .

26 July 1837

. . . Lalanne wrote to tell me that the governor had asked about me; seeing a man on horseback, he thought it was I. I have therefore decided to pay him a call. I did not find him, for he was at lunch at M. Eyma's. I don't have to do anything more, but I felt I should make this gesture to help Louis Cléret [his son-in-law], who may need the governor. This M. de Mackau truly is a cruel enemy of the colonies. We hear that he has been recalled and that M. Massieu de Clairval is to replace him as governor.

27 July 1837

. . . The governor sent me a gendarme to excuse himself for not coming to see me. He had to leave earlier than expected. I prefer this courtesy to his visit. No one knows why he came here; he plays the clever diplomat, but his cleverness is sewn with white thread [i.e., too obvious]. He is just ambitious, that is all there is to it.

28 July 1837

. . . Lalanne writes me that the governor passed by his house without stopping. No doubt that is how these [government] gentlemen behave. I remain astounded that the government is able to find planters willing to assume public office. In the old days the governors lived among our families as our friends; they treated the parish commanders with the respect they needed to run a useful administration. Today's governors consider themselves too exalted to be polite.

My kinsman Louis Littée called on me. I hear that he has applied for the mayorship. He must be very stupid not to see himself realistically; the poor devil knows nothing about public administration and also cuts a pitiful public figure.

31 July 1837

... My son came at ten o'clock. I had promised to hand over the administration of the property to him tomorrow, August 1, and he is very anxious to seize it. I myself will not mind getting some rest. If I had 300 francs a month, I would rarely be on the plantation; I would go and stay with my daughters. I am thinking more seriously than ever about going to France, for the establishment of my daughters demands it, and it is a sacrifice that I must make. ...

1 August 1837

Without fanfare and noise I have handed the administration of my plantation to my son. So I am no longer involved in anything. I hope with all my heart that things will go well. The negroes seem satisfied to see my son as their leader; a few of them are sorry to see me go, and soon they all will be sorry. Not that they have reason to complain about my son's injustices, for I am certain that he will take good care of them and treat them kindly. But a young man never has the same patience as a man matured by long experience. I used to shout a lot, but I soon forgot my anger and often gave out money.

2 August 1837

My son has had to order some punishments; they [the slaves] are testing him and will work normally only when they see that he is determined not to make any concessions. This always happens when a new administration comes in.

9 August 1837

... [Touring the plantation with Eugène, we] stopped at a field that Adrien was having worked. We saw some superb cane. My son was there with the negroes. To my distress I observed that he had given them only 18 minutes off for lunch. This is not enough time, and the negroes must be upset about it. One must be fair with these people and give them the rest stipulated in the ordinances.

[It soon becomes clear that Adrien is by no means fully in charge of the plantation. His father almost immediately begins to second-guess him, and a major generational conflict looms on the horizon. On 12 August, in a conversation with his young kinsman Eugène, Dessalles reveals his dissatisfaction with his son's work and his own philosophy of running a plantation.]

12 August 1837

The superb weather continues. I took a tour of the Caféière with Eugène Dessalles. We had a long conversation about the administration of my plantation. My son had made him see everything in a light favorable to himself and told him with the assurance of a young man that he would produce more revenue than I had done. Eugène believes him and no doubt considers me an old dotard. Young people today no longer believe in experience; born with perfect knowledge of everything, they put their entire trust in youth. I wish I could count on what Adrien says, but alas! I am not mistaken; I foresee, not the ruination of my business, but great trouble on the plantation. Adrien's reasoning is faulty, he is stubborn, and he is presumptuous; that is more than enough to fail utterly. If he could consistently produce 300 hogsheads and preserve the negroes, I would be very happy. But he will want to prove that he is cleverer than I am, and so he will plant a great deal, force everything, and in the end the net revenue will be less and the resources for the future will be destroyed. I can hear his excuse now: "One cannot," he will tell me, "make money without losing oxen and mules and even some negroes." I shall answer him—but, deaf to my voice, he will disdain my words as usual—that, in the difficult circumstances the colonists are experiencing right now, it is better to make do with smaller revenues and to preserve one's resources. If my son recognizes this truth, it will unfortunately be too late, for by then it will be impossible to repair the damage.

By planting every year 20 carrés [62.4 acres] of land in new cane and keeping as many carrés in second-year canes, one can obtain as many as 280 hogsheads of sugar. But one must fertilize the newly planted cane and take care of the second-year cane. To the best of my knowledge and belief, that is all my plantation can produce with the forces I am leaving there. The plantations are magnificent, but my son does not and never will admit this; he will even react with pleased laughter to the base flattery of those who will not fail to come here in order to tell him that it was high time that he took charge. My wife thinks he can succeed; even though I am convinced of the contrary, I put him in charge of my affairs, though not without trembling. Whatever may happen, I am determined never to return to the plantation once I leave it. If France does not suit me—and I believe it will not—I will come back to the colonies and settle at Saint-Pierre or its vicinity. My children will have to come to an agreement and steer this little ship as best they can. . . .

21 August 1837

. . . I saw the mulatto girl Victorine come out of Adrien's room. I slapped her face a few times and called her all kinds of names. I want to put a stop to this shameful commerce, which is highly offensive to me. This little hussy is of a revolting effrontery. I have never interfered with Adrien's conduct with women, but in this circumstance there are specific reasons, known only to my son—to whom I told them in confidence—to make me insist that this odious commerce must cease.[27] My son did not heed my entreaties and makes my slave persist in her reprehensible disobedience.

27 August 1837

. . . I learned that my son had a girl named Virginie come to Sainte-Marie and that he has had a child by her.[28] If he wants to take care of her, I approve, but if he means to live with her, I find him virtuous indeed!

30 August 1837

This morning I wrote to Jean Dessalles of Toulouse, who is in love with Antoinette and wants to marry her. This marriage does not seem to suit my wife and my daughter because this young man does not have the manners of a dandy. Endowed with excellent qualities, he would make a woman happy; and he has money, while we are about to lose ours. The reason for my journey is to make my daughter agree.

7 September 1837

. . . Catala came to dine with me. Threatened by his creditors, he would like to sell me his negroes so they will not be included in the assessment of his property. This comes pretty close to fraud. He brought me the list of his negroes. He would sell me 66, but I would sell 25 back to him, so that I would really buy only 41 negroes, 9 oxen, and 7 mules for a total of 43,000 francs. He wants me to pay him that sum in four equal yearly installments beginning in September 1838 and continuing in the same manner. This I cannot possibly do. I propose to pay the sum in six installments and to begin only in September 1839. I did not find his assessment exaggerated, but I cannot buy the cat in the bag; I must at least see them and find out whether they want to serve me. This affair could be very important for my plantation, my revenues would surely increase, and

27. Could this Victorine be Dessalles's daughter?
28. The child is Palmire, of whom a great deal will be heard in the 1850s [HF and LE].

this would allow me to pay off my debts more quickly. Many good things can come out of this acquisition. Nothing ventured, nothing gained! These negroes are accustomed to hard work and severe discipline; this is a precious warranty, and I have every reason to hope that they would do well for me. . . .

[Here is a description of the standard social occasion in which Dessalles took part: a dinner party attended exclusively by men, with entertainment consisting of food, ribald conversation, and business consultation.]

9 September 1837

Weather magnificent. We dined at Pierre Cardin's. Catala had sent him an excellent mutton, and the dinner was excellent. We ate and drank considerably, which is why I was very agitated all evening and could not go to sleep until very late at night. The table companions were Lalanne, Louisie Burot, Arthur Martineau, my son, Eugène, Pierre Cardin and his two grandsons, and I. The conversation was very frivolous indeed, and several ribald songs were sung. I told Lalanne about my plan to buy Catala's negroes; he approves and thinks I should not keep them separate them from my own. He is right; an immediate fusion will be proof of my trust and an incentive for them to behave well. . . .

4 October 1837

I am witnessing some curious conversations: the posturing of today's young people *stinks to high heaven*. Nothing will do unless it is the very latest. Eugène plays the scholar to settle the most difficult questions of literature. Nothing is beautiful unless it comes from the pen of Victor Hugo, Eugène Sue, etc.; it is just too funny. To avoid getting into interminable discussions, I say nothing. When it comes to politics it's even worse; legitimacy is a hollow dream, the re-public will prevail — these are the fine opinions I hear them profess with all the power of stubborn conviction. As for religious principles, these gentlemen have worked them out to suit their convenience: Jesus Christ is a prodigious *man*; to kill oneself when one is unhappy is a perfectly simple and natural thing. Seduc-ing two sisters in the same family, running away with another man's wife — all of this is considered very nice. What distresses me is that my son — often from a desire to do like these young people — shares and defends their errors. When I speak to him of Eugène's petulance and his debaucheries, he replies, "Yes, but he is a good fellow." Looking at it in this way, it is easy to find good fellows even among the most guilty of men. How I long to be by myself!

10 October 1837

. . . Eugène expresses subversive opinions about the people of color and the slaves. I do not think he will talk this way everywhere, for the principal planters would hate him if he did. Dominated as he is by republican ideas, he should never have come to Martinique. Actually, I believe that he would not have come if my son had not persuaded him to do so. He must have painted this country in beautiful colors, but it was not long before he realized there was nothing here for him to do. Given his laziness, his taste for *libertinage*, and his spendthrift ways, I doubt that he will ever succeed in business.

17 October 1837

. . . Here is a very strange anecdote I heard at Fort-Royal. I was told that M. Noguès, the attorney-general, acting on denunciations he had received, sent some gendarmes to M. Reynoird, a planter at Robert, with orders to go to a certain place on his plantation and exhume the body of a negress who was said to have died as a result of being maltreated by her master. M. Reynoird, astounded by such a mission, at first could not believe it. But when he was shown the order, he demanded to know who had denounced him. The gendarmes were unable to name anyone. Then he demanded the name of the slave, which he was told. She was perfectly alive, and he brought her in to show her to the agents of the authorities. Having examined her, the search party went to the place indicated, dug it up, and failed to find a body. M. Reynoird went to see M. Noguès, complained about this inquisitorial measure, and threatened to take him to court, holding him responsible for the troubles that would arise on his plantation. When he demanded to know who had denounced him, he was told that the attorney-general had acted in response to a public outcry. Upon his return to his district, M. Reynoird had the matter investigated, and all the planters signed a statement attesting that there had never been a more lenient administration than his and that he had for many years succeeded in keeping poison off his plantation. In a fury and armed with this statement, he returned to Fort-Royal, made a horrendous scene, and demanded justice from the governor.

What will be the outcome of all of this? It will be that M. Noguès will be supported, that he will get out of this infamy unscathed, and that M. Reynoird—after having spent a great deal of money and gone to horrendous trouble—will be only too happy to go home and plant his cane! Today the slightest misdemeanor on his part would be considered a crime by the government, and he would be pursued without mercy. I am told that [many of] his negroes, having learned of the steps taken by the public ministry and proud of the concern shown by the government, have lodged complaints or run away and that poison is causing ravages on his plantation. This was to be expected, for this is always the outcome of such ill-considered actions. MM. Reynoird are strong and vigorous, and they lack neither family connections nor resoluteness. In their place, I would see to it that this little character [Noguès] gets a sound thrashing. In this fine country we make a lot of noise and carry on fiercely right at the moment, threatening to kill everything, but soon everything calms down, and before long such events are talked about as if they had happened a thousand years ago.

I have always had a very poor opinion of M. Noguès. Starting out as attorney-general of Guadeloupe, he did not leave a good reputation there. He owed this high position to his uncle; if he still occupies it in this country, he owes it to the influence of the same uncle, M. Halgan, who knows his nephew's deficiencies. His abilities are few: he writes poorly and talks like a garrulous old woman in a shrill and fatiguing voice. Of very common family background, this little man is full of vanity and pride. Moreover, the magistracy of this country — and indeed of France — has become a matter of wheeling and dealing; money has become the main driving power for the men of justice. The magistrates who come to the colonies are a pitiful lot; their main goal is to make their fortune; if their positions are not sufficiently lucrative, they will end up selling justice. Then woe to honorable people who have a court case! One can only count on the courts if their members are independent by dint of their fortune and their social position.

6 November 1837

. . . I am told that M. de la Bretonnière, vice-admiral and a colonial, is to replace M. de Mackau [as governor]. I have trouble believing it, for the very fact of being a colonial of Martinique would rule out this favor. I do not know M. de la Bretonnière; he is said to have very little education. He married a demoiselle Camboularet, widow of a sieur Morancy, who by her intrigues and the favors she granted to ministers and men in power has furthered her husband's career. This Madame de la Bretonnière — who was the wife of M. Morancy when I came to Martinique in 1806 — was pretty but enjoyed the reputation of a woman of loose morals. It was even said that she was the mistress of M. de Villaret, governor of the colony, and that it was she who had obtained for her first husband the grade of captain and aide-de-camp. She belongs to a rather disreputable family: her sister, Mme Bontems, was openly living with a M. Prunier, whom she married as soon as death removed M. Bontems. It would really be odd and laughable to see Mme de la Bretonnière as wife of the governor doing the honors for the government of Martinique. I do not think that the wellborn women of the country will call on her, but one never knows! My daughter, Mme Cléret, will have to go to government functions because of her husband's position; this already makes me sad. I like to think that M. de la Bretonnière will be prudent and wise enough to come to Martinique by himself and that he will sense that his wife would be completely out of place here.

11 November 1837

. . . Sylvie came to ask me to let her buy her granddaughter Victorine.[29] I agreed to let her go for 800 francs. This sum will help me plug a few holes.

[At this point it becomes clear that Dessalles has not "handed over the reins" of the plantation to Adrien. Relations between father and son are becoming more and more acrimonious, the main bones of contention being money and Adrien's sexual mores. As usual, the approach of the year's end aggravates Dessalles's financial problems.]

23 November 1837

. . . This evening I had a long conversation about business with my son. He would like me to make him an associate on my plantation. I will do nothing of the kind, for I do not want my children to dictate their law to me. Actually, I am very displeased with my son.

24 November 1837

. . . I had a visit from M. Félix Fontenau.[30] . . . I talked to him about my problems; I owe about 20,000 francs to his firm's Nantes and Trinité branches. I asked him to give me 12,000 francs for my wife's upkeep for next year, whereupon he demanded that I send him 140 hogsheads of sugar per year. I wanted to show him that, in view of my other obligations, I would be unable to do so. My son, who was present, claimed that it would be possible; I had to yield, and the deal was concluded. In addition, I give him 43 hogsheads that are all ready to go for 11,000 francs, which he will pay me at the end of this year. My son, far from giving me support, made it impossible for me to fend off this demand; if

29. This is probably the mulatto girl Victorine whose sexual relation with Adrien stirred such strong feelings in Dessalles. See 21 August 1837.

30. One of the partners in the firm of Fontenau Fils, commission merchants in Nantes and Trinité. Pierre Dessalles had long done business with this firm and was deeply in debt to them.

I had not yielded, M. Fontenau would not have failed to say that I was acting in bad faith and would have believed my son rather than me. What a dreadful position to be in! I am suffering terribly! I sat down at table but did not eat. . . . I sent my wife a letter of credit for 12,000 francs payable by the firm of Fontenau Fils of Nantes.

27 November 1837

The weather has been terrible. This did not prevent Adrien from going to Trinité in order to find money to solve my difficulties. However, M. Félix Fontenau did not give an inch. Pierre Cardin had transferred to me a credit of 10,000 francs on the Richier estate, for which M. Alexandre Fontenau acts as the executor. Nonetheless, it was impossible to prevail upon this firm to accept these bills [of exchange] and to pay me the sums stipulated. . . .

I wrote to Louis Cléret [his son-in-law], sending him 1,300 francs for Sinson [a creditor?], 1,300 for Calixte [payment on her dowry, no doubt], and 3,000 francs for M. Fabre [another creditor?].

28 November 1837

Eugène was good enough to go with Lalanne to see whether Abbé Pouzet's brother might be willing to lend me money. They found him quite eager to oblige me. I feel better now, for I will be able to buy sugar to make up for the shortfall in the amount I had promised to send to M. Durant.

30 November 1837

Fine weather. I took advantage of it to go bathing in the sea. I lunched with M. Etienne Pouzet, to whom I spoke about the sum he is to lend me. He must clear this with the vestry board of the church; everything in this wretched country takes a lot of time.

After lunch I spent two hours with Lalanne; from his house I went to visit M. Louisie Burot, whom we found surrounded by his mulatto women and his bastards. In this colony, wine is a proud master. Since the death of one of his bastard sons, good old Burot has not left his place. He vaunts his [son's] good qualities; to hear him talk, the man was without faults. Yet there is proof that he was a rabid enemy of the whites, one of his class who most ardently wished for their ruin. I have gladly forgiven him for insulting me in my own courtyard and hope that God will give him peace and mercy. From M. Louisie Burot's, I went to Pierre Cardin's; he is a good man, but also surrounded by mulattoes.

His bastards live pell-mell with his legitimate children. Truly, such neglect of the proprieties is found only in Martinique. It makes me shudder.

2 December 1837

... Louis Le Vassor[31] dined with us. The poor devil is having great trouble right now: M. Morestin, the manager of [Le Vassor's plantation] Limbé, hired a supervisor [*économe*] who is compromising the plantation's tranquillity. He hit a negress for breaking wind. M. Morestin, instead of reprimanding him, supported him, which made the negroes very angry. Just as we were sitting down to dinner, a messenger came to tell Louis that the work gang had refused to go to work and was in full revolt. I advised him not to return to the plantation until M. Mont-Louis, the representative of Ferbeaux [a magistrate?], had arrived. M. Morestin's star is fading; if he continues to make such blunders, he will no longer be able to manage the Limbé plantation. That would be too bad, because so far he was the only one to make this property yield as much as it can yield — and more.

3 December 1837

[After mass] I found Louis Le Vassor [at my house]. M. Mont-Louis was at le Limbé; he upbraided the negroes, and calm was restored. . . .

[In mid-December, the conflict between Dessalles and his son reaches crisis proportions, with shouting matches in the presence of guests and days spent not speaking to each other. Adrien is clearly frustrated at not being allowed to fulfill his functions as manager; Pierre considers him incapable. Meanwhile, Pierre manages to borrow enough money for a voyage to France, where he thinks he is needed to negotiate the marriage of his daughter Antoinette. He leaves unstated the idea that his absence might cool off his relations with his son. References to the joy of being reunited with his wife are perfunctory.

Dessalles spends New Year's at his daughter's house in Fort-Royal, his mind made up to sail for France.]

31 December 1837

... Tomorrow is New Year's. . . . I am glad I am not on my plantation, for it would make my heart suffer that I cannot give any New Year's gifts to my negroes.

31. Louis and Alexandre Le Vassor, the owners of the Limbé and Union plantations, were relatives of Dessalles. Dessalles acted as their and their mother's financial and legal advisor and considered the two young men frivolous spendthrifts. He was often irritated when they came to visit him precisely at dinnertime.

CHAPTER FIVE

1838–1839

[Before he sailed for France in March 1838, Dessalles experienced a trying series of frustrations and troubles. Creditors who realized he was about to leave Martinique appeared on his doorstep demanding to be paid; in January he suffered an extremely painful and debilitating bout of bleeding hemorrhoids; and Adrien repeatedly "forgot himself" and talked rudely to his father, who in turn had no confidence that his plantation would be run properly in his absence. "I had linen cut out for the domestics and some of the negro children. I do not think that Adrien will give them what they need in my absence; I believe they will often lack clothing" (26 March).

His efforts to arrange lucrative marriages with two wealthy sisters for his nephews Louis and Alexandre Le Vassor failed because of their crude and casual attitude. These "debauched dandies" did not even pretend that they were interested in anything but the wealth of their prospective brides. Dessalles was particularly upset because the wealthy sisters were related to him and to his nephews: "It is most unfortunate that such good matches should fall to strangers," he commented.

Prominent in the entries of this period is Dessalles's ambivalence about his journey to France. On the one hand, he professes to be eager to leave "this awful country" and all his troubles behind him, fantasizing about staying in France ("if I can afford it"); on the other, "it causes me great anxiety to leave my properties behind," and "my heart suffers cruelly from the separation from my children who live in the colony" (2 March). Not much of this ambiguity is left on 28 March, when he describes his departure from the Nouvelle Cité.]

28 March 1838

I spent a dreadful night, hardly sleeping at all. I was haunted by the idea of leaving my plantation. I did not say goodbye to anyone; my women servants showed their feelings. At six o'clock I was in the saddle and took the path along the heights. When I could no longer see my plantation, I experienced such a rush of feelings that I nearly fell off my horse; I was choked by sobs. In France I will find my wife, my children, and many relatives, but not one square inch of property. This thought is horrible. . . .

30 March 1838 [on board the *Thémire*]

. . . I should give the passenger list here. There are only five of us, namely M. Félix Fontenau [whose firm owns the ship], a conceited and coarse personage who is inordinately proud of his wealth; I mentioned him earlier.[1] M. Méry Neuville the younger, a planter from my district, sixteen years old, who is going to France for his education. My servant [Nicaise] and I—and a young man of color who is also going to France for his education; his name is Norbert Thimothée. His father[2] recommended him to me, and I promised to look after him, to take him to Paris, and to report on his progress. This young mulatto, seventeen years old, seems to be pleasant, and I believe I will not have reason to be sorry to have taken charge of him. Thimothée is the mechanic of my plantation. I hope that, in view of the good turn I am doing him, he will take extra good care of my mill.

We had barely come out of the harbor channel when our young people started to vomit. This tribute one pays to Neptune is disgusting. People make fun of seasickness; although I have never experienced it myself, I have seen so many people suffer with it that I always feel sorry for those who have it. Dinner was served at five o'clock. I did not think that young Norbert would come to the table, but he was one of the first to sit down. What will my friends in the colony say when they find out that I have dined with a mulatto? I can hear them now; they will really sink their teeth into me. I don't care! In the interest of the colonies, we must wish that prejudice will end. A well-bred man of proper manners cannot, of course, live and eat with an unprincipled and unmannerly mulatto, but education must do away with distinctions, and a man, whatever his color, must be included in all social relations if his manners warrant it.

1. See 4 May 1837. Dessalles owed the Fontenau brothers a great deal of money, and they imposed harsh conditions for future cooperation.

2. Thimothée, a free man of color, was the mechanic hired by Adrien who succeeded in repairing the plantation's sugar mill that had constantly broken down under Chignac's neglectful management (8 January 1838).

The colonies can only succeed if prejudice disappears, for these prejudices keep the different classes apart and these hatreds often give rise to the most harmful dissension. The planters owe the misfortunes they experience on their estates to the perfidious advice that [free] men of color give to the slaves; all these troubles would disappear along with the old prejudices. We must also admit, however, that the colored class has done little to deserve the kindness of the white class, for hatred and vengeance inform all the actions of their lives. This class would not be satisfied with perfect equality, and it is only too evident that what it wants is superiority. There is no question that it dreams of taking over the entire colony. It is up to the government to maintain a balance and to the wise men of both classes to calm the effervescence of the population.

[On the fourth day of the voyage, 108 miles out of Martinique, Dessalles notices that the crew seems to be working overtime operating the ship's pumps. M. Fontenau assures him there is no cause for concern; he says his firm keeps its ships in good condition, since it does not insure them. Four days later, however, there is a storm, the leaks get worse, and the decision is made to return to Martinique; the *Thémire* limps into Trinité on 12 April. When Adrien meets his father on his way to the plantation, he is "terrified," no doubt thinking that he is being haunted by a ghost. Dessalles writes, "My happiness at being back at my plantation is indescribable."

The next ship, the *Espérance*, sails on April 24. It has no cabins, so that passengers have to supply their own "huts." The food is so poor that they help bake the bread and prepare the meals, especially the fish they catch during the passage. On June 2, the *Espérance* arrives safely at Bordeaux, and Dessalles is reunited with his wife and younger children.

The first reference to missing Martinique appears two weeks after his arrival. Most of the people he sees in Bordeaux are Creoles. The entry of 6 July shows the relationship between his worries about the continued existence of the colony and his distress at the wasteful lifestyle of his family.]

6 July 1838 [Bordeaux]

I went to see Mont-Rose [a fellow colonial]; M. Bence was with me. We talked about the colonies, for it is an inexhaustible topic for the Creoles. Their position is so critical that it is normal for them to think about it. But it is driving me out of my mind! I see poverty rapidly catching up with us, and it distresses me that my wife does not even try to cut down her expenses. The amount of money that is being spent at rue Saint-Fort [M. Bence's house, where Mme Dessalles and her children are living] is horrendous, but the abuses are difficult to extirpate. The cook, who is the former nurse of my two youngest children, does everything without being checked; her accounts are settled once a month.

She is a good and honest girl, but this way of running a household will not do. She does not accustom my daughters to take care of even the smallest details. One should never go to bed at night without having settled with one's cook, and one should always tell her what she should make for dinner the next day. Here we sit down to the table without knowing what we will have to eat.

We also have too many domestics. Nowadays they all want to be treated like masters; if one does not give them café au lait in the morning, they don't want to stay in the household. Nine domestics are fed in the house in rue Saint-Fort, not counting people to whom food is sent. The family will suffer cruelly when it is no longer possible to continue this state of things. I keep pointing out to my family all the horrors of our precarious situation. I do not like living in the home of my father-in-law, who is not easy to get along with and where my expenses are higher than if I had my own home. I am being patient, however, since this cannot last, and I will return to Martinique next year. . . .

[In July and August, Dessalles, his wife, his daughters Antoinette and Emilie, and his son Henri visit the Dessalles family of Toulouse (distant relatives) in connection with Antoinette's marriage to Jean Dessalles, a plan that had been hatched by Adrien. The encounter turns out to be a disaster.]

14 July 1838

. . . Toulouse is a big place, rather ugly, but with abundant resources; everything is a third cheaper here than in Bordeaux. The surrounding countryside is magnificent.

At three o'clock in the afternoon, I went to the Dessalles's. I found the old mother to be an excellent woman but appallingly simpleminded. The old father arrived a moment later; like his wife, he received me most cordially.[3] I had dinner there. The oldest son, who is mad, is all heart. The one who just arrived from Paris and whose name is François is tall, heavily built, and very gentle in his manner. Like his brother Jean, he lacks proper upbringing; this is a shortcoming that can never be repaired. This family is altogether too bourgeois; my daughter could never put up with it. I cannot understand how Adrien could have seen it in such a way that he would dream of his sister's marriage with one of these young men. I am not proud, but by God! I do not think I have fallen low enough to make this kind of an arrangement for my daughter. The abundance that reigns in this hut — and it is nothing more than the hut of rich peasants —

---

3. The Dessalles lived at rue du Pont Guilheméry no. 9, where they owned the salt depot of the City of Toulouse. The "old father" was 74 years old at the time, and the "old mother" 66 [HF and LE].

bespeaks a lot of money. Let them keep their gold; I prefer our manners and our customs to money acquired at this price. The discovery of such a family is a true calamity! I cannot get over it that my son saw these simple folks in such a favorable light. Jean—who wants to marry my daughter—detests nobles; he seems to be good friends here with a young Cassaing, a republican who has imparted his ideas to him. No, no, I have no more use for republicanism than for the bourgeoisie. I shall keep the position I have in the world.

[Dessalles's further impressions of people, places, and things in southern France cannot be included here. The rigors of nineteenth-century travel—muddy or dusty roads, crowded coaches, dreadful food, bedbugs in the hotels—often put the fragile Mme Dessalles and her spoiled daughters into "diabolical moods." When that happens, Dessalles's longing for Martinique becomes overwhelming. It should also be pointed out that the trip serves to strengthen his identity as a Creole, for he is often called upon to tell his hosts about life in the colonies. At one point he has a conversation about music with a M. Vidal, mayor of a small town in the Aveyron:

It seems [he writes on 10 August] that today people only appreciate new music and that Gluck and Piccini are in music what Corneille and Racine are in literature. It is really funny. I was asked for my opinion and replied that, in the last eleven years, I had only heard the music of the negroes and that I was therefore in no position to state an opinion. But, said M. Vidal, the music of the negroes is the whip! Monsieur, I replied with verve and indignation, the whip is practically unknown in the colonies. It is used on horses and insolent individuals, and the most unfortunate negro in our colonies is still more fortunate than the most fortunate of your peasants. No doubt he sensed how stupid he had been; he did not reply, and the conversation did not go any further. What prejudices there are against the colonists! I went to bed before everyone else.

A few days later, he continues this comparison between the peasants of the Massif Central and the black slaves of the colonies.]

14 August 1838

... I told the local landowners how surprised I was at the politeness of the peasants, who never fail to salute you when they meet you. They replied that this is not to be trusted. The peasants are indeed polite, but they become very vicious when they are provoked and upset. Vindictive in the extreme, they use the most cruel means imaginable to avenge themselves and respect neither age nor sex nor even the sacred character of the priesthood. Two priests had their throats cut in their lodgings in full daylight, and the perpetrators of the crime were never found. These churchmen had preached too much against the deterioration of morals; having too forcefully thwarted the peasants' propensities, they had finally made them angry. There is a lot of hue and cry about the morals of our negroes, but they are a thousand times preferable; doing openly what these peasants so carefully conceal, our negroes do not, at least, commit all the crimes that are perpetrated here in these mountains.

[After the family's return to Bordeaux, Dessalles settles into a rather monotonous routine. By the end of the year, his mind is made up; he will return to Martinique. The plans of the rest of his family, however, remain indeterminate.]

31 December 1838

Despite the rain, I went out with Antoinette. I bought the New Year's presents for the domestics. Since I cannot give them money, I was forced to go to a store to buy some material on credit. Our financial constraint is horrible. My wife's tranquillity frightens me; her obstinate determination to stay in France and especially in Bordeaux will bring the ruin of my family.

Adrien plays the master on my plantation. Afraid of losing the authority with which I have been kind enough to provide him, he tries to prove to me that I must stay in France; but he will not succeed. I am very anxious to go home.

1839

[Increasingly uncomfortable in the family circle, Dessalles takes to spending many evenings at Bordeaux's businessmen's club, the Cercle de l'Union; before long, he contracts a full-blown gambling addiction. Gambling losses are now added to his other financial problems. In January the diary almost exclusively mentions gains of 10 to 12 francs, but by February the losses are quite high. Here too, as on the occasion when he claims that whipping is practically unknown in the colonies, Dessalles proves himself a skillful practitioner of denial.]

12 February 1839

This evening I went to the Cercle; I played craps (*au crabe*) and had the misfortune of losing 600 francs. This loss does not take one penny away from me, since I had won this little sum at the game. At this moment, though, 600 francs less is an enormous deficit. I am very sorry that I risked so much money. Gambling is very dangerous to a man, even the most self-assured. This dismal lure of gain exposes him to terrible remorse. Henceforth, I shall be more circumspect.

13 February 1839, Ash Wednesday

... This evening, I went to the Cercle. Despite my resolution to stop playing there, I let myself go, joined a bank, and lost 450 francs. I am sick about it, particularly since I had to tell my wife in order to pay.

[Dessalles's gambling continues. Meanwhile, his wife's health deteriorates steadily; she continues to lose weight, and her doctors seem to feel that she is suffering from some kind of hysterical condition. Considering that she died only seven years later, this was probably a misdiagnosis.

News of a major earthquake in Martinique further frays everyone's nerves; in the end, however, it turns out that family members have not been harmed and that damage to the property has been relatively slight. Another great source of unhappiness for Dessalles is the recurring illness of his "*petit nègre*" Nicaise, who apparently suffers from bouts of venereal disease, a fact that absolutely must be hidden from Mme Dessalles, who dislikes Nicaise intensely. In an effort to cut down expenses, Dessalles moves his family to Poitiers, where his youngest son will pursue his studies. He then books passage to Martinique and is off on 20 May 1839.

His first stop after landing at Fort-Royal is La Rivière Monsieur, the plantation of his daughter Calixte and her family.]

27 June 1839

When I entered my daughter's room, I shuddered to see the damage caused by the earthquake. Except for Calixte's room, everything is in ruins; the house and the galleries are held up by bamboo poles. Pressing my daughter upon my heart, I thought my sobs would suffocate me. I found her aged and changed, all her features altered by misfortune, and her face covered with pimples. Arthur [his grandson] is a fine child, but not very well right now because he is teething. Georges [de Cacqueray-Valmenier, Dessalles's son-in-law] seemed crushed under the weight of enormous sorrows; he sees his fortune lost and no possibility of restoring it. I would never have imagined the full extent of poor Martinique's misery. . . .

28 June 1839

I arose at half-past two in the morning and found Georges in his sugar mill. I talked to him about my affairs. The low price of sugar has made it impossible for my son [Adrien] to fulfill the obligations I had assumed [the payment of his daughter's dowry], and the situation has grown steadily worse. I left La Rivière Monsieur at half-past five. . . .

When I arrived home, Adrien was not there. A letter explained his absence;

he felt that he should accompany his cousin's body [Alexandre Le Vassor had died suddenly] to Saint-Pierre and not abandon poor Louis Le Vassor in this mournful circumstance. My domestics came out to meet me and showed some signs of joy at seeing me. I cannot begin to express the sensations that shook me; this plantation, whose appearance used to be balm to my misfortunes, now only seemed to foreshadow impending ruin. To arrive at the house, I took the canal; I felt that the cane looked dirty and neglected. I am impatient to see my son, for he will no doubt explain to me why he has not sent any sugar since January. . . .

At seven o'clock, Adrien came from Saint-Pierre; I found him changed and gaunt. We did not talk much; I only told him that before being filled in on my affairs, I wished to have some rest. His first words were shattering; in his opinion, I am ruined, and there is nothing I can do about it.

29 June 1839

. . . Adrien talked to me about my situation. The low price of sugar has upset all calculations and ruined the country. I still do not want to look at the accounts, for I am in a state of malaise that is hard to describe. My son says I was wrong to come back and feels that in this country I will no longer obtain even the smallest credit.

I spent a very sad day engaging in somber reflections. The governor has opened the ports and permitted the export of sugar; foreign ships are crowding the approaches to our harbors and loading our sugar. This measure seems to have given movement and life to the country, but how will it be taken in France? The commercial interests will be furious, and will not the government have to fight a party [i.e., the abolitionists] that only wishes for the ruin of the colonists? In this manner we will lose the interest that the maritime ports, and indeed all of France, seemed to have in our well-being. French ships will find it difficult to obtain cargoes, and the shippers will be displeased. On the other hand, it is also possible that we will more quickly receive tax relief and that the metropolis will respond to the colonists' cries of distress. Until now, we have been disappointed so often that one does not know what to think.

1 July 1839

. . . Adrien has begun to tell me about the problems that overwhelmed him. The low sugar prices and the sums I had to pay in Martinique prevented him from fulfilling any of the obligations I had left behind. He found it very difficult to raise the money needed for the maintenance of the plantation. I had no idea of the position this country is in. If I had, I would not have come back. How am I going to deal with my creditors? How am I going to provide for my wife? How am I going to explain my position to those to whom I owe money? I am really in very deep trouble. To make things even worse, the cane does not yield anything. Adrien cannot imagine what has caused this deficit. Yet the answer is simple; he planted too much cane and was unable to care for it properly. He will not admit this and tries to prove to me that it was an effect of the earthquake, but my notion is correct. Poor Martinique! One more unexpected event such as a tornado, and all that will be left of you will be a dismal rock battered by all evils.

2 July 1839

. . . At four o'clock Adrien suggested we go down to the buildings, and I followed him. The new sugar house is handsome, but to finish it would demand expenditures that we cannot afford. When I was back under my trees with Adrien, he told me that he was discouraged and could see that he would not achieve last year's revenue. I wanted to prove to him that he had done too much planting. At this point, he said in the most absolute tone that we would never see eye to eye and that we would have to separate. I told him that no one was easier to get along with than I and that he should not reject my advice and constantly forget, as he was doing, the respect he owes me. He said that our upbringing had not been the same, but that his heart was in the right place. According to him, he sees only one way to get out of this trouble, and that is for me to sell out to my children. He said he would provide for my livelihood in France; as for the creditors, he would fight them off. Certainly, there is nothing I would not do to reestablish my affairs and save some of my fortune for my children, but this way would only compound the pattern of mismanagement and bad faith. I think it more appropriate to call a meeting of our creditors, give them an exact accounting of our position, and ask for their indulgence. If they fail to help me out, then my wife—whose rights remain intact—can ask for a separation of property, make an arrangement with my brother, and, when circumstances permit it, satisfy my creditors. It must also be said that the sugars I sent to France have never fetched good prices. One thing is certain: neither my gambling nor other misconduct[4] has made me deserve the fate that overwhelms me. For many years now, I have not been receiving anyone, and the expenses for my table amount to very little. May God examine and judge me. . . .

4. One does wonder what this "other misconduct" was.

4 July 1839

. . . M. Le Camus, manager of the Saint-Jacques plantation and brother-in-law of M. Duperré, Minister of the Navy, came to see me and brought me the governor's instructions.[5] They will promote the complete upheaval of the country. Outlawing the whip would produce the most baneful results. If these instructions were followed to the letter, we would be a thousand times better off with immediate emancipation. To make the negro think about all these ideas for improvement is to expose the colonists to the most baneful disorders. M. de Moges [the governor] contradicts himself: opening the ports and permitting the export of our sugar is an attempt to rekindle the spirit of the colonists who had for so long carried the burden of the injustice the metropolis had heaped on them; to touch the internal system designed to regulate the work and discipline of individual plantations is to promote revolt and compromise the livelihood of the Whites. Ameliorating conditions on one plantation but not on another will say to the negroes of the latter, "Go and obtain by force what your masters will not give you voluntarily."

M. de Moges is meddling in things that are none of his business, no doubt in order to look good to the Abolitionist Society[6] and to make himself a reputation. The Director of the Interior, who at the moment is M. Eyma, acts like a man who has sold out to power. He allows the government to encroach upon his rights as overseer of the state-owned plantation called Saint-Jacques. This plantation is the property of the colony, and nothing can be changed there without the approval of the Colonial Council. M. Eyma, so far from protesting such illegal and baneful acts, writes to M. Le Camus that he must urge him to execute the government's orders. It is a disgrace! I have long felt that nothing good can be expected of M. Eyma, for how can one trust a man who went over to the English in 1809 and helped them seize this colony? What is one to think of a man who, born a Frenchman and a Catholic, has abjured his religion and served the cause of his country's enemies? Despite all odds, M. Eyma wanted to be somebody; now that his affairs are completely out of order, he will make all kinds of concessions to keep a position that brings him money and prestige. He is not a bad man, but he is devoured by ambition. His brother, M. Louis Eyma, has gone bankrupt twice and ruined respectable families. On these grounds alone, his brother should have kept out of public affairs.

5. These instructions, dated 28 May 1839, provided in particular for the opening of a school for slave children under 16, material incentives for marriages between slaves, and limitations on the use of the whip, even as a means of marking work rhythms [HF and LE].

6. The French Abolitionist Society, though much less effective than its British counterpart, gained increasing support in the French Chamber of Deputies in the 1830s and 1840s.

[Throughout July, the diary is filled with complaints about Adrien's poor administration of the estate during Dessalles's absence, as well as Adrien's general muddleheadedness and the company he keeps. Worst of all is his friendship with the Ballain family, with whom Dessalles has, for reasons unknown to posterity, been fighting for years. Before long, it becomes clear that Adrien wants to marry one of the Ballain daughters.]

27 July 1839

I have begun a letter to my wife; I tell her everything and hide nothing. The poor unfortunate woman! How unhappy she will be! At five o'clock this afternoon my son arrived with [Arthur] Bence [Dessalles's brother-in-law] and Georges [de Cacqueray-Valmenier, his son-in-law]. I had a conversation with these two about my affairs and about my son's supposed plans to marry Mlle Ballain. Arthur does not think that Adrien will make this marriage; Georges was positive that he is determined to do it and that he will respectfully ask for our consent. What a blow this was for me! I will not survive such a shame! Mme Ballain is descended from mulattoes. It is only too true; her mother and her aunts had children by negroes and mulattoes, and several of these children are still alive. The reputation of the young Ballain ladies is absolutely terrible, and the morals of the one whom Adrien wants to take as his wife are rotten.

[The first step was to take the administration of the estate away from Adrien: "Since yesterday, Adrien is no longer in charge" (29 July). His father is also gathering information on New Orleans, where he wants to send Adrien to get him away from the Ballain family (23 July). Dessalles's financial situation lurches from crisis to crisis. On 3 August he receives an official notice from the Fontenau brothers, the commission merchants who have advanced him 42,000 francs (see 29 August), to fulfill his obligations or be held responsible for delaying the departure of their next ship. On 24 August he consults the justice of the peace of Trinité,[7] M. Pothuau, then meets with the Fontenau brothers.]

24 August 1839

. . . M. Alexandre [Fontenau] berated me for borrowing money, knowing that I would be unable to repay it. I apologized and pointed out that, through the fault of my son, I did not know the state of my affairs. My son was in the next room with M. Villiers. M. Alexandre took unfair advantage of his position; for twenty minutes I had to put up with the most cutting and painful talk. I had to remain silent. Asked how I was planning to repay what I owed, I referred to the proposals contained in my letter of the third of this month. M. Alexan-

7. Justices of the peace were instituted only after the Restauration [HF and LE].

dre called this disgraceful and rejected such offers. I replied that the state of the colony and of my affairs did not permit me to advance others. I recalled to M. Alexandre that his other debtors had been treated more generously and that all of them had received a reduction of their debt, while I was asking only for a deferral. He delivered a string of insolences. He permitted himself to say that, if he had finished with Mme Le Vassor [Dessalles's aunt], it was because he did not want to have anything to do with a woman *of this kind.* Offended by this last word, I reacted as I should and reminded him that he and his brothers had been that lady's servants. I added that I had not come here to insult him or to hear insolences from him.[8] He replied that he would go to court and have a brief published. "You will have it done, and you will pay for it," I told him. "I will draw up mine myself, and nothing will be forgotten." . . .

After long debates it was agreed that MM. Fontenau would give me six years to pay without interest and that I would give them the consent of my commission agent or the signature of a solvent planter. I returned to my plantation at six o'clock, totally exhausted. Adrien behaved well; he did not say a word.

[Attending a name-day celebration for M. Pécoul, a prosperous planter on the heights of Saint-Pierre, Dessalles has the opportunity to observe what he considered the wave of the future for Martinique. He is clearly baffled that M. Pécoul is prosperous and happy.]

28 August 1839

Having spent an excellent night, I went down to the salon at eight o'clock. Many guests were already there. Everyone wished M. Pécoul a happy name day. Thereafter, he received all his negroes, who delivered the same good wishes. The parish priest, Abbé Girardon, seemed to enjoy the decorum of these slaves and their air of happiness. He is an excellent priest, generally loved, and possessed of all the evangelical virtues. Of Pécoul's 300 negroes, 40 are married and getting along very well. In his case, these means of civilizing the negroes have been successful; I suppose he has been very lucky. On other plantations, they would upset everything, as I experienced on my place in 1827. I wanted to improve morality and made 12 marriages in 14 months. Yet it was precisely those whom I married who poisoned my negroes and my animals and who have caused me such losses. The negro is bizarre; what is good for one is not good

8. Pierre Dessalles eagerly grasps this opportunity to defend his family's honor and thereby save face in this painful confrontation, even though he had frequently complained about Mme Le Vassor's business dealings and her private morals.

for another. This is what often makes general regulations so harmful. Pécoul is rich, he can experiment, but everyone is not in this fortunate situation.

We did not sit down to eat until half-past twelve, and it was almost four when we were finished. There was dancing all evening, square dances, bamboulas, etc. A very tiring day. At dinner M. Segond sang a song in honor of our host. The wine flowed freely. Free men and women of color from Saint-Pierre were at this party, and a great many whites had come. Mme Jules de Loyac had come with her daughter. Pécoul ushered them into his salon where they took some refreshments.

29 August 1839

. . . At noon I went down to the Mouillage and called on M. Lefaivre in his counting house. I informed him of my affairs and of the arrangement proposed by MM. Fontenau concerning the signature of a commission merchant. He felt that in the present circumstances a merchant could not issue 42,000 francs' worth of notes, particularly for such a long term. I tried to convince him that he would run no risk, since the notes would be paid for by my sugar. He agreed, but is afraid that this would be bad for his credit. He will write me a letter, which I will show to MM. Fontenau. . . . In short, my trip was a waste of time.

[M. Pothuau, the justice of the peace, finally mediated an arrangement between Dessalles and MM. Fontenau. Dessalles was given six years to pay off his debts, but had to produce his wife's signature in addition to his own (7 September).]

8 September 1939

. . . My mulatto Saint-Just has been to see Adrien and found him torn with remorse. This slave has made him understand that he cannot marry Mlle Ballain; he agreed, but the sentiment that dominates him is stronger than everything else. He said that he would come to throw himself at my feet this evening. He did come up to my room at eight o'clock and stayed at my feet for more than two hours. He confessed all his wrongs to me and asked me to forgive him. What torments him most are all the terrible things he supposedly said about me. How can a son tear apart his father in public? Fortunately, such examples are rare; it was my special fate to experience this ingratitude after I had placed so much trust in my son. At ten o'clock my son [left], asking me to write him a letter that he could use to get away from that disreputable family.[9] He exalted the virtues of the young lady but laid out the turpitude of

9. Presumably this would be a letter denying permission for this marriage. In Martinique there was no real majority for marriage, and the consent of the parents was absolutely necessary at any

her family. How terribly guilty Mme Ballain is! For a mother to exhibit her daughters! to permit a young man to sleep under the same roof! If I had stayed away another six months, my poor son would have been lost. He promised to give up this marriage.

[Great turmoil fills the next month. Adrien "drinks" too much opium and stops eating and speaking; Mme Ballain is enraged and threatens to have him beaten up or worse if her daughter's honor is attacked. But Dessalles remains firm: "I would a thousand times rather see my son die than see him make such a marriage." Adrien vacillates from one day to the next; his father is ready to go out of his mind. His misery is compounded when he has to attend the funeral of one of his grandsons at La Rivière Monsieur. On 7 October Adrien sails for France. Life gradually returns to normal: hard work on the plantation, money troubles, gossip.]

28 October 1839

Louis Le Vassor, whom we had not seen for a few days, came to spend the day with us. He brought the news that Théotiste Fortier, the mulatto bastard daughter of M. Fortier, has died, leaving a fortune of 1,200,000 francs. This woman was singularly attached to the Whites, particularly to her father's family. She left to each of her three daughters 300,000 francs and 300,000 francs to each of her father's children. She will be missed by everyone in the colony.

29 October 1839

. . . I spent last evening at my [livestock] pens. One of my negroes, Avinet, was impudent and unruly. I had him whipped. Today the negroes did not work well.

30 November 1839

I went to visit my Caféière. The tranquillity of this place is soothing to the spirit, and I spent a delightful hour there.

We spent a peaceful day. Georges [his son-in-law] told me about his plans. An advance of 1,200 francs would enable him, he says, to produce 300 hogsheads of sugar per year; he believes that, within seven years, he would no longer owe anything. I tried to prove to him that he was wrong, but this is his fixed idea and nothing can dissuade him. He would be glad to see immediate eman-

---

age, even after the promulgation of the *Code Civil*. The opposition of the parents could be overruled only after three notices drawn up by a notary. Before the promulgation of the *Code Civil*, one also had to obtain the permission of the district judge not only for the marriage itself but also for the notices [HF and LE].

cipation because, he says, his proximity to town would permit him to rent [sic] as many negroes as he needs. How wrong! At this moment one can still find negroes for rent, because they have to work in order to pay their rent to their masters [i.e., pay their masters for the time they are given]; but if they were free they would work only if they wanted to. They would much rather rent a piece of land, which they would work for themselves, than work for Whites, against whom they would all unite, there is no doubt about that. To see it differently is pure fantasy. As for me, the day general freedom is proclaimed, I shall consider myself ruined, and I will no longer be able to inhabit this country! . . .

26 December 1839

I went to work in the upper part of the plantation and had the opportunity to see my son's negligence. The cane that was planted would have been magnificent if it had been taken care of; as it is, it will yield nothing because it has been neglected. It is distressing.

27 December 1839

I was in my cane field when I saw a young domestic come running to tell me that Mme Beaumier was waiting for me at the house. It was again about the nonpayment of the draft for 2,500 francs on Marseilles that my son had given her. It will soon be due, and she came to see if I could give her sugar. I promised to deliver to her the first ten hogsheads I will produce. This unexpected circumstance will greatly hamper me. My whole life is spent like this!

After Mme Beaumier left, I got angry with my mulatto Saint-Just, whom my son has overindulged. This young mulatto dreams of liberty and fortune. Filled with ambition, he seizes on every means of making money. I would not complain if he did his work properly, but he shows reprehensible negligence in handling everything that belongs to me. A thief, he takes everything he can. Adrien gave him privileges that increased his aspirations; he never appears at prayer, he has his own apprentices, he is associated with the master artisans and directs building projects, he has sheep in his own pen. Living with a woman who sells tafia, he runs her business for her. He has taken over the room where she sells her tafia and uses it to receive his protégés and friends. He has a tobacco patch and a small cassava field, and he speculates on everything. Once again, I would be glad to see this activity if my affairs were doing better, but the fact is that he tries to cause me as much expense as he can. All these privileges would degenerate into abuses if I were not watching out. I had promised, even though it hurt me, to maintain them if his conduct met my expectations; but ever since I came back he has shown no zeal whatsoever. On the contrary, he has become more and more casual. My outburst of this morning was caused by a very minor matter. Yesterday he had started cleaning up around the house. While repairing a wall that runs through my courtyard, he pulled out the old mortar in order to put on a new finish. Some of the old mortar was gone; I wanted it to reinforce my walkways and therefore asked him what he had done with it. "I had it put in the manure pile," he answered confidently.

I immediately went to see if I could have it removed from there, but there was no mortar. Going back to him, I asked again what he had done with it. Without losing his composure, he replied that he did not remember whom he had asked to dispose of the mortar.

"Please find out," I insisted, "what has become of this mortar, I really need it." [10]

At this point he stood up, made as if to go to the manure pile, but then returned to his work. Now I could see by his discomposure that he had had this old debris carried to his cabin. I steadily looked at him: "Well, where is the old mortar?"

"Monsieur," he said, "Léon has probably mixed it into the new mortar."

He stood up to show me, but failing to find anything, he went back to his work. At this point I blew up and heaped reproaches and insults on him. I made him give back the old debris. I informed him that I no longer wanted him to have sheep on the plantation and demanded that he dismiss his apprentices. He showed, I must admit, great resilience. I forced him to humiliate himself and to apologize for his behavior; he did so without hesitation, and his tone reflected shame rather than anger. I was unable to restrain myself, and I am desperately sorry to have let myself be carried away. But really, I have too many personal griefs against this mulatto. When my son left for France and I managed the plantation by myself for two years, his conduct during these two years was exceedingly bad. When I left the country in 1838, I asked my son not to indulge this mulatto in any way. In this instance as in all others, he paid no heed to my opinion and my advice, and instead this mulatto became his confidant and his friend. He used him to facilitate his debaucheries. When I reproached him on my return from France for having accorded so many privileges to Saint-Just, he replied: "I wanted to attach him to you."

This mulatto exerts a great deal of influence over many of my negroes and can be extremely dangerous. If ever poison were to reappear on my place, we must not hesitate to lay hands on him. I have never been anything but well

10. "Mais voyez . . . ce que ce mortier est devenu." It seems remarkable that Dessalles addresses his slave in the formal "*vous*" form.

disposed toward him, as God is my witness, but I want him to deserve my kindness by submission to my orders and zeal in doing his duty. I have freed his mother and his young brother.[11] His older brother [12] died in France in my home, overwhelmed with my favors. He [Saint-Just] would like to receive the same favors, but he will have to deserve them. What will be the result of this scene? This evening he showed up at prayers and seems most humiliated. . . .

28 December 1839

I spent the most horrible night imaginable; the anger I experienced yesterday upset me to the point of hurting me. I also had much pain in my left wrist, where I sprained a nerve.[13]. . .

11. His mother is Fortunée, his young brother is Saint-Fort, and his sister is Trop, the mother of Saturnin.

12. The mulatto Dieudonné, who died at the château of Lespinassat [HF and LE].

13. Did Pierre Dessalles not only upbraid but also strike Saint-Just?

1840-1841

1 January 1840

This is a horrible day everywhere, but especially in the colonies. When I woke up, two wretched fiddlers and a tambourine player came to grate on my ears and to remind me that it was New Year's Day. I clasped my children to my bosom, and we wished each other a better year than the one that has just ended. . . . My negroes came one by one to wish me a good year, and I told each one what his or her behavior or past history might deserve. I urged them to work well for themselves and for me, so that they would avoid punishments and create some comfort in their own dwellings. They will soon have forgotten my advice, and tomorrow I will again have to shout and punish. . . .

I had a long conversation with my mulatto Saint-Just. I tried to point out that, in granting him so many privileges, Adrien had exceeded his authority and overindulged him. He asked to be sold, but I told him that I had no intention of doing that. I urged him to return to ideas better suited to his duty and not to expand his personal enterprises as he was doing. He was very sad when he left. It is to be hoped that his conduct will change. . . .

[Early in the year Dessalles gives a wedding party for his slave Césaire.[1]]

1. Another Césaire had killed himself in 1823 (letter No. 34 [26 July 1823]). At that time a young child had probably been given his name.

10 January 1840

This morning we slaughtered an ox, a sheep, and a cow. I distributed the beef to my work gang. I invited everyone I know: if all those invited come, we will have a tremendous crowd. I can't wait for this wedding to be over, for my negroes don't work as they should; all they can think about is getting their clothes ready. . . .

11 January 1840

Early in the morning all my negroes brought me herbs and wood. At nine o'clock my daughter helped dress the bride. At ten the wedding party left for town. When the ceremony was over they came back to the plantation, accompanied by the musicians. We fired 21 musket shots in their honor. They took over my salon, and the dance began. The negroes of the whole neighborhood came to share their joy. I had a magnificent meal served to my invited guests; we were 22 at table! After the Whites' dinner, that of the slaves was served, and it was copious and good. Counter and square dances are going on right now; my courtyard is lit by torches, which produce the prettiest effect. It is nine o'clock in the evening, and this racket will no doubt go on all night. The negroes seem happy. Their gaiety makes me sad; at this moment, my family in France may well be lacking everything. How can I be happy in this thought?

12 January 1840

A few more guests arrived. My negroes danced until midnight. Many free people of color came to watch, and even danced with the slaves. I went to bed happy in the thought that tomorrow I will get back to my routine.

1 February 1840

I forgot to record here all the fuss I had the day before yesterday. I had not been satisfied with my driver[2] for some time. The day before yesterday the work was very sluggish. I pointed this out to him, telling him to do something about it. He sassed me and told me that he only knows his own way of working the negroes and that he is not in the habit of killing people. I was patient and did not say anything. At noon I had three stakes driven into the ground and

---

2. The driver [commandeur] was a slave designated as the foreman who enforced discipline in the work gang. The sign of his authority was the whip, which he used to a greater or lesser extent [HF and LE].

had him tied to them; he was given fifty lashes. Césaire, who administered the punishment, did not hit him too hard. I did not intend to take the whip away from him [the driver], but only asked him to admit that he had been wrong and to declare that he would henceforth obey my orders. Yet he persisted in saying that he would continue to act as before. So I had him put into an iron collar.

I called for my head mule driver, Charles, a young negro [originally] from Guinée, and made him the driver for the work gang. I then replaced Charles with Victor, another newly purchased young negro. All these changes will improve matters, I am convinced, because *I, the master*, have made them; a manager would have bungled everything. The work has gone much better since then, and the negroes seem content. Today at noon I finished cutting all the cane; a great quantity is piled up by the mill, which will have to run, I believe, until tomorrow.

2 February 1840

I have a small sore on the bone of my leg that hurts. I have bandaged it, but it does not seem to get better. I kept still to see if rest will be good for my leg.

[The sore keeps getting worse; Dessalles becomes increasingly worried, but does not call the physician La Peyre. Instead, he agrees to see Louis Littée's cook, who has an excellent reputation for his skill in treating wounds. His first remedy "seems to work wonders," but the pain soon comes back. Dessalles again calls the cook, who starts him on a new remedy. "So here I am in the hands of a charlatan!" he writes with a certain resignation. The reason he does not call Dr. La Peyre soon becomes apparent.]

27 February 1840

I received a letter from the physician La Peyre containing my bill for 1839, amounting to 789 francs 90. I sent him a money order on my commission merchant payable in three months. In this country you can't get sick; for five visits to Mme de Valmenier [Dessalles's daughter], he charges 230 francs! This cries out for vengeance! Yet one must keep quiet, lest these gentlemen refuse to come when one really needs them. It's a disgrace!

28 February 1840

Louis [Le Vassor] told me yesterday that the apostolic prefect and the *curé* of Fort-Royal[3] are leaving the colony. It appears that, following incendiary talk

---

3. Abbé Castelli and Abbé Goubert; both were proponents of new ideas [HF and LE], that is, ideas tending to emancipation.

at the church, the Colonial Council demanded the dismissal of these two men, who claimed that they only expressed the governor's views. How will M. de Moges [the governor] take these accusations? Calling for the suppression of the whip in the colonies means promoting their ruin; the negro would no longer do anything if he were not to be beaten.

2 March 1840

. . . Lalanne dined with me. He told me that the government had finally accorded him the 2,000 francs indemnity for the damage he suffered in the earthquake. This pleased me more than if I had been granted this sum my-self. He brought me a letter from some of the planters of Saint-Pierre who got together to write to all the planters, asking them to let themselves be taxed at the rate of one franc per barrel of sugar for the purpose of winning over a few journalists and giving M. Le Chevalier the means to continue his paper *L'Outre-Mer*. The sums obtained would be sent to Paris to MM. de Perinelle, Bilouin, and Fortier,[4] who would be in charge of distributing them. I said that I would be very glad to contribute to this subsidy, but that I hoped it would be given to our delegates [i.e., lobbyists]. To act otherwise would be to show them distrust and insufficient appreciation of the efforts they are making on our behalf. It is essential that the journalists coordinate their strategy of defending us with our delegates. M. Le Chevalier has no doubt been helpful to us by raising the colonial question, but in attacking certain powerful personalities, he has irritated them and diminished their zeal for our cause. We are too weak to go in for insulting language. . . .

13 March 1840

This morning I sent for M. La Peyre [the physician] for the *capresse* Clara. He bled her and prescribed emetic water. I acted very cheerfully so that he would not notice my bad leg. Today I am in great pain, and the sore is suppurating considerably. My leg is swollen and my skin is purple. I am worried.

[*"Mon empirique"* continues to treat the sore with different ointments and baths. It finally seems healed in early April.]

14 March 1840 (Saturday)

I gave my negroes the day off in lieu of their food rations. . . .

---

4. These men were the deputies from Martinique.

16 March 1840

The negro Calixte, former servant of my son, came to ask me for a certificate of liberty, but I refused to give it to him. This young negro conducted himself well while in France. On his return to the colony, he thought that a royal decree according freedom to all slaves who had touched French soil would apply to him; I myself believed it too. But when Calixte left for France, the matter was governed by a different law; unless the royal decree has a retroactive effect, Calixte never ceased being a slave. He applied to the governor, who refused to give him his certificate of freedom. This matter must be resolved, and I will look into it.[5]

At dinnertime the negress Joséphine was being insolent. She wanted to quit working early. The driver sent her back into the ranks, and that made her furious. Passing by the house, she called out the most insolent words, screaming at the top of her voice. I had her tied to three stakes, and she was made to pay the price for her insolence.

27 March 1840

At one o'clock, I had a visit from MM. de Percin and his brother Northumberland.[6] . . . We talked about emancipation and the neighboring colonies. The news from France is not good, although we do understand that the debate on the [emancipation] law has been postponed until 1842. This would gain us some time; between now and then, what happens in the English colonies is bound to make things clearer. . . . One can only hope that France will give up these absurd projects, which would ruin our colonies. M. Thiers ended a very long speech by saying he hopes that within three years the French flag will no longer fly over a slave territory. He added that France is essentially a continental power and that it does not need colonies. Listen to the Great Statesman! M. de La Martine[7] also speaks against the colonies and serves up the greatest absurdities in pompous phrases. Why don't they send him back to his *Méditations*!

5. See Susan Peabody, *"There Are No Slaves in France": Law, Culture, and Society in Early Modern France, 1685–1789.* Ph.D. diss., University of Iowa, December 1993.

6. Claude Charles Marie de Percin [54 years old, a contemporary of Dessalles] and his brother Louis Auguste Ferréol de Percin Northumberland [44], often called Northhum or even Norton [HF and LE].

7. The poet Lamartine, one of the future leaders of the Revolution of 1848.

5 April 1840

Yesterday MM. Louisie Burot, his nephew, Pierre Cardin, and Lalanne came for dinner. We talked about the colonies. They brought me the paper *L'Outre-Mer*, which I read with pleasure. It warmly defends our interests, and I believe that even in the Chamber there are deputies who understand our position. The government does not want our loss; but even supposing that France were in a position to afford an indemnity, how would we deal with the slaves? All hope is not lost, and I flatter myself that nothing will be changed in the status of the slaves.

7 April 1840

Three negroes from Gros-Morne came to ask me for work. I rented them at 35 francs per month, and I give them three pounds of cod and three pots of flour per week. I set them to cleaning up my grassland; they started this afternoon. I will keep them if I am satisfied with them.

12 April 1840

I went to mass; the heat was excessive. The church was full of negroes. I was back at home at one o'clock. Louis Le Vassor dined at the Nouvelle Cité. Together we read a pamphlet by M. Huc, a former attorney and member of the Colonial Council, in which he seeks to prove that the absurd ideas of philanthropy go back to the time of the Reformation. It is a strongly reasoned piece of work, and the style is good. He also proves that slavery has existed at all times and that Christianity has sanctioned it. He clearly establishes that the Macchiavelism of England has struck its blows in every part of the globe and that this perfidious nation is the source of all the woes that threaten the colonists. I also read a letter by the colonial delegates [i.e., lobbyists] to the deputies of the Chamber. Its meek tone clearly shows that they feel the cause is lost, so they talk of indemnity as a favor. Showing such discouragement is no way to defend the interests that have been entrusted to them. The rights of the colonists are obviously just and sacred; this being so, they must be asserted firmly and with conviction. The uncertainty that weighs on our future is dreadful.

1 May 1840

I cut cane all day long, and I manured at the Corbière with my sick slaves and the negro children from the courtyard.

My financial trouble is awful; I don't have two francs to rub together. The term when I must pay the Fontenaus is approaching, and my sugar is not ready.

I am afraid that Fourniols [a section of the plantation] will not yield as much as I had expected.

2 May 1840

We were able to carry straw until 11 o'clock, then it started to rain. With the small gang and the negro children from the courtyard, I manured all day long at the Corbière. At eight o'clock we stopped boiling: working all week, I have produced fourteen hogsheads of sugar. This slowness of the process is harmful to my operation. As soon as the mill starts running, my negroes are exhausted; then they have to be kept going by the whip.

[On 8 May the important royal ordinance of 5 January 1840 reached Martinique. Calling most notably for the inspection of individual plantations by royal judicial officers, it outraged Dessalles and his friends, who immediately planned a letter of protest to the governor.]

9 May 1840

I gave my negroes all Saturday off in lieu of their food rations. . . .

I had to chastise the negress Manette, who works in the plantation hospital, for unseemly talk. She accused my servant Adée of reporting to me everything that is happening on the plantation and of slandering her. She stirred up all her kin and all her partisans, and serious threats were made. I personally gave Manette a thrashing, whereupon all this talk stopped instantly.

15 May 1840

. . . Lalanne sent me a decree of the governor providing for the execution of the royal ordinance [on plantation inspection]. We certainly had not expected such a prompt decision. We thought that the Colonial Council would be consulted. . . .

The negroes know exactly what is going on; since the arrival of the royal ordinance, I find that mine are less pliable and more difficult to handle.

21 May 1840

. . . Pécoul[8] is of the opinion that we should put up with the consequences of the royal ordinance without complaining; so we must just stand by as we are being despoiled. I immediately informed Lalanne of this opinion.

8. Pécoul was the wealthy, progressive planter at whose house Dessalles had met socially with most of Saint-Pierre's prominent people of color in August 1839.

This evening a free mulatto by the name of Dérose came to see me. He told me that a meeting in town had been well attended and that several men of color had been there. Everyone approves the letter [of protest] to the governor.

9 June 1840

... At noon, Lalanne arrived at the Nouvelle Cité accompanied by M. Bonnet, the royal judicial inspector [*procureur du roi*, as called for in the ordinance]. After the customary courtesies, we brought the conversation to the purpose of his visit. He tried to make the government's intentions look as good as possible, even while acknowledging the measure's bad effects. He stayed with me for 45 minutes. I expressed my reservations so as not to be out of step with the defenders of the colonies, but of course I have no means of resisting force. I think that the royal inspector was pleased with my conduct, for this time he limited himself to a simple visit. My negroes did not even know that he had come to the plantation. I am told that the negro who follows him and carries his trunk is very dangerous because of what he communicates to the negroes. This is good to know.

29 June 1840 [Dessalles's name day]

When I woke up, the dean of my negroes came to congratulate me on my name day. The others did not bother with this courtesy, and I was glad of it. Ten years ago they would not have failed to come, but today they no longer owe their masters anything. Without the whip they would not even work in our cane fields any more. I gave my negroes the day off and paid for the fiddler, so they danced until two o'clock in the morning. Many negroes from other places came to share their pleasure.

[The dinner celebrating the name day was attended by 11 of Dessalles's friends, all men.]

4 July 1840

I gave the negroes the whole day off.[9] Yesterday I forgot to mention what happened in my field gang. The negro La Prière refused to obey the driver and actually hit him. Having recently been a driver himself, he should have realized the gravity of such an offense. For a moment I felt like handing this negro over to the law, feeling that the case was serious; but then I thought it

9. He does not say whether again it is in lieu of food rations.

would be better to get it over with right away. We can always get in touch with the law when we are forced to do so. So I had 75 lashes administered to this negro and had him put into an iron collar. Since the ordinance of 5 January, the negroes have become very difficult to handle. The negress Félicité, who is five or six months pregnant, does not work at all; when I spoke to her about it, she sassed me. Since I cannot punish her in her condition, I did not say anything, but once she is delivered, I will remind her of this occasion. She is the sister of Nicaise, to whom I have given his freedom,[10] so I must be extra severe with her. If I acted otherwise, the negroes would not fail to object and to say aloud that I let her get away with things because of her brother. . . .

6 July 1840

Very early in the morning, I went up to the Bananière with the field gang and part of the small gang and had them hoe until noon. The negro children put straw in the cow pen. I went to my Caféière, where I did not find Nicaise. I sent for him, and he administered in my presence 15 lashes to all the negroes attached to the Caféière. These scoundrels do not want to obey him and work very poorly. Yet they are better off than my negroes down below [at the Nouvelle Cité]. On my return to the sugar mill, I went to the cabin of the negro Toussaint, had all his belongings taken away, and had him locked into the loft of my storehouse. This scoundrel, in order to get out of work and to die, keeps up a stomach ailment that puts him into a horrible state. I will not give him back his cabin and his things until he is completely cured. Sometimes one is forced, against one's inclinations and in the interest of these wretches, to employ means repugnant to one's conscience. If I had closed my eyes, Toussaint might well have been gone before the month is out, whereas, if I take care of him, I might succeed in prolonging his days. These are things that the abolitionists would not understand; they would not fail to say that the despair at being a slave drove this negro to destroy himself. Laziness and dread of work, these are the motives that cause him to let himself die. If he were free, his entire life would be devoted to theft and pillage.

14 July 1840

One of my negresses returning from town gave me a letter for Saint-Just, my mason. I opened it; it is from the son of Chéry Magloire [a prominent mulatto

---

10. This is the first indication that Nicaise had obtained his freedom, apparently without having to pay for it.

of the district] who asks him to send him a few pounds of lead if he can get it. I was quite surprised and quite indignant, for I had suspected for some time that the free men of color incite our negroes to rob us, and now this proof that came into my hands by chance corroborates my hunch. Pity the proprietor, for he does not have on his place one slave whom he can trust.

22 July 1840

... Today I read M. de La Martine's speech about bringing back Napoleon's ashes; it is full of admirably formulated ideas. Like La Martine, I think that it is too early to bring to Paris a body that may well give rise to riots. People find it admirable that Louis-Philippe had the idea of bringing back to France what remains of the great man. This idea is politically motivated, for he hopes to consolidate his own dynasty on the throne of France. But whatever he does, he will eventually have to yield to the legitimate monarchy or to the Republic.

[In late July Dessalles again suffers a bout of ill health: a heavy cold, stomach troubles, hemorrhoids. Was there any relation between this and his unusually harsh behavior, followed by self-righteous self-pity? Or was it the fear of impending emancipation that caused both?]

31 July 1840

... In the last two days my young negress Clète, who is excessively lazy, has not appeared in the field; she insists that she must be admitted to the hospital. I administered a whipping to her myself. She said some extremely offensive things. I wanted to have her arrested, but she disappeared. This perked me up a little. When I returned to my salon, lunch was being served. Maximin[11] testily said, in the presence of the domestics, that one must not discourage the negro. I repeatedly asked him if he was mad, if he had gone out of his mind. He sensed his impropriety and replied that he was sorry to have expressed himself in this manner. I was chomping at the bit; if I had not reminded myself of my friendship for his father, I don't know what I might have done. I defy anyone to find two plantations where the negroes are treated better than on mine. A few lashes of the whip offended this young man, who may well have slept with this negress yesterday or the day before. All my life I will be the victim of my kind heart. I am truly sorry to have brought this young man with me. Born lazy, he spends his life sleeping and does not do a lick of work all day. He hopes that his friend who has gone to New Orleans will succeed and that he can join

11. Eymar, a young relative of Dessalles, who had been living with him for several weeks.

him there. He thinks that he can get a managership.[12] Living on illusions in this manner, he will continue to wallow in idleness.

[On 19 August the negro Toussaint, who had "given himself" stomach trouble, dies. "The criminal!" Dessalles exclaims. He is the fourth member of his family to do this to his owner! He therefore asks the mayor for permission to have Toussaint buried on his plantation rather than in consecrated ground. "This," he writes, "may have a salutary effect on the attitudes of the other negroes. It is very important to them to be buried in consecrated ground." Christianity had apparently penetrated slave culture to some extent.]

31 August 1840

My young negro Nicaise [who is free] told me about his plan to get married. He would like to marry a daughter of M. Humeau, who has some 15,000 francs. I would be very glad if he succeeded, but a mulatto by the name of Dérose, this girl's brother-in-law, will do all he can to prevent this marriage.

10 September 1840

At three o'clock I was brought three letters from France, two of them from my wife written on 23 June and 11 July. She informs me that M. Durant refuses to continue paying her pension. She therefore turned to Mont-Ferrier, who agreed to furnish her 600 francs per month. I immediately wrote to my wife to urge her to stay in France if she had not yet left. I wrote to Mont-Ferrier to thank him and to tell him that he would not receive his sugar until next February or March. I also wrote to M. Durant to reassure him about the money I owe him. . . . This news from France has given me a trembling fit that I am unable to stop.

11 October 1840

Almost everyone in the district went to Marigot [for the inauguration of a new church]. Maximin stopped by at Le Limbé for M. Morestin. Knowing that Saint-Just and Trop had gone off without a *billet*,[13] I asked Maximin to have them arrested. It is a lesson they deserve. These two think that they are so much above their fellow slaves that they do not have to submit to this formality. Their relations with free people of color will be their ruination.[14]

12. Forty years after the Louisiana Purchase (1803), French still seems to have been the language used on sugar plantations there.
13. All slaves needed written permission to leave their homes [HF and LE].
14. Saint-Just was the mason on the plantation who had frequently irritated Dessalles with his

26 October 1840

This evening M. Michaud brought me letters from France which I wanted to open only in the morning, so that I would be able to sleep tonight. But since Maximin hoped to find a letter from his father in the packets, I broke the seal. . . . Seeing a letter from my wife, I opened it and learned that she must have left France on 30 September last and that she will perhaps arrive here before three weeks' time. I also learned that my brother is about to land in Martinique and that he has hostile projects. It seems that I am to be driven from the plantation and replaced by a manager and that all my family shares this opinion. Deeply shaken by all this news, I retired to my room to reflect on my position.

[Dessalles's reunion with his wife and daughters gets off to a very bad start.]

11 November 1840

I received a note from Adelaïde La Perelle telling me that the ship *Le Hâvre & Martinique* has arrived at Saint-Pierre. Great joy in the family! [Dessalles was waiting for the travelers at the home of his daughter Calixte near Fort-Royal]. I asked Georges to go immediately to Saint-Pierre to be with my wife and my daughters. While he was dressing, a messenger brought a letter to Calixte from my daughter Antoinette. It says that the ship had arrived last night at 11 o'clock, that many longboats came alongside, and that only they had no news from their family. I cannot begin to express my indignation on hearing such a thing, for I had taken every precaution; a servant girl has been waiting for the ladies at Saint-Pierre for several days. Having learned that the ship was to go on to Fort-Royal, I decided to wait for it here, as much for reasons of economy as to avoid a great deal of fatigue. Georges had not yet left when a longboat sent by M. Lefaivre brought me a letter from him inviting me to use it to fetch my family [at Saint-Pierre]. I quickly dressed. When I was about to leave, I read in Calixte's eyes that, if I went to fetch the ladies, she would not see them right away and that her happiness would be put off. I therefore decided to stay. I wrote a note to my wife, and Georges left. We were hoping that he would bring back the ladies that evening. Adelaïde La Perelle joined us, and we waited in vain until almost ten in the evening. Every movement, every yap of a dog made us think that a longboat was arriving.

---

entrepreneurial activities. Trop was the mother of Saturnin, who came to play such a large role in Dessalles's later years.

12 November 1840

My wife and my daughters did not arrive until ten o'clock in the morning. I was struck by the change in my wife; she is extremely weak in spirit and in body. My daughters are unchanged. My poor Calixte experienced sad and tender feelings on seeing her mother and her sisters. The conversation was almost always general, but I did have a few moments to talk with my wife about her son [Adrien]. While she does admit the wrongs of this wretched child, I seem to notice that he made her believe whatever he wanted her to believe. I shall need much patience and resignation! I hope that Arthur [Bence] will set his sister straight. . . .

16 November 1840

. . . My daughter Emilie, who talks more than her sister Antoinette, said clearly that she hates this country. I am sorry that my affairs do not permit me to maintain these ladies in France. Given these feelings, no doubt shared by my wife and Antoinette, I can see that I have cruel moments ahead of me.

17 November 1840

We spent our day en famille [still at Calixte's home]. At dinner an extremely disagreeable thing happened. I asked for some water to wash my hands; when a washbowl was brought to me, I plunged my hand into it but very quickly pulled it out again, because it was full of shit! Georges took this with his usual calm. His negroes relieve themselves into the canal below the house, and this mess comes into a bathtub that receives water from some spigots especially adapted to this use. I got mad; Georges tried to make excuses for his negroes, and I said nothing more.[15] This apathy of my son-in-law upsets me terribly.

> [Dessalles returns to his plantation while "the ladies" stop to see various acquaintances en route and do not arrive at the Nouvelle Cité until the 29th. Their belongings—piano, harp, etc.—arrive ahead of them. Meanwhile, Dessalles has a new problem to contend with.]

27 November 1840

. . . I received a complaint from M. Etienne Ballain, which prompted me to have four of my negroes punished. A pig that I killed because it was devastat-

15. Characteristically, the slaves are blamed for a situation caused by the planter's failure to install proper sanitary facilities.

ing my cane turned out to belong to one of M. Ballain's negroes. This negro was upset and spoke fighting words. The two work gangs exchanged insults and would have come to blows if they had not been separated. Such disputes between gangs are always dangerous and lead to disorders. The only way to stop them is to chastise the negroes of both gangs. I have had mine punished, and I believe that M. Etienne, as he promised, will not fail to whip his.

I asked M. Pascal for the big bathtub of l'Union for the ladies, and he sent it right away.

28 November 1840

My negroes had all Saturday off. At noon I dispatched ten negroes, two horses, and a mule to Lamentin [to fetch the ladies]. This evening my negroes informed me that M. Clovis [Ballain] did not have his negroes beaten and that he said he was not enough of a bloody fool to do that. How very like him. . . . Tomorrow I will send M. Jules [Michaud, his manager] to demand justice.

29 November 1840

. . . I was brought the message that my negroes and those of M. Clovis [Ballain] were fighting. I quickly sent over M. Jules, who separated them by hitting them with his big whip [*rigoise*]. He then went to M. Etienne Ballain and told him that this disorder was caused by his weakness. Maximin was at [the Ballains'] prayer assembly, and he witnessed the whipping M. Clovis had administered to his negroes. My gang expressed its joy at hearing of the punishment administered to the negroes of Fourniols. I believe that this will put an end to the matter.

[On 2 December, the Dessalles' daughter Calixte gives birth to a little girl at the Nouvelle Cité. A local midwife directs the delivery. Madame Dessalles is useless, wandering about aimlessly and wringing her hands.]

18 December 1840

. . . The priest of the district came for dinner and administered a private baptism to Calixte's little girl. I was as polite as I could be with him, but I must say that I do not like to have him at my house. He is full of ambition. He again mentioned his hope of becoming the curé of Mouillage. Lalanne, who also dined with us, brought me letters from France and one from Pécoul. The latter tells of events about to happen. It appears that the abolitionists are pushing very hard for emancipation and that the government lacks the strength to resist. 1842 is mentioned as the date for this new legislation. If this is so, 1842 will see the ruin of the colonies. . . . Louis-Philippe wants peace at any price,[16] while the people want war. France will soon see a revolution that will be more bloody than the first one. Then what will become of us? This is very difficult to predict.

22 December 1840

. . . I had a long conversation with my wife about the New Year's gifts we must give. I had noticed from the time of her arrival that my young negro [Nicaise] offends her. She now spoke about it and said that she does not want me to keep him on the plantation. I pointed out that I cannot abandon him, but she claims that he is harmful to the interests of the plantation, that he treats the other negroes as if he were the master, and that, of course, everyone is jealous of him. This is pure speculation and indeed perhaps the result of gossip that was brought to her. I will resist as long as I can, for I have only praise for poor Nicaise and I do not want him to fall into misery. We also talked about my brother. She is supposed to write to him to tell him the whole truth of what is happening on the plantation, and she does not think she will be able to reassure him. I am resigned to everything, but I will not be pushed around. I will always fight what is unfair and unreasonable. I am convinced that Adrien told a thousand tales to his mother, who still has for this wretched boy a tenderness that I am far from sharing. I cannot forget his bad conduct toward me.

31 December 1840

. . . Tomorrow we will begin a new year. I shall give to each negro three meters of linen cloth; this is not much, but it is a lot in my straitened circumstances. My wife received a letter from her sister: my children in France are very well.[17] Sugar has fallen from 34 to 27 francs. This decline is upsetting my calculations and will retard my liberation.[18] God's will be done!

16. Dessalles refers here to the Near Eastern crisis between Britain and France in 1840. The French government did back down amidst the protests of the chauvinists.

17. Louise, married to Louis Cléret, and Henri, studying law at Poitiers [HF and LE].

18. Dessalles's subconscious seems to play a trick on him when he calls "getting out of debt" his "liberation," a term that was used interchangeably with "emancipation."

1841

10 January 1841

This evening, just as we were about to retire to our rooms, the servants came to tell me that there was no more oil in the lamps. I was angry at their negligence and used this opportunity to urge my ladies to pay attention to this matter. Oil, candles, and soap are used up with terrifying speed. I will never be able to pay my debts if we don't economize on everything. My daughters, especially Emilie, appear to be surprised that anyone should speak to them of economy; what I say to them seems to offend them. And yet what I am trying to achieve will profit only my children. What good does it do me to deprive myself of everything? In twelve or fifteen years I will no longer be here. . . . My wife, my children, everyone is asking me for money; when I don't give them any, it seems that I am showing ill will. I am annoyed and very tired of my position.

21 January 1841

Day of mourning and of sorrow for the friends of legitimacy: 48 years ago today, Louis XVI was dragged to the scaffold. France still feels the effects of this abominable crime.

At five in the morning M. Jules came to tell me that the weather was too bad to cut cane. I told him that we had to do it anyway because I need money. . . .

[Family life increasingly grates on Dessalles's nerves. On 1 February the first shipment of dresses—which Dessalles finds "pretty ugly"—arrives for the ladies from Bordeaux. Two days later they buy more dresses from some local dress merchants. "They are very happy to be able to spend money." The presence of Calixte and her children, with their constant whining and crying, further aggravates the situation. Still, on 9 February, he does the proper thing and gives a great dinner party for 33 for the baptism of Calixte's baby daughter. "Many free people of color from the town came to watch us through the windows."]

22 February 1841

Today at dinner my daughter Emilie permitted herself to criticize me for failing to do something for an old negress who took care of all my children and who is still in France with Mme Cléret [the other daughter]. She said a lot of extravagant things about this subject, and my wife agreed with her. I got angry and forcefully expressed my astonishment. They seem to think that I have the riches of Croesus! Surely I am no more cruel than the next man; indeed I believe that so far I have been only too kind. I have no property in France, and I am having an extremely hard time sending over enough money to provide for my children. I gave this negress her freedom; let her come to Martinique and I will see to it that she is cared for on my plantation. But I am not stupid enough to maintain her at huge cost in France.

This negress, a libertine like all women of her class, had lovers in this country; she even has a son, with whom she would do very well. My daughters were not informed of this particular fact. I brought it out in a moment of impatience; after dinner my wife berated me for not sparing my daughters' modesty. How very nice to be given lessons in propriety at my age; I am just delighted! So what did I say? I said that this negress had a son. Is that something to offend anyone's modesty? Why would she be different from all the women of her class? Surely my daughters, since their arrival in this country, have seen that our servants are having babies even though they are not married? To tell the truth, it is enough to wear out the patience of the most even-tempered of men. This put me in a terrible mood, and I went to bed earlier than usual.

26 February 1841

My daughter Antoinette is losing a lot of weight and has constant headaches. This country does not suit her at all. It is too bad that my wife did not receive the letters in which I urged her to stay in France in time; the presence of the ladies here causes me more expenses than if they had stayed there. . . .

[In the first days of the year, Dessalles establishes contact with Thyrus Littée in view of forming a partnership for exploiting the Caféière.]

28 February 1841

. . . I received the contract that Thyrus wants me to sign. I carefully read it and was surprised that it was signed by the son of M. Richard de Launay, who can only represent his father if he has a proper power of attorney. The contract stipulates that a third of the net yield of the sugar and syrup will be delivered to me at the end of each pressing (*roulaison*). Since I am not to incur any cost whatsoever, this article must be stated more clearly. These are the two observations I felt I should submit. If they are amended, I will sign the contract. One cannot be too explicit with these small planters, who always want to pull the blanket over to their side and who twist everything to their advantage.

17 March 1841

. . . I sent my servant Trop to Saint-Pierre, asking her to rent me a place for the ladies. . . .

22 March 1841

. . . While we were at dinner, our servant Trop came back from Saint-Pierre; she found a little house that might suit us, but she was unable to tell us what it would cost. Mme de Valmenier [his daughter Calixte, who has just returned to her own plantation] wrote to the ladies, telling them about her children's illness and saying that she has only one doublon in the house. My wife asked me if I could send her some money.

"Not a penny," I replied. The wisest thing to do would be to stay here at Sainte-Marie and send to my daughters Mme Cléret and Mme de Valmenier the income from the five hogsheads of sugar that I had planned to use for our expenses at Saint-Pierre.

I don't know what she will decide. . . . I am really very annoyed with these constant demands. My children should be the first to help me, yet they are the most demanding.

23 March 1841

My wife is anxious; she would like to go to Saint-Pierre and also send money to her daughters. It seems that it is my fault when there is no money. Accustomed to spending it freely, she does not know how hard it is to come by. . . .

24 March 1841

The ladies have decided to go to Saint-Pierre. They will make do with 300 francs for their expenses. This will permit us to send 500 francs to Louise and as much to Calixte. Our large belongings ["piano, harp, etc."?] will go by boat; the rest we will receive later.

[The stay at Saint-Pierre lasts until 30 April and proves most unsatisfactory for everyone. The small house is not suitable, the heat is excessive, the ladies are "unwell," and Dessalles is bored. Aside from a little shopping, the only outings are to church. After about three weeks, the family finally makes some social calls, but Dessalles is often disgusted with the lack of "class" of Creole society. Here, for instance, he describes Madame Lefaivre, the wife of one of his commission merchants.]

17 April 1841

... I was struck by the luxury of the dwelling and could not help remarking that these commission merchants do not stint on themselves. We, the poor planters, are the ones who pay for the enjoyable life of these gentlemen. Mme Lefaivre was once a beautiful woman, but she is over the hill and her manners are not those of a proper and well-bred woman. She did, however, receive us rather graciously. What is most striking about her is her madras kerchief, which she wears in the most pretentious fashion: little pins with attached chains jingle at every movement she makes. This headgear is really very funny; it reminds one of both a mulatto woman and a Chinaman.

[Genuine emotion and fond memories are expressed in the diary in early May, when Dessalles learns of the sudden death of his old friend Jacques Lalanne. In mid-June he is called upon to help draw up the inventory of Lalanne's estate.]

14 June 1841

At ten o'clock Louis Littée and I arrived at Mme Lalanne's; the notary was already there. . . . At five o'clock the whole operation was finished. The appraisal came to more than 250,000 francs. But the description of his furnishings upset me terribly! What a miserable household! These good people only have six pairs of sheets, six tablecloths, twelve towels, five glasses, six platters, twelve plates. . . . Any poor person would be outfitted better than that! Poor Lalanne is really blameworthy—how could he let everything go to the point of leaving his house in such a state of destitution! His plantings also look very sad; there is almost nothing to make sugar with. And yet Octave [19] complacently struts his pretensions and hopes to make enormous amounts of money; unfortunately, I am quite sure he will not amount to anything. Never have I seen greater apathy; all he cares about are his clothes! His mother is crazy about him and believes him to be a phoenix. . . .

[A week later Octave Lalanne dies of a fever, helped to his grave, in Dessalles's view, by Dr. La Peyre, who "stuffed him with quinine" and failed to administer soothing and cooling potions and rubdowns.]

24 June 1841

... I have fallen into deep sadness since the death of Octave Lalanne. It is a frightening thought that the only physician we have in the district is so inept at

19. Lalanne's son, who had failed miserably as Dessalles's manager some years earlier.

treating fevers. The people of color are so afraid of him that they take advantage of his absence to send for another physician. That is what Chéry Magloire did when his son had a fever; he called M. Blot, and the young man was saved.

20 July 1841

. . . I received M. La Peyre's bill for 1840. Although I did not call him often, it comes to 225 francs. It is not difficult to make a fortune if one flays people! He charges more for his solicitude than for his visits. When will the district be rid of such a creature!

24 July 1841

At the moment I have several negroes seriously ill with tenesmus [a dangerous constriction of the muscle system]. The physicians know so little about these kinds of illness that I am afraid to call them.

30 July 1841

Last night I was awakened with the news that the negress Joséphine had given birth to a boy. I got up and provided everything that was needed. . . . Our negress Idile is in labor since Sunday [this is Friday]. M. La Peyre claims that everything is in good order, but I am afraid it will be necessary to use instruments. That will mean an extra expense.

31 July 1841

Since the negress Idile was not improving, I called M. La Peyre, and she was delivered by forceps. Mother and child are doing well.

1 August 1841

. . . M. Dorval La Peyre came to see the negress whom he delivered. He stayed and talked to me for a long time and told me the most peculiar things. An ambitious man, he is looking to make a fortune by every means and pays more attention to his business and his ships than to his profession. He hates everyone who can compete with him, for he would like to handle all of the district's shipping. He even criticizes the way people administer their plantations. And from the way in which he talked to me about Ferbeaux's plantations, I would not be surprised if he had set his sights on getting Ferbeaux's power of attorney. That would give him absolute power over the Limbé and the Charpentier plantations. . . .

2 August 1841

... Emilie has had a fit of nerves brought on by the boredom of this country. The ladies do not know how to resign themselves to their fate, and my wife is the first to foster their disgust with the colony. How I wish they could leave.

12 August 1841

A gendarme came with an order of the mayor to provide manpower for a public *corvée*. Tomorrow I am to send ten negroes to work on the roadways of town. Many planters pay no attention to such orders and don't ever comply. I informed the gendarmes that I would no longer send anyone if I learned that the mayor had failed to punish delinquents.

[The complaints about Dr. La Peyre continue all summer; in August one of Dessalles's female slaves dies, he assumes under the physician's ministrations. On this occasion the local priest also comes in for criticism.]

29 August 1841

Bad weather, impossible to go down to town. My negress is still in the same state. The priest, whom we have been calling for four days to confess her, sends word that he does not have a horse. I proposed to send my mule, but he claims that his legs would drag on the ground. This is how these gentlemen fulfill their calling. They only work, it must be said, for money, and so nobody trusts them. . . . This evening my wife, seeing that my negress was desperately ill, sent a saddled horse to M. le curé, who replied that it was too late and that he would come tomorrow. This is the kind of priest they send us. . . .

9 September 1841

Weather not as bad as yesterday. Several negroes came to the hospital. Tripoli is still in the most worrisome state [with tenesmus]; his throat is closing up and he is growing weaker. For what physician can we send? We need a second one in the district. . . .

10 September 1841

A dreadful and distressing day. Since Tripoli had gotten worse, we had to send for a physician. A letter was written to M. Fénion, who could not be found. I myself wrote to M. Blot, who replied that he was resting in order to take a physic. I again sent to M. Fénion, who was still not there. Then we had to decide to do something. Since the patient had nausea and intermittent hiccups, we felt that ipecac would do him good, so we administered it to him with all due caution. He vomited green matter, and often. The nausea continues despite the chicken broth and the hot wine I had given to him. I am extremely worried. I wrote to a neighbor who is rather good at treating these illnesses, and I also wrote to M. Duveau, physician at Trinité. What is M. La Peyre going to say? It is exasperating! The district will seize on this circumstance to spin a lot of tales, and soon no dog will take a bone from us. I can see that it is quite dangerous for my ladies to live in this district, for what would we do if they fell ill? All this is very worrisome to me. . . .

Louis Littée sent me a letter he received from the mayor of Robert concerning a subscription in favor of M. Granier de Cassagnac. The planters of Robert, electrified by the writings of this defender of the colonies, have without hesitation subscribed for a sum which—in conjunction with what could be raised from other communities in the colony—would be used to buy him a property in France that would give him a sufficient tax rating to run for elective office and possibly become a member of the Chamber. In these notes,[20] I already expressed my opinion of M. de Cassagnac, who is a mere confidence man, although his fiery pen can usefully serve our interests. It is really quite humiliating to see a man of talent sell his writing. M. de Cassagnac would write equally well against us if he found people who were willing to pay him for it. How horrible to be unable to respect the man who defends our cause. I replied to Louis Littée that he had to decide for himself what he would do and that I would subscribe if everyone else did; I do not want to make myself conspicuous.

[Tripoli dies, and Dessalles finds a new physician for his plantation. We learn that this man, M. Mouleng, works under contract for individual plantations; if he can obtain enough contracts, he will settle at Sainte-Marie and practice from there. Dessalles will do his best to persuade other planters to give him their contracts; this will be the only way to get rid of M. La Peyre.

The mulatto woman Adèle dies.]

12 September 1841

. . . We spent a very sad day; two burials in one day, not something to gladden one's heart. My daughters were sick over it. The negroes, on the other hand, looked happy; a funeral is a party for them, and they have been busy getting their clothes ready since yesterday. Tripoli's body was taken to town with great pomp; no one was missing from the procession. Adèle's body went off alone,

---

20. There is no mention of this person between 1837 and 1841, another indication that there were other volumes of Pierre Dessalles's diary that have been lost [HF and LE].

carried by two negroes whom we had trouble finding. This unfortunate woman had no kin on the plantation; I do not think she was too sorry to leave this life. A bastard daughter of the younger Dupin, she belonged to a large family on the left hand. Before her father died, he had said that she should be given her freedom, but he left so many debts that his creditors made the family sell his bastards in order to get their money. When I bought this mulatto girl, she told me about her position, which made me hesitate to buy her. I only decided to do so because of her entreaty: "As long as I have to live as a slave," she said, "I would rather be owned by you than by anyone else." She was not lazy, but suffering for the last 25 years of an incurable disease of the foot, she spent most of her time at the hospital. May God grant her peace and mercy!

13 September 1841

My hospital matron [*hospitalière*], still suffering from a pain in the womb, asked to be treated by a certain negro whom they call a sorcerer, so I sent for him. The remedies he gave her have already made her feel better. . . .

[Nonetheless, the woman dies a few days later, much to Dessalles's regret: "This negress was most useful to my hospital; she knew about illnesses and took good care of the sick."

There seems to be a crescendo of illnesses on the plantation at this time. The contract with M. Mouleng does not materialize, and soon Dr. La Peyre is back, bleeding the patients, prescribing emetics and quinine.

The deaths continue; Dessalles has lost ten slaves in eight months. "If this goes on any longer, I soon will have no negroes left to work my land" (29 October).]

19 November 1841

This morning a letter from Dr. Mouleng informed me that the piano tuner, M. Letavernier, is at Trinité and that he will come to my house if I send him a horse, which I did instantly. He arrived at four o'clock, just as we were sitting down to dinner. He has not left the piano since.

21 November 1841

The ladies went to mass. After their lunch, I asked the piano tuner what I owed him, and he was shameless enough to ask for a doublon. This made me mad, and I expressed my astonishment in overly strong terms. He had the insolence to say that he did not want anything and that he was happy to have been of service to the ladies. I had to return insult for insult, and I gave the doublon to my wife, telling her that I did not want to see him before he left. For this behavior he would deserve to be chased ignominiously off the plantation.

[Throughout December, Mme Dessalles suffers from intermittent fever, and her daughters are also more or less "unwell." "The ladies do not know how to deal with adversity; they are frightened of everything. They keep me from doing my work and—far from diminishing my financial troubles—they serve only to increase them" (28 November).]

11 December 1841

Yesterday I received news from France: M. Cléret writes to me . . . in favor of Adrien. I really don't know what they want me to do. They ask me to forgive him, even though I have done so long ago. But this is not enough; he wants money. I am giving him 1,200 francs a year; that is all I can do, and I will not give more.

31 December 1841

The day passed quietly. Tomorrow will be painful; I have no New Year's presents for my negroes.

CHAPTER SEVEN

1842–1843

17 January 1842

This morning M. Jules Cardin [the manager] came to treat me to great news; 29 wooden planks have been stolen from my sugar buildings. I am not surprised at all; nobody is watching the place. I blame my workman Saint-Just; he went into my woodshed four and five times a day, and he should have noticed it. He pays court to my wife and all strangers who come here, for he wants to create supporters for himself; he knows that I have caught on to him. This evening I warned my negroes that they would have no more free Saturdays as long as my planks are not returned and as long as I do not know who has stolen them. They listened to me in profound silence. After prayer they formed several groups, and I was told that they are accusing my mulatto Tapté, who has long been in the habit of stealing. I will be severe in this circumstance.

18 January 1842

This morning, as soon as it was light, Nicaise came to tell me that he and several other negroes had run around all night and that they had finally found the thief; it is definitely Tapté. It appears that he sold these planks to a free mulatto by the name of Jean-Baptiste, who had them picked up at night and taken to Mme Dégorce's, where they were used to build a cabin. I immediately informed Louis Littée [the mayor of Sainte-Marie] of these particulars, telling him that in the public interest, I do not feel I should let this matter go by. He came here this evening in person and in my presence took the following deposition from Saint-Just [Saint-Just is speaking]:

"I was told by Césaire that a few days before New Year's he saw one evening in the barrel-making shop four negroes belonging to Mme Dégorce and the free mulatto [le nommé] Jean-Baptiste, also known as Coyau, and that, informed by Pierre that the said Goyau [actually Coyau] had come to meet Tapté, he had no doubt that it was Goyau who had bought these planks from Tapté."

Louis Littée believes that in the interest of the Dégorce and Dessalles plantations, it would be better to settle this matter out of court. If the judiciary became involved, these plantations, which are already short of negroes, might find themselves, perhaps for a long time, deprived of several of their most valuable slaves. I was inclined to take this advice and declared that I would be willing to settle if Mme Dégorce were also so inclined. Littée will therefore sound out Mme Dégorce as to her intentions. After he left, I sent for the negro Césaire, who repeated to me what he had said to Saint-Just; he added that he did not know the names of Mme Dégorce's negroes, but that he would recognize them if he saw them. I also sent for the negro La Disette, who told me just what Nicaise had said and repeatedly assured me that MM. de Survillié's driver had told them he had seen Mme Dégorce's negroes carry these planks. Now we will have to see what turn this affair will take. I am determined to place it into the hands of the judiciary if Mme Dégorce should hesitate to act with severity.

19 January 1842

Since Louis Littée had asked me to give him a letter for Mme Dégorce, I sent it to him early this morning. Nothing has been heard from my mulatto Tapté. This evening I again interrogated La Disette and Nicaise; they now say that the driver of MM. de Survillié had indeed told them he saw some negroes carrying planks, but that he had not said he recognized these negroes as being Mme Dégorce's. One can never get an exact deposition from negroes.

20 January 1842

. . . This morning I had the visit of a gendarme who asked me for some information about Tapté. He told me that yesterday he had carried a letter from the mayor to Mme Dégorce and that Mme Bonneville [Mme Dégorce's daughter] had insisted that he, the gendarme, take cognizance of its contents, even though he had refused to listen when it was read. What is becoming of the mayor's recommendation that this matter be handled quietly and discreetly? But this is the temper of the Creole; he can never keep anything to himself.

At two o'clock Mme Dégorce's cook, accompanied by a young negress, came to ask me for an explanation. He claimed that my negro Césaire had implicated him in the affair of the theft, but I told him that Césaire had not named him at all. He demanded to see Césaire, whom I called in, and who repeated several times that he had not spoken of him. It appears that his masters and some other people criticized him for having communicated with Césaire. He left greatly troubled, and I admit that he looks guilty. His name is Henri.

21 January 1842

[Emotional remembrance of the death of Louis XVI.]

I had the visit of two gendarmes who brought me a letter from the mayor. He sent for my information M. Bonneville's response on behalf of his mother-in-law [Mme Dégorce], and it is just what I expected; according to her, her negroes are not guilty of anything. Truly, these uncultivated Creoles are quite pitiful. I wrote back to Louis Littée that I am holding back my formal complaint and that I would make a final decision about it only after Tapté has been arrested. Consequently, I gave Césaire a warrant to go looking for him.

22 January 1842

I have punished my negroes by taking their free half-day. I made them dig up the recently cleared patch.

25 January 1842

It has been learned that Mme Aimée Ernoult's big longboat was taken by some negroes who wanted to flee to a neighboring colony. It seems that the longboat has sunk; the bodies of two negresses and a child have washed up on the shore at Sainte-Marie. It is not yet known what has happened to the other individuals. My mulatto Tapté may have been among the fugitives.

[The plot concerning the stolen planks thickens when a free man of color, the father of the accused man, produces witnesses who testify that they heard Césaire and Tapté tell Nicaise where they put the stolen goods. Dessalles does not believe for a moment that Nicaise has anything to do with the theft, but he becomes discouraged and considers dropping the investigation.]

26 January 1842

. . . I know the people of color, having studied them for a long time. If this affair went to court and if it were a matter of prosecuting Nicaise, this Boniface would find as many false witnesses as he wants, all of whom would testify as he would wish. Justice is very difficult to practice in a corrupt country like this one. Even whites have been known to commit perjury. The true principles of honor are upheld by very few individuals.

[A few days later the entire family is invited to a baptism at Louis Littée's; Antoinette is the godmother.]

31 January 1842

. . . The meal was most handsome and very good. Mme Littée, an uncultivated Creole, found herself surrounded by free mulatto women who were brazen enough to sit down next to my wife and my daughters. I found out about this only after we had returned home; otherwise, I would have spoken to Louis Littée and made him feel the impropriety of it. I cannot understand why the Creole ladies love to surround themselves with mulatto women.

5 February 1842

I punished my negroes by taking their half-Saturday; as long as Tapté is not brought back to me, I am determined not to let them have it. . . .

11 February 1842

A week ago I ordered irons to be put on the negress Joséphine because she twice hit the negress Cristaline with her hoe and swore to kill her. She is living with the negro Joseph, by whom she has two children. This negro has three women, and there is constant fighting. I shall be forced to use strong punishments if these scenes continue. I released Joséphine, who promised to behave herself.

18 February 1842

. . . M. Silvain Gaillard, the assistant manager, left me today. Touchy like all uncultivated Creoles, this young man took offense at being criticized; when he came to work for me, he promised that he would not see any negresses, but he has forgotten that condition, and the negroes have complained. So I asked M. Jules Cardin to speak to him, and he took offense. There was always a negress in his room; besides, it was said that he had a nasty disease.

28 February 1842

Today I had the visit of a free mulatto by the name of Jean-Baptiste Giles, who has just been released from prison, where his brother Vénérant died under the blows of his nephew Florimont. Jean-Baptiste, though he escaped death, has wounds to show that Florimont did not hold back when he hit someone. Yet this Florimont did not have his prison term increased, which I cannot understand. So now the very large Giles family will never forgive him for this kind of murder. They have already started their campaign of vengeance; the only purpose of Jean-Baptiste's visit was to inform me of a series of thefts committed by my mulatto Saint-Just, an intimate friend of Florimont who also profited from these thefts. He says that they took from me lime, nails, pitch, pilings, and lumber, which they used in the construction of Florimont's cabin at Pain-de-Sucre.[1] If it were not for this hatred that has sprung up between Florimont and the Gileses, I would not have known about any of this. But how am I to deal with Saint-Just? He has long done nothing but rob me and never misses an occasion for doing so. How does one get rid of such a scoundrel? I am in a very difficult situation.

[Dessalles once again develops a painful boil, which is treated, as in 1837, by Louis Littée's cook. The healer prescribes baths and applications of cassaba to clean the wound; he also has chickens peck at it on two occasions. By 1 April the boil finally begins to itch and heal.]

8 March 1842

. . . While we were at table, a planter of this town, M. Thierry Mont-Rose, came to see me to inform me of an unpleasantness he is experiencing. One of his negresses, who was punished, disappeared from his place and went to denounce him to the royal prosecutor. He has been summoned to appear next Saturday. I gave him a letter for M. Pujo [the royal prosecutor] and also made out a certificate [of good character] for him. One can no longer chastise one's slaves, for they know that they are being protected without rhyme or reason by

---

1. Small hamlet belonging to the town of Sainte-Marie, about 4 km from town and 3 km from the sea. Not to be confused with the plantation of the same name that was located not far from there but closer to the coast [HF and LE].

men who have the confidence of the government. This being the case, they no longer respect their masters' authority. If things don't change, it will become dangerous to live on a plantation.

9 March 1842

Louis Littée writes to me to ask in what terms he should recommend M. Thierry Mont-Rose. I replied that by examining himself he would see what he had to do. I only know M. Thierry Mont-Rose from what I have always been told about him, and I have always heard him praised.

4 April 1842

I went on horseback to my sugar buildings and my cane fields. My work gang is getting smaller: once again I lost a young negress of 35 years to stomach trouble. I can't understand why my negroes are so discouraged. After all, I do take very good care of them. This evening I distributed linen cloth to them.

11 April 1842

I went to my sugar buildings, where I found the greatest disorder. M. Jules only worries about the cane and neglects everything else. An old ox, exhausted by work, would have died if I had not given orders to put it into the grassy pasture. I also lost a young mule that was overworked.

15 April 1842

... While I was in my sugar buildings, the negro Valentin showed disrespect to his boss by threatening him three times with his knife; when the gang boss gave him three lashes with his whip, he [Valentin] seized the whip and cut it in two. I had him put into the iron collar, and he was given 29 lashes. Quite uppity, that young one.

19 April 1842

... The negroes are spreading the most terrible rumors about M. Le Grand de Launay: they claim that he killed a young negress with prolonged mistreatment. No doubt this is a calumny. In the last 18 months there have been three such accusations. Although I am his closest neighbor, I would be hard put to give an idea of his character.

30 April 1842

... M. Jules complains about the negroes. If he treated them with severity and if he were fair to everyone, things would go well; unfortunately, he is not consistent. He is sometimes severe and sometimes indulgent, and he gives special favors to the negress with whom he is sleeping as well as to her brother Elie. The other negroes do not come to tell me this, but they make sure that I hear them talking. Right now they claim that Augustine and Elie are always in the sugar buildings when the mill is running and that they are never in the cane fields. Augustine, they say, is doing the work of an old negress.

30 May 1842

The negress Joséphine has disappeared, taking her youngest child with her. I am trying to have her caught; this negress is temperamental and can be quite dangerous when she gets a notion.

31 May 1842

The negro Césaire, whom I sent in pursuit of Joséphine, came back at eleven o'clock with the information that he had been told everywhere that Joséphine had said she was going to seek justice. An hour later the negress Joséphine arrived, brought in by a mulatto woman belonging to Mme Catala, who entreated me not to punish her. She [Joséphine] had declared that she had not gone off to seek justice but to find her mistress [Mme Dessalles] who at this moment was at Le Bochet. I asked her what had prompted her to leave; she replied that when M. Jules had taken away part of her time for lunch, she had become exasperated. I agreed not to do anything to her, but I warned her that, at the first infraction, I would not miss her.

4 June 1842

My mill has once again broken down; I desperately need a new large roller. Meanwhile, we will make do with the one I have so I can process all the ripe cane.

I wrote to my wife and to Mme de Valmenier; I am sending them a letter from Adrien, who wrote to me imploring me to forgive him. His letter is most unseemly, for he accuses me of being too severe. As if his conduct, which is without precedent, could have deserved the slightest indulgence. ... The ladies urge me to answer him; they have no feeling for what I have been through and what I am still going through. I am convinced that they make excuses for Adrien and that they blame me. I am completely isolated within my family.

However, I will write, but I am determined never to live under the same roof with my eldest son.

10 June 1842

Two of my women servants asked permission to go to Fort-Royal for their own affairs; I will use this opportunity to send a letter to the ladies [who are visiting Mme de Valmenier].

My mill is running more and more poorly. We had to stop it at 11 o'clock, for the wall threatened to cave in; I never saw anything like it. Five stacks [*grandes*] of cane were still lying on the ground, so I asked M. Roque to have them ground at Mme de la Salle's. The neighbors sent me their mules; by six o'clock everything was moved to Mme de la Salle's. This is the first time I have seen such a thing on my plantation. All of this has greatly fatigued me and put me in a rotten mood.

11 June 1842

Mme de la Salle's mill has so little water that it took all day to put through the cane, and the boilers will not stop until nine this evening. It is a great setback. . . .

12 June 1842

. . . Dr. La Peyre brought me some letters from France, which I will read only tomorrow because I am afraid of the news they may contain. Dr. La Peyre sent me his bill for 1841; I shuddered when I found out that I owe him almost 1,200 francs! Three hundred francs for one delivery! Surely this is reason to protest a thousand times! How can one hope to get out of debt if one is fleeced like this?

13 June 1842

I sent to Trinité to see if a large roller could be found there; there were indeed several, but they are not suitable. M. Jules went to the Limbé plantation; M. Morestin [the manager there], to oblige me (he says), is willing to sell me a set of rollers that he no longer uses for 500 francs more than it is worth. So I am more at a loss than ever and just don't know what to do. I read the letters from France. Adrien writes me four pages, talking about our relatives in Paris; he does not sound repentant. Mme Cléret depicts her circumstances as extremely straitened; she appeals to me for help. I am truly to be pitied; how will I get out of my difficulties if I do not have my family's help?

14 June 1842

Yesterday M. Morestin told me he would abide by the estimate of two mechanics; this morning I sent him the two he had designated. One estimated [the value of the set of rollers] at 1,300 francs, the other at 1,400. This morning he declared that he would be criticized [by the owners] and that the best he could do was to let it go for 1,800 francs. I have decided to make this sacrifice and am sending for this set of rollers this evening.

15 June 1842

I finally have the set of rollers from Le Limbé here. Jean Bart, my mechanic, is busy fitting it to my mill. . . .

25 June 1842

I punished my negroes by taking their half-Saturday because they stole three bunches of bananas from me. Theft is a violent crime that cannot be allowed to continue on a plantation.

I went to see Le Camus at Saint-Jacques [the state-owned plantation]. I learned from him that the Charpentier plantation has suffered heavy losses. One negro there was caught spreading poison and has been handed over to the royal prosecutor. M. Le Camus also told me that M. de Sanois was in dire trouble because of the unruliness of his negroes, an unruliness that was in part brought on by his own misconduct. Here is what he [Le Camus] told me: M. de Sanois, infatuated with one of his negresses, obtained her favors by giving her money and jewelry; but the negress, who did not like him, supposedly listened to the sweet talk of the negro men on the plantation. In his jealousy, M. de Sanois appears to have inflicted on his negroes punishments that exasperated them. Twelve of these negroes—among them the negress who was the object of his passion—thereupon ran away. It appears that these negroes were hidden by those of the Saint-Jacques plantation, who provided shelter and food for them in a cane field. M. de Sanois, accompanied by five or six gendarmes, came to Saint-Jacques in the middle of the night and awakened Le Camus, who summoned the most culpable negress. This woman admitted everything and even named the town's free men of color who were planning to facilitate their escape. One of these free coloreds escaped through the indiscretion of Louis Littée, namely, the son of Mme Sainte-Rose, a woman of color who is an intimate friend of Mme Louis Littée. Warned by Mme Littée, she helped her son get away. What an infernal country! The whites and the local authorities are often the first to forget their duty.

3 July 1842

I had received a dinner invitation from Hosten, but just as I was about to leave, M. Jules told me that he had lent his horse to Nicaise. I was so indignant that I sent someone to fetch this horse and to tell Nicaise that I forbade him to go to Gros-Morne, which has its municipal fête today.[2] He took my order with calm and resignation and came to apologize. I reproached him for consorting with too many free men of color and urged him to pay more attention to his work. His submissiveness disarmed me. Since Saturnin was not well, Nicaise followed me to Hosten's, where I arrived at noon.[3]

5 July 1842

A grand marriage today at Marigot: Mlle Crassous is marrying M. Victor Hervé. This young lady was educated in France; she is ugly and rather unpleasant. Her family is from this area and has played an unfortunate role in our revolutions. A M. Crassous de Médeuil has left unfortunate memories. M. Hervé's family are good people; his oldest brother, who has established himself at Saint-Pierre, has acquired somewhat of a fortune and a good reputation, which I believe he deserves. His conduct toward the Lalanne family has won him my respect. I only wish these people were not so self-satisfied.

In our town there is also a marriage of people of color today: the bastard daughter of Louisie Burot is marrying the son of Chéry Magloire. I hear everyone has prepared finery that will be curious to see; the people of color exaggerate everything, and so the ladies will be covered in silk and the men resplendent in their suits. The fanciest mulattoes of the district will be at the wedding. These Magloires used to be good people; but ever since political rights were bestowed on the people of color, they have become pretentious, and the one who is getting married is particularly distasteful in his stuck-up manner and his self-importance. I believe he hates all whites. My young mulattoes want to see the wedding, and I allowed them to go to town.[4]

[Ceaselessly moving about between Saint-Pierre, Fort-de-France, Sainte-Marie, and the plantation, Madame Dessalles and her daughters are now at Mme de Valmenier's, where Dessalles regularly sends provisions in a vain effort to keep down expenses. In their absence he tries to relax and enjoy a few pleasures.]

2. Remember that Nicaise is no longer a slave.
3. Nicaise presumably rode a mule or walked.
4. Does this mean that Dessalles's black slaves did not want to see the wedding? If so, this may imply a certain cultural separation between black and mulatto slaves.

12 July 1842

. . . I continue my cold baths [in the river]. Aside from the good this does me, it is a distraction. I have food brought to the water's edge, I watch my little domestics[5] bathe, and I have the pleasure of seeing them dig into their food with great relish.

[As soon as the ladies return to the plantation, trouble resumes.]

2 August 1842

My wife is in a rather unpleasant mood. She spoke to me about Antoinette and wants me to make sacrifices to attract a husband for her. I told her that as long as my debts are not paid, I am determined not to make any sacrifice. She tried to convince me that with such an attitude, I was not fulfilling my duties as a father. . . . Everyone pesters me with demands, and no one seems to care about my situation.

4 August 1842

. . . Apropos of marriage, I told Saint-Léger in confidence that I would like to establish Antoinette and that I would be pleased if M. Duquesne of La Case Pilote were to think of her. This M. Duquesne is a close friend of Caderousse, the present manager of Mme Ferdinand Le Vassor, and so he will probably come to the district. I asked Saint-Léger to speak to M. Caderousse about it. It is in these ways that marriages are often made. This young man enjoys a good reputation; he has a plantation on which he owes money, but with organization and economy he can succeed. . . .

6 August 1842

Mme Saint-Léger is in the district. The ladies are distressed at the idea that she will call on them; she may be the daughter of a blacksmith, but she is still a respectable woman. There is no way to avoid her visit, unless we want a falling out with her husband. We don't need an extra enemy; we have enough as it is.

24 August 1842

I went to have lunch with Saint-Léger and was kept there by a horrendous rain that continued all day. At Saint-Léger's I heard that a servant girl of Mme

5. Nicaise and Saturnin [HF and LE].

Lalanne had had a miscarriage on the floor of Mlle Idile's room; the latter did not notice anything. But when she got out of bed in the morning, she stepped into this horrible stuff. Thinking that dogs or cats had dragged this mess into her room, she called for somebody to take care of this and had everything tossed out of the window. The young servant kept quiet and did her work as usual. Five days later she felt unwell; when the doctor was called, he judged that she must have had a miscarriage. She admitted everything. What an abomination! The things a young lady is exposed to in this country! Yet—would one believe it!—Mme Lalanne will probably keep such a creature in her house.

28 August 1842

Saint-Léger and his wife came to dine with me [the ladies are again absent]; the wife has a good appetite.

5 September 1842

The mason Putiphar has been insulted by one of my negresses; I had ten lashes given to her for the sake of appearances. If their dispute had taken place outside of work, I would not have punished my negress, but the workman was quietly doing his job. It seems that he sought this negress's favor and that he bragged about having enjoyed her. Her pride was hurt, and she vented her anger.

26 September 1842

. . . My mechanic Faustin [a free man of color] was summoned by the mayor in response to a complaint brought against him by a free negro named Guiambon. Guiambon denounced Faustin for having inflicted very harsh treatment on one of his negresses. The mayor should not have accepted this denunciation, or he should have called in the negress herself. These kinds of informers are dangerous; nobody is safe from their calumnies. I know that free men of color are usually very hard on their slaves, but Faustin offends the men of his class by the mere fact that he is prosperous. Although he plays the devout, this Faustin has many bad traits: he is a liar, a drunkard, and unscrupulous in his business dealings. Other than that, he is not a bad fellow.

27 September 1842

[Last night] I had just gone to bed when Faustin appeared in my courtyard. He told me that Guiambon had come to his house, threatened him, wanted to beat up his wife, and made his negress run away. So he [Faustin] went to lodge a complaint with the mayor; this morning he told me the mayor had sent for Guiambon to appear in his presence at eight o'clock.

Faustin returned in triumph from the mayor's; Guiambon admitted that he had been wrong and apologized. . . .

2 December 1842

I am having terrible trouble with the mason Faustin; I had sent four hogsheads of sugar to Saint-Pierre and was to pay this Faustin with the proceeds. We had agreed that he would collect this sum and return a fourth of it to me. He did go to collect the money but kept all of it, claiming that the sugar had not yielded what he expected. The hogsheads of sugar produced 55 francs less than we expected, so it was 41 francs less for Faustin. I have never seen anything like this piece of swindle! The man had the gall to come and see me, and I talked to him as he deserves. This evening Louis Littée [the mayor] came to see me, and I lodged my complaint; he has summoned Faustin before him. We shall see how he will get out of this one. I had counted on this sum for my trip to Fort-Royal; if I fail to get it, I am in dire difficulty. This evening I heard from the ladies; they await me with the greatest impatience.

3 December 1842

Louis Littée writes to me that he has looked into Faustin's case and ordered him to bring me 100 francs. Always these half-measures! Poor Louis can't ever do things right. Faustin came to my door to see me; I was about to go to bed and refused to see him, declaring that I do not want to have anything to do with a swindler.

10 December 1842

After lunch I left for the Case-Pilote plantation. On my way I stopped to see M. Guignaud, whom I found in his sugar buildings. This M. Guignaud is the son of the M. Guignaud[6] who played such an honorable role in our civil wars. Brought up in France, the son has acquired unusual expertise since he came here. Unfortunately he loves experiments. Being a chemist, he undertook — first at Spoutourne on the Saint-Prix plantation and then on his own place — improvements that have ruined all those who have tried to implement them.

---

6. Guignaud or Guignot. See Pierre Régis Dessalles, *Historique des troubles survenus à la Martinique pendant la Révolution* (Courbevoie: private printing, 1982), 32–38 [HF and LE].

Tilting, filters, side pieces, etc., all have made for better looking sugar, but the expenses have not been recouped by better prices. I have not made any changes in my old method; I am waiting. I will make changes only after experience has proven that they offer substantial benefits.

[Case-Pilote was the property of M. de Percin, known as Fanfan Percin and "the oldest son of M. Percin known as Percin Canon for his bravery; at the time of our unfortunate civil wars, he performed in this country acts of bravery worthy of the greatest captains."]

... I had a long talk with M. de Percin about the unhappy position of our colonies, and he told me a few rather curious anecdotes. A fierce royalist like all his family, he makes no bones about his opinions; a colonial above all, he is fighting a war to the death against the liberals and repulses to the best of his ability all that can be harmful to his country. When the ordinance of 5 January [providing for government inspection of plantations] was implemented, he received the royal prosecutor who had come for the inspection very harshly; he also stood up to Governor de Moges to whom he spoke with all the vigor produced by a clear conscience and great independence. M. de Moges, seeing that he would be unable to convert M. de Percin, admitted to him that we were still in '93 and that the Revolution was not over. This admission would seem to indicate that M. de Moges is a legitimist, which I would not have believed. . . .

M. Northumb, M. de Percin's brother, is the father of a large family; he owns the Garnier plantation, whose granddaughter he married [sic]. He enjoys general esteem, which he deserves by the loyalty of his character and his devotion to his country. Although I do not know all the members of the Percin family very well, I have the greatest affection and esteem for them. Birds of a feather flock together, they say; it is certain that I am never happier than when I find myself with frank and loyal men who uphold the principle of legitimacy.

We dined rather late and had an excellent meal over which M. and Mme de Percin presided with that casualness and bonhomie which are a thousand times preferable to the stiff formality prescribed by fashion and custom. M. de Percin's family is charming. His eldest son, a notary at Gros-Morne, will walk in the footsteps of his father, whose opinions he shares. M. Lacoste Montrose was also at M. de Percin's. I had not met him before; he is M. de Percin's brother-in-law, in other words, an honorable and good man; his family is of Fort-Royal.

Also present at M. de Percin's was a man by the name of Duluc [a free man of color], formerly a tailor who used to make suits for me and who, having made a fortune, wanted to become a planter. He bought the Cools plantation adjacent to M. de Percin's. This Duluc is not a bad man, far from it. He has been cheated and duped by ruthless schemers, and his fortune, which was once considerable, is much reduced. We drank to the health of Henri V; may he soon return to the throne of his ancestors!

I returned to town in the most beautiful moonlight. It was ten o'clock when I arrived home [he is visiting his family at Mme de Valmenier's]. The ladies had not yet gone to bed, so I was able to tell them about the fine day I had spent and about the contentment I felt in my heart.

25 December 1842 [Christmas Day]

A great day for the entire Christian world! To my distress I was unable to go to mass, for I was afraid of the roads. M. Alexandre Thébault is with me since yesterday; he came again to find out if I now wanted to sell my plantation. He offered me 500,000 francs for the lower section (Nouvelle Cité exclusive of the Caféière) with 100 carrés [312 acres] of land and an equal amount of woods.[7] My last word was that I would sell, but not for less than 550,000 francs.

[The end of the year finds Dessalles once again at Mme de Valmenier's, where his wife and daughters have been staying for months. Almost everyone is suffering from fevers and various malaises.]

1843

[In December, Mme de Valmenier's doctor had recommended a cure at the thermal station of Absalon to take the waters of the warm springs which, flowing at a temperature of 30 degrees centigrade, contain bicarbonate and iron. Located some 10 kilometers north of Fort-Royal, the thermal station is dominated by a series of *pitons*, or volcanic mountains: the Piton Daumaze, the Piton de l'Alma, and especially the Pitons of Le Carbet, which dominate the landscape of Fort-de-France. This thermal station can still be seen today (HF and LE). Dessalles leaves La Rivière Monsieur on 4 January to prepare lodgings for his three daughters. Mme Dessalles does not come.]

4 January 1843

... On my way I stopped to see Cools, whom I found in a tattered dressing gown. He told me about Mars Faure, who is today relegated to a small country place that he rents from M. Duclesmeur. The wretched fellow is always drunk; he eats and drinks with mulattoes and negroes. The last of his family, he has

7. The size of the Dessalles plantation, 200 carrés (624 acres), half of the land in woods, is about average for plantations in this area of Martinique.

devoured an immense fortune and dragged a once honorable name through the mud. . . . When I arrived at the Pitons, I set all my people to work. I made them clean three rooms, took a bath, had dinner, and went to bed early.

[Dessalles and his daughters take the waters for two months, enduring a great deal of boredom and the company of various "insignificant" Creoles. Their health does improve somewhat. On 31 January a letter from M. Lefaivre, his commission merchant, disturbs the routine.]

31 January 1843

M. Lefaivre informs me that rumors to the effect that I am selling my plantation are being circulated. He urges me to tell him if this is true and proposes to find me a very solid buyer who will give me a better price than the one I am offered. I immediately replied that I did not want to sell, but that exceptionally advantageous offers might prompt me to consider it. I must make up my mind, for old age is upon me and death soon thereafter. If I do not sell, I will never be able to pay my daughters' dowries, considering that I am barely able to pay the income on them. This means that my sons-in-law will never be satisfied. This situation makes for discontent and irritation in my family.

1 February 1843

I spent a stormy night; my business affairs turned around and around in my head, and I did not shut an eye. I wrote to my wife, who probably will not share my opinion.

4 February 1843

My wife, now that there is a possibility of selling, feels we should keep the property. . . . I must return to my plantation for a week to hear the proposals of the new buyers.

7 February 1843

M. Alexandre Thébault had lunch with me. He was sure that the new buyers who had presented themselves are MM. Ludovic Littée and Lagarigue. I told him positively that I would not sell for less than 700,000 francs.[8]

---

8. A few weeks earlier (25 December 1842) his "last word" had been 550,000 francs.

[Nothing more is heard about the sale of the plantation until October of the same year; even then, it does not materialize.]

10 February 1843

... Michel Martinau [one of the assistant managers] asked my permission to have a pen built for keeping his sheep. I curtly turned down his demand, which greatly offended me. Managers and their assistants must exclusively concern themselves with the owners' affairs; that is what they are paid for, and they are no longer suitable if they are distracted by personal interests.

[On 4 March, the family leaves the Pitons; the women stop at Rivière Monsieur, while Dessalles goes straight to his plantation.]

5 March 1843

... En route I stopped by to see MM. Hippolyte Tiberge and Dallard. They told me that M. de Moges [former governor] had hastily left for Saint-Domingue; that country is engulfed in revolution. Boyer [president of Haïti] is dead, Niginac would like to succeed him, the negroes and mulattoes are massacring each other. M. de Moges went to the rescue of the Whites, who are in the towns.

The legislative bill on the sugar question [i.e., sugar cane versus sugar beet] has been vigorously debated in the relevant committees. It is thought that, once the deputies are better informed, they will be calmer when this question reaches the Chambers. M. de Tocqueville sees this matter in the light of national interest and reasons with great sagacity. One of the two industries will have to cede the terrain to the other; that is inevitable. As it happens, the cane offers real and positive advantages, so it is for the beet to yield.

8 March 1843

In my absence I lost a strong young negress to yaws; that makes two in a very short span of time. ...

I sent a messenger to my wife with fifty eggs and six pots of flour. ...

Every evening, a comet appears in the west; it is terrifying by the bright light it casts. The length of its tail is prodigious. The negroes believe that it presages the end of the world, and many Whites attribute the disasters and misfortunes that have befallen the world to it. I myself am afraid that it is the precursor of a dreadful drought.

10 March 1843

Philippe [the cook] brought me letters from my wife. I groaned when I read those from my son Henri. This wretched child will inflict upon me sorrows perhaps even more stinging than those that Adrien has caused me. In speaking of his income, which I reduced to 1,200 francs, he proffered the most unseemly threats; if it were not for my wife, I would let him know how displeased I am. My position is aggravated by the demands of my family. Louis Cléret [his son-in-law] constantly asks for money; his office does not provide a sufficient livelihood. What a foolish marriage my poor Louise has made!

My negroes have again stolen from me, and I will be forced to make them work tomorrow [Saturday]. M. Jules is no help to me; he seems to disapprove of my severity, and this produces a very bad effect. I went to check on my sugar buildings; all the wood above the boilers has rotted. It has barely lasted four years.

12 March 1843

... The astronomers of the United States have announced that there is some disturbance in the march of the heavenly bodies, and my wife believes that our grandchildren will see the end of the world. Everyone reasons according to his or her lights and ideas, and everyone is most certainly mistaken.[9]

13 March 1843

We cut cane this morning. I made arrangements for Ignace to build 12 negro cabins. My negroes are sleeping under the stars and are exposed to the inclemencies of the atmosphere. . . .

18 March 1843

My harvest and sugarmaking [*roulaison*] are finished; I have produced 14 hogsheads of sugar, which is nothing.

[In late March Dessalles suffers another bout of poor health: ringing in the ears, bleeding hemorrhoids, dizziness. A week later, Mme Dessalles and her daughters return to the plantation. This time, they stay only two days before spending the entire Holy Week in town, lodging with Mme de la Salle. On their return, acrimony and tension are worse than ever.]

9. It is rather amusing to read that a few days later Pierre Dessalles was quite worried that he had been one of 13 dinner guests at a friend's table, having read "in manuscripts" that following such reunions of 13, several of the guests have been known to die.

21 April 1843

Yesterday at six in the morning my two daughters and I went on horseback to check on the Caféière. This caused me to reflect sadly on the size of my land and the impossibility of cultivating it because of the lack of negroes.

We worked on the statements sent by MM. Durant. The ladies thought I owed them only 45,000 francs. Indeed, that is all I will owe them when the 42 hogsheads I earmarked for them are sold; however, they first have to be sold. My daughters complained about their situation; they constantly hurt my feelings and do not even notice how unseemly their words are. My wife has accustomed her children to argue about what they should have and to challenge their parents' actions. I would like to see Arthur [Bence, his brother-in-law] and my wife challenge their father's actions to his face; I believe they would be roundly rebuffed! But I must take everything without a murmur. I find the evenings long and wearisome. I get up at four in the morning, and the ladies cannot understand why I want to go to bed early. It is not really hard to understand, is it?

25 April 1843

Adrien writes to his mother that Mme Le Vassor, through her connections, can arrange a rich marriage for him, but I doubt it. I don't care about a good alliance, as long as he marries a rich girl. This unfortunate young man allows himself to be led on by everybody! My wife wanted me to ask Mme Le Vassor to lend me 40,000 francs; I did it with horrible repugnance, firmly convinced that I will be refused. My relatives have treated me shabbily before, and I know exactly what my dear cousin will say.

The ladies are complaining that they do not see anybody and yet do nothing to be friendly to strangers. My wife complains that the air of Sainte-Marie does not agree with her.

[The series of complaints by the ladies seems endless.]

4 May 1843

M. Lefaivre has trouble selling my sugar, and the difference between his weights and mine is horrifying. . . . The cane does not yield much, and I don't know if I will obtain the 45 hogsheads for which M. Jules is hoping. Lucky if I make 36! This young man [M. Jules] just goes along where the Good Lord takes him, and I will have been led astray by his faulty calculations.

9 May 1843

My cane yields so little that we must start cutting in another section. I will not have enough to satisfy my creditors. It breaks my heart.

13 May 1843

The English packet boat[10] that stopped at Saint-Pierre brought the news that the Chamber had put off debate on the sugar legislation until 26 April. Our uncertainty thus continues, and we still have to fear that we will not obtain anything.

17 May 1843

. . . We received letters from my son Henri, who tells us about the opposition the sugar legislation has encountered. Indeed, M. de Broglie[11] has once again called for emancipation, but it seems that this measure is not to be adopted until 1853. This would mean that our existence will be prolonged for another ten years, for once the negroes are freed, it will be impossible to maintain this country. God have mercy upon us!

14 June 1843

My wife had news from Adrien, who informs her that he is about to leave for the island of Cuba. He has obtained a post as head manager with power of attorney on a plantation and will earn 4,400 francs per year. May he succeed![12]

22 June 1843

M. Michaud left yesterday for Saint-Pierre; the ladies gave him 200 francs to bring them two dresses they would like to have for the fête of Gros-Morne, to which they may not even go. The weather is rainy and the heat is excessive. My wife has taken a dislike to Saturnin;[13] she harassed me with ridiculous argu-

10. This was almost certainly one of the first steamships, which delivered the mails more quickly and reliably than sailing vessels. Nonetheless, sailing vessels also remained in use for a long time thereafter [HF and LE].

11. Duc de Broglie, deputy in the Chamber and a leader of the French Abolitionist Society.

12. He did not; by the end of the year he was ready to leave Cuba.

13. Dessalles was as fond of this house slave as he was of Nicaise. As in the case of Nicaise, he never explicitly stated why Saturnin was such a favorite, except that he was "very docile." But unlike Nicaise (*"mon petit nègre"*), the French editors seem to believe that Saturnin (*"ce jeune mulâtre"*) was Dessalles's son by the "very docile" and "promiscuous" (4 July 1823) house slave

ments because I had given him the morning off to work in his own cane. This is to give him a special favor, she says, which is bound to make him proud and spoiled. This young mulatto is very docile, yet she claims that he has an air of independence. If she continues to bother me about it, I will set him up in a craft, and he will no longer appear in the house.[14]. . .

15 July 1843 [Saturday]

I took the negroes' morning, giving them in exchange a pound and a half of codfish. My cane fields are so messy that I saw myself forced to put off the cutting. Before we can make sugar, we must clean up. One of my negresses, Marie-Angèle, is so sick that I asked the abbé to come and hear her confession. He came but did not stay with her long. . . . The curé attributes all of the district's misfortunes to M. La Peyre. I certainly share his opinion; such a creature is a true scourge of society. . . .

1 August 1843

We started up the mill at two o'clock; the slowness with which everything is run is frightful. In the three years M. Jules has been with me, he has not done anything right; my vinegar plant is gone, my carts are in the most pitiful condition, my negroes perish and diminish in numbers, the mules and oxen are painful to behold. In short, everything looks perfectly dismal. My books are in disarray. Things cannot continue in this way; if I did not owe him money, I would fire him right now.

The negro Célicour is very ill today; I doubt that he will see tomorrow.

Trop. In a letter of 17 November 1823, Dessalles writes with studied casualness to his mother: "Trop has not yet been delivered . . . it is something she brought back from the Morne Moco. The opinions are divided; most think that the child is that of an old *béqué*. Chignac, who must be better informed of what goes on in the negro cabins, assures me it is that of a mulatto whom he often sees at Fortunée's. Frankly, I don't care one way or the other." A few days later he reports the birth of a boy and says that the father is a mulatto by the name of Favo.

The fact that Saturnin received special treatment is naively laid out in the entry of 1 April 1843, from which it appears that Dessalles gave Saturnin large quantities of new and used clothing, including one pair of German silk trousers, for a total of 10 shirts and 12 trousers. Nicaise received approximately the same quantity of clothes. "The other house slaves received two blue-striped trousers each." See letter of 4 July 1823.

14. Setting up a young mulatto in a craft was indeed a way for a white father to provide for an illegitimate son.

2 August 1843

Upon awakening, I learned of the death of the negro Célicour. Another one gone! These losses of negroes are frightful.

7 August 1843

Marie-Angèle and Phanor have gotten worse; the former again began to vomit, and the latter is becoming weaker every day. The negress Augustine, who was bitten by a small snake last Friday, only came to the hospital yesterday [Sunday]. The negro Jean-Philippe whom we consulted first said it was nothing; then, when the swelling appeared, he examined her more closely and recognized the problem. The belated application of a dressing has aggravated the condition of the patient, who developed a flux of the chest. At that point I sent for Joseph Coco [another healer?], who said he was ill and could not come. I called M. La Peyre, who bled the patient, and I then sent for Marcellin, Joseph Coco's son, who came immediately and administered his remedies. All this produced a good effect, and the patient is out of danger—at least I hope so. . . .

8 August 1843

I lost the negro Phanor to yaws. These continual deaths are very hard to take, and I don't know why they are happening. After all, the negroes are as well off here as any place else. I am often tempted to think that it is poison, but then I reject this idea.

11 August 1843

I asked M. Lefaivre to reserve shipping space to Marseille for 25 hogsheads of sugar. The net revenue of this shipment is to be paid to M. Charles Dessalles. An old negress whom I have freed, the woman who took care of me when I was a child, by the name of Praxcède, arrived on the plantation last night. In 1823 I married her to my mother's cook, a free man of color [nommé] Honoré; they went to Spanish Trinidad to seek their fortune, but found nothing but misery there.

13 August 1843

Yesterday M. Michaud sent my negro Elie to me to let me know that the manager of the Perrinelle plantation has been assassinated by the negroes. Louis Littée, in our conversation about the district, told me the most dreadful things about certain individuals. When will I be able to get away from such an unsociable place? I have six children, and not one of them can help me. My situation is most unfortunate and makes me suffer cruelly.

20 August 1843

I am alone on the plantation. It rained last night. Saturnin, to whom I had given permission to go to mass under the condition that he be back by half-past ten, did not return until half-past seven in the evening. I gave him the whip myself; I flew into a rage, which was very bad for me. This young mulatto is incorrigible; he gives in to all his passions. I truly fear that he will come to no good. And yet he is very gentle and not at all insolent. He wept a lot.

28 August 1843

I had long promised Pierre Cardin's bastard children to give them a dance. Yesterday morning I sent them some refreshments and in the evening a fiddler. Then I went to dine with Pierre Cardin in order to see a mulatto ball close up. The ball came off quite well. These mulattoes are poor copiers of white people. The colored girls were charming, but they acted like loose women. Their manners were casual, they are familiar and bold, and even those who still have their dignity are true courtesans. I felt so out of place in this company that I was glad to leave.

3 September 1843

Pierre Cardin dined with me; all his bastards came to walk around at the Nouvelle Cité. I had a collation served to them, and they danced to the fiddle until ten at night; they even slept here and will leave in the morning. You can't be polite to these free coloreds without being taken advantage of.

I had a visit from M. Quemin, who brought me a letter from Saturnin asking for five francs for having captured his horse. M. Quemin complains that the style is too familiar. I read the letter, which is really stupid. Because this young mulatto can write a little, he abuses his skill and writes all the time. This obsession may cause him a lot of trouble; I will scold him about it in private.

4 September 1843

I am finally rid, thank God, of all that miserable scum. After a copious lunch, they all went home. Poor Pierre Cardin must often be embarrassed. What a shameful family!

17 September 1843

. . . At Fort-Royal, I learned that Admiral de Moges, commander of the naval station and ex-governor of Martinique, had gone to M. Vatable's place and asked the manager for permission to examine the negroes, their cabins, and everything concerning their life. The manager refused to comply on the grounds that his proprietor would reprimand him. I understand that, despite this refusal, M. de Moges insisted and went ahead. I also hear that he asked the negroes if they were happy and if they were treated well. Satisfied with their answers, he again questioned them about their work. "Are you working well?" he asked. "Yes, Monsieur," the negroes replied. "That is very good, my friends. If you continue to work well, your master will be content, you will be happy, and you will be prepared for the benefits of emancipation, which will come to you soon."

I can hardly believe that M. de Moges would have permitted himself such a breach of all the proprieties. Yet that is what is asserted, and all the colonists are indignant. I suspend judgment and prefer to think that these stories are exaggerated.

29 September 1843

This morning they brought me nine dead guinea hens and two sick ones. I had them opened, and they were found sound. There was no sign of snake bites. It is really discouraging. If they had been poisoned, there would be some trace of it. If they were killed out of spite, those who did it were careful not to let it appear, for I tried in vain to find any blows or injuries. It all made me sad.

30 September 1843 (Saturday)

I made my negroes work until lunchtime to punish them for the death of my guinea hens; it appears that it was they who killed them out of spite. Two are missing; they have not yet been found.

2 October 1843

We have resumed the work of the plantation. We are hoeing young cane that should have manure. This evening a free man of color, a mason, complained to me about a mule driver who supposedly insulted him. I would have had my negro whipped, but when I learned that the free man had struck him, I only ordered that he be put on the bar for the night. The free man was not pleased by this decision, but I told him off as he deserved, and I exempted my negro from all punishment. The workman, whose name is Yoyo Blampuy, came to apologize before I went to bed. He said he was drunk, and so I forgave him; he will continue his work tomorrow. . . .

3 October 1843

This has been a most difficult day for me; things went wrong from the moment I woke up until I went to bed. Mlle Perrinotte [a woman of color] came to ask for the hogsheads of sugar I had promised her for September. I lost my composure and vomited a thousand insults on her; I was later sorry that I forgot myself, but I simply could not control my anger.

I sent my wife [who is visiting at La Rivière Monsieur] a messenger with 12 chickens and 50 oranges.

[On the next day, he sends "100 oranges, some avocados, jam, a brick of soap," and so on.]

19 October 1843

Monrosier came to dinner. While he was with me, two of the town's mulattoes, Sully Jean-Bart and Ernest, came to see me. They brought along a negro whom I bought for 864 francs payable in four months with a 5 percent interest charge. Sully Jean-Bart sold him to me, but he had brought along Ernest, the scholar of that class, to draw up the contract of sale. The negro is Caplaon; he is young and handsome, and he consented to serve me.[15] He used to have the unfortunate habit of running away, but since he has relatives on the plantation I think he will break himself of this failing.

22 October 1843

At seven o'clock we started up the mill; by nine everything had broken down. Impossible to go on. What will become of the 24 stacks [*grandes*] of cut cane?

23 October 1843

The mill will not be finished until this evening; the mechanic hopes it will work. . . .

15. Cf. entry of 7 September 1837.

24 October 1843

. . . Since my mill still did not work properly, I sent for Jean-Bart, whom I upbraided in lively terms. He accused M. Jules Cardin, who [he said] never gives him the kind of wood he asks for. I confronted these two and witnessed the most unseemly scene in which swear words and insults were exchanged. Jean-Bart has been extremely negligent in his work, and M. Jules himself has not properly supervised Jean-Bart. And I am the turkey that is stuffed with this farce. I will have to stop the mill so everything can be repaired. A great loss of time!

25 November 1843

At noon MM. Thimoléon du Fougeray and Pierre Cardin arrived. The latter had barely greeted us before he told me that his son-in-law was charged with asking for Antoinette's hand for Léopold Camouilly. Knowing my wife's ridiculous ideas, I was distressed by this démarche. Thimoléon joined me under the trees and acquitted himself of his mission. I replied that there had been public talk about this marriage and that I thought my wife would second my efforts to persuade my daughter to accept such an honorable proposal, which was bound to ensure her happiness. He gave me some details about this young man's fortune. We dined at three o'clock, and these gentlemen left at five. Only then was I able to inform my wife of Léopold's suit; I found her most displeased and had no trouble guessing that Antoinette would share her mother's opinion. I said all I could in favor of this young man, who does have the finest qualities and is destined to have a fortune of 500,000 francs. My daughter, called upon to give her opinion, declared that she would never consent to this marriage. Since she has her mother's support, I felt that I would not obtain anything and said no more. But this refusal pains me enormously. In the three years that the ladies have been in this country, no one of our own class has presented himself. This young man is the only one who appreciates my daughter and wants to marry her. To be sure, his birth is not as good as mine, but in today's circumstances, should one be so particular? And is his father's misconduct a reason to hold it against him, who combines in his person so many estimable qualities? I confess that I had not felt such stinging pain for a long time. If I were to act on my first impulse, I would abandon my whole family and go far away to find rest and affection. I wrote to M. Thimoléon telling him that my daughter is resolved not to marry in this country. . . .

27 November 1843

M. Chignac informs me that Trop and Saint-Just have asked him to rent them his house in town so they can receive their brother Saint-Fort, who will soon arrive in the district with his wife and children. I am stunned; this is certainly to snap their fingers at me. When I gave this young mulatto his freedom,[16] it was under the express condition that he would never again set foot in Sainte-Marie. . . . But no! He is coming and means to deal with my family on a footing of equality. This country is no longer tenable!

8 December 1843

. . . My wife spoke to me about my weakness for my domestics. She finds that I spoil them. I really do not know what she means. I am good to my domestics because I need their care and because I can sense how difficult it is to serve an aging man. If I did not compensate them a bit for the constant trouble I am giving them, they would become disgusted and take a dislike to me. It is hard to owe other people's care to fear; I try to owe it to their zeal and affection. They are being blamed for being too well dressed and for being familiar; that is their crime. My domestics are not insolent at all; I would not allow it. I suppose they should go around in rags and live in perpetual constraint. Truly I think these ladies' ideas are quite unreasonable.

9 December 1843

I lost my negress Brigitte, who was barely 38 years old. She was ill and had not done any work for a long time. Her mother asked me to have a funeral for her, but I refused because she had not been a good subject. It is a favor I accord only to those who behave well; the others I just send off to the cemetery without any religious ceremony. Her [Brigitte's] mother asked my permission to pay for the funeral herself. I consented and even lent her the money she will need for the ceremony. I will probably never see this money again, but my initial refusal will have produced a good effect on the other negroes.

12 December 1843

Big events today. The negress Jeanne has given birth to a pair of twins, who are so weak that one could safely bet they will die. M. Peu Duvallon of Marigot

16. For Saint-Fort, see letters No. 21 (15 July 1822), No. 53 (6 December 1824), and No. 62 (26 May 1825); also chapter 3, note 16.

writes to inform me that six of his negroes had apprehended in the big woods my mulatto Tapté, who has been missing [*marron*] for two years. Not having a dark cell [*cachot*] on his place, he sent him to the police commissioner at Marigot. He claims [the reward of] five francs for each of his negroes. I sent M. Michaud with a negro to fetch this scoundrel. What am I going to do with such a villain? Accustomed to stealing, he will no doubt resume his roguish tricks. . . .

13 December 1843

M. Michaud returned very late last night. My mulatto is in bad shape, with his face and feet all swollen. The life he has led greatly contributed to making him so sick. I had 29 lashes given to him. I have written to M. Duvallon and sent him the 30 francs he claimed for his negroes.

CHAPTER EIGHT

1844-1847

1 January 1844

This day is tiresome and boring everywhere, but particularly in the colonies, where one has to put up with the compliments of negroes whose only aim is to thwart one's every effort to earn money by their thievery and their buffoonery. My morning was spent in receiving felicitations and giving advice.

The drumbeat continued until we went to bed. It gave me a migraine. Louis Le Vassor dined with me; he has not sent a single candy, just as I had predicted. I sent a bag of candies to Mme Catala and conveyed my good wishes to Léopold Camouilly.

5 January 1844

My daughters' servant girl was stopped by Mme Catala's maid, who asked her why Mlle Antoinette did not want to marry M. Léopold, such a fine young man. She replied that she knows nothing about it and went on her way. Such a thing can only be seen in this country, where the domestics know all about confidential family matters.

9 January 1844

I went several times to Fond-Saint-Isle [a section of the plantation] that is now being planted, but I never found M. Jules there [M. Jules has already received his notice], for he spent almost the entire morning in M. Lagarigue's sugar buildings. The negroes do just about what they want. It is high time to put an end to this situation.

11 January 1844

My work is progressing slowly, and M. Jules pays very little attention. Just before going to bed we were presented with a most disagreeable episode: I was playing cards with Antoinette in the little salon where the ladies had been doing their fancy work. We hear rustling in my wife's sewing basket, and Emilie says to her mother that it is being stolen. We all get up, and indeed the basket is gone. I call together all the negroes, who fan out in every direction to catch the thief. We leave the scene of the theft for one minute. When we return we find the basket on the wall of the terrace; the material for a vest that had been inside was found on the ground. The negroes, amazed by such boldness, loudly lament this infamy, yet the thief was among them!

Never have I seen a more horrible nocturnal scene! In a thunderous voice I dismissed the lot of these rascals; we resumed our game, not without making some sad reflections. Twenty years ago such things did not happen; one slept with the doors open, and everything that belonged to the masters was sacrosanct. Ever since the ideas of philanthropy have come to corrupt our negroes, they go in for every kind of brigandage; soon, alas, our very lives will no longer be safe. More than a half-hour after this event, a young domestic brought my wife the lining for a vest which he had found on the walkway near the kitchen; we had not noticed that the lining was missing. What brazenness!

14 January 1844

M. Jules has settled the accounts with me. I owe him 3,900 francs. . . .

We dined by ourselves. I gave the work orders, since M. Jules will leave tomorrow. Nicaise, who talked to the negroes, said they would like me to manage my plantation myself. I passed this on to my wife, who seemed annoyed. She is afraid that this will make me stay in Martinique; this is indeed the best thing for me to do in the next three years.

[However, a successor to "M. Jules" is hired. He is Alfred de Gaalon, 33 years old. "He understands the management of colonial properties very well and seemed to me judicious in his way of reasoning. . . . He is well brought up and has a fine wit" (17 January).]

30 January 1844

Today Philippe [the cook who had served the family well for many years] got drunk, and our dinner showed it. We had to go through the motions of having him whipped. After three lashes I gave orders to stop it; it made all of us sick to see it. M. de Gaalon had him put in irons; I will pardon him tomorrow.

[Returning home after a week's absence Dessalles expresses his first doubts about the new manager.]

17 February 1844

I did not find that much cane had been carted off. M. de Gaalon has made the rule that mule and handcart drivers will continue to work, even on Sundays, as long as any cane is left in a field. This will get them going a little better.

20 February 1844

The negroes are working listlessly; I spoke to them and pointed out that it would be in their interest to have the plantation freed of debts soon, because we could then improve their lot. Césaire replied that I only owed money to my brother. They told M. de Gaalon that I had lots of doublons and that I was demanding too much work from them. I learned that M. de Gaalon is going after the young negress Jeanine. If this were true, he would be breaking his word; when he arrived here he told me that he would take his mistresses from outside the plantation. Alas! Men are all the same.

12 March 1844

This evening the negro Césaire showed himself uncooperative; when M. de Gaalon ordered him whipped, he ran away, although he soon came back. Then M. de Gaalon wanted to make him spend the night under the bar, and he ran away again. The ladies aggravated each other's fright. This rogue needs a thorough punishment.

13 March 1844

. . . We were enjoying the evening cool at the side of the house when we saw a negro coming toward us. He threw himself at M. de Gaalon's feet. It was Césaire. He received 25 lashes at prayer time. May he benefit from this lesson.

22 March 1844

... Within a few days I have lost two old oxen and a mule. M. de Gaalon does not show his teeth enough; he is dissatisfied with the slowness of the negroes and constantly says so, but he does nothing to make them work better. He reasons with them, but that is a language the negro does not understand. The whip alone can make him work; that is the cruel truth. It is the only means that has ever done me any good.

5 April 1844 [Good Friday]

Rain all last night. We gave the negroes the morning off so they can adore the Cross.

16 April 1844

Three negroes had disappeared; two came back of their own accord, one is still missing. The work gang finds the work too hard. M. de Gaalon keeps them constantly occupied, but I see that he takes very good care of them.

[Throughout March and April Dessalles complains of pain in both eyes and poor vision. M. La Peyre, the physician, admits that he can do nothing for him and recommends that he go to France for treatment. During this period Dessalles employs a kind of outside accountant, a M. Durieu, who examines his entire financial situation and comes to the conclusion that his debts amount to 280,000 francs. "It is clear that I will have the greatest difficulty liquidating this sum and that I will die in debt. . . . In this situation, I wonder if we should even think of going to France" (22 April).]

25 April 1844

... M. de Gaalon arrived from Saint-Pierre at five o'clock, bringing a horse back with him. He did not say much about my affairs, but I see that he wants to spend money to improve the quality of the sugar. To this end he has bought horse manure. He paid no attention when I said that this plantation has always gotten along without outside manure and yet has produced handsome revenues; it was as if I had not spoken at all. . . .

28 April 1844

M. de Gaalon is impatient and does not feel that things are going as he would wish. This evening he told me that my recommendations to the carters concerning the care to be given to the oxen had done more harm than good and that threats discouraged the negroes, as he had noticed. So here is a young man who has been on my plantation for a mere three months, yet knows my negroes better than I do! Really, one can only shrug one's shoulders. His remark, totally out of place as it was, would have prompted me to dismiss him on the spot if certain considerations for others were not involved. I told my wife about it, but she thought that it was just a simple remark. This led to a most disagreeable conversation between us. I was subjected to the most scathing reproaches. I in turn stated openly that I could no longer live with my family and made it clear that I would not leave the colony until I had an assured income of 4,000 francs.[1] A stranger within my own family, I can no longer bear it. . . .

[Dessalles's relationship with de Gaalon deteriorates rapidly, particularly since his wife and daughters have great faith in the manager's abilities.]

13 May 1844

Miserable weather; impossible to go to mass. A letter from the jail warden at Fort-Royal informs me that my negro Modeste, who was caught at Rivière-Salée, has been brought to his jail. This is an unexpected expense. Such contre-temps do not upset M. de Gaalon at all, for they don't cost him anything. Poor proprietors! The losses are all for you. As for the manager, come hell or high water, his salary goes on just the same, and he pockets it, whatever the circumstances.

[From mid-May to early June, Dessalles is very ill with bleeding hemorrhoids, eye trouble, migraines, and an itching skin rash. Doctors in Saint-Pierre advise a return to France, so passage is booked for late June. But before Dessalles leaves, many of his creditors, white and mulatto, come to demand their money. He seems to treat each one of them differently, depending on who they are and how much he owes them.]

10 June 1844

I had barely come out of my room when I saw Montout Laquiote arrive. This mulatto spoke to me most insolently. I asked him to use a different tone; other-wise, I would send him off to fuck himself. I did not mean this as an insult, but he spat out every invective he could think of. I was stupefied. The ladies overheard everything from their room. Antoinette had a fit of nerves about it. I asked him [Laquiote] for his papers, which he did not have, so I told him to

---

1. In 1847, when he is promised an income of 6,000 francs following the sale of the estate to his children, he complains bitterly that they mean to let him starve to death. See entry of 6 June 1846.

fetch them. He came back at three o'clock, but my wife did not want me to see him. She called him in and told him that, in view of his behavior this morning, we would no longer deal with him and that he could go to court if he wanted to.

At noon the son of Kar Chatenay [a mulatto woman] also came to claim 300 francs that we owed her; this was the fifth time he came to see me about this. Sure that I had paid this sum, I examined—my bad eyes notwithstanding—the accounts of Victor Raynal and found that I had signed a draft of 300 francs in favor of Kar on 17 December 1836. The young mulatto said nothing more. They are a sad lot, these free men of color: as soon as they are in financial trouble they try to think of a way to bilk the whites. This Kar family had no doubt hoped that I would not find my documentation. They threatened to take me to court; when they were finally proven wrong, they did not offer the slightest apology. One can never win with these wretches.

Chéry Magloire [also a free man of color] came to settle his accounts. This one has always been most precise. He asked me if I wanted to sell my young mulatto Ernest, and I replied that I would do it to give him a good position; he [Chéry Magloire] accepted this condition. Consequently, he counted out 1,000 francs, and I signed the contract of sale.

That beggar Castandet brought me a negress, asking me if I wanted her in exchange for Saturnin; she was obviously suffering terrible stomach trouble. This villain wanted to cheat me once again by selling me this negress for 1,000 francs, although he probably did not pay more than four doublons for her. I could not refrain from pointing out his duplicity to him.

14 June 1844

I settled my accounts with the blacksmith, M. Pra, and with MM. Octave and Dorval La Peyre. I was very satisfied with the manner in which they handled themselves. Durieu read me the contracts he concluded with the various creditors. . . . What I have to pay frightens me. M. Hauchecorne [a commission merchant of Le Havre, who henceforth will receive all the sugar from the plantation and pay the Dessalles family a regular income] may also get frightened and want to withdraw from the arrangement. What a terrible position! What are we going to do when we arrive in France? What would become of us if M. Hauchecorne refused to furnish us with enough money to live on? I am terrified of all the things that can happen. M. Durieu's calculations are no longer valid if the plantation does not produce 300 hogsheads [150 tons] of sugar annually. . . . What I feel inside myself cannot be described. I am suffering more than the damned; life is a burden to me. How happy I would be if God took me from this world!

15 June 1844

Today I signed all the contracts. I signed a draft for 8,000 francs on M. Paul Hauchecorne, payable to M. Lefaivre in 120 days, and one for 2,337 francs, payable to Fournier frères of Marseille on 3 June 1845.[2] I assume this obligation in fear and trembling.

20 June 1844

A very fatiguing day; I had to settle accounts with several persons. Chéry Magloire came to an agreement with me about Saturnin, whom I sold to his grandmother.[3]

21 June 1844

Same kind of day as yesterday, and even more fatiguing, because my negroes pestered me with their goodbyes. These poor people. . . . I am sorry to leave them, for I am used to the service of my domestics who took care of me with affection. I will find it hard to have whites serve me.

[The family, along with Nicaise, finally embarks on the *Gustave-Edouard* on 4 July.]

16 July 1844 [on board the *Gustave-Edouard*]

. . . This morning Arthur de Sanois [a fellow passenger] told me—in the presence of Nicaise and the maître d'hôtel—about some of the atrocious things he had done to his negroes. I could not help but express my disapproval. This was only braggadocio on the part of this young man; I am convinced that he has not done any of the things he said he did. He also told me that M. Huyghues-Désétages—who had applied to manage my plantation—was excessively hard on the negroes. Here is one example he gave me: a negress who had broken

2. This debt was still not paid in 1847 when Dessalles was quite embarrassed to find himself at dinner with M. Fournier because he owed him 2,500 francs. "I was brazen about it and cavalierly talked to him, and he was most amiable" (13 February 1847).

3. There seems to be a family connection between the Magloire family and Dessalles's favorite, Saturnin. In the present passage it is unclear what role Chéry Magloire plays in the sale of Saturnin to his own grandmother. The latter, Fortunée, soon frees Saturnin.

her thigh complained in the hospital about his negligence in taking care of sick negroes. Upon hearing of this, he had her taken out and given 50 lashes. This action is so ferocious that I have trouble believing it. Nicaise told me the maître d'hôtel was so indignant that he could not wait to tell the crew about what he had heard. These are things that, if they are spread about in France, can do us a great deal of harm. . . .

[The ship lands at Le Havre on 15 August. Dessalles grandly gives a dinner for MM. de Sanois, his kinsman Adrien Coppinger, and Paul Hauchecorne, his new commission merchant. Meanwhile, Nicaise gets into trouble.]

15 August 1844

Just as we were about to go to bed, we were treated to a horrible scene. They brought me Nicaise, half dead; sailors had taken him to the café and got him drunk. He does not respond to any question. I could not possibly express how upset I am; I am so fond of this young negro that the idea of seeing him in such a humiliating state saddens me to the highest degree.

16 August 1844

I did not close an eye; I kept a candle lit, and the sight of Nicaise broke my heart.[4] At five o'clock he woke up and did not know where he was. He cried so hard that I did not dare scold him too much. He did promise me that he would not put himself into such a situation again. . . .

[A week later the family moves into an apartment in Paris, 14 rue Caumartin. Dessalles does some sightseeing, consults a doctor who inspires confidence, suffers through boring tea parties which have become fashionable in some circles, bickers about money with the ladies, deplores the cold climate (in August!), and already dreams about returning to Martinique. This dream does not come true until November 1847.

The three-year stay in France, briefly described here as the transition to a renewed residence in the colony, was an ordeal for Dessalles. Money was the root of the problem, but the relationship with his wife and all his children deteriorated in other respects as well. At one point, for instance (12 September 1844), his wife accuses him in the presence of his children of loving his servants more than he loves them. One is surprised at so much perspicacity on the part of Mme Dessalles. The word "separation" is pronounced.

De facto, the two spouses are separated. Madame, in poor health, stays in her room or goes shopping with her daughters; Monsieur strolls on the boulevards in the morning, sees some Creole friends in the afternoon, and attends the theater at

---

4. Nicaise slept in his master's room, as has been clearly conveyed earlier [HF and LE].

night. He has again succumbed to his passion for gambling and loses considerable sums of money. He is bored, disgusted, and homesick for Martinique:

> Spending one's life in this manner is really dreary. Why did we come to Paris, for God's sake? To eat badly and suffer privations of every kind? In Martinique I could at least distract myself with the work of my plantation. I enjoyed the freshness of my trees, and I varied my food. Dessert is one of the things I always liked most, and there I had fresh fruit all year long, fresh compotes every day, and cream custard at every meal. Here it's those miserable almonds every day, which don't do the stomach any good. . . . [19 February 1846]

Mme Dessalles dies on 21 May 1846, apparently of consumption. Dessalles fills his diary with highly rhetorical expressions of loss, mourning, and love; he even experiences a religious conversion in honor of his dead spouse. As the French editors put it, "Pierre Dessalles now founders in a mysticism and bigotry whose constant expression is so tedious that we see no reason to subject the reader to it. Lasting for more than a year, this bout of piety had more or less abated by the end of 1847, although some vestiges of it remained with him for the rest of his life" (III, 217).

Less than three weeks after his wife's death, Dessalles comes to an arrangement with his children. On 5 June, Louis Cléret, Dessalles's son-in-law, persuades him with honeyed words to accept an agreement.]

1846

6 June 1846

I sold La Nouvelle Cité to my children. Everything is gone; I no longer have any property in Martinique, all I own is 21 carrés [65.5 acres] of land in Guadeloupe. I am reduced to an annuity of 6,000 francs. In the provinces and by myself, I would have enough; but in Paris and with my daughters, I will always be poverty-stricken.[5]

3 July 1846

. . . Pécoul [an acquaintance from Martinique] and I went out together. When we arrived on the boulevards, I suddenly had a colic, and I could not

5. The sale was made "*sous seing privé*" [that is, privately] and dated 10 June 1846. Since Louis Cléret found that it was too costly to have it registered in France, Cacqueray-Valmenier offered to have it registered in Martinique. It appears that this contract had certain legal flaws, a fact that— in conjunction with the purchasers' failure to fulfill their obligations—subsequently allowed Dessalles to have the sale invalidated. Certain of the plantation's creditors also seem to have acted in this sense. See the entries for 1848 [HF and LE].

hold it in. . . . Imagine my mortification! When I arrived home, Nicaise washed me off. It was another attack of cholerine, brought on no doubt by yesterday's fatigue. What a dreadful affliction! People wonder why I am attached to my domestic. Alas! Here is why I am attached to him; it is because he takes care of me without disgust and because I trust him. If my domestic had been white, this would have made me feel terrible; indeed I might not even have dared ask him to help me. My little negro spent his evening cleaning my underwear and my trousers. When I said that I felt sorry for him, he laughed and kept repeating, "It's nothing, Monsieur! Don't you worry about it!"

18 July 1846

The weather is dark and gloomy, and my sight is waning in an alarming manner; I have a great deal of trouble writing and reading. At half-past seven I went out by myself and walked on the boulevards. I am living in isolation; without my religious books, I don't know what would become of me. I am a burden to my children, and I must not ask too much of them. I am bound to annoy them. That is why I miss Martinique so much. There I could at least talk to my little negro children, and I could ask my negroes about their work on the plantation. I was never bored. Here I take no interest in anything, and I have no one to talk to. . . .

12 August 1846

In January I had given the wood merchant a draft on Paul Hauchecorne, which the latter refused to pay. So I had to pay today; the bill was 728 francs. It was paid with Nicaise's money. . . .

2 September 1846

[I wrote to Bence] about my intention of returning to the colonies, telling him that I wish I could live close to my daughters, but that the climate of France is harmful to my health—and that other reasons as well call me back to the colonies. My daughters, having shunned my advice, now seem to want to follow it, but it is too late. . . . My heart will never cease to desire my children's happiness, but I do not wish to depend on their caprices. That phrase spoken by my poor wife in the presence of my children—"you love your domestics more than your children"—has done irreparable harm. If I go to Guadeloupe, Saturnin is there; there will surely be talk that I am going to Guadeloupe to join him. I would only go to that colony as a last resort, for I prefer Martinique in every respect. But since it is possible that certain people there fear my presence because of the influence I might exert over my negroes, I would make the sacrifice of not going there.

[In November, Antoinette asks for her father's consent for her marriage to Jean-Jacques Cléret-Languavant, brother of her sister Louise's husband. Dessalles considers this marriage "foolishness" and predicts that it will be "the most miserable marriage in the world." [6] However, he does give his consent, and the marriage is celebrated in December, though not without a great deal of bickering about who will pay for the dinner that is held at Louise's home in Chatellerault. After the wedding, the weather turns very cold.]

16 December 1846

. . . Nicaise left me alone from ten to half-past three. At four I went to see Louise; her cook has not been sober in the last four days! Snow is falling in big flakes, and the weather looks very threatening. I am frozen. What wouldn't I give to be in Martinique!

26 December 1846

Louis Cléret [his son-in-law] brought me more papers to sign. I am asking for certain changes, without which I will not sign anything. I told him flatly that, if everything that was offered and promised to me were not given, I would sue for it and that I meant it. He believed what I said. . . .

Louise came to my room to whine and to tell me how much she suffered because of what is happening. I opened my heart to her; I told her about my own pain and laid particular stress on the fact that my children will not allow me to live at the Nouvelle Cité.

It was a very sad day for me.

1847

1 January 1847

I had a two-hour conversation with the priest. He approved of my conduct. I went to my daughter's [he is still at Chatellerault] to receive my children's New

6. A few months later, he again notes, "Languavant had dinner and lunch with me. The more I look at him, the less I understand Antoinette; he is ugly and there is nothing pleasing in his demeanor" (7 August 1847). Yet Antoinette should have been very easy to understand; she had nowhere else to go.

Year's wishes. Louise's house is freezing cold; however much I try to warm my hands and feet at the chimney, a minute later I turn to ice. I would not be a bit surprised if I had caught cold. This accursed climate! . . .

8 January 1847

I had a fever for five days and stayed in my room. Louis came to see me, and we talked for more than two hours without coming to an understanding. They want to get out of paying me the 3,000 francs they are supposed to add to my income in 1850. . . .

9 January 1847

Louis Cléret came with his wife, and we had a perfectly dreadful scene. The situation got so out of hand and I had such a violent fit of anger that I obtained everything I wanted.

My poor Louise, the daughter whom I love so much, suffered greatly. And I myself, who always fear to make others suffer, I truly deplore what has happened!

[In mid-January Dessalles returns to Paris with Nicaise; he now fights with his sons Adrien and Henri, neither of whom show him what he considers proper respect. He does, however, have a fairly lively social life in the circle of Creoles living in Paris. It is becoming increasingly obvious that he feels himself to be a Creole.]

21 January 1847

. . . Adrien stopped by for me, and we went to Pécoul's house at half past six; we were thirteen at table! The dinner was handsome, but I did not really enjoy anything. I met Pécoul's older brother, a very affable man. This family is weighted down by its wealth, but are they happier because of it? It is probable that, consumed by ambition, they regret not being noble. Alas! with what pleasure would I give up my nobility for an income of 10,000 francs! At Pécoul's house I also met a Creole of Martinique, M. Aminthe de Maupertuis, who is involved in land speculation. He belongs to a company that has bought land in the American South [probably the West of the United States]. Pieces of this land are then sold, and the profits already amount to 300 percent. He told me a lot about this type of colonization, and I must admit that I am tempted to get into this speculation. . . .

27 January 1847

By the packet boat, I received a letter from Saturnin, who asks me to let him buy his mother [Trop]. I wrote to Georges to consent to this sale at the price of 1,200 to 1,000 francs. . . .

11 February 1847

M. Engler had lunch with me; I talked to him about the land in America, and it looks as if he might go and establish himself there. If one has an agitated life and has not accomplished anything, it is good to find rest in a new and tranquil country, which will no doubt have its torments some day, but in such a faraway time that one can hope not to see it. In this old Europe that is becoming demoralized with all these ideas of progress, people are so dominated by their thirst for gold that it is not safe to form new relationships.

5 March 1847

As I was getting out of my bath, Nicaise made me impatient, and I reproached him for his flightiness and his character flaws. He had the audacity to tell me that he would leave me if we were not going back to the colonies soon. I replied that, since I was accustomed to being rewarded with ingratitude, I was not at all surprised by his threats. He told me that he loves no one more than he loves me, but that I am too impatient and never pleased with anything. I confess that I had not expected to hear such language. This young negro is too dissolute and too fond of his companions. It is high time to return to the colonies; on whom can I rely today?

11 March 1847

. . . Nicaise put on a costume and went to the Opera ball; I found it impossible to keep him from going. Oh dear! In what state and at what time will I get him back tomorrow?

12 March 1847

I had to light my fire myself. Nicaise did not appear until ten and in such a state of drunkenness that there was no way of speaking to him. This young negro will never correct himself; for his sake it is more than time to take him back to Martinique. What would become of him if he were left to his own devices in Paris?

[In the following weeks Dessalles succumbs to another bout of gambling mania, this time at the instigation of a M. Dupau. Here is how the French editors describe the situation:

> This M. Dupau, who seems to be a friend of Adrien, suddenly appears here without any explanation. But from this day forward, he will be a frequent and soon daily dinner companion of Pierre Dessalles: he comes to dinner and then *plays a hand*, an activity that soon occupies Pierre Dessalles every night until all hours. We do not know how much he won or lost, but M. Dupau seems to be very short of money. He introduces P. Dessalles to a Sieur Collasson, a native of Toulouse like M. Dupau, a professional gambler and owner of a gambling den: fortunately, however, Dessalles senses a trap and does not get caught. . . . Dupau is mentioned too often to hold the reader's interest, but this episode serves to illustrate the low caliber of personal relations of the author, who was clearly deeply depressed throughout this period (III, 244).]

23 March 1847

My soul is sad; I wish I were already in Martinique! I see problems about money and position that may prevent me from leaving soon. Adrien's jeremiads and the indelicate behavior of Mauny [a confidence man who has fleeced Dessalles] give me the spleen. The ceremonies at the [church of the] Madeleine are very long indeed; they contribute not a little to the fatigue I feel.

3 April 1847

I had a visit from Jabrun,[7] who talked to me about the colonies. Emancipation is inevitable, but MM. de Broglie and de Montalembert told him that the Chamber would start by granting the colonists a fair and appropriate compensation. Jabrun outlined to me a plan which pleased these two rabid abolitionists. This plan would keep the blacks on the estates by giving them an interest in the net yield. They would be given their cabin, a piece of land, one day a week, and one-third of the property's net revenue.[8] I hope this plan will be quickly adopted if it will give us peace and quiet and especially if it means that colonists will cease being looked upon as pariahs. The greatest misfortune of the colonists is that they do not speak with one voice: Jabrun was not authorized

---

7. Jabrun of Guadeloupe was, according to Dale W. Tomich, "one of the most technically advanced planters in the French West Indies" (*Slavery in the Circuit of Sugar: Martinique and the World Economy, 1830–1848* [Baltimore: Johns Hopkins University Press, 1990], 194).

8. This system was later to be called "Association."

to present this mode of emancipation [in the name of all the colonists]; he presented it as his personal idea.

[In mid-April Dessalles books his passage to Martinique; to pay for it, he pawns almost all his silverware and receives 2,451 francs. His creditors, headed by Lefaivre, want to have him arrested, and Paul Hauchecorne seems ready to stop paying the annuities. What to do?]

27 April 1847

. . . M. Jollivet has asked the colonists to come to a meeting at his house tomorrow. No doubt it is to plan our protest against the words of M. Rollin-Ledru,[9] for the session of the Chamber was horrible. The entire population of Paris is stirred up against the colonists, who are being accused of deeds that can only be calumnies. It would be desirable for emancipation to happen soon, if it is to give rise to more such debates.

28 April 1847

Today we met at the house of M. Jollivet, lobbyist for Martinique. We recognized that the only way to defend the colonies was to use the press. Today that is what governs public opinion. Six colonists—MM. Bernard-Feyssal, Bence, Adolphe Perinelle, Froidefont de Farges, Adrien Fortier, and Filassier—have been designated to conduct an inquest into the facts alleged by M. Ledru-Rollin [this is his correct name] at the Chamber of Deputies. If they are libellous, we will make it known by way of the newspapers, and we will brand as a liar the orator who has so shamelessly proclaimed them. If they are true, we deliver their infamous authors to public outcry. It is not right for the colonists as a group to be held responsible.

22 May 1847

I received . . . a letter from the elder Cléret, who tells me that there have been fires[10] at seven plantations in Guadeloupe and that, in one place, they found a prison cell [*cachot*] holding a negro who told tales of horror about his master. This affair, he says, is of such a grave nature that it is liable to do the greatest harm to the colonies. . . .

9. No doubt Ledru-Rollin, one of the future leaders of the Revolution of 1848.
10. The implication is that they were caused by arson.

5 August 1847

I received a visit from Henri du Chayla, who brought along the Superior of a Trappist monastery who is planning to settle at Saint-Jacques. He was accompanied by a Trappist brother who had returned this year from the colony, where he had been sent to explore the country. The Superior is to go there with five brothers. They will free the negroes who work this property, and whites and negroes will work there pell-mell. Will this experiment succeed? I hope so. . . . The Superior, it seemed to me, acts from the best intentions; but the race of men they will have to civilize is very difficult to manage. After they left, Nicaise asked me who these priests were, and I explained it to him. He shook his head and told me that this experiment would not succeed. "But then," I asked him, "is there no way to do anything with people of your kind?" "There is," he replied, "but these men themselves, who go there with the best of intentions, will not withstand the climate; before a year is out, half of them will be gone, and you will see that, with respect to the morality they will preach, many of them will be the first to forget all proprieties and to set the most unwholesome examples. The negroes have always followed all their natural impulses; if these priests succeed in making them devout, they will turn them into hypocrites."

This reasoning is unfortunately not devoid of sense. If God does not come to our aid, the colonies are done for; this much seems certain to me.

7 August 1847

Nicaise received a letter from Saturnin, who has returned to Martinique. In the newspapers one can read the address of the Colonial Council of Guadeloupe, which seemed dignified and calm to me. That colony is resigned to emancipation, while Martinique is more firmly committed than ever to its system of resistance.

[Meanwhile, the revenues of the plantation fall to such a low point that Hauchecorne threatens to cut off the credit; the new owners, Dessalles's children and their spouses, want to reduce his monthly income from 500 to 200 francs. Emilie writes that she has consulted a priest who has approved their conduct: "I confess that when I heard this, my indignation was such that the idea of cursing these unworthy children occurred to me. But the thought of God gave me the strength to bear such an awful insult" (30 August 1847).

A long reflection about his relations with his children and with his servants reveals a great deal about Dessalles's Creole or Caribbean identity.]

30 August 1847

... At half-past 11 [after an evening of gambling], I arrived home, but before going to bed I wanted to find out what Adrien had heard from his uncle [Arthur Bence]. It seems that Emilie is saying vile things about me, so the family fears I will use my influence to harm them; they are also afraid I will attach myself to Nicaise's daughter and to my old domestics [presumably Trop and especially her son Saturnin]. This is nothing but women's gossip! My indignation and exasperation are at their height! Surely I would not have believed that anyone could be jealous and take offense at my kindness to a child of seven. I need affection, and my children do not give it to me. I would attach myself to the lowliest animals if they showed me some sympathy. Abandoned by my family, which always refused to stay with me in Martinique, is it any wonder that I am attached to the domestics who have served me with zeal and affection? I love these poor unfortunate people, that is true; but I love them as one loves people who are totally dependent on one for their livelihood and their happiness. Is there any justice and any charity in my children's reasoning? Truly, I am to be pitied!

[On 6 November 1847, Dessalles finally embarks for Martinique, where he arrives on 12 December. The first person to whom he speaks is "a M. Fleuret, a friend of Adrien, who informed me that the court had annulled the sale." A great round of social visiting ensues, and Dessalles finds that colonial society is changing.]

20 December 1847

... M. Amédée Joyau has married the widow of a free man of color by the name of Faure, who committed suicide. This does not disturb De l'Horme, for it is said in public that he is on excellent terms with the lady of the house. I also heard about Mme Béroine, the wife of my former tailor. Those who form the colonial society now have ties to tradespeople, whom in the past we did not receive. . . . Our poor country has certainly been diminished by this!

[However, Dessalles soon starts spending his evenings at Amédée Joyau's house. The last diary entry for the year seems to suggest that the unhappy years Dessalles spent in France have made him slightly more tolerant of the nonwhite elements of colonial society and that he is beginning to feel himself a Creole.]

31 December 1847

The last day of the year. . . . I went to all the shops to find some candy, but it seemed so expensive and so bad that I only bought a bit of apple sugar, which I sent to the Joyau ladies along with some oranges and a pineapple that were sent to me from Gros-Morne by a mulatto woman to whom I once did a good turn. This poor woman wrote me a note filled with feelings of warm affection and great gratitude. I replied with a few lines and sent her some candy. I spent the evening with M. Joyau. All I have left is one doublon to buy my soup with. . . .

CHAPTER NINE

1848

[Having come to know Pierre Dessalles as an increasingly disgruntled, irascible, and fundamentally unhappy man, one should not be surprised that the desired return to his beautiful island does not lift his spirits or improve his health. He is still penniless. Since he has not yet regained possession of la Nouvelle Cité, he has no work except to prepare for the court proceedings against his children with his lawyer, M. Cazeneuve. On a less personal level, however, his malaise may well have arisen from his status as a marginal in the original meaning of this sociological term, that is, a person who has claims to membership in two overlapping cultural spheres without being fully integrated in either.

In any event, as early as 17 January, he roundly declares that he is "disgusted with this country, where I find nothing but disappointment."]

20 February 1848 [Sunday, visiting at Rivière-Monsieur]

I had barely awakened when three negroes from my place arrived, among them the driver. They seemed to be in good health. I asked the driver if the work was going well. "Not as well as in the old days," he replied.

[While awaiting the trial, Dessalles stays with his friend Mauny and visits other planters. He is generally pleased with the reception he is given.]

27 March 1848

This day will mark an era in my life. We had been talking under Fougain-ville's tamarisks for two hours, and I was just reading Victor Hugo's famous piece on the Jew when two riders appeared. They sat down in our midst until I had finished reading the piece. One of these gentlemen, a M. Gaubert, then asked if we knew about the events that had occurred in France. "I just came from Le Marin, and M. Pelet showed me a letter from his son-in-law, M. Schef-fler, informing him that the government of Louis-Philippe no longer exists. He himself has fled to England, and a provisional government composed of La Martine, Rollin-Ledru, Garnier-Pagès, Dupont de l'Eure, Arago, Crémieux, Marie has been formed on 25 February. The Republic has been proclaimed and emancipation with indemnity declared. Calm reigns everywhere. M. Ros-tolan has arrived in the colony with special powers, and M. Husson, notary at Fort-Royal, has been appointed Director of the Interior."[1]

We were astounded, stunned! We sent word of the news to Mauny, MM. de Venancourt, and de La Guigneraye, who lost no time joining us. We wrote to M. du Chastel and to Meillacq. The local curé and some other planters came to confirm what we had heard. This evening Thimoléon received from his brother in Paris a letter providing a detailed account. Louis-Philippe's flight was as cowardly as that of 1830. Paris is quiet. Nothing has yet been said about emancipation, but with this government it will be one of the first acts of the Republic. Jollivet [the lobbyist for the planter interests] is said to have been killed. Froidefont, Pécoul, and Bence are members of the colonial committee.[2] I am glad that it is they rather than I. . . .

28 March 1848

Our day was spent in conjectures about the events. I see many excitable idealists in this provisional government, men who are the declared enemies of

1. For the early signs of the Revolution of 1848 in Martinique see the special issue of the *Annales des Antilles, Mémoires de la Société d'Histoire de la Martinique, no. 15–1983*: Léo Elisabeth, *L'Abolition de l'esclavage à la Martinique* [HF and LE].

2. On 2 February, the day when Arago became minister of the Navy, the colonists of Marti-nique residing in Paris held a meeting. A committee was formed to identify the colony's most pressing concerns in this new situation. Present at this meeting were Le Jeune de la Motte, Hus-son, de Montlaur, Desmases, de Maupertuis, Froidefont-Desfarges (presiding), Tanguy Duchatel, Lucy de Fossarieu, Adrien Dessalles, Filassier, de Fougainville, Martineau, Desfontaines, Gibert, Langlois, Pécoul, Le Pelletier de Saint-Rémy, de Bence, Perrinon, Le Chevalier, de Lavigne, Blon-del, Billouin, etc. It was decided not to debate the question of slavery until the return to France of Schoelcher, who at the time was in Senegal. This information comes from a letter of the younger Le Pelletier published in the *Courrier de la Martinique* [HF and LE].

the colonists. We have everything to fear from this new order of things. The appointment of M. Husson as Director of the Interior tells us that the government is not well disposed toward us, for this M. Husson is controlled by the class of mulattoes and detests white people. It will be very hard to contain the class of mulattoes, for they have cruel vengeance in store. If the scenes of '93 are reenacted, God only knows where they will stop. I am prey to dire premonitions.

29 March 1848

Oscar Duplessis met an individual who told him that there was some agitation at Fort-Royal. M. Mathieu [the royal governor] is said to have handed over all power to M. Rostolan [the special envoy from Paris]. . . .

30 March 1848

. . . Fougainville has received a proclamation by M. Rostolan, who has seized power. It is judicious but poorly written. M. Husson has also written a letter, in a style that is hardly French. I see the horizon filled with dark clouds, and all these first acts of the provisional government look damnably like those of '93. So far, the scaffold has remained silent. . . .

[On 1 and 2 April, Dessalles visits an acquaintance, M. Pelet. At his table he eats meat on Friday ("contrary to my principles, which upset me very much"); on Sunday he does not go to mass "in order to please Pelet." No doubt an impecunious guest feels that he has to adapt to the mores of his host's household. "Christian morality is not honored much here," Dessalles writes, noting also that the son of the house is "a character, but his manners are quite poor."]

4 April 1848

Pelet has received letters and newspapers. The paper makes much of the visit that the new Director of the Interior has paid to Saint-Pierre, an occasion that permitted the population to express joy about the new order of things. In a moment of enthusiasm and happiness, M. Husson threw himself into the arms of M. Pory Papy, the mulatto lawyer,[3] and then into those of the negro

3. Member of a prominent and politically engaged free family of color, Pory Papy had studied law in France and returned to Martinique in 1835. In 1836 he was sworn in as barrister and solicitor at Saint-Pierre. In 1848 he became a member of the city council, then provisional mayor, and finally deputy for Martinique. After the 20-year interlude of the Second Empire, Pory Papy was reelected deputy in 1871. A convert, he became a fervent Catholic and a political moderate. He died in 1874 [adapted from biographical notices in HF and LE (4: appendix)].

Alexandre Sauvignon;[4] this reunion of the three colors cemented the harmony among the inhabitants. Truly, a great sight! The newspaper expresses surprise that Bissette was not included in the Parisian committee of colonists. . . .

7 April 1848

. . . Thimoléon de Fougainville has received from M. Husson a proclamation to the negroes, to be posted in town and even on the plantations. Written in French and Creole, this piece informs the negroes of the government's intentions concerning their liberation. M. Husson goes a bit far; he is trying to curry favor with the mulattoes and the slaves. Since this proclamation is to be posted in the neighboring districts, it would be dangerous not to post it here.[5]

10 April 1848

. . . The packet boat expected for yesterday arrived this morning; there was a riot at the post office, where people snatched newspapers and letters out of the director's and the mail carriers' hands. The most outstanding news is this: the committee appointed to implement the emancipation of the slaves is composed of MM. Schoelcher,[6] Mestre, de Gatine, Gaumont, Perrinon, Wallon, and Louis

4. Jacques Léandre Alexandre Sauvignon, associate mayor of Saint-Pierre, became municipal registrar in 1849 [HF and LE].

5. In reality, this proclamation, written in French and Creole, stresses the beneficent role of the masters, who have called for emancipation, and enjoins the slaves to continue working and to show themselves good Christians until the Republic has assembled sufficient funds to pay indemnities. The proclamation reads, in part, *"Long live work, long live Monsieur, long live Madame, long live marriage,"* and so on [HF and LE].

6. Victor Schoelcher was born in Paris in 1804, the son of a renowned porcelain maker. As early as 1829, he became sensitized to the problems of slavery by traveling in the Caribbean, Mexico, and Cuba. With strong literary skills and a polemical temperament, he became involved in the struggle for emancipation. Pamphlets and books published between 1833 and 1843 made him widely known. In 1840 he once again traveled to the Caribbean to study conditions in the French, Danish, Spanish, and English islands. He happened to travel on the same boat as Adolphe de Perinelle, and the two men became friends.

Following the Revolution of 1848, he became undersecretary of state in the ministry of the Navy and the Colonies. As chairman of a committee, he wrote the legislation on emancipation (the decrees of 27 April) that his good friend Perrinon, as commissioner of the Republic, proclaimed at Saint-Pierre on 6 June 1848.

Deputy of Martinique in the Constituent Assembly, then of Guadeloupe in the Legislative Assembly, he fought on the barricades at the time of Louis Napoléon's coup d'état of 2 December 1851 and as a result was exiled from his country. Living in England until the end of the Second Empire, he was reelected as a far left deputy on his return and became a lifetime senator in 1875. He died in Houilles near Paris in 1893, leaving numerous polemical works [adapted from biographical notices in HF and LE (4: appendix)].

Percin of Saint Lucia, all men hostile to the colonists.[7] Perrinon[8] has been appointed government commissioner in charge of transforming slave labor into free labor. The provisional government is no longer quite as self-assured. Elections are to be held on 10 April—which is today!—and the Constituent National Assembly will meet on 20 April. . . .

12 April 1848

. . . There is much concern about the demonstration in Paris by a deputation of mulattoes and negroes, headed by Bissette and students of the Ecole Polytechnique, to demand that Bissette return to Martinique to proclaim the freeing of the slaves and at the same time to plant the liberty tree in the place he had designated for it. The Bissette family is moving heaven and earth to enhance the importance of Bissette who—if we are to believe what is being written—was thrown out of Perrinon's house. The shouts of the populace have a ring of ferocity that has many people deeply worried.

15 April 1848

. . . I went see De l'Horme, Joyau, Henry Pompignan, the latter's mother, and Paul des Grottes. We talked about the events of the moment. There is general consternation. The slaves are already leaving their masters. The men of color are also worried, for they are afraid that the Republic will not last. A number of families are emigrating; d'Oysonville writes to me that the scenes of '93 will be repeated. . . .

7. Mestre, an adversary of the colonial system, replaced Husson as Director of the Interior. Gaumont was a working man. De Gastine, a lawyer, had drawn up the appeal procedure for the insurgents of Grand' Anse; appointed commissioner of the Republic in Guadeloupe in June 1848, he remained in this post only until September, when he was replaced by Colonel Fiéron. Wallon was the secretary of the commission [HF and LE].

8. Adolphe Perrinon was born at Saint-Pierre in 1812. His biographies indicate that "thanks to the protection of one of the island's colonists, he was sent to France to be educated at Rouen." Admitted to the Ecole Polytechnique in 1832 and to the Ecole d'Application in 1834, he became a naval artillery officer and was stationed at Guadeloupe from 1842 to 1845. Having attained the grade of battalion chief, he later directed a foundry. In 1848 he was sent to Martinique as commissioner of the Republic charged with proclaiming the emancipation of the slaves. Subsequently elected deputy from Guadeloupe, he sat at the extreme left and opposed all counterrevolutionary measures. When he was reelected to the Legislative Assembly along with his friend Schoelcher, his election was nullified because it had been marred by violent incidents. However, he was reelected in 1850. In 1852 he left the military and retired to private life. An officer of the Legion d'Honneur since 1848, he left two works on naval artillery and several smaller brochures [adapted from biographical notices in HF and LE (4: appendix)].

The notary Cazeneuve told me that at this point I should not be so anxious to have my plantation back; but I feel it would be better to be there than to float around as I am doing. . . .

20 April 1848

A young mulatto from my plantation came to see me. I reproached him for his brother's and his mother's conduct. I talked to him about a plan to form an association with my negroes, and he thinks they would be glad to adopt it.

There are efforts to send Bissette to this country, but Schoelcher has pronounced himself against it. If this mulatto came back, he would most certainly cause a great deal of harm here, and the former members of the court would not be forgotten.[9] Nicaise tells me that many petitions demanding the return of Bissette are being filled with signatures.

22 April 1848

M. Husson has arrived [at Saint-Pierre] and quickly established contact with all classes. The mayor was pressured into issuing a proclamation by the men of color. Léonce, an ex-convict mulatto who is free on bail,[10] has permitted himself the most foul language. He said that, since his fellow blacks have been branded, it was now the turn of the whites to be branded. His hatred of the white race will never die; he is suspected of being the rouser of this rabble, yet the authorities are not doing anything to stop him. Their conduct is incomprehensible. It would be very easy to preserve order, but it would demand different means than those being employed.

24 April 1848

. . . Today M. Husson is giving a banquet for a group of whites and people of color, among them M. Hervé, the mayor, and MM. Braffin and Raynal [municipal councillors]. I saw the men of color go by my door gloved and dressed to the nines. If our situation were not so critical, it would really be quite funny. . . .

9. In 1823 three members of the high court—among them the author—had voted to condemn Bissette to death. See chapter 2, first letter of 1823.

10. Louis Nicolas Léonce was first punished for insolence in 1823, even before Bissette; exiled for a time, he remained one of the leaders of the people of color of Saint-Pierre after his return. In 1833 he was preventively arrested as soon as word of the affair of Grand' Anse was received, but the army had to disperse the crowd that refused to let him be arrested. In 1847 he was convicted of breach of confidence; when his first appeal was rejected, he appealed to the highest court [HF and LE].

M. Husson pursues this fusion [11] without looking right or left; eventually he will be swamped, and God knows how he will get out of it. . . .

A ship that arrived in 28 days brings news of 25 March. A great many states experienced revolutions; all of Europe will be engulfed. . . . France was fairly quiet, but business was dead and there were many bankruptcies. . . . In this wretched country here, the negroes, unable to continue their disorders in the towns, are pushed by evil men of color to fan out into the countryside. At the Case-Pilote, M. de Saint-Rémy was assaulted by a band of criminals who forced their way into his home. Mme de Saint-Rémy was forced to pay a bill of 200 francs;[12] his granddaughter and her child spent the night in a cane field. M. Husson, informed of this disorder, responded that he could not do anything about it; however, an examining judge did go to the premises. At Le Prêcheur, the mayor experienced the same scenes. The crowd wanted to make him sign "Vive Bissette! Vive la République!" but he replied that he would blow out the brains of anybody who tried to do him violence. When he showed his pistols, the whole gang ran away. One act of vigor and firmness would be enough to bring these fractious people to heel, but as far as I can see, those in authority are not about to take any measures whatsoever.

27 April 1848

A ship arrived from France with letters and newspapers. There have been differences of opinion within the committee on emancipation. Schoelcher and Perrinon wanted immediate emancipation, with indemnity to come later; but the others felt it would be dangerous to launch uneducated people into society without first establishing rules for work and conditions to prevent disorder. It appears that this last opinion prevailed and that Perrinon, displeased, had a letter that offended his colleagues inserted in the *Constitutionnel*. This circumstance may well prompt the government to abandon its plan of sending him to Martinique to proclaim emancipation. Aware of this circumstance, the men of color seem to be crestfallen. . . .

11. *Fusion*, a new expression, went beyond fraternization and would even include marriage. The policy of fusion preached by Bissette and Pécoul came to grief during the Second Empire [HF and LE].

12. It was not customary to pay cash, and to demand to be paid was considered insolence. In this case the insolence was no doubt caused by the fact that although the name of Le Pelletier de Saint-Rémy's son appeared on the posted proclamation, the father did not accept this evolution [HF and LE].

28 April 1848

As we were playing our hand of boston, the cannon announced the arrival of the packet boat, and shouts of joy immediately sounded from every side. The rabble filled the streets, and I had a terrible time reaching my lodgings, for it was pouring rain and the crowd was tightly packed. What is the news this packet has brought? I do not expect anything good.

29 April 1848

It was barely light when I was at the post office, where I did not find one letter for me. On the Place Bertin I met many merchants, men of all colors and shades of opinion. M. Meynier has been appointed attorney-general, M. Ardouin councillor at the royal tribunal, M. Papy king's attorney at Saint-Pierre.[13] M. Perrinon will arrive with his family by the first steamer available; that was the news. . . .

1 May 1848

Louis-Philippe in exile will remember that today is his name day and that, for seventeen years, France did not fail to celebrate it. May God forgive all the harm he and his family have done to France!

Nineteen bandits from Fort-Royal came to Saint-Pierre yesterday. They rebuked their fellows for missing the opportunity of committing murder and mayhem. It is known who they are, and the police are watching them.

[At a court hearing at Fort-Royal on 13 May, Dessalles's sale of the Nouvelle Cité plantation to his children is annulled. He immediately fires the manager de Gaalon and mulls over Nicaise's report on the situation at the plantation.]

15 May 1848

Yesterday I wrote to M. Michaud [former manager] to place the plantation under his care and to tell him to receive the keys from M. de Gaalon and have my room readied for me. I am planning to go up to the plantation at the end of the week. Nicaise has arrived from Sainte-Marie. He found my negroes well disposed, although some of them have very bizarre ideas. The mulatto Saint-

---

13. "Royal tribunal," "king's attorney," and even "Fort-Royal" were clearly misnomers, now that the Republic had been proclaimed, but Pierre Dessalles was slow to change his vocabulary. He also continued to refer to "my negro" and "my mulatto" long after emancipation had been declared.

Just, he tells me, means to rent the plantation and become its absolute master. Saturnin has gone in for all the progressive ideas of the moment and has assumed the leadership of the people of color in town. I think this young man will go overboard; I will not take any chances with him. It appears that even Philippe [the family's longtime cook] does not intend to stay with me and that he has said some very improper things.

16 May 1848

First thing in the morning, I received a letter from Durie [financial adviser] telling me that my brother's orders, received by the last steamer, instruct him to use sequestration, takeover, and expropriation [against me]. . . . So it is clear that he has decided to treat me without the least consideration. . . .

19 May 1848

The night, it is said, brings good counsel. Since I did not close an eye, I thought a lot about my affairs. Considering my brother's rather unfavorable disposition, I think it would not be wise to return to the plantation. Why should I go to all the trouble of organizing my association and the work it will do if I am to be chased off the place?

My domestics came from Sainte-Marie. Michaud writes that my negroes listened without much interest to what I had instructed him to tell them. They smiled and repeatedly said they were already free. Nicaise claims it will be very difficult to get any work out of them, but that I will be able to do it. M. de Gaalon misses the plantation; he is sick about leaving it. He has used his influence over the mulatto Saint-Just to make him conceive absurd and exaggerated hopes concerning the new arrangements that will be made on my plantation. This mulatto has muddled the ideas of my negroes, who have now become very difficult to handle.

21 May 1848

The streets are more congested than ever with negroes, who are running about in every direction. I went to see Duclary, who offers a pitiful sight; he has just returned from his plantation, where his negroes declared that they were free and refused to do any work. He lodged a complaint with M. Husson, but he will receive no response. The conduct of M. Rostolan is inconceivable; he compromises everything by his weakness.

22 May 1848

Very early in the morning I was awakened by a great popular commotion. I quickly dressed and went out with M. Turpin to see what had caused all this noise.

M. Léo Duchamp, having been threatened at knife-point by one of his negroes, reported the incident to the authorities, who jailed the negro. When the work gangs of neighboring plantations found out about this, they staged massive uprisings, armed themselves, and came to town demanding that their comrade be released. The authorities made a show of force, and M. Hervé at the head of the troops was just about to read the riot act when the mulatto Papy, as adjunct mayor, ordered the negro released. In several places, men of color ripped up the pavement. Some thought that this act of weakness would appease the population, but it only served to unleash more and more threats. "We want the heads of the whites," the people said aloud.

More than twenty thousand negroes crowded the streets, uttering the most horrible cries of fury. Anxiety was painted on every face. The night was what we all feared most. That awful night did come and with it the fire at the fort.[14] In this situation, Nicaise asked me what I wanted to do. "Let's find a ship," I told him.

Quick as lightning, he went off; ten minutes later he came back to tell me that Captain Deschappelles[15] was expecting me. Nicaise accompanied me to the shore, where I met Duclary and his family and many other persons. I jumped into a launch and a moment later was on board. The wind was blowing furiously. We spent the whole night on the bridge, deploring the fate of our poor Martinique and that of its unfortunate planters whom the government had delivered to the fury of the blacks and people of color. The fire was spreading in several directions in the Prêcheur and the Fort areas. We heard the ferocious shouting of the negroes. At ten o'clock we were told that M. Rostolan had arrived. Alas, we said, as if with one mind, this man is incapable, yet determined to remain in his post.

Day finally came; but what anxiety and what fatigue!

14. That is, the neighborhood of the fort at Saint-Pierre.
15. Captain Deschappelles had brought the author to Martinique in November 1847 (see above). He had also brought Mme Dessalles and her daughters in 1840 [HF and LE].

23 May 1848

I stayed on board all day. The other ships were just as full as the *Ballochant*. The day was spent bringing women and children on board. On one nearby ship I saw the Lagarigue ladies embarking. Visitors from the shore came to see us, and we learned of the horrors of the night: 34 persons locked in the house of M. de Sanois have been consumed by the flames (MM. Désabays father and son, Mme Désabays and five children, Mme Valton and two children, five Le Sueur daughters).[16] Atrocious things were said by the mulattoes. At Prêcheur a M. Dujon was massacred; plantations were put to the torch. M. Rostolan, calm as can be, called a meeting of his council. The men of color who belong to it gave him to understand that he would restore calm if he proclaimed emancipation. Consequently, amidst the most awful disorder, but with great pomp, emancipation was proclaimed. Rejoicing now took the place of rage; processions marched through the streets, and shouts of joy were heard: "Long Live Bissette! Long Live Perrinon! Long Live the Republic! Long Live Liberty!"

That is what we heard all day long. Gun and pistol fire was interspersed with these shouts. Never have I heard such noise! There are more than 300 of us on the *Ballochant*. What a night is ahead of us! Sad reflections on all sides, from every mouth. Children were crying from hunger or just from naughtiness. Women were weeping and bemoaning the fate of their children, their husbands, their parents; men of all ages had come on board for various reasons. . . . God! what a sight! Nicaise had arranged for me to have the quartermaster's hut [on deck], and I crawled into it early, missing my own bed. Captain Deschappelles was wonderful to everyone, but among those whom he obliged, I noticed many who acted without discretion.

---

16. Ever since the uprising of the Grand' Anse in 1833, in which the elder Désabays, at the time military commander of that town, played a major role, that name was anathema in the colored community. Moreover, the elder Désabays was in town to testify on this day, 23 May, in a law case against Pory Papy. Unfortunately, from the beginning of the troubles, he believed he would be safest in the Sanois house, where too many people were already living. As it happened, the people of color also loathed the name Sanois because of a militia colonel who bore it.

For these reasons, the rioters made for that house, where they had heard that the whites had assembled a weapons depot. The elder Désabays shot and killed one of the assailants—Michel Michay, 28 years old, a mattress-maker—prompting the rioters to set fire to the house. The arrival of the fire brigade was held up by the rioters.

Government troops in a state of alert were posted to avoid a massacre on the eve of the emancipation proclamation. The elder Le Sueur seems to have escaped, which is why only his wife and six children are mentioned. To be added are Ruire, his wife and three children, two women by the name of Fadat and Blaye, someone named Laserre, and some ten domestics of color. This would account for 36 victims [HF and LE].

24 May 1848

A letter from M. Michaud informs me that M. de Gaalon called the negroes together and told them that the plantation no longer belonged to me. I decided to go into town to seek advice about what to do. I did not meet any business advisors. All law offices are closed, all shops boarded up. The streets are full of shouting and screaming negroes who stop all passers-by and force them to shout, "Long Live the Republic! Long Live Liberty!"

The women in particular are rabid; one has to shake hands with all of them. Everyone has a long face; when meeting someone of one's own kind, one almost does not dare speak to him. Tricolor flags are hanging from every window. One is supposed to wear three ribbons in one's buttonhole, and those who do not have them are forced by the populace to put them on. M. Rostolan's conduct makes everyone indignant.

27 May 1848

Two of my former negroes [i.e., ex-slaves] came from Sainte-Marie to see me. They told me what M. de Gaalon has done. This impertinent character already made certain propositions to the negroes; he offered four gourdes to those of the field gang and three gourdes to those of the little gang [which does lighter work], plus all day off on Saturday. Such an arrangement would be ruinous; one could not possibly carry it out. Clearly, his aim was to annoy me. I will send Nicaise to Sainte-Marie, thereby taking possession of the plantation.

29 May 1848

We have good news from Guadeloupe: emancipation has been proclaimed there in the greatest tranquillity, and it appears that the negroes are making arrangements with the owners. . . .

30 May 1848

Nicaise left by himself at five o'clock this morning. A rumor is circulating that the negroes will set fire to the town, for they want to pillage and steal. There was pillaging at the house of M. Simonnet of Lamentin, whose money and silverware were taken. The government keeps quiet and by its silence seems to condone everything. It is asserted that at Robert, a demoiselle Osier-Bellevue was raped by forty of these criminals. More and more people are emigrating. Turpin came to tell me that I have been designated as the first person to have his throat cut at the first scuffle. . . . I went to consult some trustworthy persons, and they believe that before I decide to leave this country, I must go to my plantation and establish some kind of arrangement with my negroes. I will therefore leave by boat tomorrow [sailing around the island], especially if the news from Nicaise is good. . . .

31 May 1848

. . . It was not Mlle Osier-Bellevue who was raped, but rather a lady named Coquelin de l'Isle, and instead of forty, only ten negroes made her suffer this outrage. One does not feel quite so sorry for her, since she has already had intimate relations with men of these two classes. When 200 free blacks swarmed out all over the countryside in order to pillage, M. Husson at the head of an imposing force went out to meet them. Thirty were arrested and taken to the Fort-Royal jail. The officers of the regiment of Fort-de-France[17] wanted to depose M. Rostolan, whose weakness has compromised everything. This man may well boast of having lost the colony. . . .

2 June 1848

The Duchamp family and M. Raynal left for New York. Many others are emigrating as well, and the situation is deteriorating. It appears that the negroes are arming themselves and that the ringleaders are coordinating their projects. Not a word from Nicaise. It seems that there is unrest in the district of Sainte-Marie. M. Octave La Peyre, who came to see me, told me that his brother Dorval disappeared last Sunday and that no one knows what has become of him. The negroes of Prêcheur have let all the whites know that they should leave if they do not want to be slaughtered. Everyone has left, even the parish priest. . . .

One of Lagarigue's negroes has told Adée that my negroes do not want me and that they want to keep M. de Gaalon. It is evident that this dreadful person has used his position to win the hearts and minds of my negroes.

3 June 1848

Today a horrible scene took place at the fort: to commemorate 3 June 1790,[18] the populace wanted to hang a white man. They first picked the physician

---

17. When the Republic was proclaimed, Fort-Royal once again became Fort-de-France, but the force of habit often makes the author forget to use the new name [HF and LE].

18. On 3 June 1790, which that year was Corpus-Christi Day, the "patriots" of Saint-Pierre had perpetrated a horrendous massacre of men of color. See *Historique des troubles survenus à la Martinique pendant la Révolution* by Pierre Régis Dessalles, the author's father. The elder Dessalles attempted, at the risk of his life, to save a few of the prisoners that the populace wanted to kill [HF and LE]. The "populace" in 1848 was clearly different from the "populace" in 1790; that of 1790 was white.

Rufz,[19] but when some people pointed out that his skill is useful to the public, he was spared. A M. Prévoteau happened to come by; he was arrested and already had the rope around his neck when a young man of color had him released.[20] The guilty parties have been arrested and procedures are being initiated.

At half-past three, word came that the steam frigate carrying M. Perrinon was about to land. Flags immediately appeared at the windows, and the forts and the outer harbor prepared to greet the government commissioner. Ferocious joy burst out everywhere; never have I heard such a racket. I went for a walk on the Desnots Battery, where groups of people were discussing the day's events. There are differing opinions about the intentions of the new governor who, in my opinion, will find it difficult to restore order. Papy, Alfred Agnès, and Meynier have been asked by Perrinon to go immediately to Fort-Royal. The latter two have obeyed, but the first is needed too much at Saint-Pierre and has stayed.

4 June 1848

M. Husson, we hear, has been removed from his post because of his proclamation to the negroes; this document displeased Schoelcher, who had declared that the negroes were civilized enough to be given their freedom. Papy, who was designated as Husson's successor, has refused because he wants to preserve his popularity. He wants to become mayor of Saint-Pierre and a national representative. The men of color are divided; Papy is of the Bissette party, Alfred Agnès of the Perrinon party. The latter is upset that freedom was proclaimed before his arrival. Meynier was bold enough to tell him that the prettiest feather was pulled out of his cap.

I finally heard from Nicaise. He informs me that my negroes no longer want me and that they only want M. de Gaalon. They received Nicaise very badly, telling him to get off the plantation if he wanted to stay alive. Nicaise responded very well. M. de Gaalon declared that he would not hand over the plantation until he was paid in full and until he had seen the court verdict. On Friday evening, when he had heard from Valmenier, he consented to hand over the plantations [the Nouvelle Cité and the Caféière]. Nicaise therefore seized the two properties, and M. de Gaalon, having caused terrible disorder, was obliged to go to Fort-Royal. . . .

I told [Louis Littée] about the decrees that are being printed at this mo-

19. Dr. Etienne Rufz, member of the municipal council of Saint-Pierre, who favored immediate abolition [HF and LE].

20. It appears that this action was purely symbolic, but it did create an uproar [HF and LE].

ment; since landowners do not owe land or a cabin to their former slaves, the latter might just as well leave their erstwhile masters. I wrote to Nicaise to do his best and to send me the names of all those who are willing to accept Association, so that I can draw up a contract that I would send him so he can sign it in the presence of the authorities.

[On 6 June the commissioner of the Republic, M. Perrinon, formally enters Saint-Pierre, accompanied by his family, General Rostolan, the apostolic prefect, and a "numerous escort." "I want to see work and order," he declares, "and to obtain them I will make use of all the means that have been entrusted to me." Dessalles is impressed.]

6 June 1848

With one voice, everyone praises the noble heart of M. Perrinon. When I find good breeding and noble sentiments in a man, whatever his color, I like to honor him.[21]

The town was illuminated, and the rabble obstructed the streets, yelling "Long Live Perrinon, Long Live Bissette."

8 June 1848

Nicaise writes me a most satisfying letter: my negroes are clamoring for my return. . . .

10 June 1848

Yesterday M. Perrinon went to Prêcheur and harangued the negroes, who gave him an enthusiastic reception. When speaking of the events of 22 and 23 May, he broke into sobs and was unable to continue. Recovered from this strong emotion, he said, "Let us draw a veil over these sad scenes." Then he urged his audience to resume work as soon as possible.

Lagarigue and Saint-Isle seem to favor Association [a kind of revenue-sharing arrangement with the ex-slaves]; they feel that it would be very important for all landowners to adopt the same system. M. Rémy,[22] the new Director of the Interior, is to go to all communities to help the planters. MM. Maillet, Borde, and several other planters went to see the commissioner-general and were very satisfied with the interview.

21. By 20 August Dessalles had changed his mind; Perrinon was now a "communist mulatto."
22. Jean Joseph Rémy-Neris, 35 years old, a man of color, doctor of medicine, and member of the Saint-Pierre municipal council [HF and LE].

"Messieurs," he told them, "I will employ all possible means of gentle persuasion on the new citizens. If these do not succeed, I shall make use of all the powers that have been entrusted to me. As for troublemakers and those who give pernicious advice, I shall find them, even if they were hiding in mouse holes, and I will know how to punish them."

I only hope that it will not be too much for him! Already the people of color are beginning to grumble, and one even hears that the most rebellious among them claim they will know how to bring him to heel if he does not behave.

14 June 1848

[Dessalles finally returns to his plantation.]

... It was painful to see this plantation again, for it brought back sad memories. As soon as I am able to leave it, I will be happy to do so. The good subjects of my plantation came to present their respects; those who had been won over by M. de Gaalon and who had declared that they did not want me hesitated to come to greet me. I acted as if I knew nothing about what has happened here. Several are asking to work for wages, but I explained that this was impossible. I announced that on Saturday I would make them propositions that they could take or leave. Tomorrow I will give them an ox and pay a fiddler, and they seemed to be satisfied.[23]

17 June 1848

Three men of color—Regis, Thimothée,[24] and Castandet—called on me, and I could not avoid shaking hands with them. Louis Littée[25] sent for my horse and came to have lunch with me. He was present when I made my offers to the negroes. I explained as best I could the system of Association, and I made it clear to them that wages would not give them a secure position, while the system of Association would, as long as they adhered to the established conditions. If they were paid a wage, one could fire them at any time. The mayor, Saint-Just, and other workers joined me in making them understand what advantages

23. It was traditional to provide for a celebration when the master or an important member of his family returned to the plantation after an absence [HF and LE].

24. Régis, called Régis Luce, born circa 1780 and freed in 1823 under Governor Donzelot. Thimothée (whose name seems to be Plainval), born circa 1778, was a mechanic who repaired mills; he was the brother of Saturnin's mother-in-law, Mme Cognet, of whom a great deal will be heard in the 1850s. Recall that in 1838 Dessalles had agreed to take the mechanic's son, Norbert Thimothée, to France for his schooling (see chapter 5) [HF and LE].

25. Apparently Louis Littée is still the mayor of Sainte-Marie.

they would have. All our efforts were in vain. In the end they did say that they would accept if Perrinon urged them to do so. Louis Littée therefore wrote a letter to the commissioner-general; Nicaise will take it to him tomorrow. A little Creole,[26] Louis Igou, had lunch with us and listened to all my propositions. I could see right away that he was not going to leave. They are so indiscreet and tiresome, these little Creoles! . . .

19 June 1848

Nicaise came back at ten o'clock in the evening. M. Perrinon received him extremely well. This government leader approves of Association by halves [in other words, sharecropping] and is opposed to wages, which are reminiscent of slavery. Meanwhile, nothing is done to make the negro go to work. The position of the landowners is horrible. . . . M. Prunier [a prospective new manager?] told me that a dragoon of Sainte-Marie, a man of color who had given pernicious advice to the workers, has been arrested at Gros-Morne and taken to Fort-Royal. It is clear that, without the people of color, our negroes would have behaved well. Montrose Magloire is one of those suspected of having given malicious advice; what makes one believe this is that he refused to serve on the committee appointed to make the rounds of the plantations for the purpose of persuading the negroes to go to work.

21 June 1848

This morning, in the presence of Saint-Just and Nicaise, I finished drawing up the sectioning of my land and the articles of Association.[27] My negroes are not talking. I am determined to go to Fort-Royal tomorrow to consult M. Perrinon. The state of anxiety in which the freedmen are now living will take a bad turn.

24 June 1848

We are preparing to start work on Monday. Saint-Just already has 33 workers, Nicaise has no more than five; but by this evening more will no doubt show up. . . .

---

26. What we would call "poor white."
27. See appendix A to this chapter for excerpts of these articles.

26 June 1848

The negroes have cut cane all day long, but the work went very slowly. Saint-Just is being patient. When Nicaise heard some of the field hands talk about a second Association,[28] he decided to quit, so that now Saint-Just alone is in charge of the work.

[There was still a dispute about the ownership of the cabins and garden plots on the plantation. Dessalles hoped that it could be resolved by a public commission denying the ex-slaves any claim to their cabins and garden plots. This would permit the owner to charge rent for them.]

28 June 1848

Louis Littée came at ten o'clock. We were finishing lunch when the commission appointed to talk to the negroes arrived. It consisted of Numa Littée, Sully Rosier, and Ernest Cesilia [the last two were men of color]. I received the group cordially and without affectation. The two men of color seemed to be satisfied. When the negroes were assembled, the commission spoke to them, but they were not interested in any of their proposals. In the end the commissioner-general will decide the matter.

4 July 1848

One of my former slaves came to ask me to get him a doctor for his wife.[29] I replied that I could no longer commit myself to paying the slightest sum, but that, if the ex-slave workers were to guarantee me the payment of the doctor's visit, I would call him. They want to keep all the conveniences of slavery and reject all the burdens that come with freedom.

14 July 1848

. . . M. de Lorge, bailiff at Trinité, came to notify me of the court order confirming the verdict annulling the sale [of the plantation] to my children. . . . M. de Lorge spoke to me of a letter from Bissette that will be published in the colony's newspapers, saying that he [Bissette] is distressed that his name is being used as a flag. He urges everyone to let bygones be bygones; to prove that he himself has forgotten, he says that he has frequented the son of M. de Lucy and shaken hands with my son, both of them children of two members of the

---

28. It was not a second Association but only a second team within the Association [HF and LE].

29. Under article 8 of the Association the worker was entitled to this service, but the act had not yet been signed [HF and LE].

court who had condemned him to death [in 1823]. I feel sorry for my poor son if he indeed had to shake hands with Bissette.

[Commissioner-General Perrinon comes to the district to explain the system of Association.]

15 July 1848

. . . At nine o'clock we were at Saint-Jacques; a high mass was sung. A half-hour later Perrinon emerged from the church, accompanied by three or four work gangs. I wanted to cut through the crowd to see him but had to give up. I finally reached him at ten o'clock. I spoke to him briefly, and he answered politely. I talked to him about my contract and about letters concerning work and Association, which I had submitted to the mayor. I was not exactly bowled over by his response; he said he was only passing through Sainte-Marie and would have to study the matter in greater detail. I confess that his entourage frightens me; nothing but mulattoes and negroes everywhere, it is really repulsive. M. Pory Papy came toward me, looking very jaunty. I did not know him, but he held out his hand. I asked him with whom I had the honor of speaking; he gave his name. I could not refrain from telling him that this was the first time I was speaking to him.

I went down to town, where M. Perrinon arrived at three o'clock. He spoke for two hours, explaining the system of Association to the workers; all the work gangs were present. I saw that my negroes listened very carefully to everything M. Perrinon was saying, but I do not dare hope that things will go better. Before I saw M. Perrinon, I had a high opinion of him, but today I think quite differently. I now see him as a man completely given over to the mulattoes, although I am not sure of his motives; either he is afraid of them and wants to curry favor, or he shares their hatred for the whites. The fact that he agreed to dine at Montrose Magloire's, the composition of the guests there — all of this does not give me a very positive idea of his sentiments. The casualness with which he treats the fears people express to him strikes me as inappropriate; after all, May 22 and 23 are not very far behind us. . . .

The curé, with whom I came back to town, told me that at M. Thénos de Gage's, where M. Perrinon dined yesterday, he had expressed the wish to have at table next to him one of the plantation's negroes. M. de Gage turned a deaf ear. When the request was repeated, he replied that he had been asked to give this dinner and that it was not a political banquet.[30] Moreover, he could not

30. For which the guests paid. Political banquets were the rage in France in the 1840s. Attended by middle-class men, they dramatized political issues. Reform banquets sparked the Revolution of

possibly seat at the same table his wife and one of his former slaves. Since he had no intention of continuing this kind of fusion, he did not even want to start it. So M. Perrinon was obliged to give up this bizarre idea. All of this does not speak well for the commissioner-general. When I reached home, I was glad to have gotten out of such a black population.

16 July 1848

. . . This evening Césaire came to tell me that I had been mistaken, that he had heard M. Perrinon state positively that if there was a parting of the ways between the landowner and the worker, the latter would have the right to keep his cabin and his garden plot for three months. I tried to prove to him that he had misunderstood, but he insisted and so I said no more. Then he told me that his wife no longer worked on the plantation. "In that case," I said, "she will not get a garden plot." Thereupon he loudly protested and added that I did owe her a plot.[31] So now I shall have to bother M. Perrinon and ask him to make these awful negroes understand reason. This country seems very, very sick to me; if the system of government does not change soon, whites will not be able to stay here much longer. . . .

17 July 1848

First thing in the morning I wrote to M. Bontemps, secretary-archivist of the government, asking him to report on Césaire's claim to M. Perrinon. As soon as my letter was written, Nicaise and Saint-Just were to go with this negro to see the governor, but the latter declared that he would only go with me. Not feeling well, I said that I could not ride a horse. At this instant all the negroes, called from their work by Césaire, came into my courtyard. I heard them murmuring from afar, then Nicaise and Saint-Just informed me that they did not want to continue working. I stepped forward and asked them why they had stopped. "It's Césaire," they said. "He came to warn us that you are only going to give us ten square meters [*trois pas*][32] of ground for our plots." I calmly explained

---

1848. Transferred to a multiracial society, this form of political organization could sharpen racial tensions.

31. Under articles 2, 4, and 17 of the Contract of Association, Césaire's wife was not entitled to a plot. As for the delay within which a dismissed worker had to vacate, it was not stipulated in the contract of the Nouvelle Cité, but it was eight days in certain other contracts, such as that of the Dubuc-Dubuffet plantation. These contracts, however, were signed later, in April 1849 [HF and LE].

32. That is, about 10 square meters instead of the 1,000 stipulated in article 4.

Césaire's claims and my intentions. There were more murmurs, and I heard some of them saying in a low voice that they did not want me to be involved at all[33] and that they would only obey Saint-Just. "Speak up," I said, "so that I can hear and understand you!"

Thereupon, brandishing their machetes and all roaring at once in horrible tones, they repeated that they did not want me because I had left orders to kill them, as they had been told by M. de Gaalon. In a stentorian voice, I declared that they would all leave the plantation before they saw me agree to an act of weakness, that they ought to know me, and that I was not afraid of them. I gave orders to have my horses saddled and told them that they would have to follow me. A half-hour after this dreadful scene, I was in the saddle, followed by Nicaise, Saint-Just, and all the negroes. At two o'clock I arrived in the court-yard of the mayor of Trinité, M. Eleuthère, and explained the situation to the commissioner-general. "Where is this M. de Gaalon?" he asked me. "I will have him arrested." I did not fail to tell him that this wretch had caused me a great deal of trouble. "Where is he?" he asked again. "He has gone off to France," I replied.

M. Perrinon and M. Eleuthère received me in the most courteous manner. Everyone was very anxious to please me. I met Edouard Fortier and some other planters who, like myself, had come to seek help for their problems. M. Perrinon spoke forcefully to my negroes, once again explaining to them their rights and mine, and stating that, if they did not improve their behavior, he would be seriously angry. . . .

18 July 1848

The negroes have resumed their work this morning; it is going as slowly as it possibly can.

19 July 1848

. . . At lunchtime I heard the negroes grumble; they seem discontented, and several said they were going to ask me for land that they could work in groups of ten. I pretended not to hear them.

---

33. They wanted him to respect articles 3 and 13, which provided for no more than "general supervision" of the landowner [HF and LE].

24 July 1848

My mulatto Philippe [the cook] came to find out about errands at Fort-Royal. I rebuked him for his behavior since emancipation and gave him a letter for my daughter. Because Saint-Just has been insulted by a young negro by the name of Charlery, I wrote to Louis Littée, asking him to notify Charlery, as well as his mother and five other individuals, that they have to leave my plantation. We can no longer put up with this; there is a constant stream of horrible talk and insults. He [Littée] gave them until Saturday to leave the premises [this is Tuesday].[34]

25 July 1848

Two negresses whom Littée ordered off the plantation came to see me and cried so hard that I was foolish enough to let myself be moved. I am pleased to see that the mayor's [i.e., Littée's] decision has had a salutary effect. The negroes were more conscientious today. My contract is not being ratified; this is becoming tiresome. I sent Louis Littée the covering letter he must write to the governor.

26 July 1848

The workers sent a messenger to M. Perrinon to find out whether they must pay the freight and the commission for the sugar assigned to them.[35] The governor had already pronounced himself through M. Bontemps, whose letter I have. I never saw such recalcitrant negroes; their constant quibbling must be very tiresome to the authorities. As for me, I have had it up to here!

Jean-Bart [former slave, a mechanic] went to see M. Mont-Fleury [a man of color, manager of the state-owned Saint-Jacques plantation and the labor commissioner] and told him a pack of lies. Among other things, he said that he was given only until Saturday to leave his cabin and harvest his foodstuff. M. Mont-Fleury believed him and gave him a paper asking me to give him a month to harvest his foodstuff. I had already given him two months and even more, so this consultation will prove quite costly to him. These people!

M. Mont-Fleury, the labor commissioner, came this morning. Together we went over the act of Association that is to keep my former slaves working. At

---

34. Under article 13, ex-slaves can now be dismissed from the plantation with the consent of the *conseil des prud'hommes* [workers' council]. In this case, Dessalles appears to have circumvented this body by appealing to his friend Littée, the mayor of Sainte-Marie.

35. This is a matter of interpreting article 14. The author is correct [HF and LE].

two o'clock we called all the workers together; they listened to the reading of this piece, which three-fourths of them did not understand at all. Such shouting, such insults! In the end they accepted everything; tomorrow morning they are to appoint their workers' council [or *conseil des prud'hommes*]. My head is swimming. . . .

28 July 1848

. . . Saint-Just has gone to Saint-Pierre; he charged me 1,800 francs for his work. I had 22 hogsheads of sugar loaded onto M. Simonneau's ship, one-fourth for the workers, three-fourths for me.[36]

4 August 1848

First thing in the morning I wrote to M. Mont-Fleury, asking him to be present when I distribute the sum of money I owe my workers, but he was not there. I am bothered by the reading lessons Saturnin is giving on the plantation. This young mulatto always has a newspaper in his hands and goes from cabin to cabin. . . .

5 August 1848

I spent all morning counting out the money from the sugar sold by Saint-Just; what a bore! The workers had to share 818 francs; that is not very much, and I am afraid they will lose interest.

In addition to charging the 1,800 francs, which I have given to him, Saint-Just also brought me a small bill for some wheelwright work. I will be as patient as I can possibly be, but I do not believe that things can go on like this for too long. Ernest too brought me a bill for some minor jobs. It is just a small sign of things to come.

[When the first elections for the National Assembly under universal male suffrage take place in August 1848, Dessalles and his white friends agree to vote for a specific slate of white candidates. Stories that the local authorities (mostly men of color) are coercing the "new freedmen" (i.e., ex-slaves) to vote for candidates of color are circulating.]

36. This was called for by a transitional article of the act of Association: "The cane presently on the plantation shall become part of the partnership; however, the workers will only be entitled to one fourth of the cane presently ready to harvest." This article is justified since, at the time when this cane was planted and growing, the workers were entirely maintained at the expense of the plantation. But this too was to become a source of conflict [HF and LE].

7 August 1848

. . . Louis Littée and the curé came to see me. Littée wanted to consult me about something that happened to him. One of his negroes, he said, was stopped in town by two men of color who asked to see his voting card. He gave it to them, and Eugène Yotte inscribed on it the names of Bissette, Schoelcher, Pory Papy, France, and Mazouline.[37] Somewhat taken aback, the negro showed his astonishment. At this point, the younger Zozo pulled from his pocket a letter and said, "Listen to what the governor writes: he recommends that the new freedmen name the five individuals designated above if they do not want to run the risk of seeing the election of a general who would come here with a white flag and reestablish slavery."

The negro lost no time telling Louis Littée about this incident. Abbé Jeune-homme [the curé] is of the opinion that we should keep quiet about this, for it might expose Louis Littée to cruel vengeance. I share this opinion. But this is what we are reduced to by the critical position into which we have been cast.

9 August 1848

At ten o'clock I went to town; there was a huge crush of people at the town hall. Thanks to the mayor, I was able to enter by a back door and placed my ballot into the urn. Robert Littée informed me that the men of color of Fort-Royal declared they would force the whites to vote with them. Consequently, M. Perrinon has landed 500 sailors in case there is trouble. I immediately returned to the plantation, where M. Mont-Fleury joined me shortly thereafter, and we went to work. . . . We distributed to fifty of the workers the money to which they are entitled. They uttered cries of indignation as they were paid, and some even intimated that they had been robbed.[38] My head is throbbing; I am sorry that I involved myself in this distribution and will never do it again. M. Mont-Fleury does not display sufficient firmness; he looks as if he were humoring them.

---

37. To explain this episode: It had been decided on 27 April 1848 that the vote would be secret. But because of the large number of voters, the ballots could be filled out in advance instead of being written out in the presence of the election board. Illiterate voters, meaning most of the former slaves, therefore asked the supporters of their candidate to help them [HF and LE].

38. There were 80 altogether. Their indignation is understandable, for it was not clear whether they were to receive a fourth, a third before expenses, or a full half of the proceeds; nor was there any mention of the price of sugar, which was very low. It is not easy to unravel these issues [HF and LE].

14 August 1848

Robert Littée brought me the *Courrier de la Martinique*, which discouraged me. It seems that the question of indemnity has been treated [in the National Assembly] and that we will get only 500 to 600 francs[39] per head of negro between six and sixty years and that half of that sum will have to go to the creditors, while the other half would be paid only as long as the workers are employed. This is a dreadful spoliation. But how could we expect anything else from people who have no understanding of colonial affairs. . . .

16 August 1848

. . . [We have just learned] that M. Perrinon has been recalled and that all appointments in this colony have been nullified. The credo he had published in Guadeloupe has undone him in public opinion. Troops and a new governor will be here soon. This news has been a very great pleasure to me.

[On 18 August, the workers of the Nouvelle Cité plantation finally accept the contract, not without voicing a specific demand for a foreman to replace Saint-Just, who has gone to see his brother in Guadeloupe. Dessalles rejects these demands; clearly, there will be more trouble.]

20 August 1848

. . . I picked up the *Courrier* and read it to M. Prunier in its entirety. M. Perrinon's creed is quoted in full. . . . The commissioner-general now proves as clearly as possible that he is nothing but a communist mulatto and the agent of that criminal Schoelcher. He did not expect such publicity. I think he is finished. . . .

I worried all evening about what happened to Louis Le Vassor on election day. When two or three of his negroes showed him their ballots, he told them that they had voted for incompetent men who would not be good for the country and because of whom the sugar of the Union plantation would not sell as well. They went to see the mulattoes in town and blamed them for this choice. When Louis went down to town, fifteen men of color surrounded him and told him that he had insulted them. "I did?" said Le Vassor. "Yes," they replied, "you said to your workers that we had betrayed them by writing the names of Bissette, Schoelcher, Pory Papy, France, and Masuline on their ballots." "I told these new freedmen that these men were not suitable; that is my opinion, and at a time when everyone has the right to state his opinions publicly, I did not

39. This was half of what they expected [HF and LE].

mince my words. In short, gentlemen, if you feel offended, I apologize, I deeply apologize. Will this satisfy you?"

They said "yes" and Le Vassor walked away. Today they are bragging that M. Le Vassor apologized to them, adding that it was a good thing for him, because otherwise they would have buried him the next day. I can't get over it!

23 August 1848

The sun had been on the *morne* for 35 minutes when the workers came to work. I reminded Saturnin that he should be on the spot in order to write down the absentees. Instead of one hour, they take an hour and a half for lunch. The negresses in particular display an affected insolence. They parade up and down before you without saying anything and disdainfully look at you until you get mad, then they pour out the most biting insults. The more time passes, the less I think that work will resume. The mulattoes are getting the better of us. When the horn was sounded for the two o'clock shift, the workers did not come out of their cabins until three. This evening the representatives of the workers' council came to complain about this irregularity and about the insolence of Joséphine, who does not want to take orders from anybody and who stands in the field leaning on her hoe without doing anything. I told them that it was up to them to call a meeting of the workers' council and to get rid of all those who do not work and who behave insolently. They seemed determined to do just that.

30 August 1848

This morning Saturnin came in, swaggering insolently and with his hat on his head to tell me that the negroes want him to be their *économe* or sub-manager.[40] If I agreed, he would promise to run the plantation. I showed him my astonishment and thanked him for his services. I asked him to do his uncle's [Saint-Just's] job until his return, then I will decide what I want to do. He informed me that he had found someone else to take over his school. I said that he should not have done this without my permission. He said that he knows the law as well as I do and that he would not get into any trouble. I confess that I needed all my reason not to get mad. I did, however, remind him that four years ago he was my slave and that his tone was improper. This young mulatto is lost, and what he has done hurts me terribly. . . .

---

40. This was a revolutionary stance; the hat was a symbol of great importance, and the post of *économe* or sub-manager was usually reserved for whites only [HF and LE].

11 September 1848

First thing in the morning Césaire and Charles came to tell me that the work gang no longer wanted Saint-Just. I said that this was fine, that he would work for me and I would pay him. They added that they did not want him to supervise the work and take attendance.[41] I told them that since I am the main manager of my property, they would not dictate whom I take as sub-managers, that they would obey those I hired, and that otherwise, they would leave the plantation. At noon Man [a female worker of a certain standing, former mistress of de Gaalon] stopped the mill, declaring that they would now enjoy the noon hour. La Disette, who just then arrived with the mule drivers, declared that this would not do, turned the water for the mill back on, and began loading it. This spontaneous action made those who had abandoned their work change their minds.

Joséphine said horrible things and incited her fellow workers to disorderly conduct. At a quarter past six I went down to my sugar buildings and asked how many vats [*grandes*] of cane juice [*vésou*] had been made. "Not even four," replied M. Michaud and Saint-Just. I reprimanded the negroes for their slowness and tried to make them understand that things would never work out unless the contract was executed and that they could quit if they were not satisfied. My words seemed to have made some impression; but at this point, Philibert joined the group and told them that they were stupid. During slavery, he said they had not been afraid of anything, and now that they were free, he was surprised to see them tremble. Shouting now broke out, with Man yelling at the top of her voice and Robert saying that machetes would soon come into play. Gustave clacked a whip and playfully asked one of his comrades to give him a few lashes. The mill and the boiler were shut down. . . .

[In the days following this incident, Dessalles summons both the mayor (Louis Littée) and the labor-commissioner (Mont-Fleury) to his plantation to reason with the workers. Dessalles hopes that some of the ringleaders will be removed from the plantation by a court order (see 27 September). For the moment, he feels there is some improvement in the work habits.

Meanwhile, he learns that Perrinon has nominated him as a candidate to the municipal council; but when he finds out that his "presence would be offensive to the black population," he declines to accept the nomination. He is confirmed in his decision when he hears the words of a crowd of women assembled in front of the town hall: "What do these whites want, anyway? We have no use

41. Under the contract, this was indeed the job of the foreman, who was elected by the workers, and not of a sub-manager. To understand the subsequent events, see article 6 of the contract [HF and LE].

for them here; there are more than enough men of color, the country belongs to us" (24 September). An improvement for Dessalles's private life appears on the horizon when his old servant Adée Maximin, alias Telcide, comes to see him.]

21 September 1848

... Adée Maximin arrived from Gros-Morne. I had not seen her for a long time and so felt a strong emotion when I embraced her [sic]. She is still beautiful, although changed. But what pleased me most was to see that she still has the same perfect attitude and the same admirable devotion to my person. If my fate were decided, I would take her with me.

27 September 1848

The work continues to go very badly; at half past two a gendarme came to tell me that M. Joannet[42] would come with armed police and that he had dismissed 21 workers from the Limbé plantation. I called the workers together; at half-past three the president of the tribunal [Joannet] arrived. I talked to him, telling him about the disorder that exists, and he took note of everything. He addressed the negroes, reprimanding them for their laziness. He dismissed Césaire, Man, Joséphine, Clète, Isaac, Gustave, Philibert, Tobie, and Robert. The rest of the work gang seemed stunned and unhappy. The negro Charles in particular looked indignant. This M. Joannet speaks well, he has self-assurance and great firmness. I received him with all the courtesy called for.

[Adrien is on his way to Martinique. For the first time we hear about his illegitimate daughter, Palmire, who will become a great source of dissension between father and son.]

4 October 1848

To my great astonishment, M. Durieu [a financial adviser] arrived here. At first I gave him a very cold reception, but he was so friendly that in the end I did speak to him. My brother has given orders to pursue me legally, but he thinks it is more advantageous for everyone if we come to an arrangement. Here is what I propose: an annual income of 3,000 francs, the Caféière and ten carrés [31 acres] around it for my lifetime use, plus eight carrés with full property rights, the ratification of a sale made to Nicaise,[43] and all my furniture here and in France. Durieu is going to see Valmenier and will report back promptly.

42. Dessalles refers to Joannet as "royal judge," giving him a title that no longer exists [HF and LE].

43. Profiting from the presence of the lawyer who drew up the contract for the Association,

[Starting on 30 October, Nicaise directs the work of the plantation; he intends to be "very severe," but only 18 workers report to the field.]

15 November 1848

Saint-Isle sent me the last issue of the *Antilles*,[44] which reports the resignation of Bissette and has a long article expressing the indignation and the surprise of the editors. It is announced that Bissette will be in the colony in a month; he is coming with Pécoul, who seems to have won him over. The mulattoes of the town are all upset, and they are trying to stir up the new freedmen. A mulatto by the name of Beaubrun reportedly said that, if the blacks did not do what they [the mulattoes] want, they would push them back into slavery. . . .

24 November 1848

Yesterday the gendarmes came to close the school. This is an excellent measure, for all the bad advice is due to these wretched rogues of the town who had fanned out all over the countryside on the pretext of teaching the negroes to read. I went down to my sugar buildings; Nicaise was angry with the negroes who started the mill very late and work incredibly slowly. I believe that they are being secretly manipulated.

5 December 1848

Against my advice, Nicaise wanted to distribute the money received for the syrups during the noon break; of course, this interfered with the work. These kinds of distribution should only take place on the workers' time, on Saturday and Sunday. Charles refused to hand over his work book,[45] but Nicaise made it clear to him that he would get his money only if he submitted to this condition. Gustave followed his example. La Disette and Desbattes first wanted to do likewise, but then did submit. This refusal on the part of Charles is particularly improper because he is a member of the workers' council. That is why, if he does not obey, I will go to court. . . .

Dessalles had sold a piece of land, less than two hectares [4.8 acres] in size, to Nicaise. This piece of land was not part of the plantation, but had been purchased separately by the author in 1828 [HF and LE].

44. Biweekly paper founded in 1842 by Carles [HF and LE].
45. A booklet used to keep track of a worker's hours and wages [HF and LE].

15 December 1848

This evening I received a letter from the Director of the Interior asking, on behalf of the governor, for my opinion on several very important matters. I will give my response right away [see Appendix B, in this chapter].

20 December 1848

The negro Youcar left the plantation with his wife and went to work for Mme de la Salle.[46]

31 December 1848

. . . Dieudonné came to bring me a letter from Adrien, informing me that he has arrived. I immediately had the horses to fetch him readied, and Nicaise insisted on taking them to him. This news has moved me greatly. Far from my children, it is a consolation to me to see the arrival of the one who has never denied the family ties. I must hope that harmony will be reborn. But I consider it impossible, for my soul has been too badly bruised to forget soon what I have been made to suffer. The negroes danced until midnight. Adée sent me a superb New Year's present, which I accepted; she also sent Louis Le Vassor some fruit of outstanding beauty.

46. Landowners who could pay were beginning to compete for workers. Youcar was the first to leave Dessalles voluntarily; contrary to expectations, there was no large-scale migration to the towns [HF and LE].

Appendix A

Excerpts of the Articles of Association for the Dessalles Plantation (1848)

Article 2: The assets brought to the partnership by the workers consist of each individual's labor and diligence. The assets brought by the proprietor consist of the use by the Partnership [*Société*] of the plantation's land, agricultural buildings, workers' cabins, utensils, and farming implements. . . . Consequently, all these objects will remain the exclusive property of citizen Pierre Dessalles, and the Partnership will have their use only as long as [the present contract] remains in effect. The dwelling and all its dependencies are not included in the Partnership.

Article 3: The proprietor will be the sole administrator of the plantation and the ultimate director of its operations, either in person or through a manager or representative of his choice. He will be assisted in this task by a foreman [*chef de l'atelier*] to be elected by the workers.

Article 4: The workers will keep, as in the past, and for as long as they are members of the Partnership, the use of their cabins and their gardens . . . which are not to exceed 10 ares [0.24 acres].

Article 5: [Although traditionally the workers were not given Saturday off during the harvest,] the workers assume the obligation of devoting the first five days of each week to the work of the plantation. . . . The workers will have the free use of Saturdays, holidays, and Sundays. . . .

Article 6: It is expressly agreed upon that in exceptional circumstances, work will be performed on Saturday for the cutting of cane and the manufacture of sugar under the express condition that this day will be repaid to the workers during the following week. . . . During the actual sugarmaking [*roulaison*], work in the mill and the sugar house will never be interrupted for meals. Workers will take turns eating and will immediately return to work in such a manner that the work will not suffer. The nine-hour day ends at sundown.

Article 8: Workers belonging to the Partnership who become ill will seek care and treatment at their own expense at the plantation's hospital. Not included in this expense are the cost of the physician and the medications, which will continue to be borne entirely by the proprietor. However, major surgical interventions, such as the setting of broken bones, amputations, etc., will always be paid for by the individual worker, unless the worker sustained the injury while working for the Partnership.

Article 10: The working day will be nine hours. It will begin at sunrise and end at sundown. However, at the time of sugar production, the proprietor will be allowed to lengthen the working day by two hours. This span of time will be interspersed with periods of rest following the usage of the plantation, but these periods may not exceed a total of three hours.

The proprietor will be required to furnish to each worker at the beginning of each year a new hoe in exchange for the old one. He will also furnish for the cutting of the cane and other work on the plantation 48 machetes per year. The old machetes will also be handed over to the proprietor for new ones. If in the course of the year these tools were to be broken through the fault of the workers, lost, or diverted to other uses, they will be replaced by the workers at their own expense but nonetheless remain the property of the proprietor.

Article 11: The proprietor will keep a register in which each worker will have an individual account. Every evening the foreman will report to the proprietor the hours of work furnished by each worker, and these hours will be recorded in the above-mentioned register. . . . Work missed for reason of illness or leaves of absence granted by the proprietor with the approval of the Workers' Council will be noted in the individual accounts. In this connection . . . it is expressly agreed that nine hours of absence from work, whether consecutive or not, will be counted as the equivalent of one working day. Any absence from work for reasons other than those stated above will be sanctioned by withholding the pay for a number of days double that of which the delinquent worker has deprived the Partnership (unless the worker has replaced himself within 24 hours by a worker approved by the proprietor and the Workers' Council). The sums resulting from such withholding will be used for paying day laborers who in such cases will be hired by the Partnership to make up for lost working time.

Article 13: [Provides for the election of a five-person Workers' Council which includes the foreman, himself to be elected.] The proprietor or his representative may always be present at the deliberations of this Council but will have no voice in its deliberations.

[This Council is also the intermediary between the proprietor and the workers.] The Council will have the right to exclude from the Partnership, with the consent of the proprietor, workers who deserve such punishment for their bad behavior. . . . The Council will meet every Saturday at noon and can be summoned to an extraordinary session whenever the proprietor or his representative deems it necessary.

Article 14: The workers will be entitled to one-third of the sugar before expenses. The third belonging to the workers will be delivered to them in kind as it is being produced. . . .

Article 17: Any worker who withdraws from the Partnership before its term has expired will lose his right to the dividends that have accrued to him since the last distribution. Nonetheless, such a worker will have the right to harvest the foodstuffs of his individual garden, unless the proprietor prefers to pay him for these foodstuffs upon estimation by the Workers' Council. [The grace period for this is not stated.]

Article 22: The proprietor reserves for himself and excludes from the Partnership 12 ha [hectares] 92 a [ares] 60 ca [centiares] [about 31.2 acres], which will be taken by him, to wit: 2 ha 68 a 58 ca in the section called Jardin Madame, and the rest in the sections called Herbes de Guinée, Bananière, Hyppolite, Avocat. . . . M. Dessalles will have the right to cultivate these pieces of land for his own account. . . .

Appendix B

Pierre Dessalles's Letter to the Director of the Interior (1848)

[This is Pierre Dessalles's response to the questionnaire sent by the Director of the Interior to the plantation owners of Martinique in December 1848. It is an unfinished draft, and we do not know whether the letter was actually sent. However, since it reflects a certain mentality, it seemed appropriate to include it here (HF and LE).]

Sainte-Marie, 17 December 1848

Citizen Director of the Interior,

Retired from public affairs for about seventeen years and determined never to return to them, I am exclusively concerned with my private affairs. Since my retirement I have twice traveled to France and have thus followed the events that have taken place only as a private person. The confidence M. le Gouverneur is today kind enough to show me is too great an honor for me to permit me not to respond to it. My opinions are bound to reflect the gap created by my long absence from public affairs.

Having long foreseen emancipation, and indeed fervently wishing for it [sic!], I had returned to Martinique in October 1847 with the sole objective of considering my slaves already free and forming with them an Association on an equitable footing. Although I had to consider them free, I would not have undertaken anything that would have compromised the indemnity to which I might some day be entitled. Unfortunately, I had sold my property, which was not restored to me until 14 May, a few days before the dreadful and deplorable events of the 22nd and 23rd of that same month [May 1848]. I was therefore forced to renounce all of my plans. Retained at Saint-Pierre for reasons of health, I was unable to take personal possession of my property until 14 June. I found that my former slaves had fallen prey to the same delirium that gripped the entire population at that time and that the plantation was almost deserted. It was only twelve days later that I was able to motivate them to produce sugar with the stipulation that the citizen Commissioner-General himself establish the share to which they would be entitled. It took 4½ weeks to produce 22½ hogsheads of sugar. Never have I seen work performed more negligently and irregularly; yet whenever I made a critical remark, I triggered disrespectful scenes and indeed serious threats of disorder that ceased only after the inspection tour of the president of the tribunal of Saint-Pierre. As for the work, it may no longer be quite as slow, but the irregularity with which the workers attend to it remains staggering. This irregularity is documented in the record of absenteeism.

The workers believe that because they are free, they do not have to honor any of their obligations. They take days off whenever they feel like it and without permission; if one criticizes such behavior, they show great astonishment and ask you with the greatest self-assurance whether they are not free. Reasoning with them in their own interest and with the utmost patience has as yet been unavailing to make them understand their duties and their rights. The women in particular are irascible, mock everything one tells them, are always ready to forget their obligations, and freely express all their passion and their anger. This, then, M. le Directeur de l'Intérieur, is the true state of affairs. I shall now address the four questions to which you wish me to respond and present my observations concerning them.

The number of workers attached to the plantation and participating in the Association was, originally and until 1 September, eighty-three, including the guard. Since 1 September, this number has been reduced to seventy-three. I must point out here that the number of active workers has never exceeded forty.

It took three weeks to produce 29 ½ hogsheads of sugar. One-quarter carré has been planted, and 1 ¾ carrés of new shoots and planted cane have been hoed [1 carré = 3.12 acres].

Manuring: none.

The average number of hours spent working per day has been 7 ½; under the system of slavery, the work that was done in the whole month of September would barely have taken twelve days.

From the moral point of view, the changes that should be brought to the present state of things are not as many as one might imagine, but they would demand a great deal of supervision on the part of the authorities. Above all, it would be important to put only trustworthy men of stable opinions in charge of undoing the bad attitudes that the new freedmen harbor about proprietors in general—attitudes that may have been spawned by the memory of slavery, but which most certainly have been fomented and strengthened and are kept up by secret influences. Because of this influence, communist ideas that they [the new freedmen] do not understand any better than anything else have spread, and many are still dreaming of property distribution. Men who consider the cultivation of cane a dishonor because it was so closely linked to slavery do not today set a good example by working together with the new freedmen in order to make them feel better about working the land and contribute effectively to the country's prosperity. Instead they prefer either to wallow in the most pernicious idleness or else to go from plantation to plantation in order to foment trouble and disorder. This is one of the most serious scourges that must be addressed. And the community where I live is suffering more than most in this respect. It is also one where the obstacles to work are the greatest.

Now there is another matter that deserves the government's most urgent attention, namely that of education. This is the most important area in which one can obtain good results for the unity of purpose and the success of the changed system. But this teaching, in which the proprietors must participate, since it involves their interests, must only be entrusted to moral and essentially Christian men. Unfortunately, the proprietors—especially myself—have had the unhappy experience of unauthorized schools that were set up on their plantations. It will be very difficult to make the new freedmen—especially those who have reached a certain age—lose the vicious habits of slavery. It will be very difficult, I repeat, to instill in them the new attitude of a free man, for they do not understand what true freedom means. However, by means of religious instruction, it might be possible to modify bad habits and to instill ideas of family, which would be extremely useful for promoting their happiness and the tranquillity and prosperity of the colony. Especially the young freedmen urgently need the solicitude of men who will spread morality and instruction; once their intelligence has become more flexible, they will become accustomed to new ideas and will guarantee that . . . [unfinished]

CHAPTER TEN

1849

1 January 1849

I was awakened by the sound of a wretched fiddle and a noisy kettle drum. My former slaves came one by one to wish me a happy New Year. I am planning to give them a speech when they are all here. Ernest and Madeiras had the effrontery to come right into my little back yard. Héloise saw my indignation and had someone tell them to get out, which they did. Inconceivable behavior!

Adrien arrived at one o'clock and showed great pleasure at seeing me; I too was very happy to embrace him. He brought me a letter from Henri and one from Antoinette asking for my approval of a marriage that she hopes to arrange for Emilie.[1] Henri continues his *démarches* for finding a position, which will be very difficult. . . .

Saint-Just came this evening; I dressed him down in a masterful way and spoke to him in the strongest terms about his brother, his nephews, his mother, and his sister.[2] Adrien too lit into him and called him all kinds of names. Idoine

---

1. In the end, Emilie did not marry at all; she became a nun.

2. His brother, Saint-Fort, freed by Dessalles's mother and now living in Guadeloupe; his nephews, Saturnin and Ernest, the latter now called Ernest Trop; his mother, Fortunée ("all our troubles have come, and always will come, from Fortunée's cabin" [Dessalles to his mother, 1825]); his sister, Trop ("as long as she is promiscuous anyway, I would at least like her to have many children, who would someday make good slaves [*sujets*] for us" [Dessalles to his mother, 1823]).

and Tapté had the nerve to show up, but I sternly chased them away. It has been a very painful day, and I was glad when it was over.

6 January 1849

Adrien went to see Saint-Isle and M. Le Grand [neighboring white planters], finding them encased in their old prejudices, which they will never lose. Such individuals will always hinder the march of the new transformation. The negroes show my son great interest; he speaks to them, and they seem to listen to him. But those who give them perfidious advice will soon destroy the confidence they are showing him. The men of color have not come to call on him, even though they told me that they would be glad to see him. How can one count on such perverse creatures?

10 January 1849

. . . I received a letter from Nicaise and one from Pécoul [in France] of 28 October. Nicaise informs me that the best sugar fetches fifteen francs at Saint-Pierre and that he would be forced to leave the workers' share in the warehouse if the prices did not improve when the packet boat arrives. What a situation! How can we meet the plantation's expenses with such prices? . . . Pécoul takes credit for the recall of Perrinon and the nomination of M. Bruat.[3] There is no question that he has made great efforts to defend our interests.

12 January 1849

The negroes came out of their cabins late. They are hatching a new project, namely, to be put on wages. Césaire and La Disette have asked me for land

---

3. Armand Joseph Bruat (1796–1855) was born in the Alsatian town of Colmar. Joining the navy in 1811, he attained the rank of first mate in 1827. Having shown outstanding boldness in the expedition to Algiers, he was captured during this operation and delivered by the French victory. He subsequently rose to the ranks of frigate captain (1831), captain of a battleship (1838), governor of the Marquesas Islands and then the Islands of Oceania. As the king's emissary to Queen Pomaré, he—together with Dupetit-Thouars—compelled her to consent to a French protectorate. After serving as counter-admiral in 1846, then as maritime prefect of Toulon, he was named military commander of Martinique, Guadeloupe, and their dependencies in 1848, a post he occupied until 1852. As vice-admiral he participated in the siege of Sevastopol and was named admiral in 1855. On his way back to France after a brilliant expedition to the Sea of Asov, he died on the high seas. His widow was appointed governess to the Children of France [children of Napoleon III] in 1856 [adapted from the biographical notices, HF and LE (4: appendix)].

and want to become sharecroppers [*colons partiaires*].[4] Adrien thinks this is the surest way to solve our difficulties, and I will try it. France has compromised everything by emancipating the blacks without first establishing a system of work. M. Rostolan was guilty of great slackness.

16 January 1849

Nicaise and Emile have returned from Saint-Pierre, where misery is at its height. Sugar does not sell.

People who want to plant are offering themselves everywhere. We are just beginning to negotiate with our former slaves for several pieces of land. This sharecropping would save us a great deal of trouble, if it can be made to work.

We have learned that Ferdinand Blampuy has been appointed mayor and that the adjuncts are Ernest Yotte and Eudorçait [all men of color]. This is pretty strong; by confirming these nominations, M. Jouannet [a judge at Saint-Pierre and a man of color] proves he is only interested in his own class. MM. Saint-Isle, Le Grand, Papin-Dupont, Bonneville, and Numa Littée have resigned.

[Nicaise reports what he has heard in town.]

18 January 1849

. . . All the mulattoes in town were eager to greet Nicaise, even though they do not like him. At Latulipe's they talked about the resignations handed in by five whites [see above]. Even though they are in fact humiliated, they [the men of color] act arrogantly, saying that they can get along very well without the whites, who have been in power in this country only too long. One man by the name of Deterville[5] pointed out that union would be a good thing for the general good, but the others replied that it would never happen in this community. And it is true that as long as all the ne'er-do-wells are chosen as town councillors, honorable people will not want to be associated with them. But if they put in honorable mulattoes, the whites will be eager to fraternize with them. This we cannot tell them too often.

[Dessalles renews negotiations with the family about ownership of the plantation.]

4. Under this system, which was similar to sharecropping, the landowner was paid a portion of the harvest in kind [HF and LE].

5. Actually Detervid; a carpenter and property owner, he had kinship ties to the mulatto artisan elite of Sainte-Marie, people like Sully Jean-Bart, Monrose Dérose, Ernest Yotte, Adophe Moïse, and Faustin [HF and LE].

31 January 1849

. . . My children do not want to fix my annuity at 3,000 francs. They would give me the entire Caféière and not a penny to go with it. I do not see how we can come to an arrangement. I would prefer an annuity of 3,600 francs to any arrangement: in that case I would go to France and settle there. This would be the only way to escape the importunities of the creditors.[6] . . .

9 February 1849

. . . The colored girl Palmire—supposedly Adrien's daughter—seems nice enough, but quite insignificant. My son spoils her to the point of making himself ridiculous; I don't know what he has in mind for her. During my absence, he permitted himself to make her dine at the table with the Lalanne ladies, which has greatly upset me. I only keep her in my household because I consider her a member of my domestic staff and would not have her as my equal. One must be kind to these people, but one must keep them at a distance. To act differently would be immoral. My poor son has no idea of the proprieties; if this were his home he would wallow in dirty linen. In a conversation he had with me, he told me in all naiveté that he was anxious to straighten out his affairs and that, having decided not to marry, he would surround himself with his bastards. I was so dumbfounded by such a bizarre plan that I just looked at him without saying anything. . . . As for myself, I hope to die as a man who respects the proprieties.

10 February 1849

Thimothée and Anicet, two men of color of this town, deplore what is going on in our town hall; they asked me if I believe that such things can last long. They understand that these men are doing great harm, but they would do nothing to stop them! There is simply no way that one can count on this intermediary class.[7]

---

6. Note that Dessalles no longer praises France as a better place to live than the colony.

7. The nineteenth century had developed a theory about race in the colonies. In the eyes of the white Creoles, Caribbean society was divided into two classes, the *free* and the *slaves*. Since the true *free* were the whites, the *free* people of color (freedmen or the descendants of freedmen) enjoyed a status midway between the two classes; hence the term *intermediary class*. This notion, which permeated the society depicted in the present story, was violently rejected by the majority of the men of color. They considered themselves "people of blood" [HF and LE].

8 March 1849

. . . The new freedmen are saying loudly that Bissette's only purpose in coming to the colony is to give them land. Jean-Bart, formerly a farmer on my plantation, has permitted himself to pull out vegetables in the field he used to cultivate. A complaint against him will be lodged with the justice of the peace.

16 March 1849

We have received the *Courrier*. Bonaparte [i.e., Louis Napoleon Bonaparte, elected President in November 1848] is consolidating his power. The French government has granted 50,000 francs to those who emigrated from the colonies in the wake of the events of May 22 and 23 of last year. M. Bruat failed to inform us of this circumstance, which was known only in Guadeloupe. It is a disgrace! This man has just appointed to the post of police commissioner of Fort-Royal a mulatto, sieur Waddi, the most cruel enemy of the whites. May God soon deliver us from this red revolutionary sent to the colony at the tail end of the provisional government!

19 March 1849

After lunch I went with Valmont to Numa Littée's, where we stayed until four. We played a good bit of dominoes and talked a lot about California, where we all decided to go.[8] But since night brings good council, tomorrow we will give up this bizarre plan.

22 March 1849

. . . We have learned that Bissette has arrived at Saint-Pierre. . . .

26 March 1849

[An acquaintance] told me that Bissette had called on many whites, who in turn will go to see him. People cite his many speeches to the negroes, which reflect an excellent attitude. He accepts all the donations made to him and it appears that he has received a great deal of money. To shouts of joy, he has asked the negroes never to lump his name together with that of Perrinon and has declared that he would become deputy only if Pécoul were elected with him.

---

8. The gold rush was on.

2 April 1849

I went to lunch with Adolphe Perinelle, with whom I talked about the current events. I told him that Bissette intends to see him; he said that he did not believe it and that it would be to deny his entire past to shake hands with and receive Bissette. I feel the same way and therefore will make sure that I am not at Sainte-Marie when he comes. . . .

5 April 1849

. . . Adrien arrived at four o'clock, soaked to the skin. He called on Bissette last Saturday and found himself in his salon with more than sixty persons of all colors. He embraced Bissette, who praised him to everyone present. He [Bissette] promised my son to come to the plantation, which means that I am condemned to receive him. The mulattoes of Sainte-Marie are spreading the rumor that I fled the town in order not to receive him, which is an additional reason for me to return home. That is what Nicaise advises. The fact is . . . that I am not going out of my way to meet this man, but that he is coming to me. So I will receive him politely, with all the dignity that is called for.

13 April 1849

Before our dinner the curé and Robert Littée paid us a visit. The former has received an invitation to dine with Bissette next Tuesday or Wednesday. We talked about this personage. M. Jeunehomme [the curé] asked me what I would do if he came to see me; I replied that I would receive him. He agreed with me. Adrien, however, thinks I should not appear, that to do so would be to compromise my past record. But I think it would be cowardly to avoid him. "What would you do," my son asked me, "if he embraced you?" I admit that this idea had never occurred to me, and it really shook me up. These gentlemen do not dare give me any advice. Back in my room, Nicaise again told me not to leave my house, because that would produce a very bad impression. I agree with him. Still, it will be very painful to find myself face to face with such a man, whose conduct is pure calculation. It is better, of course, that he has embraced the flag of order, but can we be sure that he will be followed?

20 April 1849

Following a mild critical remark I made to my son at dinner, he seriously failed to show me proper respect. It is no longer to be hoped that he will correct himself, but at least he no longer has that violent temper. He forgets that, by keeping his bastard daughter here, he places me in a most awkward position. Nothing, to be sure, would give me greater pleasure than to be useful to this girl if I saw that she was being occupied and treated as a servant, but I see with dismay that Adrien looks upon her as if she were one of my legitimate grand-daughters. She enjoys a room that Héloise must make up every day; when she goes to town, she must have a horse, and Adrien makes a spectacle of himself by accompanying her. This does not suit me at all, but I must put up with it, although I get no thanks from anyone.

22 April 1849

Letters from Saint-Pierre tell me that serenades are being exchanged between the Bissettistes and the Schoelchéristes. The mulattoes want to force a white man, M. Garcin, who has debauched a girl of their class, to marry her. Apparently there is talk of duels between the two classes. Someone tried to poison Bissette at Basse Pointe. Petit-Frère Roche, a mulatto of that town and rather a bad lot, stopped here on his way home. The only reason he did so was to find out whether I was making preparations for receiving Bissette. I avoided talking to him.

Bissette is at Grand' Anse, and Mazuline is conducting his own campaign. The situation is becoming more complicated. I find that the negroes have been less docile in the last two days. It is quite obvious that Schoelchérist agents are abroad in our countryside.

26 April 1849

All the white landowners of our town have decided to meet Bissette as he approaches and have offered him a banquet *at my house*, which he has accepted for next Saturday. Thus I will find myself face to face with the man whom I condemned to death 26 years ago! This does not upset me in the slightest, for my conscience is clear. But the trouble these preparations are going to cause me! We have nothing here with which to receive 40 persons and will have to borrow everything. Adrien could have kept this burden from me, but he seems to enjoy the idea that I will find myself in this false position.

[Dessalles tries in vain to change the venue of the banquet; his workers insist that it must take place on his plantation and offer to construct a tent to accommodate the 40 guests and to borrow the utensils necessary for such an affair.]

28 April 1849

I was up at five o'clock this morning. The negroes did bring a few leaves and a few bamboo poles, but not enough to finish the tent. They worked hard at it until one o'clock, but then the weather turned bad, so we gave up on the tent and decided to break down one wall of the former salon. As if by magic, everything was decorated by four o'clock. Adrien went to meet Bissette, who only arrived at half-past six. Salvoes were fired, and great outbreaks of joy showed him the happiness his presence had brought to the black population. I was in the salon, and Adrien led him to me.

"M. Dessalles," he said, "I am very pleased indeed to find myself in your presence. As for the court verdict that condemned me, I no longer think about it. In fact, it has made my political fortune and has afforded me influence that I will use for the good of our common fatherland. In France I formed close ties with your eldest son and have shaken hands with your younger son, who is your very image. Allow me to embrace you; the past is entirely forgotten."

"M. Bissette," I replied, "my presence here proves to you that you are received without any ulterior motives. I know about your ties to my eldest son and therefore found his desire to receive you here perfectly normal. I have never had to reproach myself for any resentment toward you. Today our feelings are identical, and the flag you have adopted guarantees you the sympathies of all honorable people in this country."

After this address, I led him to the sofa, where we exchanged a few banal phrases. I asked Adrien to present to him all of the town's planters who had come and told him in a loud voice that he was in the midst of friends determined to give him their support in all circumstances. I then slipped out to see how our domestics were doing. Returning to the salon a half-hour later, I asked if all the men of color invited were present, and someone brought me Sainte-Marie Magloire, for whom I had asked by name. "I am very glad," I told him, "to see you here. For fifty years our two families have liked and respected each other. I have warm feelings and esteem for your mother and your sister-in-law Mme Chéry; your elder brother, for whom I have never had anything but praise, is my friend."

Bissette was listening most attentively to every word I said. Sainte-Marie Magloire bared his chest to me and, speaking with his hand on his heart, told me with great emotion that he had long carried me *there*. I then shook hands with all the other men of color. Thereupon, Bissette spoke and presented a very long account of Schoelcher's turpitude and Pory Papy's ridiculous behavior.

At eight o'clock we sat down at table. I had placed myself at one of the ends. Bissette was in the middle, with the curé to one side and Valmont to the other. Adrien was seated across from him; on his right was the workers' representative [*prud'homme*] Israel and on his left M. Bonneville, who had his workers' representative to his left. All classes were thus represented. Before the soup, Adrien offered a toast to the democratic republic, whose blessings he described. Several other toasts were made. Bissette proposed a political toast and then drank to my health; he rose and came over to clink glasses with me. I met him halfway and thanked him. The curé drank to the health of Bissette, and the meal ended with a toast to the workers' health. Everything came off very well and with dignity. After the coffee—which we took in the salon of the pavilion—Valmont and Arquen, at the request of Bissette, sang a few pieces. We drank to Bissette's success at the National Assembly. At half past eleven he took his horse and returned to town.

I was exhausted. Barely able to reach my bed, I slept until daybreak. My impressions are by no means painful; since my conscience is clear, I was not upset by seeing this man—a man to whom in all fairness one must grant a certain merit and whose conduct is noble, grand, and deeply marked by the stamp of Christianity. Religion alone can produce such a conversion. What will people not say about all of this? Let them talk; my name is forever inscribed in the history of this country. When he left, Bissette shook hands with Adrien and said, "My friend, your race will save this country!"

30 April 1849

The negroes are out of their minds! Some claim that Bissette said the owners can no longer evict them from their cabins, which belong to them. Some say that Bissette has declared they are entitled to two-thirds of the gross revenues. Some even said that they were entitled to three-thirds! Our former slave [*nègre*] Césaire told Adrien that he had some accounts to settle with him, since Bissette had said that he was supposed to receive two-thirds of the gross receipts for sugar.

"All right," Adrien replied, "the cantonal jury will decide this question next Saturday. Go on home and go back to work, or I will throw you off the plantation."[9]

A moment later three or four others came to voice the same demand with the same insolence. My son has reported them to the justice of the peace, who

9. "Retourne chez toi, reprends le travail, ou je te chasse de l'habitation." Adrien used the familiar "*tu*" form in speaking to this worker. As we noted earlier, Dessalles used the formal "*vous*" in speaking to a slave.

has summoned them for next Saturday. They have gone to see Bissette and will no doubt come back humiliated. It is a negro from M. Thénos's place who came here and has spread all this bad talk among our negroes; he is the reason for what is happening. Adrien has written to the mayor to request that the gendarmerie come to make an official report.

1 May 1849

. . . We have settled the account for the banquet; the expense came to 360 francs 55, and we took in 425 francs 95. We will distribute the surplus sum of 65 francs 40 to the servants.

2 May 1849

The negroes who returned from Trinité last night came to work this morning. They were very quiet about what they had obtained from Bissette and the justice of the peace. The work is going poorly, bad talk is circulating, and insolence, which had ceased, seems to be starting up again.

We hear that at Trinité Bissette had to fight against terrible opinions. It appears that a man of color by the name of Jules Néron had praised Schoelcher, declaring that only the principles of that criminal could save the colonies, whereas those of Bissette promoted their destruction. Bissette, furious, expressed his anger and called the men of his class all kinds of names, and there even seem to have been challenges [to duels]. The whites gave a banquet [for Bissette] at M. de Saint-Albain's.

[Once again Dessalles's children and his brother attempt to expropriate him. This time he agrees to leave the plantation and to divide the indemnity he is to receive (laws published in the *Journal Officiel* on 13 June 1849) with his brother and his principal creditors, MM. Durand. It is not clear what the amount of the indemnity will be.]

13 May 1849

Adrien returned from Trinité last night with a young mulatto who had traveled with him. He is the bastard of a sieur Sandras who had him educated in France. Seventeen years old, he received all of his schooling there, but has no experience of men and the world. Without a profession, he will soon be at the level of the men of his class if he does not do something about it. I received him very well, but I admit that it was not without repugnance. My son embraces fusion[10] in a manner that frightens me and will very often place me into such predicaments. . . .

15 May 1849

Today M. Alexandre Cardin came to take up his post as assistant manager [*économe*]. The negroes showed their pleasure at seeing him, but asked if Adrien and I would stop supervising them; it appears that they detest us. The villains! We cannot be too severe with them. . . .

24 May 1849

Yesterday Robert Littée had brought us 3 Madeirans who agreed to work for us: two men for 25 sols a day, a woman for 10 sols. But they did not come. I had expected this: they must have been dissuaded by the men of the town. Our workers have made up their minds to do absolutely nothing, for they want our ruin. And that has been put into their minds by the advice they have received, particularly from Saint-Just and Mont-Rose Magloire, who act as campaign managers and go from plantation to plantation. Villains that they are!

30 May 1849

At six o'clock in the evening I received from the president of the Saint-Pierre committee a package containing printed ballots, a written appeal to his compatriots by Bissette, and sixteen flags bearing the names of Bissette and Pécoul. I am asked to distribute these appeals and flags to favorably disposed work groups[11] and to urge the landowners to go down to town at the head of their workers.

3 June 1849 [election day]

At half-past seven I went to town, where I heard mass and stayed for the benediction of the Eucharist. Then I went to the town hall and deposited my ballot. I found that all the mulattoes had assembled there. Ferdinand Blampuy greeted me most graciously and offered me a seat; I was curt and decisive and refused everything. Moïse Adolphe and Eudorçait came over to me; I shook

10. We would call it "integration."
11. "Gangs" no longer seems the appropriate translation of "*ateliers*," but Dessalles continues to use the same word.

hands with them. That villain Castandet looked at me askance and from below; he did not know what to do with himself. Just as soon as I had voted I left. . . .

I then went to the curé's and found him distributing ballots to the negroes who had asked for them. He took away from them the ballots inscribed "Bissette and *Schoelcher*" that had been given to them by the villains of the town. In one of the rooms of the town hall I had seen Eugène Godard and the younger Zozo giving out ballots. My former mulatto Saint-Just spoke to me in a wheedling voice, apologizing that he had failed to pay his respects to me for so long. I answered brusquely and left him standing there. This evening I learned from Nicaise that he [Saint-Just] has been seen giving my negro Catharie a ballot inscribed "Bissette and *Schoelcher*"; when he saw Nicaise he changed color and motioned to Catharie to hide his ballot. A moment later he came over to Nicaise with a stack of ballots in his hand and offered one to him, pointing out that it was for "Bissette and *Pécoul*." Nicaise left indignantly. He went to Latulipe's, where he told people about this shameless piece of cheating. Ernest Trop, who was present, asked him who could have committed such an infamous act. "It is your uncle," Nicaise replied, "and you can tell him so from me." "The monster! Wait till he comes to see me! I will let him have it!"

4 June 1849

. . . Paul Ballain stopped by at half past seven. The ballots have been counted: Pécoul had 555 votes, Bissette 776, Schoelcher 250, Papy 20, and Robert Littée 1. So it was a complete victory.

5 June 1849

The elections at Gros-Morne have yielded the following results: Bissette 750, Pécoul 540, Schoelcher 12, and Papy 3. Those of Trinité were more favorable to Schoelcher; Pécoul obtained no more than 250 votes. M. Gérard, who came from Saint-Pierre, informed us that Bissette and Pécoul had achieved a complete success there. In short there is every hope that Pécoul will be elected. Adrien and Valmont claim that the men of color of Sainte-Marie have expressed their sympathy for Pécoul. The wretched opportunists! They can see that they are bested, and so they must arrange for a way out. . . .

6 June 1849

We have learned that except in three towns, Pécoul has obtained the majority everywhere. That's wonderful! Upon his return from Trinité, Adrien reported that some people tried to take away the voting urn. Bissette had gone through the streets of Saint-Pierre declaring that if the mulattoes wanted civil war, they should say so, for he would place himself at the head of the blacks, and they [the mulattoes] would soon be done for.

[Nicaise has been beaten nearly to death by some men in Trinité to whom he expressed his "excellent opinions" about politics. He sends them a challenge via Adrien, and Dessalles is hard put to find a decent set of pistols for Nicaise. Duelling seems to have become an ingredient of political life in the newly emancipated colonies; the diary twice mentions duels between Bissettistes and Schoelchériens, in addition to brawls between the two groups.]

25 June 1849

Adrien's bastard girl told someone that, once I am off the plantation, she would eat at the table and stay there even if the governor came to dinner. My wretched son does not realize that he is ruining this girl.

22 July 1849

. . . Adrien has announced to the negroes that the Association no longer exists and that starting tomorrow everyone must find work on a tenant farm [*colonage partiaire*].[12]

25 July 1849

Letter from Valmont: yesterday he had the occasion to see M. de Percin, notary at Gros-Morne, who talked to him at length about current affairs. He apparently told Valmont under the seal of secrecy that his uncle Northumb Percin had met with Bissette and that the subject of this interview was exclusively the political course pursued by M. Bruat [the new Bonapartist governor]. Both equally indignant about the partiality of that admiral, they decided that they would ship him off to France, along with MM. Meynier and Jouannet, and continue to administer the colony in the name of France—the military being

12. Under this system, an estate was worked by individual tenants and the landlord received rent [*fermage*] from each *colon partiaire*. In practical terms, the landlord usually had to advance the money for paying the workers. In the case of the Dessalles plantation, Nicaise became a *colon partiaire* for 23 ha 9131, Michaud together with Joseph Israel (a former slave) for 24 ha 5594, and Césaire and La Disette (also former slaves) for 2 ha 1542 and 5 ha 6512 respectively. While all of these *colons partiaires* were obliged to grow sugar, they fell into two categories: those who did everything by themselves and those who were entrepreneurs. Nicaise and Michaud employed sixteen workers each, and La Disette employed six, while Césaire and his wife worked by themselves [based on HF and LE (4: 167n. 17)].

almost won over. Valmont adds that he has trusted me with this project because it is of such grave consequence and that he recommends it to my discretion and my reflection. I wrote in reply that I cannot consign my thoughts on paper but that we would discuss the matter when he comes here. There is no doubt that Admiral Bruat is greatly to be blamed and that, a Schoelchérien at heart, he is still hoping that the party of the Mountain will triumph.[13] In that expectation, the governor protects all his partisans who are in power and takes only half-measures for maintaining order; as a result, everyone's interests are compromised. Those who are intent on order are discouraged. I do not approve, however, of the remedy conceived by MM. Northumb and Bissette. This would be an affair similar to that of MM. Ricouard and de la Varenne,[14] but circumstances are different now, and France, agitated by various parties that vie for power, is in a situation that would make such a coup d'état an even more serious event. It would be wiser to be patient and to go on suffering; after all, why could the colony not lodge a massive complaint with the Legislative Assembly? If we want to preserve the colonies and get people to work, it is obvious that Bissette's ideas must triumph. If Bissette launches himself into such an enterprise and fails, he will be finished forever and this country will no longer be inhabitable. . . .

3 August 1849

During dinner Adrien again uttered one of those improprieties that he dresses up in the fine mantle of philanthropy. Here is what happened. M. Michaud has established a business on the plantation selling all kinds of things, but mainly codfish. Adrien knows this; he also knows that, once I leave the plantation, I am to receive part of his profits. Well! Under the pretext of his great interest in the negroes' well-being, he has stated his intention of buying them codfish, which all of those who work on the plantation would share and which they would be able to buy at moderate prices—an enormous boon for them! To be sure, I would be very happy indeed to participate in such a worthy undertaking; but since I know the negro's character—excessively suspicious— and especially since I know his propensity to suspect one's best intentions, I could not help but point out to Adrien that this undertaking would give rise

13. Dessalles mixes the revolutionary terminology of '93 with that of '48, employing such terms as "the Mountain" and "communism," "terror" and "the Reds" almost interchangeably.

14. This is known as the Gaoulé Affair. In 1717 a revolt against the central authority broke out in Martinique. The colonists arrested the governor, Marquis de la Varenne, and Ricouard, the intendant, both of whom had just arrived, and put them onto the next ship bound for France [HF and LE]. Dessalles probably read about this incident in his father's history of Martinique.

to unfortunate clashes and that I would urge him not to go too far in expressing his interest for a class that has pushed its ingratitude vis-à-vis its masters to an extreme. "Besides," I added, "this project will go down the drain just like that of teaching them to write and of instilling morality." "I will not be accused," he replied, "of having acted against my conscience for motives of personal interest." It was an insolent remark which, for the sake of peace, I had to swallow quietly. I truly feel sorry for this wretched Adrien and hardly dare predict what will happen once I am off the plantation. Alas! he will utterly wallow in dirty linen! . . .

22 August 1849

. . . At nine o'clock Sully Jean-Bart, a good mulatto of the town, came to tell us that Abbé Ladret had been ordered to leave town and to go immediately to Basse-Pointe. The mayor and some of the town councillors worked for this move because this priest had advised the new freedmen against voting for Schoelcher. Adrien immediately drew up a petition to the governor, which all the inhabitants, white, yellow, and black, covered with their signatures. He will deliver it to the Governor on Friday, accompanied by Sainte-Marie Magloire. I had planned to go to Gros-Morne for three days, but in Adrien's absence I do not want to leave the plantation without one of us present.

24 August 1849

. . . My former slave Césaire came to collect three sols which I owed him. I talked with him about his *colonage*; he has great expectations for the results of his work. He now understands the benefits of hard work. He told me that the bad advice of the mulattoes in town had held back and stopped the negroes. "Yes," I replied, "I know that the evil came from these wretches, but today I believe they are no longer listened to." "They're not, they're not, they're not!" he said again. "No one listens to them any more, although they keep talking." He then named Eugène Yotte and his mother-in-law as those who constantly tell the negroes that they are not free and that they are still working for the whites.

25 August 1849

Adrien came back from Fort-Royal this morning. When M. Bruat agreed to receive him, he did so under the condition that there was to be no publicity for the petition; it is evident that this brave admiral is afraid of the press. He told the delegation of all colors that he was sorry that he could not reverse the decision once it was made. Adrien explained to him that the dismissal of the vicar would do great moral harm. He understands this and finally gave the delegation a letter to the Director of the Interior. Adrien spoke of the revolutionary municipal government of Sainte-Marie. "Yes indeed!" he [Bruat] exclaimed, "your municipal councillors are revolutionary, all right! I am glad of it! Once people have learned about universal suffrage, they will not be reelected." "Meanwhile, however," Adrien pointed out, "honorable people are suffering, and everything is going badly." "Can't be helped, can't be helped," he [Bruat] added.

These are excellent and sublime words for an administrator. . . . It is pitiful, and quite frankly M. Bruat is no more made for the role he is playing than my slipper. As they were leaving the office, Calixte, Adrien's former domestic who was part of the delegation, said that however hard the admiral tried, he would never be anything but a peasant. . . .

23 September 1849

A man of color by the name of Aulien, formerly a slave [*nègre*] on the [state-owned] Saint-Jacques plantation, came this morning to ask Adrien to serve as a mediator for him. . . . The Director of the Interior, to whom Adrien had referred him, told him that he had to leave Saint-Jacques and produce an appraisal of his work. Consequently, Adrien went to the premises. M. Mont-Fleury [the manager] received him well, and everything went very smoothly. In dealing with the mulattoes, Adrien is extremely courteous and benevolent. He is hoping to instill good attitudes in them, but he is mistaken; these men will not appreciate what he does for them nor will they love him.

[In late October Bissette again visits Sainte-Marie and the surrounding area, presumably to win over the Schoelchéristes. Here is what Adrien reports to his father.]

23 October 1849

. . . The landowners of Sainte-Marie and their farm workers joined Bissette at the Charpentier plantation.[15] He was delighted to see them and expressed warm feelings to Adrien. He knew that the blacks of Saint-Jacques were planning to kill him. When he reached that plantation, Mont-Fleury, all red in the face, received him. Bissette told him that he had not intended to stop there,

---

15. This plantation belonged to Comte Ajax de Ferbeaux, a cousin by marriage of the author. Situated 4 km north of Sainte-Marie near the village of Marigot, it still exists [HF and LE].

but that upon learning about the blacks' hostility toward him, he had come so
that they could find out about him. The blacks, hearing these words, protested
their innocence and started to shout "Vive Papa! Vive Bissette!"

When M. Mont-Fleury walked over to Adrien to express his regrets that he
had not yet come to call on him, a new freedman addressed this manager in a
loud and threatening voice and told him that if he knew that anyone here was
a Schoelchériste, he would grab him by the skin of his belly and throw him to
the ground. Mont-Fleury, trembling, pale, and beside himself, replied that he
was a *good* Schoelchériste. "Don't repeat these words," the freedman told him,
"or you'll be done for."

At that moment cries of rage and indignation resounded from all ranks. My
son, using his influence, tried to make them understand that everyone was free
to have his own opinion.

"No, no," they insisted. "We must finish with these wretches who have taken
advantage of our trust and our ignorance to give us bad advice and push us into
evil deeds."

The situation was becoming very tense, so they called Bissette, who was in
the house. He scolded the blacks, and everyone calmed down at the sound of
his voice. The group then moved on and shortly thereafter arrived in town.
There, not many flags were hanging from the windows, and the houses of the
Schoelchéristes were shut. In their anger the new freedmen yelled insults at
the mulattoes, heaping abuse on them for their deceit. They hit all the closed
doors with their sticks. The mayor, who happened to be at the town hall, came
out to restore order; they grabbed him by the shoulders, roughly pushed him
forward, and made it clear to him that they no longer wanted him as mayor,
that he was vile, a Schoelchériste, and so forth. . . . He got away more dead than
alive and was not seen again. . . .

[Bissette and the landowners then went to the curé's house, where the dinner
"came off beautifully."]

27 October 1849

[During a game of dominoes before dinner, Adrien tells a group of Dessalles's
friends about Bissette's visit to Gros-Morne.]

. . . We were listening with interest when suddenly the scene changed. Describing a dinner at the home of a mulatto woman by the name of Estelle,
he enumerated the guests. Bissette had to his right Adrien's bastard daughter
Palmire, whom he kept calling Mademoiselle Dessalles. When I heard this, my
blood boiled up, and I angrily pointed out to him that he should have cor-

rected M. Bissette. He replied that he couldn't care less and that he had just laughed about it. I was overcome by indignation and expressed my feelings in the strongest terms. I explained to him that I had legitimate children and that I would never allow anyone to usurp their name. He said that this name was his own and that he could give it away. I asked him if he intended to legitimize this girl, for in that case I would not remain 24 hours under the same roof with him. "You should be ashamed," I added, "to expose such immorality to the light of day. What is this shamelessness of going around with your bastard girl and introducing her everywhere? Is this not a grave breach of morality and, above all, is it not to mock your family?"

He talked a lot of confused nonsense and uttered the most outrageous improprieties. The gentlemen present were embarrassed. We sat down at the table but did not eat or talk much. The party broke up early. How I am to be pitied!

1 November 1849

. . . Adrien, who has been to town, told us that the mulattoes are fretful and uneasy. A circular letter asking landowners willing to receive M. Bruat in their homes to place their signature at the bottom of the sheet was not signed by anybody. This is the first time that such a thing has been seen in Martinique, where the governors have always been so well received. The conduct of this one must really have been harmful to the interests of the colony for people to treat him this badly!

4 November 1849

Adrien . . . had the opportunity to talk with some men of color [in Sainte-Marie], whom he found more hardened than ever. They complain of the haughtiness with which the whites treat them; their pride is choking them. They hope that the town council will remain in place. "No more than M. Bruat," Adrien replied.

They are hoping that the governor who will replace M. Bruat will be even more democratic. The mayor, Ferdinand Blampuy, has written an excessively polite letter to Adrien to invite him to the banquet the town council is planning to give for M. Bruat. They also wrote a rude one to the curé, who will not appear at this banquet any more than my son. That poor curé will be subjected to persecution by these wretches, for he committed a serious blunder when he accepted to preside over the banquet in honor of Bissette. A priest, the curé of a community, should keep out of all hatreds; his duties and his ministry must come first.

[On 25 November, Bissette pays another visit to the Dessalles plantation.]

25 November 1849

What a lot of noise! What fuss! It has given me a fever, which I still have, and it is two o'clock! The escort arrived, headed by the hero of the day. Our meeting was very cordial, and I embraced his two daughters. The dinner was very pretty and very well served. Before the soup, I addressed the following words to Bissette: "Monsieur le représentant, by inviting you to this family meal, I have been very happy indeed to give you another proof of my confidence and my warm feelings for you. [Speaking to the other guests:] Gentlemen, let us drink to our honorable representative, M. Bissette, who by his noble and magnanimous conduct has acquired in the history of the colonies an admirable page that even the scythe of time will not be able to erase."[16]

M. le curé and Bissette vied for the honor of proposing a toast to me and said the most flattering things. We left the table at ten o'clock, having emptied more than 80 bottles of different wines. The meal was very convivial. Now our rooms are invaded by the farm workers, who have eaten and drunk more than we have. A horrendous amount was simply wasted.

26 November 1849

After an excellent night, everyone arose in very good humor. Bissette, surrounded by all my farm workers, dispensed the most admirable advice to them. He vaunted the advantages of association and *colonage* and thundered against working for wages. At ten o'clock a fine breakfast was served. At table Bissette reminded me of the time when I was in plays at Fort-Royal[17] and even sang two songs from *La Jambe de Bois*. He was really full of wit and charm. At two o'clock everyone left for town. I suddenly went from the most dreadful commotion to the most delicious peace and quiet. I enjoyed my dinner and was in bed by eight.

[The municipality also gives a banquet for Bissette; Pierre Dessalles does not participate but gleefully conveys all the bad things he hears about this event.]

16. It is not the fault of the translator that these metaphors are mixed!

17. Dessalles had both a taste and a talent for the theater. We have a few short plays (in verse or prose) that he wrote in the 1820s and performed on the occasion of social gatherings in the salons of Fort-Royal or Saint-Pierre, where they were much appreciated. They were not lacking in style, inventiveness, and wit [HF and LE].

28 November 1849

A huge crowd has been coming through my courtyard since this morning. Forty marriages were made [at the town hall]. Then the banquet took place: everything was poorly done, there was not enough wine, and one could not even get a drink of water. Several toasts were proposed, and they so excited the participants that in order to hear they broke down everything, climbed on the tables, and crushed the food under foot. They attribute all the disorder that took place to enthusiasm. . . . Maybe so. The fact is that this demonstration was a heavy blow to the Schoelchéristes. Nicaise, I am told, did a fine job delivering the speech I had prepared for him. Bissette is delighted.

29 November 1849

At two o'clock more than 200 riders and 4,000 negroes and negresses went down to town and escorted Bissette all the way to Trinité. Never has such a procession be seen. No shouting, no insults, everything came off in perfect order. All the houses in town had the flags out, and the Schoelchéristes did not show themselves. Bissette walked the streets until midnight and went indiscriminately into all the houses that had a flag at the door. What a blow for M. Bruat! His presence provokes disorder, that of Bissette calms all passions. . . .

[On 4 December, a farewell banquet is organized for Bissette. Adrien and almost all the plantation's farm workers leave very early in the morning for Rivière Blanche, about twenty kilometers from Sainte-Marie, where this celebration is to be held.]

4 December 1849

. . . They returned this evening, not very satisfied. . . . The hungry negroes had fallen upon the meat and bread that had been distributed to them. Bissette was so displeased that he cried out to them: "What are you doing, my friends? You behave like cannibals, like savages! The more I try to raise you up, the more you lower yourselves. You make me ashamed. Am I not a negro like you? Then do as I do, imitate the Whites! They alone will civilize you. Do not imitate the mulattoes. What use is the drum? Don't you see what the Whites use for their dances? Like them, use the violin. Then my daughters and I will come to your dances."

CHAPTER ELEVEN

1850–1852

1 January 1850

Upon awakening I received the wishes of my good Nicaise and then those of almost all the farm workers [*cultivateurs*], to whom I distributed salutary advice. Arquen and Numa Littée came to wish me a Happy New Year. . . .

[His son-in-law Georges de Valmenier having died in late December, Dessalles has to visit his daughter and participate in a memorial service at Fort-de-France, which he continues to call Fort-Royal. Among the social calls he pays during his stay is one to the Bissette ladies, who "received [him] very well."]

21 January 1850

A dreadful day for all hearts devoted to the true principles of order and religion! Fifty-seven years ago today Louis XVI, the best of kings, carried his head to the scaffold. My pain is as keen as on the first day, and I am humiliated to belong to a nation guilty of so great a crime. . . .

17 February 1850

. . . I went down to town to hear mass. The church was very crowded, and without the help of some young people I could not possibly have reached the pew of Pra, who kindly let me have a seat there. Adrien's bastard girl had asked me for one of the two seats I rent in Louis Littée's pew, but I did not care to have the public see me there with her. On the contrary, I want everyone to know that I do not share the weaknesses of that wretched son of mine.

[New negotiations for the sale of the plantation to Dessalles's children had resumed early in the year. They were completed on 5 March.]

5 March 1850

Adrien arrived late last night. Everything has been settled for 200,000 francs.[1] For this my children will have a property that cost me 750,000. I will retire with an annuity of 3,000 francs, which may well be paid irregularly and cause me all kinds of annoyances. So now my son is satisfied; he will take over the authority he so badly wanted, and he does not blush at the position into which his father is placed. Here I am bankrupt, and many people will consider me a fraud. God is my witness that I wanted to pay everything I owed, but the demands of my family have ruined me, and those I expect to face in the future have made me decide to adopt the course I have chosen. . . .

[On 11 March, Dessalles moves to the Caféière. His household there consists of Adée Telcide, the housekeeper; his old servant Adée, who helps out as needed; Ernest, the young handyman, a son of Dessalles's former servant Trop who is also Nicaise's nephew; Ernest's younger brother Léopold; and of course Nicaise. Here is what he has to say about Adée Telcide.]

19 March 1850

. . . I wish [she] would leave for good. It is true that she is very hard-working and very conscientious and that she never forgets the respect she owes me; but she sends lots of things to her mother and uses everything that is mine with a familiarity that does not suit me at all. I really dislike this woman. I do not want to have a row with her, but I wish I could get rid of her in some honorable manner. Impropriety of every kind offends me. . . .

[A few scenes from Dessalles's domestic life at the Caféière.]

6 April 1850

Landais came from Gros-Morne, and a few moments later Louis Ballain arrived. We played Impériale all day long. Adée gave us pork with all kinds of sauces; I hope it won't upset our stomachs too much.

1. By contract signed on 18 February 1850 in the presence of Me. Durieu, notary at Lamentin, and M. Gilmaint, notary at Fort-de-France [HF and LE].

8 April 1850

Yesterday after mass, which I said in my room with my domestics, we continued what we had been doing yesterday; today we led the same life. Paulius Pra brought us newspapers from which we did not learn anything.

11 April 1850

After our dinner Ernest and Léopold took the horses to the river, but instead of returning right away they played around with the ropes. Adée noticed it and felt she should give Léopold a little beating with a creeper. It was even more the fault of Ernest, who is older, and I wanted him to be punished in the same manner, but he ran away. I let him know that he could only get back into the house after he had been punished. He hid and I did not see him again. He is a scoundrel whom I no longer want around.

12 April 1850

Ernest slept in the salon. Nicaise saw him there after we had gone to bed. I could have used this opportunity to whip him, but I preferred to throw him out. He has left, taking with him all the things I had given him. He is a heartless child, and I am glad to be rid of him. . . .

I . . . wrote to my young godson, son of one of my Albis cousins, to invite him to come and stay with me. Landais assures me that he would suit me and that I will be pleased with him. His father, Gigon Désormerie, is crazy and stupid. Nicaise dined with us.[2]

15 April 1850

Young Désormerie has arrived. The child is pale, and one can see that he has suffered utter poverty. He has no linen and no shoes. I had some shirts and pants cut out for him. He is gentle and does not speak French too badly. He went to work right away. I hope that he will be useful to me and that I can do something for him.

24 April 1850

Young Ludovic Gigon [Désormerie] takes care of my cows and works with me on the small garden; he seems to be a good fellow. My goddaughter, who is

---

2. It may have been improper for Adrien to dine with his bastard daughters and other people of color, but for Dessalles to share a meal with Nicaise is clearly a different matter!

the daughter of Saint-Olympe [a man of color], arrived Monday and is mending my table linen.

30 April 1850

. . . I had the visit of three men of color, whose names I will not mention.[3] They talked to me of this bad town council, to which they attribute all the problems of the community. Ernest Yotte is the most culpable of them all, for he is the only one who has some qualifications. If he had wanted to, he could have calmed and straightened out everything. These men assured me that Castandet was saying very bad things, such as, "As long as the whites are alive, the colony will never be tranquil."

Nicaise says this is mere talk and urged these men not to spread it around. Despite Saturnin's ingratitude, I would not want anything bad to happen to a member of his family. Adrien has had some fits of anger against the negroes and has said awful things to some individuals in town. What a temper!

["Retired" and living at the Caféière, Dessalles avidly watches developments at "his plantation."]

3 June 1850

. . . Adrien is displeased with his workers, who don't do much. The mulattoes have succeeded in making themselves heard; they are again engaging in their foolish talk about the Republic and are acting with great insolence. They are led to believe that Perrinon is on his way here and that he is coming to divide up the land. The newspapers from France seem to foretell trouble. Bissette's writings and his speeches to the farm workers indicate that he fears a civil war. All these things are quite unsettling, and I am very much afraid that the whites will have to desert the colonies.

5 June 1850

Adrien's bastard girl Idoine,[4] whom I had thrown out of my house, came to ask me to forgive her. I briefly lectured her and forgave everything.

M. l'abbé Carbonel, pushed by Adrien, offered to buy Nicaise's *colonage* from him. Nicaise asked 10,000 francs, but the abbé wants to give no more

3. Why not? Planning to publish the diary? Showing it around? Or fear that people will go through his papers?

4. She must have been born about 1830. Adrien had brought her to the plantation earlier in 1850.

than 6,000, payable in 1,000 franc installments over 6 months. This proposition is laughable. M. Jeunehomme [the parish priest] found Nicaise's appraisal too high. These good priests do not think that their masses are too expensive, and they say as many as anybody wants. They would like to have everything for nothing. The clergy in this country is not very honorable; it is time for us to get a bishop who does away with the abuses the local priests have instituted. These gentlemen are planters; they lend out money and speculate in ways that do not square with the Gospel. And they want the respect of the public! It is enough to make you shudder![5]

10 June 1850

At six o'clock in the evening, in the middle of a terrible rainstorm, my dear and beloved Nicaise arrived, telling me that he had not felt well since this morning and wanted me to treat him. I immediately ordered a leg-bath for him, but he could not stay in it. He has a strong pain in his right arm and a sore throat; he has trouble swallowing. I suspect he will come down with influenza. I had him rubbed with oil and with camphor and gave him sugar-water and orange blossom tea to drink. He took a little milk soup. He has trouble spitting. I am very concerned about his state. Could he have caught a chill? God of Kindness, do not take this friend, this good servant, away from me.

14 June 1850

For the first time since I began taking down these notes, I spent three days without touching them. God of Justice! God of Mercy! Give me the strength to tell all the circumstances of the great misfortune that has befallen me.

[There follows a long, detailed description of Nicaise's painful but controlled death. Dessalles, probably correctly, eventually identifies his illness as tetanus or lockjaw, contracted when he was bitten by a small dog. Like any middle class Frenchman, the dying Nicaise calls for a priest, a physician, and a notary. The priest hears his extensive confession, but the illness makes the patient shake so much that two physicians are unable to bleed him, and the notary cannot make him sign his will. After the confession, Dessalles tells us, "a negro from Guinea, who is considered a sorcerer, came in with a remedy. The sight of that liquid terrified him [Nicaise]; he screamed dreadfully and asked for me. 'Monsieur,' he said, 'after the action I have just performed, how can I place myself in the hands of

5. Nicaise's *colonage* was not worth more than 6,000 francs. It is true that the local priests engaged in business; the notarial archives indicate that Abbé Jeunehomme and Abbé Decavata were the most active. Since priests had no need for an expensive lifestyle, they had relatively large amounts of liquid capital in a rural area where money was scarce [HF and LE].

a charlatan!' Sublime words, which prove how much he appreciated the forgiveness of his sins." After a series of increasingly terrifying fits, Nicaise mercifully expires at the end of the second night.

Dessalles is deeply distressed by the death of this companion and devoted servant. Nicaise may well have been the only person for whom he ever felt anything that can be described as love, protestations of love for the wife who ruined him and the children who despoiled him not withstanding.

A few weeks later he is invited to the wedding of his goddaughter, a young woman of color whose family he respects. On this occasion he happily drinks to the prosperity of "our beloved Martinique" with his hosts, ex-slaves though they are. For once he seems able to foresee a future in which people of different races will live together in harmony, although one does sense that Dessalles likes Saint-Olympe and his family because they treat him with the utmost deference and endeavor to act like whites.]

17 July 1850

Big wedding today at Saint-Olympe's, a former slave of Mme Le Vassor. By dint of his excellent qualities, his good opinions, and his sensible behavior, he has earned a small fortune and deserved the esteem of honorable people. He is marrying his daughter to a young mulatto, a bastard of M. Gruet,[6] whom he has brought up, so that he knows his temper and his principles. He preferred him to another man, for here he can be sure of his child's happiness. Since I am the godfather of this young woman, to whom at the time I gave three acres of land as a present, Saint-Olympe felt he should invite me to his daughter's wedding. I accepted the invitation without hesitation. At one o'clock I arrived at Saint-Olympe's sugar building, where I found only his eldest daughter, who is married at Trinité to a boat captain by the name of Ularisse. I was received with all possible marks of respect. They had transformed the mill into a dining room. A few moments later Louis Littée arrived, so I could wait without becoming impatient until dinner would be served. Saint-Olympe and his family are Bissettistes and hence not on good terms with the municipal council. The mayor, that vile Ferdinand Blampuy, and his secretary Eugène Godard, a kind of budding little Robespierre, had been in possession of all the papers needed to draw up the documents for a week. But no! In order to do a nasty turn to Saint-Olympe and his family, and probably also to Louis Littée and myself, whom they knew to be invited to the dinner, they did not perform the marriage until four o'clock. Sérano, Saint-Olympe's eldest son, vigorously showed his displeasure and is determined to withdraw from such a municipal govern-

---

6. This young man, Alexis Dorinville, is a carpenter; M. Gruet is a relative of Dessalles's mother and successful manager of the Dessalles plantation in the early years of the century.

ment. So the wedding party did not arrive at the plantation until close to six o'clock. We sat down at the table at half-past seven and were not finished until a quarter past nine. The meal was beautiful and tasty, the wines of good quality. Everything came off admirably well, with all the seemliness and propriety that govern the gatherings of the most distinguished and well-bred people. During the dinner we had a violent storm that disrupted everything: rain, wind, and thunder forced the guests to stop the meal for ten minutes; the hosts finally placed sheets over the doors, and the dinner continued. Before I sat down at the table I proposed a toast to the bride and groom, Littée drank to the health of Saint-Olympe, Sully Jean-Bart to my health, Serrano to that of Littée, and the toasts ended with that brought by Saint-Olympe to the prosperity of our beloved Martinique. The weather, the darkness, and the roads did not permit me to return home. I therefore slept at the home of that good man Saint-Olympe, who heaped every possible attention and the most exquisite marks of respect on me. May God bless this excellent family!

[Meanwhile, conditions in Adrien's household at the Nouvelle Cité are exactly what his father had foreseen. Having attended a special memorial mass for Nicaise, Dessalles spends a day at the plantation.]

21 July 1850

. . . This evening, Léopold[7] was accused by one of Adrien's mule drivers of stealing some money from a drawer. I did not know what to say to this. It just proves to me that I must come to the plantation as rarely as possible, for as soon as any little thing disappears, my people will be accused of having stolen it. Adrien is giving room and board to three or four mule drivers,[8] asking them in return to take care of his horses and serve at table when they are at his house. These young men play cards all day long after they have finished their work, which they perform with remarkable slowness. Most of the time the horses are without water or food. They bring all kinds of characters to the house. Louis Ballain and M. Auguste have seen Idoine delousing the fellow named Alexandre in the kitchen, and it even seems that she lets that young mulatto climb up on her. Adrien's only guest room is occupied by these boys, four or five of whom sleep on the same bed. It is a terrible mess. Palmire herself is in the middle of all of this and is happy to live in this filth. And Adrien sees all of

7. The young handyman who lives and works at the Caféière.
8. One would like to know exactly who these mule drivers were; they may have been close to Adrien's children [i.e., half-brothers of Palmire and Idoine]. This would account for his blind indulgence. Significantly, his daughters treat them as their equals [HF and LE].

this and does not say a word! When he comes back they will tell him about the theft, and he will be the first to claim that Léopold is guilty. Anything these bandits say is Gospel to my son. Really, his way of life is disgusting! I wish I were 1,800 leagues from this country!

[Between 14 August and 24 September, Dessalles spends time at Gros-Morne and Fort-Royal, where he complains about the excruciating heat and spends much time gambling and making social calls. On his return to the Caféière, he finds that his children have taken steps to replace Nicaise in their father's household and, if possible, in his affection.]

25 September 1850

What an excellent night I had! Thanks to the cool weather, I woke up only once. I forgot to mention the return to this colony of Saturnin.[9] He came back, I am told, with excellent sentiments and ideas that he should never have given up in the first place. Mme de Valmenier praises him highly.[10] Are they by any chance thinking that I will take him back into my service? I have forgiven the wrongs he has done, but they are too recent to forget. By his conduct he stirred up my former slaves against me, and this could have led them to kill me. Nicaise, on the other hand, saved me from death and remained faithful to me until his last breath. That is the difference between these two. I used to love Saturnin more than Nicaise and might perhaps have done more for him than I did for Nicaise. His ingratitude was horribly painful to me and made me suffer dreadfully. It also increased my attachment to Nicaise, who came to have for himself all the affection I used to give to both. Today, seeing Saturnin can only increase my sorrow. In the future I will not be able to trust him; I will always consider him a perfidious ingrate, whose kinsmen, with the exception of Saint-Fort, are my most cruel enemies. I therefore hope I will not hear anything more about him.

Régis and Faustin, two men of color, came to talk to me about Saturnin. The former told me that he was sent to me by him [Saturnin]. Adeline, whom

9. Saturnin, 26 years old, is a son of Trop. "Entrusted" to his grandmother Fortunée in a *sale* concluded with the author's permission, he had been freed by Fortunée. He had been living for some time in Guadeloupe with some of his uncles who, as we shall see, were soon to arrive in Martinique as well [HF and LE].

10. The French editors note that the pressure brought to bear by Mme de Valmenier [Calixte, Dessalles's daughter] seems to indicate that she feels nobody will take better care of her father than a "half-brother of color." One must add, however, that Dessalles himself indignantly denies such a paternity. On the other hand he eventually does incorporate Saturnin, his wife, and his children into his household. As in the case of Nicaise the relationship remains fraught with ambiguity.

I had sent to town, was called in by Trop, Saturnin's mother. She was asked how I was, and Saturnin said that he would come to see me one of these days. Apparently he also added—the insolent fellow!—that he was my son and that, if I was strong, so was he. These are insolent words that I do not understand and which I will ask him to explain if he is brazen enough to appear in my presence.

I saw with pleasure that nothing has been neglected at the Caféière during my absence. I really should have two extra workers. Adée has to do all the housework by herself; fortunately, she is not afraid of work. . . .

28 September 1850

. . . Chéry Magloire came to sound me out about Saturnin. I told him all of my grievances against that family and explained to him why it was impossible for me to take him back into my service. He left dejected. Saturnin passed by very close to the Caféière on his way to Montout Léandre. It would have been very wrong of him to come to see me.

30 September 1850

When I was least expecting it, Saturnin appeared. He looked embarrassed. When I saw him I could not help remembering my past kindness to him and his ingratitude. I put him at ease, and my first question was, "What are your plans?" "To stay with you," he replied.

I pointed out that I was in no position to be useful to him, given my straitened circumstances. I explained my situation to him, and in order not to come to harsh reproaches I asked him about news from Guadeloupe. He depicted that colony as an infinitely unhappy place and told me that the horrors he had witnessed there had caused him to change his opinions and that he was today a man of law and order.

"Living with rabid Schoelchéristes," I said, "it seems difficult to believe that you do not share their erroneous opinions." He assured me that he was finished with them. "All the better for you," I added to this.

Sadness was painted on his face. Although he worked very hard [in Guadeloupe], he did not bring back one gourde [five francs]. I did not hide from him the contempt with which I have come to view his family. At this point my dinner was served. He probably expected to eat with me, but when I sat down I said to the servant girl, "When I have finished my dinner I want you to give Saturnin everything he needs."

After my dinner I went to lie down on my bed. After he had eaten, Saturnin came to join me. I showed him Nicaise's portrait; when I talked about the qualities of this excellent subject, I broke down in tears. He too shed a few tears. At that moment, Adée came back from town and told me everything she had seen. Yesterday at mass the curé reproached the newly freed men for the choices they had made in the recent elections and revealed to them the aims of the wicked people who make up the municipal council. It seems that Florine's daughter loudly said in the church, "What business is it of his? He had much better keep quiet."

Saturnin's brother Ernest, sitting in the choir with his uncle Castandet, apparently grimaced and shrugged his shoulders. These are the men whom the curé has admitted to their First Communion!

As he left, Saturnin asked me when he might be allowed to return to see me. "Whenever you like," I said. . . .

[Apparently, nothing is said about Saturnin's "insolent" claim that he is Dessalles's son. Clearly manipulated and in desperate need of companionship, Dessalles spends several weeks reassessing his opinion of Saturnin. A humble gesture on the young man's part tips the balance in his favor.]

16 October 1850

Saturnin arrived yesterday; I spent my day alone with him. He has begun to speak about the wrongs he has done, and I have lectured him long and hard, trying to make him understand that it would take a great deal of effort on his part to obliterate the memory of all the errors in which he had become involved at the time of [the founding of] the Republic. I kept him at arms's length. When it was time to go to bed, he refused the bed that had been prepared for him. Instead, he took the mattress of the small sofa and slept in my room like in the days of slavery.

[Saturnin will live with Dessalles, who can only offer him some land, room, board, "and even laundry service." But since he does have his *état*, he will be able to earn his own money if he can find work. As soon as he has moved in, Saturnin announces that he is in love and wishes to be married. This worries Adée, the housekeeper.]

15 November 1850

At ten o'clock Mme Cognet, the mother of Saturnin's beloved, arrived. I received her politely. I reasoned with her about her political opinions, pointing out how harmful they are to her interests and to her family. She did not seem to be very firmly attached to them [her political opinions]. . . .

I spoke to her of Saturnin's love for her daughter. She agreed to everything, for she adores Saturnin, whose praises she sang. I told her that the marriage could not take place until after the memorial mass for Nicaise that I must celebrate next June 11 [first anniversary of Nicaise's death]. So we have almost eight months to discuss this. Saturnin is enchanted. When she left, Mme Cognet promised me to give up her Schoelchérism.[11]

[Beginning on 1 December 1850, Dessalles no longer makes daily entries in his diary. Until now, the gaps are due to the French editors (with additional cuts by the translators). Henceforth the text still has a certain continuity, but there are gaps of several days, which by 1856 can amount to a whole week (HF and LE).

At the very end of the year, in a complicated transaction, Dessalles buys from Adée a house "for Saturnin" at Gros-Morne. He plans to live there with Saturnin and his wife, who will have a small and as yet unspecified business there.]

1851

12 January 1851

I have seen Saturnin's mistress, whom I found cheerful, amiable, and very gentle. I believe I will be very pleased with her. . . .

25 January 1851

. . . Saturnin's future wife spent 24 hours here [at the Caféière]; she is charming, and the more I see of her the more I congratulate myself on this marriage, which I now wish had already taken place. I have decreed that the wedding should be held at Saint-Pierre. In this manner there will be no fuss and no expense for me and no fuel for a lot of gossip.[12]

29 January 1851

I noticed that more than 30 boards were stolen from my pavilion. I shouted and threatened until the worker Léon declared that he had seen these boards at the house of a mulatto by the name of Saint-Cyr. I wrote to the mayor and the field warden came to take down the particulars. Arthur [who works for Dessalles] is compromised in this theft, for Saint-Cyr stated that it was he who sold or gave him these boards. Poor Adeline [Arthur's wife] was in tears and went to fetch her husband. The latter confessed his guilt and asked my forgiveness

11. This encounter certainly looks like a meeting between the parents of bride and groom!
12. Presumably he means the nature of his relationship to Saturnin.

a thousand times. Young people whose marriage I sponsored less than four months ago and for whom I have shown such warm interest! What appalling conduct! Adrien is of the opinion that I should pursue this matter, but how can I decide to harm two young people of whom I was fond? Arthur is asking me to take him back and promises to make up for his wrongs. Night brings council; I will decide tomorrow.

30 January 1851

This morning I have forgiven everything and written to the field warden not to pursue his investigation. Arthur has gone back to work for me in order to pay back what he owes me [13] and has promised to behave well. It makes me happy that I have been able to do a good deed.

[Saturnin and Rosélie are married February 17 and arrive at the Caféière a week later. "Saturnin's little wife," the author notes on the very first day, "has already taken over the keys, and I think she will do a good job. She seems to be careful and thrifty." The next passage is somewhat puzzling and allows for a number of different interpretations: either simple sexual jealousy of an aging man whose days of "amorous *a partes*" are over; actual erotic interest in one or the other of the young spouses; or the guilty realization that the mulatto Saturnin (possibly his biological son), his wife, and their future children are his true family, and that indeed—just as his wife had said years earlier—he loves them more than his legitimate children.]

26 February 1851

Magnificent weather. Saturnin's wife is suffering from a slight scratch and walks with difficulty. Saturnin neglects all his work in order to stay with her constantly. These amorous *a partes* fatigue me and make me feel more lonely than ever. They do not understand the role they are supposed to play. I hope to God that their devotion to me is not based on a calculation that would mortally wound my soul. It is my misfortune that I love too strongly, and my attachment to Saturnin is above human scheming; I do not fully understand it myself. Right now my imagination and my head are making me into a most unhappy human being. I hide in order to weep. How my children would laugh if they knew what I am feeling.

13. "This incident illustrates the situation rather well: a former slave can live for months on a plantation and perform all sorts of services that are more or less remunerated by *kindnesses*. . . . There is no such thing as pay scales; everything is seen in terms of affective ties. In order to pay for the stolen boards, Arthur—who remains a member of Dessalles's household—will work for a certain number of days like any paid employee" [HF and LE].

I should speak here of Saturnin's wife; she has been near me for five days now. I can see in her all the germs of excellent qualities: she is gentle, and I think she is pious, more by instinct than by knowledge of the Christian doctrine. She adapts to me in a manner that delights me, for she has a kind of reserve that strengthens the good opinion I have of her sentiments. I am convinced that she will become attached to me as much as I am disposed to become attached to her. She is not pretty, as well as short and without a waist, but she is clean, healthy, and endowed with a playfulness enhanced by her youth. I wish her all the happiness she deserves.

Saturnin has no understanding of his business affairs. Before he came back to me, he had contracted a debt of 1,000 francs, and like a fool buckling under to his pride he did not have the strength to prevent his mother-in-law and probably his brothers-in-law from making him acknowledge in his marriage contract that he had received furnishings in the amount of 1,300 francs! All this makes me regret that I was so trusting and so generous. If I do not change the limitless confidence I have in him, he may well have nothing some day; and yet my main preoccupation is to ensure a happy existence for him as well as for his children, if God gives him any.

[From now on the entries often record visits of many days, sometimes weeks, of Rosélie's mother Mme Cognet and many siblings. Dessalles does not seem to mind and only objects rather vehemently when Saturnin's mother Trop joins the throng of visitors. Adrien and his sisters take a dim view of their father's lively household. In April they all spend Easter in Gros-Morne.]

1 June 1851

At the Caféière since last Monday, we have enjoyed perfect happiness and calm here. We love this place and will stay here after the town fête of Gros-Morne. . . .

3 June 1851

. . . The new servant girl we have has complained that she was made to eat a barely green fruit and that she was being treated like a dog. She forgot the respect she owes Mme Saturnin to the point that I had to scold her severely. She is threatening to leave. Mme Cognet is with us. Rosélie and [her sister] Luxine quarrelled in a most unseemly manner; I was afraid they would come to blows.[14]

14. From now on, Rosélie is frequently referred to as "Mme Saturnin."

10 July 1851

The town fête of Gros-Morne has been under way since the 6th (Sunday). On that day many worthless strangers came to town, gamblers, peddlers, and such. Young La Salle [a distant relative] came; he gambled, dined, and slept at Saturnin's.[15] This unfortunate young man has taken to drink. Being very sanguine, he might have to pay dearly in this country. He drank much too much and was so sick that I spent all night nursing him.

13 July 1851

The fête is more brilliant since yesterday. The gamblers do not really like to come to Saturnin's place. Even the whites prefer Adée's low dive. I had trouble finding a group for my whist.

21 August 1851

We hear a great deal of news. It is said that Marlet, the editor of *La Liberté*, and Pory Papy are going around in the countryside, the former in the north, the other in the south, campaigning for their spot on the ballot for the National Assembly. They certainly are starting early. . . . People also say that Marlet, the editor's brother, went to his old plantation, where he called together his former slaves and criticized them for preventing the triumph of Schoelchérism. Apparently he added that within three months the negroes and the whites would be massacred. Three of these negroes made a statement to this effect at the town hall, which immediately notified the higher authorities. The elder M. Massel, who had come from Fort-de-France, reports that a straw dummy representing a white man was carried through the streets and that the populace had beaten it up. The town fête of Sainte-Marie was canceled because of violent scenes among mulattoes. The mayor, it seems, has called for armed support.

How will M. Vaillant [the new governor] handle this? They say he is favorable to us.

23 August 1851

The editor of *La Liberté*, the vile Marlet, arrived last night, accompanied by Alexandre Léandre of Grand' Anse and Exentus of Gros-Morne. These two mu-

---

15. According to the French editors, this is an oblique reference to Saturnin's illegal gambling establishment in Gros-Morne. One assumes that the author lived there too and possibly shared the profits. Adée has set up a competing establishment.

lattoes carried their heads high and seemed proud of the role they are playing. A man of color named Roas had the honor of receiving M. Marlet, who this morning is lunching at Exentus's. Could it be possible that M. Marlet will become the representative of Martinique?! This would be well-nigh incredible. . . .

26 August 1851

. . . *La Liberté*, that vile newspaper, has been condemned to a 1,000 franc fine, suspended for two months, and its editor condemned to a year in prison. The latest issues are incendiary and filled with calumnies. . . .

21 October 1851

This morning Adrien and Charles Bissette [who is visiting Adrien at the Nouvelle Cité] came to see me. The latter promised to come spend a day with me. I shall let a few persons of Gros-Morne know about this, so that I can invite them for the same day. He indicated that Mme Vaillant [wife of the new governor] told him that M. Bruat [the former governor] had made a great mistake by not supporting his [Bissette's] father and that her husband would not make the same mistake, in fact, that he is impatiently waiting for Bissette in order to use his influence over the masses.

28 October 1851

Yesterday Charles Bissette, Simon of Marigot, and another young man, the son of a white woman and a negro whom M. Coutermont has adopted since childhood, came to dinner. Adrien had brought these guests. Saturnin gave us a very pretty dinner. I talked with Charles Bissette about Saturnin, of whom Adrien had spoken very badly. My son looked very uncomfortable, and I could easily see that he is aware of having done wrong. The mulatto Montout Léandre, whom Castandet has legitimized, was introduced to Charles Bissette as a Schoelchériste. "I salute you," Charles said to him. "Monsieur," Montout replied, "I am a mulatto first and foremost." The fool! He would not have had the courage to explain these words. But they are clear, and they mean that M. Montout is quite simply a Sénécal, as all of them are, and that if he had a chance of success, he would do what Sénécal did. But fortunately there are fines, prison sentences, and the galleys.[16]. . .

16. Sénécal was an influential mulatto in Guadeloupe who was just then being tried on charges of inciting black workers to burn white-owned plantations in 1849. He was condemned, although he never confessed [HF and LE].

9 December 1851

... After lunch I went to see Le Camus, who told me that Bissette is arranging the marriages of his son and his two daughters. Thus Palmire will have to look for another husband—if she ever counted on Charles Bissette.[17]. . .

19 December 1851

Yesterday I paid my visit to M. Vaillant [the new governor]. "Monsieur, [he said], I have the honor of knowing you by reputation; you are the father of Mme de Valmenier, whom everyone here loves and respects, and whom Mme Vaillant has highly praised to me."

"M. l'Amiral," I replied, "it touches my heart to hear the praise you have just given to my daughter, for it is well-deserved: it is the truth that forces me to acknowledge this, even though I am her father. A planter of Martinique, where I have occupied high office, I felt it my duty to present my respects to you before leaving Fort-Royal."

"I am delighted," he added, "to make your acquaintance."

Pelet was with me. Invited to take a seat, we sat down. "Now then, Monsieur," the admiral said to me, looking at me inquiringly, "the colony is doing well and I am pleased with its position. We will produce more than 45,000 hogsheads of sugar this year, and attitudes are improving. The fomenters of disorder are aware of my firmness and my resolution; I will not compromise my duty and I pledge to maintain tranquillity as long as I am governor."

"M. le Governeur," I rejoined, "your words are reassuring, and I see with the utmost satisfaction that the confidence bestowed upon you by the partisans of order and of the government is fully deserved."

At this point Pelet spoke up, delivering a long, confused speech and professing his love and sympathy for Louis Bonaparte as well as his happiness in recalling that Empress Joséphine had caressed him in Bordeaux when he was eight years old. I could see that the admiral was most uncomfortable. . . .

Pelet returned to the admiral's impending tour of the colony. "I have already begun it," said the admiral, "and I shall continue it." (Looking at me) "Your countryside is quiet, is it not?" "Yes, M. le Governeur, but the work is not going well, theft is more prevalent than ever, and production is slow." "The proprietors," he replied, "must be patient. There are still a number of measures we can take to safeguard order; until laws have been passed, the proprietors must

---

17. Adrien may have had such a project, although his father had never mentioned it [HF and LE].

put up with a few expenses, allow sick workers to stay on their estates, and provide medical attention for them. After all, they cannot expect to reap great advantages without carrying some expenses."

Here I kept quiet, for I could see that the admiral took me for my son. The latter has recently sent a man suffering from yaws to the municipality of Sainte-Marie. The man was sent to the hospice of Fort-Royal, which sent him back to the municipality of Sainte-Marie with orders from the governor that he be treated at the expense of the municipality. Not knowing all the details of this affair, I did not respond to the governor's challenge. . . .

I went back to my daughter's house, rather fatigued by having had to dress formally. I have come to dislike all ceremonies, and I doubt that M. Vaillant will often see me at his house. The colonists will have trouble adjusting to the grand-seigneurial manners which, I am told, this chief will never give up.

20 December 1851

Yesterday I spent four hours on the Savane [town square]. I was glad to hear a number of different opinions on the situation of France and that of the colony. I met nothing but men of little competence, as well as opponents of the government [*frondeurs*]. I have not yet been able to form a just opinion of the governor, whom I have seen only for a few moments, and whom I will most probably never see again. But I noticed that he did not have the sympathy of those who strolled in the town square; they were making fun of his grand-seigneurial manners and of his cocksureness about maintaining order. Some even went so far as doubting his firmness. All of this is most unfortunate, for if M. Vaillant really means to do the right thing, everyone should help him and acknowledge his good will; after all, he has only been here six months.

1852

1 January 1852

The year began poorly for me, for I was not well at all. Nonetheless I went to mass to thank God for giving us bread until now and to recommend to Him my children, my people, France, and the colonies. May He hear my prayer!

5 January 1852

On the third I left Fort-Royal at half-past seven in the morning and reached Gros-Morne four hours later, not too fatigued. Bailiff de Lorge came to bring me a summons and told me that there had been unrest at Sainte-Marie during the night from December 30 to 31. The Schoelchéristes held a meeting, ate and drank, and swore to burn down the town, to tear open the bellies of six white ladies who are pregnant right now, and to kill the curé. The devout women of the parish were alarmed and urged the curé not to sleep in the parish house, but he declared that he would not leave it, that, on the contrary, it would be a safe haven for those who would take refuge there, and that it was protected by faith and by the law. Twenty-five persons slept in the parish house that night. The farm workers were getting ready to betake themselves to town, but M. Jeune-homme [the curé] sent word to them that they absolutely must not budge from their homes, since the criminals were laying a trap for them. They obeyed their pastor, but more than fifty of them, armed with machetes, did go up to a hillside [*morne*] overlooking the town. All this came off peacefully. Once the authorities are informed, they will no doubt act against these troublemakers. Three negroes of Gros-Morne were told about these events. Two disapproved, and the third declared that from the year 1852 on, everyone should go around armed with daggers and machetes because they should make rivers of blood flow. The mayor, M. Nogig, had him arrested and taken to Saint-Pierre. . . .

6 January 1852

. . . Mme Cognet's [18] daughter, who arrived from Saint-Marie, tells what happened there in a light favorable to the Schoelchéristes; this little girl is caught in disorder up to her neck. These wretches compare what is happening now to the events of 1824. Yet how different it is! In 1824 there was a conspiracy,[19] and the judicial system acted with great severity. The government felt compelled to mete out far-reaching punishments to the colored class; the local authorities eagerly cooperated, and many men of color were unjustly driven out of the country. At that time there were privileges, and the whites, who did everything they could to preserve them, prepared the way for what has happened since.

Today all distinctions have been effaced, equality before the law exists for everyone, and the whites who have lost everything have accepted everything. The people of color, who have gained all they wanted through the events of 1848, should have been satisfied, but they have shown no sign whatsoever of being content, for they were hoping that the colony would fall to them and that

18. Mme Cognet is Saturnin's mother-in-law.
19. The Affaire Bissette: The "conspiracy" amounted to demanding for Martinique what was being demanded in France, namely, the end of special laws for people of color. A pamphlet distributed in Martinique was called "subversive," even though it had freely circulated earlier in France and even in Guadeloupe [HF and LE].

it would be their turn to replace the whites in their position of privilege and power. The government, which was instituted to maintain order and the rights of everyone, showed itself to be equitable. Bissette, the man who had sacrificed everything to the interest of his class, was satisfied with what he had obtained. He came to the colony and preached forgetting the past, reconciliation, unity, work, etc. This admirable policy has been rejected by the proud and the ambitious within the colored class; these wretches have thrown in their lot with the Montagnards and have inscribed Schoelcher on their colors. Today prosecution is directed not against men of color but against revolutionaries who want to put the whole country to fire and sword in order to achieve this changeover. It is unfortunate that the majority of the guilty are mulattoes; they are not blamed for the color of their skin, but for their hateful projects. . . .

13 January 1852

The mail boat arrived on the tenth at seven in the evening, and by eleven we had all the news here at Gros-Morne; Bonaparte has saved France by his firmness and resolve. Perrinon hid during the battle, and Schoelcher was wounded on a barricade. Berryer, Lamoricière, Cavaignac, Changarnier, de Broglie, and 200 representatives were arrested on the eve of the coup d'état. The most severe measures were taken, and the government [of the colony] has received positive and most reassuring orders. Now that the Schoelchéristes have been removed from public offices, we have nothing to fear. Those mayors who do not share the government's opinions will have to resign immediately, and suspect functionaries will be dismissed. Bravo! Bravo! President of the Republic, you are fighting disorder and protecting order. Given such a tactic, France will owe you its salvation and you will be the chosen of the People. What will the wicked municipal governments of this country do now? . . .

14 January 1852

Having left Gros-Morne at eight in the morning, I arrived at the Caféière two hours later. I always feel the greatest pleasure when I find myself in that place, which I found well taken care of. Before leaving Gros-Morne I wrote an address to the president of the Republic, which must have been filled with signatures in the course of yesterday. Adrien sent me one from Sainte-Marie, which I signed. MM. Château-Desgattes, Littée, and Boulanger have handed in their resignations,[20] on grounds that are most damning for the mayor, the

---

20. The de facto conspiracy of the large landowners would thus succeed, for the municipal council was dissolved on 31 January. Jean-Baptiste Roland Château-Dégat was to become acting mayor, soon to be replaced by Etienne Bonneville-Bonneterre [HF and LE].

assistant mayor, and all the municipal councilors. M. Bontemps is even more blameworthy than these men of color [*hommes de sang*]; if he had not kept and protected them, this community would not have become as perverted as it did.

19 January 1852

. . . Saturnin, who went to the Bourg yesterday, brought us the newspaper containing the atrocities committed wherever the reds have triumphed. Our lot in this area would have been dreadful if the Schoelchéristes had had the upper hand. What will we do about all these wretches who keep our communities in a state of malaise? M. Vaillant must make an appearance, or this country will no longer be inhabitable. . . .

21 January 1852

It is 59 years today that our excellent king Louis XVI was led to the scaffold. France has paid very dearly for this horrible crime. . . .

Adrien came to see me yesterday. He told me about a conspiracy headed by Ferdinand Blampuy, Ernest Yotte, and Amédée Thimothée. They were going to set fire to the town and massacre the whites. Adrien was supposed to be one of the first victims. The first two have been sent to Fort-de France, and my son believes they will be shipped off. I do not share this opinion. Protected thus far by the vile M. Bontemps who kept them in power, they will be treated with indulgence.

Just as I am writing these lines, Ferdinand Blampuy is walking across my courtyard, returning from his trip. Although hanging his head, he seems rather tranquil.

I have written to Oysonville and to Pécoul. I am frankly telling the latter that M. Vaillant would be a scourge to this country if he were not firm. I would be happy if my children took over the Caféière by adding 600 francs to my income. I would leave this community with great pleasure indeed!

22 January 1852

Nothing new. I live here in ignorance of what is happening; if it were not for the newspapers, I would know nothing at all.

10 February 1852

I have planted and sown onions and flower seeds that were sent to me from Brest. M. Michaud writes that the president has been named emperor; I am not surprised. I shall be pleased indeed to see the fall of this Republic!

[Throughout these insecure days, Dessalles vicariously enjoys a kind of family life by participating in the events of Saturnin's family and keeping in touch with Adrien, notwithstanding his disapproval of his son's fondness for his "bastard girl," Palmire.]

18 February 1852

Nothing special has happened in these last two days; I had work done around the house and had the yam roots dug out. Ferdinand Blampuy stopped Saturnin's brother and asked him about the news; he was pale and trembling. "Schoelcher must leave France," Ernest told him. "Some people will be deported in this country," Blampuy rejoined, looking dismayed.

Godard threw up when reading the newspaper.

Rosélie [Mme Saturnin] has had labor pains since last night. I have written to the midwife, asking her to come here. I also informed Mme Cognet about her daughter's state. Adrien's bastard girl came up, sent by my son to tell Saturnin that he needed to see him and me that he would like to talk to me. Saturnin therefore went down with Palmire. The midwife and Mme Cognet arrived, but the young woman no longer has labor pains.

21 February 1852

Faustin came up and told me that Adrien had refused to subscribe for the banquet to be held on the 24th, and so has Le Vassor. The new mayor really fails to live up to his dignity; it seems to me that he could have received the head of the colony at his own expense. I am sorry that my position does not permit me major expenditures; otherwise, I would have invited him to come to my place.

Mme Saturnin's state is unchanged; the midwife will leave tomorrow and return as soon as she is called. Castandet, Saturnin's uncle, came this morning to present his apologies [for his role in the recent unrest]. He declared to me that he felt humiliated by his position, that he had been mistaken, and that he begged me to forget the wrong he had done me. I gave him a good dressing-down, urging him to follow a better path henceforth and to be more straightforward in his conduct.

22 February 1852

Since Rosélie's pains were getting stronger, the midwife stayed. M. Michaud told me that the banquet would indeed take place Tuesday and that Adrien and Le Vassor had subscribed after all. Castandet's visit amazes everyone. It is politically wise to receive those who come back and humiliate themselves.

23 February 1852

At two o'clock in the morning Mme Saturnin was safely delivered of a daughter. She was given the names Rose, Marie, *Théodorine*.[21] The midwife left us; she will return Saturday [this is Monday]. The new mayor, M. Château[-Dégat], has invited me in the name of all the planters of this community to attend the dinner to be given for the governor at Mme de la Salle's home. I replied that the poor state of my health does not permit me to leave the house. I am glad I have an excuse for not being at this gathering. I hope that things will go well, but who will be the host of this party?

24 February 1852

. . . Amédée Thimothé came here, like Castandet, to present his apologies. After having upbraided him in the strongest terms, I urged him to perform an action that would provide a guarantee to the government and to society. "Write a letter to those who are to collect the money for the indemnity to be given to Bissette," I told him. "Confess your wrongdoing and add that you are hoping that M. Bissette will be generous enough to admit you to the ranks of his admirers."

26 February 1852

Adrien came to spend an hour with me. It seems that the governor, prejudiced by M. Bontemps, at first received the planters rather coldly. Adrien explained the needs of the community and made the excellent attitudes of the landowners known to the governor. At dinner at Mme de la Salle's, he offered a toast to the admiral and again explained the needs of the community. At each sentence the admiral looked at M. Bontemps in astonishment, as if to reproach him for having misled him. Bontemps would have liked to crawl into a mouse hole. In the end M. Vaillant, delighted with the reception he was given, expressed his wholehearted satisfaction.

29 February 1852

. . . This evening Mme Emile Burot[22] and Mme Cognet's children arrived from Gros-Morne.

21. This name is the Greek version of the French *Dieudonné*, Dessalles's second name. This child's younger brother was to be named *Théodore*.

22. Louisie Burot, a friend of Dessalles, had died in 1843, leaving a large number of descendants of color. Mme Emile Burot may well have been a daughter-in-law [HF and LE].

3 March 1852

On Monday Rosélie's godmother arrived from Trinité with her daughter and her son. We are more than twenty at the Caféière now. All these people are having a great deal of fun and are eating heartily. . . .

Rosélie's godmother left this evening with her children. She looks like a nice woman, but the way she brings up her children shows that she has pretensions.

5 March 1852

Mme Emile Burot and Mme Cognet's children have returned to Gros-Morne; our house is emptying out. Adrien has brought his bastard girl here to pay a visit to Rosélie. Bissette, it seems, is sick.

7 March 1852

Last night Mme Cognet returned to town. So today we are alone, which delights me. This evening I learned that Sénécal and Aristide Thom have escaped from the Fort-Royal jail. It is clear that they had help. M. Bontemps is the main culprit, and yet the *Courrier* had urged him more than once to be careful and to watch the jail warden.

9 March 1852

No news from the fugitives. We still do not know what the administration is planning to do about it. M. Vaillant does not have the stomach for drastic measures. As long as an example is not made, the Schoelchéristes will think that they will be treated with leniency.

Our maidservant left us this evening because yesterday she was asked to carry a few baskets of manure to the cabbage patch.

11 March 1852

. . . Since this morning, Saturnin's daughter has not been well. I sent for two neighbor women, who approved of the remedies I had given her. The child's bowels have loosened, and I believe that the obstruction is gone. I felt it was necessary to administer emergency baptism to her. . . .

26 March 1852

A letter from Gros-Morne informs me that M. Northon Percin and two other planters have been arrested for making insulting statements about the president. If this is true, these gentlemen have been very rash. Besides, how can we fail to recognize the services rendered France and the colonies? These gentlemen are not better legitimists than I am; no doubt they wish that the Duc de Bordeaux were in Louis Napoleon's place? But in these difficult circumstances, would this prince have crushed the revolutionary hydra as Napoleon has done? Patience; and while we are waiting for legitimacy to triumph, let us bless Bonaparte for the good he has done us.

19 April 1852

Last night, when my people came back from mass in town, they told me that the farm workers, especially the women, had wrought terrible disorder there. The mayor had announced to the sound of the drum that the municipal elections would take place on the 25th and that he was counting on the calm and proper behavior of the population. This is when the tumult broke out, and then seditious cries were heard: "We want M. Ernest Yotte," the farm laborers called out.

And one furious woman apparently cried that the time had come for a bloodbath. Agricole—considering that many whites had heard these words—expected this woman to be arrested, but no authority was moved to act, and the gendarmes did not even appear. These planters of Sainte-Marie are scared to death, and none of them will have the courage to show himself under these circumstances.

21 April 1852

The justice of the peace of Trinité came to investigate the affair that took part at Sainte-Marie last Sunday, and the woman who said those bad things has been indicted. It also seems that five negroes have been arrested.

25 April 1852

The rain prevented me from going to town. Great consternation seems to reign there. The elections did take place, but the government had sent 160 soldiers and a canon. The public prosecutor and the new Director of the Interior, M. de la Rougerie, had come in person, armed with the most far-reaching powers. One could have heard a pin drop.

28 April 1852

Yesterday Adrien came to visit me. Ernest Yotte and several others have been arrested and in five days will leave the country for seven years. Twelve blacks[23] have been arrested. Only 276 persons voted, and all the ballots showed the same name. Order has triumphed. Castandet narrowly escaped arrest.

2 June 1852

The workers are leaving the plantation down below, complaining that Adrien is treating them badly. I see that manpower is diminishing every day and that the plantation is no longer in a satisfactory state. I also see that Adrien is personally in financial difficulties, and I fear that this will end badly for him. He spends a lot of money on his bastard girl, whom he treats as if she were legitimate.

7 June 1852

Yesterday, since I did not have a horse, I did not go to town. I said all my prayers at home. Saturnin went to Trinité yesterday, they were having their fête. Adrien took his bastard girl there. One must have lost all shame to show oneself in public in this way with the fruit of concubinage.

17 June 1852

I have given 518 francs to the widow Cognet [Saturnin's mother-in-law]. This sum is for her granddaughter, Théodorine Ransay. It has been agreed and decreed that Saturnin will give to his mother-in-law a room in his house at Gros-Morne, for which she will not have to pay rent. She will be given a second room to store the merchandise she will purchase at Saint-Pierre with these 518 francs belonging to her granddaughter. She will conduct her business as a partnership with her granddaughter; the earnings will be shared half and half, but the sum of 518 francs will be paid back as soon as the earnings permit. Mme Cognet promises to collect the rents for the house and to hand over the exact amounts. The rent for the storeroom for the merchandise will be paid by the business at the rate of 5 francs per month. I made it clear to Mme Cognet that I hope she will not later break up the partnership in order to work by herself, pointing out that I think she would not forget that, of all her children, only her granddaughter had offered her shelter and the means of working.

26 June 1852

Saturnin and his wife left on Tuesday for Gros-Morne, where they will stay until their house opens, and I was left behind with Agricole [Saturnin's uncle],

---

23. Note that until now Dessalles has always used the term "negroes" (*nègres*).

his wife, and children. Today I had good news from Mme de Valmenier. She sent me a letter from Languavant from which I learn of the safe delivery of his wife on 26 May.[24] She also sent me a draft for 300 francs, which I immediately passed on to Languavant, asking him to pay 280 francs to my tailor, M. Flavien.

29 June 1852

Saturnin came back the night before last. He has made enormous purchases for Mme Cognet and has promised to pay for everything within three months: 2,500 francs! I am afraid he has gotten himself into terrible trouble. Impossible to give him advice—he always charges forward without thinking of the future. He hopes to sell 2,000 francs worth at the fête of Gros-Morne. He went back yesterday and informs me from there that his wife, as well as Elmire [Nicaise's daughter] and Théodorine [his baby daughter] are sick and cannot leave there. I expected to hear this, and would not be surprised to learn that Théodorine is dangerously ill.

1 July 1852

Last night Elmire arrived from Gros-Morne; shortly thereafter I received a letter from Saturnin. His wife is better, but she came close to having pernicious fevers. Mme Agricole has been running the household; yesterday she said to the servant-girl that her body was tired. I think she just wants to be appreciated, because she is doing the cooking for six persons. . . . Elsewhere she would have no choice but to prepare their food, and I feel that the least she can do here, where she has no expenses, is to put out a little bit. Agricole seems preoccupied. Of that entire family, Eugène seems the only one whose character seems good to me. I can't wait for Adrien to rent the Caféière to them and to pay me my income from the lease. This place, though delightful for its climate and its healthy surroundings, tires me because of its remoteness from town and because of the composition of my household.

16 July 1852

Agricole came yesterday morning to tell me that he would return to Guadeloupe; he will come back later to fetch his family. The poor fellow has lost his mind because of his money problems. He accuses Saturnin of causing him to move, claiming that he [Saturnin] had assured him that Adrien and I would

24. This was the birth of the first child of Pierre Dessalles's daughter Antoinette, Anna Cléret-Languavant. Four others were to follow [HF and LE].

give him work. This is not true; we only promised to tide him over. All I could do was to cede to him my lease of the Caféière or to lend him a sum of money with which to establish himself. This I am still willing to do. As for Adrien, I surely would not have promised anything in his name. There is something improper and unfair in Agricole's behavior, and I am getting tired of it. Saturnin, who arrived this evening, does not know what to say about his uncle.

27 July 1852

It is eleven days today that Saturnin has not come to the Caféière, and this disturbs me greatly. The fête of Gros-Morne ended on Sunday; he certainly could come back.

6 August 1852

Adrien left for Fort-Royal with his bastard girl. What a spectacle he gives the world! I do not think that he will take her to see his sister. Saturnin came back yesterday.

9 August 1852

... Agricole comes to sleep at the Caféière every night; sometimes he has supper here, and sometimes he does not. One evening he locked himself in his room and did not make an appearance at all; he sulks. What a strange temperament. I am tired of all of this, and I can't wait to be delivered of this family, which is all puffed up with pride. The wife is a stupid thing who, it appears, exerts influence over her husband. I have been told that she is saying things about me and that she does not like me. I wish I never had to hear about her again.

9 September 1852

... A letter from Antoinette [in France] responds rather coldly to the wish I had expressed to join her. So I will no longer talk of leaving. ...

29 September 1852

I received a strange letter from M. Languavant-Cléret [Antoinette Dessalles's husband]; he is cudgeling his brains for reasons why I should not go to Brittany. Good Lord, yes! I certainly get the point. Because if I thought about going where my children are, it was exclusively for the purpose of showing them that

I have nothing against them. But now, if I do go to France, they won't even know where I am going to settle. . . .

21 November 1852

Adrien came to see me a week ago. He has received from M. Michel Duchier a payment-due order for an obligation given by M. de Gaalon to the physician Dartignave. He is being threatened with expropriation. I have no knowledge of this affair. Adrien is very worried. It seems that he is being hounded by Durieu and by his uncle Charles, who also speaks of dispossession. I do not know what is going on among my children, but I would not be at all surprised if they were dissatisfied with Adrien's administration. I do not meddle in anything; I play my role of the one who has been done in. But just in my own little mind I would not be surprised if Adrien were in very bad financial shape. He told me that he does not intend to manage the plantation for very long and that if I went to France, he might well move to the Caféière. All of this does not sound good.

16 December 1852

Many things have happened in the last 16 days. The meeting of the municipal representatives of the Island took place at Fort-Royal. Adrien represented Sainte-Marie. M. Vaillant was most gracious. . . .

[The local priest, Abbé Jeunehomme, has died. Rumor has it that he has been poisoned.]

19 December 1852

M. Jeunehomme has been opened. The doctors stated that there was no trace of poison; he died of yellow fever and a cerebral hemorrhage, and his liver was horrendously enlarged. I am told that my son spoke at his graveside. I also hear that he was bled yesterday and that he has a fever. Given the life he leads, he has no resistance to disease; he will die if he does not give up the management of the plantation.

28 December 1852

On the 20th, when I was just sitting down to eat, a messenger from Adrien came to tell me that he was dying and wanted to see me. After a violent fit of emotion I mounted my horse and by dreadful paths went to the Nouvelle Cité, where I found the doctor. That morning Adrien, having gone out too early, suffered a fainting spell and thought he was about to die. He became frightened, sent for me, asked the doctor and the priest to come, and made his last wishes known to his friend Charles Bissette whom, I understand, he named his execu- tor. The doctor applied scarified leeches, and an hour and a half later Adrien was fine. All he needs is care, rest, and proper food. His temper is killing him and compromising the interests of the entire family.

By now he can only produce by spending money. A man of color by the name of Petit, whom he pays five francs a day, has taken command of a work group that cultivates his cane; he gives each worker 1.40 francs a day. These people do just about what they want; this Petit is cheating my son who, fear- ing that his workers will disappear, does not say anything and closes his eyes. His situation is deplorable, for he has few workers left, and those who are still with him are dissatisfied and threaten to leave. M. Michaud's *colonage* is well cultivated, but the good man is treated so poorly by Adrien that he does not want to do anything for him. My son seems to trust Charles Bissette more than anyone else. Palmire told someone in confidence that Adrien was giving her in his will 6,000 francs, six mules, some oxen, and a fully saddled horse. My son's hatred for Saturnin is frightening; he does not dare speak to me about it, but I am only too well aware of it. . . .

I am sending 86 francs 40 to my grandchildren in Fort-de-France and several silver spoons for serving sugar to Calixte.

CHAPTER TWELVE

1853–1856

1 January 1853

In the past, my house was [on this day] full of individuals who always came to present to me good wishes the insincerity of which I was fully aware. I was rich then, and I kept a good table. Now that fortune no longer smiles on me, I have not seen anyone except for a few men of color who, out of habit, came to wish me well. Even my son kept the most profound silence. I have not grown old without getting to know people, and my conclusion is that it is better to see them from afar than close at hand. My solitude would please me if it were not in this country and if I had a church close by.

Yesterday I received news from my children at Fort-Royal, to whom I had sent some modest New Year's presents. Mme de Valmenier sent me a dressing gown, and her eldest daughter a skull cap of black velvet.

[In the first three months of this year, Dessalles is greatly concerned about his son Adrien's health. Adrien suffers repeated episodes of arrhythmia and generalized agitation, brought on, as Dessalles and the French editors suggest, by the stress of attempting to manage a plantation under very adverse conditions and aggravated by the constant clamor for money of an entire clan of siblings, a father, an uncle, at least two illegitimate daughters, and a host of creditors. In fact, the symptoms seem to cease altogether after Adrien leaves Martinique and after his father dies.

Considering his son mentally unbalanced, Dessalles also worries that Adrien might actually legitimize one or both of his "bastard girls" or even marry one of their mothers.

In late February, Adrien goes to Fort-de-France to seek medical care and boards Palmire with Mme Bissette.]

2 March 1853

Adrien arrived yesterday with his bastard girl; his state is still the same. He is more preoccupied with his nerves than ever. He went to town because, he says, he wants to celebrate his jubilee and his Easter. May this resolution change his temper! His bastard girl speaks only French[1] and has learned at Mme Bissette's certain mincing ways that will elicit mockery and hatred from her class. Her mother [Virginie] came to speak to me about her unhappiness: "M. Adrien," she said, "is making Palmire's misfortune, but she is too stupid to realize it. I can no longer make any objections, for she replies that her father knows what he is doing and that she will always obey him."

My son's worst illness is this bastard girl, whom he seems to want to put on a ridiculous footing. He cannot impose her on his family which, I think, will not accept her.

6 March 1853

... [On Thursday] I went to the plantation for dinner. As I sat down I noticed five settings[2] and heard the servant call Palmire. I was preparing a strong reprimand when Virginie and Palmire had one of the settings removed. I silently thanked God. Even if my legitimate children were to accept this girl — which, I hope, will never happen — I would crawl into a hole and wait for death there; never will I hurt myself by dragging my name into the mud. Adrien will cause me grief as long as he lives. ...

[At the Nouvelle Cité, Palmire and her mother Virginie are causing a great deal of trouble by interfering in the work of the manager and different workers during a renewed absence of Adrien. Dessalles, who supervises the operations of the plantation, is very tired of "these women," who also cause extra expenses by wanting fine food (shades of "the ladies" of earlier years!); he wishes they would go away. On a brief visit to his beloved Caféière he finds more trouble from women; here it is Saturnin's mother-in-law, Mme Cognet, and her daughter Elisabeth, who bother him by "their pride and their horrible opinions." Since Dessalles is not in

---

1. People of color of her social class usually spoke only Creole [HF and LE].
2. For himself, Adrien, the manager, the assistant manager, and Palmire [HF and LE].

the habit of mincing his words, he "tells hard and terrible truths to this mother of a family who, she says, wants to convert although she does not know the first thing about Christianity."]

1 July 1853

. . . Judging by what I hear from Adrien, I am afraid that he is going out of his mind. His private behavior, the disarray of his business affairs, the bad state of the plantation, all brought about by his utter mismanagement, are well suited to impair his reason and give him tremendous remorse. I am really sorry that I have agreed to look after this plantation where I never should have set foot again. For all my troubles I will get nothing but insulting suspicions and ingratitude. . . .

Mme Saturnin, who went down to town on the 28th with her newborn, had him baptized on the 29th. His godfather is Fofo [Joseph Simon, called Fofo, the young mother's brother-in-law] and the godmother is Trop, the child's grandmother [Saturnin's mother]. There was a great gala at the Caféière, at which this Fofo was not present because, Saturnin told me, he had sworn never to eat at a white man's house. This is hatred pure and simple, or I know nothing about it!

3 August 1853

The last 24 hours have been dreadful. Adrien did not close his eyes all night, and nobody slept. He went in for the most hideous extravagances, he danced and sang horrible songs, declaring that he was damned. He wanted to tell everybody present about his presumed crimes, but I stopped him from doing that. He went to get his bastard girl, brought her into the main room and, presenting her to all who were there, said, "Here is the Queen of Sheba, the devil will take us both." "Papa," he also said, "we will go to hell together. You don't believe anything, do you?" I calmly pointed out to him that he was raving. "The devil has gotten hold of me, I wanted to betray God and have sought human consolations. Everything pushes me away from the Church; I do not believe anything." "Here again you are mistaken," I said, "you are afraid, and therefore you believe. Your conscience is speaking, and therefore you believe. You repent of your past sins, and therefore you believe. A man who does not believe anything lives a life of crime in all tranquillity and has no thought of confessing it."

Tired of arguing, he finally calmed down. The priest came at two o'clock, and they stayed together for a long time. After he left, Adrien was more calm and said that the next night would be better. He did not want to see his bastard girl who, I am told, has decided to move away. Her mother came to speak to me, and I advised her to do the same thing.

9 August 1853

Yesterday M. Trevor Daney came back from Fort-de-France; Mme de Valmenier will send a new manager. So here is a plantation that will fall into the hands of businessmen and speculators; it will soon cease to belong to my children. . . . Mme de Valmenier told M. Trevor that I had tried several times to manage the plantation myself and that I had always failed. The poor woman! When in fact I am—after M. Gruet [manager for Dessalles's father]—the one who produced the most sugar! Well, they can do as they please, if only they give me back my tranquillity; that is all I aspire to.

[Adrien's state does not improve for a long time, and the dissensions within this dysfunctional family become increasingly obvious. At one point Mme de Valmenier asks her father to dismiss "his people," that is, Saturnin and his family who have come to help him, from the Nouvelle Cité; at the same time she tells him that she has had a falling-out with her brothers-in-law and therefore only corresponds with her sisters. For a time Mme de Valmenier no longer even responds to her father's call for help, so that he has to take sole responsibility for the decision to take Adrien to the insane asylum at Saint-Pierre against his will. Adrien eventually relents and enters the asylum voluntarily on 21 October. Dessalles returns to the Caféière and a new manager, M. Camille Roy, takes charge of the plantation.]

24 October 1853

Friday night I went to town; on Saturday I spent all day with the agricultural committee. All the members except Adrien and de Launay were present. We received propositions for rewards to be given to agricultural workers. In my opening remarks,[3] I pointed out to these gentlemen that they should defend their chairman, keep our deliberations secret, and not become upset if the persons they had proposed [for a reward] were eliminated. The parish priest and the mayor were present. In his first comment the priest opposed me concerning the [unspecified] reward which I wanted to be given to the negro Israël, an excellent subject. The curé, with incredible vehemence, rejected my demand out of hand, declaring that Israël did not fulfill his religious duties and that he was unmarried. I pointed out to him that this did not affect Israël's merits as a man of order and a good worker. Still in the same heated manner, he refused

3. Pierre Dessalles seems to be chairman of the committee.

to vote for this reward. I offered to withdraw my nomination, but the committee did not want to hear of it, and so Israël was proposed for a silver medal of class I. Yesterday, when the time came to sign the minutes of the deliberation, the curé did so only after he had denied making yesterday's statements, realizing no doubt that they were improper and stupid. He had the imprudence to state in the presence of Robert Littée, Pierre Martineau, M. Chauvet, and the two young Doguerres that if Israël obtained the votes of all the members of the committee, it was because these gentlemen had not dared reject him because of me. I admit that at that moment my indignation was extreme and so I said what I thought of the cowardice of such individuals. "They told me so themselves," the curé added.

At this moment Louis Littée came into the room; it was clear that he had started all this gossip. I told him the harshest truths and announced that henceforth I would certainly avoid sitting on a committee with such people. The curé, sensing that he had done a stupid thing, tried to repair the damage. I called on these gentlemen for a new vote: M. Chauvet was the only one who dared support me, the others kept quiet. I left very displeased. Today I had lunch with the curé at Mme de la Salle's. We both played it close to the chest and . . . we got along quite well.

5 November 1853

Staying here in town is terrible. Saturnin, his wife, and their children came to join me. We are tightly packed together, and we don't find anything to eat.

Last Monday, leaving the confessional, I was not a little surprised to see Adrien come in. As soon as he arrived he called Palmire to the town hall and met her there. . . . He has come to Sainte-Marie only to see these wretched women.

7 November 1853

. . . Adrien arrived, sicker than ever; he thinks he will die any moment. He is today tormented by only one thought, that of getting back to his wretched women. I told him that he should not stay in this country, where he would never accomplish anything. He wants us to sell the house in Bordeaux so that he can have his share.

10 November 1853

. . . He wants to live under the same roof with his bastard girl and her mother. . . .

21 November 1853

. . . Adrien arrived yesterday at two in the afternoon. Since then he has almost always been lying down and shows the most profound sadness. He told me that he takes pleasure in defying God, even though he is convinced of the truths of our religion. He feels pursued by the demon and is expecting the arrival of Msgr. Le Herpeur who is to exorcise him. The demon that pursues him is Palmire and no one else.

[Adrien's illness continues to bring confrontations, gossip, and painful scenes until Mme de Valmenier persuades her brother to return to France.]

1854

3 January 1854

New Year's Day was very sad for me. The young girls who are staying with Mme Saturnin took advantage of the fiddlers who came to serenade me at four o'clock and danced until six and again this evening until seven. This savage gaiety made me sad and I spent the day in prayer. I received from my daughter a box of candy and letters from my granddaughters. MM. Roy and Michaud called on me. I am busy cleaning up around our house so that my guests will find it clean on Saturday.

10 January 1854

On the seventh at eleven in the morning MM. Louis Littée, Pierre Martineau, Desgates father and son, Jules and Gustave Littée, Chauvet, Vincent, the police commissioner, and Harold de la Salle arrived. A few moments later M. Roy Camille [sometimes called Camille Roy, the manager at la Nouvelle Cité] also came. We dined at two o'clock. MM. Louis and Gustave Littée left after dinner. M. Michaud came only for the supper, which took place at ten o'clock. Saturnin distinguished himself by the manner in which he had prepared all his dishes. On the eighth the same guests stayed; after the supper at eleven o'clock Martineau and Vincent left. On the ninth I had only MM. Desgates father and son, Chauvet, and Harold de la Salle, who only left me at five o'clock. We drank and ate considerable quantities and played *brelan*. Everyone seemed to be delighted. . . .

13 January 1854

This morning M. Ferdinand Blampuy [a prominent man of color and former mayor], coming through my courtyard, called over Saturnin and told him that he knew for a fact that M. Marchet had accepted the powers of attorney of my daughters and my son and that he would soon be on the plantation. How interested everyone is in the affairs of my family! Everyone covets this plantation and would be happy to see our ruin.

25 January 1854

Last evening I had the visit of M. Roy Camille. He brought me a letter from my daughter informing me that M. Marchet is the legal representative of my children in France.

Four thousand francs for M. Roy, 3,000 for me, 3,000 at least for M. Marchet . . . what will be left to divide among my brother and my children? [We have here] a run-down plantation that needs an immediate expenditure of at least 30,000 francs to bring it back. . . . The future looks horrible for my unfortunate children. . . .

4 February 1854

. . . Mme de Valmenier tells me [by letter] about an errand that Harold de la Salle was simple-minded enough to carry out: Palmire apparently entrusted to him a silver place setting, asking him to show it to Mme de Valmenier in the hope that she would buy it. My daughter has perfectly understood these women's [i.e., Palmire and her mother] purpose, which is to let her know that they are in distress. When I sold these two place settings I did so under the condition that the coats-of-arms be removed. But what reason would my daughter have to help Palmire rather than Idoine, Ernest, and Montout, who are also her brother's bastards? Was Mlle Palmire born to be a salon-lady? Born a bastard, she should expect no more than a few acts of kindness; destined to live by her own work, why would she want to free herself of that constraint?

[On 13 February Dessalles learns that Adrien has left for France on the 10th. He feels relief, but also concern about his son's future, given his mental state.]

30 March 1854

Mme Saturnin went into town last night. She left Théodorine with me. Since her [Mme Saturnin's] sister Elisabeth is sick, I sent for Cécé, who has been with me since eight this morning.

M. Roy Camille came to see me this afternoon; he complains about everything that goes on down at the plantation, the mill out of order, the boiler slipped off its mounting, the sugar sticky and awful . . .

Mme Saturnin went into town to see to it that the nails, shucks, and tiles that were to be sent to us from Saint-Pierre arrive in good order, and also to be there when the building is set up today.[4] This young woman has more work than she can handle, she is tired out.

I have given in to the wish of M. Roy, who is consequently farming out the last sugarmaking operation to Saturnin. I did not want to say no, but he should never have proposed this idea, knowing the absurd opinion of my wretched children, who feel that my influence and that of my people is harmful to their interest! I now stop down there only if I absolutely have to, and I have decided to take out my furniture, since I will never sleep there again.

1 April 1854

MM. Roy and Michaud came yesterday to inform me, the former that he is leaving the plantation and the latter that he is in danger of having to do the same thing. M. Roy confessed that he had found in Mme de Valmenier very little sympathy for me. Turpin had also told me this; of my six children she is the one of whom I have the most reason to complain.

26 April 1854

M. Roy has left the plantation. On the ninth I had lunch with him at Mme de la Salle's, and that evening he went to Gros-Morne. The man who replaces him—M. Lalung, whom I met in town and yesterday on my way back to the Caféière—seemed intelligent to me, and I had the impression that things were going better. I spent eighteen days in town staying with Mme de la Salle. Every day I played a few hands of *brelan*. Twice we had a dinner prepared by Saturnin and once we met at Numa Littée's.

M. de la Martinière the younger is M. Lalung's assistant. I only know him for his awful past. Our poor Nouvelle Cité will be exploited by strangers.

---

4. It appears that Saturnin—or Pierre Dessalles—is having a house built at Sainte-Marie [HF and LE].

2 May 1854

. . . Tomorrow the planters of this town are to meet at the town hall to discuss cutting the wages of the day laborers. They will not agree on anything, and I predict that nothing good for the general interest will be decided.

4 May 1854

Robert Littée writes me that almost all the planters responded to the mayor's call, but that they did not come to an understanding among themselves.

Israël came to me to lodge a complaint against the manager and the assistant manager of the Nouvelle Cité. I urged him to calm down and told him that I have nothing to do with the plantation.

16 May 1854

. . . On Sunday M. Lalung and his assistant came to see me for the first time. M. Lalung, though telling me that his orders were to treat me with every possible courtesy, has surely received from M. Marchet [attorney for the Dessalles children] instructions coming from MM. Cléret [sons-in-law] and perhaps dictated by my daughter Emilie. My son's servant Calixte—he boasted of it—is charged with watching Saturnin. To attack Saturnin is to attack me, for everyone knows that whatever he does he does on orders from me. Is M. Marchet going to be to me what Hudson-Law[5] was to Bonaparte? May God soon call me to himself!

[In May, Mme de Valmenier pays a brief visit to her father in order to check on the plantation.]

19 May 1854

Madame de Valmenier went down to the plantation early in the morning yesterday. She was not exactly delighted with how the house was kept. M. Michaud dined with us and told my daughter about all the trouble M. Marchet is giving him.

At noon M. Marchet sent word to my daughter that he had arrived. She immediately started down, went over everything with him, and was back at five o'clock. She told me that this new business manager had written to my children urging them to take over the Caféière and to compensate me by adding 600 francs to my pension.

5. Hudson-Law was widely believed to have poisoned Napoleon.

5 June 1854

I hear that M. de la Martinière has had scenes with the farm workers down below, that he beat some of them, and that he got drunk. My poor children!

I had asked M. Lalung to inquire of M. Marchet to whom I should address myself for the payment of my pension. Yesterday he sent word through Saturnin that he had spoken to him and that M. Marchet's only response had been a shrug. The insolent fellow! I have written to Mme Valmenier, informing her of this behavior. . . .

9 June 1854

Césaire went to Fort-Royal to complain to Mme de Valmenier about the bad conduct of the new managers of the Nouvelle Cité. I don't think that he obtained any redress from my daughter. . . .

I don't hear anything about my pension, and I am short of everything. . . .

13 June 1854

I finally received a letter from Mme de Valmenier authorizing me to draw on MM. Monguy et Douettes for my pension due on the first of this month. She had written to M. Marchet, who did not feel it necessary to respond. The men working for M. Marchet continue to be in conflict: M. Lalung has confessed that his assistant, M. de la Martinière, was beginning to be a burden to him. This young man drinks heavily, and he has beaten up a farm worker by the name of Zéphir. The latter was determined to lodge a complaint, so the matter had to be settled by means of money. M. de la Martinière continues to tell people that the plantation will eventually belong to him. "My father," he says, "has tons of gold, and he will buy it one of these fine mornings."

My children don't even know all of these braggarts' plans.

15 June 1854

Yesterday I received a messenger from Mme de Valmenier. . . . My daughter tells me that M. Marchet has not yet answered her; she is afraid that my draft will not be honored. That would really put me in a fine position! She invites me to come to her so that we can figure out together what is to be done. I replied with a long letter that will not amuse her.

5 July 1854

Yesterday the most dreadful scene took place: Mme Saturnin forgot the respect she owes me and said that henceforth she only wants to serve those people who suit her at my house. I tried to make her understand that she must serve without distinction all those who come here, but she rejected this view, and Saturnin sided with her. So, hard as this was, I found it necessary to tell them some rough truths, and I ended by asking them to leave me. This morning I repeated to Saturnin that his wife's temper made it impossible for me to live under the same roof with her. She made no effort to come to see me and is preparing to take her things to town. I shall not retain her.

8 July 1854

Yesterday M. Marchet, who had arrived on the plantation, sent me a draft for 750 francs. . . .

15 July 1854

I meant to go to town today, but since Mme Saturnin went down on Thursday I did not want to leave the Caféière unattended, so I stayed. My life is one of continuous sacrifice. M. Michaud dined with the managers; he is scared of M. Marchet, as he has been scared of all his predecessors.

19 July 1854

Yesterday a negro of the Nouvelle Cité by the name of Francis, a rebellious subject whom Adrien had brought in, came to lodge a complaint against the assistant managers with me. I dismissed him by telling him that this was not my business. He left railing against them: "They are bad men who want to run everything into the ground so they can get the plantation for nothing," he cried in rage.[6]

8 August 1854 [after a three-week stay in town]

I returned to the Caféière, happy to find my accustomed solitude which I use to take care of my flowers and my little garden and to pray. Saturnin's chil-

---

6. The French editors write, "This scene is characteristic of the visceral attachment that slaves and then former slaves had for the plantation—and frequently for the proprietor and his interests as well. This attachment existed for a long time. Sometimes one wonders if it does not exist to this day." This interpretation is debatable.

dren are an immense resource for me, although they often tire me out. I heard that Saturnin is having a house built in the Bourg and that he wants to put a forge there. He had not told me about this. I took the news calmly, but I am far from happy about it. How will he be able to do this?

12 August 1854 [again in town]

... It is very hot, and there is serious talk of cholera. *La France d'Outre-Mer* has a letter from Dr. Rufz about this epidemic; its opinions are no doubt very wise but rather inconclusive as to the means of protecting oneself from an illness against which medicine has not yet been able to find a remedy. Dr. Rufz's reasoning would probably be more consistent if he were talking about the best means for making a quick fortune.

20 August 1854

The entire past week was spent in burning heat. A letter from my daughter [Mme Valmenier] informs me that the Pelet family called on her in order to ask her for her daughter Anna's hand, which she felt she should accord them. The young man, whom she praises highly, has no fortune and no position; but he loves Anna who, as far as one can tell, shares the same feelings. I could only approve this choice.

On Assumption Day, we celebrated our Holy Patroness [Saint Mary], the Protectress who speaks for us to God; we also celebrated Napoleon III. The entire town council was present at the ceremony. The curé brought in a newly ordained priest to preach. A young man of lively temperament, he did not confine himself to extolling the virtues of the Virgin Mary, but instead thundered against the vices of this town's planters; certain of his expressions were reminiscent of Abbé Gailhat's [the local priest's] endlessly repeated complaints and seemed to be directed against the members of the town council. Great uproar after mass. . . . I noticed that the planters were most displeased; in order to avoid having to express my opinion and to get involved in the discussion, I abstained from going up to the curé and saying anything about this sermon, which I had found as inappropriate as it could be.

A complaint against the curé had already been formulated and was going to be sent to the higher authorities when MM. de Gage, Bonneville, and Sainte-Marie Magloire [7] went to see the curé and made him understand the seriousness of his situation. Thereupon the curé went to the town hall, where all the mem-

7. The former two are white, the third is a man of color.

bers of the council severely berated him; he told them that he was very sorry about this sermon and swore that he had nothing to do with what was said. In the end he promised to repair the damage from the pulpit. At this morning's high mass, he did indeed take to the pulpit. But far from presenting his apologies, he aggravated the situation by extolling the other preacher's virtues and his intentions of sacrificing everything to bring salvation and eternal bliss to those whom he had excoriated the week before. So far as I am concerned, this is another insult. After mass Thénos de Gage came to me and said that the best thing we can do is keep quiet and not let our opinions be known. The planters will never see eye to eye with the curé, for the planters are upset and feel deeply offended, while the curé is highly excitable and listens too easily to things he is told. Among his flaws are frequently uncouth manners and an iron will. "They can break me," he often tells me, "but they cannot bend me."

This unfortunate friction makes for difficult social relations. I have so many reasons to leave the Caféière! But where can I find a place that would compensate me for leaving this delightful place?

[In the middle of August, Dessalles spends ten days at a modest spa, "les Eaux de Mouth," where his daughter is taking the waters. Although he feels that bathing and drinking the ferruginous waters is good for his health, he is so bored that he even is glad to talk to strangers.]

15 September 1854

New bathers have arrived at the spa. I had the occasion to talk to a Sieur Nicolas, a *capre* [offspring of a mulatto and a black] who seems to be a fairly educated man. He went into business and is said to have earned 300,000 francs in four years. He has traveled in France and in many other countries, which he describes rather interestingly. This morning I took my last bath; I am anxious to get out of this awful hole.

[Meanwhile, M. Marchet is very slow to pay Dessalles's pension. In early October he is finally told that M. Monguy will send him a written statement to the effect that his drafts will be honored at the end of each trimester. "So now that is taken care of," he writes, "until things change again."

Dessalles spends all autumn at Fort-de-France, with intermittent visits to his daughter and grandchildren at Rivière-Monsieur and to Saint-Pierre, where he visits old acquaintances and indulges in gambling. The following entry exemplifies his desultory existence rather well.]

9 November 1854

Yesterday I paid a few visits. I saw my old friend Mme de Pompignan, who was glad to see me. She is 74 years old (five years older than I) and has fifteen children, all of whom are doing well. At four o'clock I went to notary Gandelat's house, where I played a three-handed boston; I lost thirteen francs, which did not amuse me. I am terrified at how my money is running out. Today I had lunch at the house of Le Tourneur of Gros-Morne; there I also saw Mme Pellerin-Latouche and her brother Vergeron. After lunch I went to the shop of a man by the name of Meilhié, who is from the same place as I. He was very pleased to see me and I bought some linen goods from him. At two o'clock I went back to Le Tourneur's where we played boston until six, and then I went home to Mlle Anna's [a woman of color who keeps a kind of boarding-house] in a terrible downpour.

14 November 1854

Still no boat [by which to travel to Sainte-Marie]. I am bored and tired of my situation. I will therefore go back by land. . . .

20 November 1854

I left Saint-Pierre on the 16th and was with my children [at la Rivière-Monsieur] at half-past eleven. . . . Yesterday, Sunday, I left my children, who seemed somewhat sorry to see me go. At ten o'clock sharp I arrived at the chapel of Rivière-Blanche where I heard high mass and a sermon on the respect one owes to the temple consecrated to God. I was very pleased with the solicitude everyone showed me. At half-past eleven I got back in the saddle. Between Gros-Morne and the Caféière, the trails I took were regular death-traps; if I had had any idea of how bad they were, I would have returned to Saint-Pierre and waited for a boat. I did not arrive home until half-past five. I am all tired out, my rear end is reduced to a pulp, and every one of my limbs feels broken. I can barely place one foot in front of the other. I was in the saddle for ten hours without taking so much as a glass of water.

At the Caféière I only found one young girl and Saturnin's two children. The children recognized me right away and were happy to see me. Mme Saturnin is ill and has gone to town for treatment; it seems that she was in great danger.

25 November 1854

Saturnin came up on Tuesday night and stayed until Wednesday. On Thursday he came back with his wife and Mme Cognet [his mother-in-law]. I was struck by Rosélie's looks; she has come back from afar! Yesterday I was happy to see Mme Cognet leave. Mme Saturnin eats nothing but salted meat. . . .

To my great astonishment I had the visit of M. Lalung, who stayed for more than two hours. I did not want to talk about the plantation; but when he stayed on and on I did ask him if everything was going well *down below*, and he told me that he was satisfied. He then entered into details that proved to me that things are indeed going well and that the plantation is being brought back; in the last seven months he has sent to the commission merchant 155 hogsheads of sugar. M. Roy had earlier sent at least 50. This means that the plantation has produced 200 hogsheads [about 100 tons] of sugar in 1854.

7 December 1854

. . . M. Marchet has authorized M. Michaud to pay my pension due on the first of this month.[8] Marchet was offended by two words he saw in my letter to Michaud, namely *"ce Monsieur,"* and he used them to refer to me in his authorization. This is the small vengeance of small people, the touchiness that comes naturally to them. . . . M. Marchet does not like well-bred people because, however brilliant a position he may attain by his various schemes, they will never consider him anything but a pipsqueak parvenu.

Dr. Chauvet, who came to the Caféière today to see Mme Saturnin, told me that the curé [Abbé Gailhat] continues in his inappropriate ways and that his relations with his white parishioners are worse than ever, whereas the blacks are putty in his hands.

1855

7 January 1855

. . . Last Thursday Mmes Saturnin and Cognet provoked a scene I felt obliged to make, and I told the former that she would have to give me my tranquillity and move to her own house. This young woman has a very difficult temper; puffed up with pride and pretensions, she thinks she is the equal of the colony's best families. And her mother, that old fool, sustains her in these notions. She

---

8. This payment came out of a sum Michaud owed to Marchet.

manages to drive from my house all those who were here as servants. Why, for a while it looked as if I would have to serve myself!

The cause of this scene was a young girl by the name of Cécé who had befriended us and for this reason had been living with us for a year. I liked her because she took such good care of Saturnin's children. Mme Saturnin took a dislike to her and talked roughly to her. Rose, that wicked little animal, also became involved and insulted Cécé. These women of color can think of the most diabolical things, and their pretensions are as farfetched as they are foolish. I told Saturnin to please take his wife to her own house, because I can no longer live under the same roof with her.

[After a stay at Sainte-Marie, where he has lost 85 francs and 40 centimes gambling, Dessalles returns to the Caféière.]

13 January 1855

. . . I found Mme Saturnin ready to leave the Caféière and to go to town [where she will live]. Saturnin had hoped that she would apologize to me and promise to change her bad manners, but she said the same improper things. Then, more stubborn than ever, she left without saying a word. She left Théodorine with me because Saturnin had demanded it. She moved everything out, taking not only her things but mine as well. I wrote to Saturnin to claim them back. I am sorry that they left me his daughter; I would have made the sacrifice of not seeing the children, since someday I will have to let them go anyway.

I am very happy in my isolation, and I am hoping that the Caféière will be restored and taken care of by a man of color who will soon move in here. Then this place will be more pleasing to me than ever. . . .

25 January 1855

Mme Désormerie [a distant relative], her sister, and two of her children came to spend 24 hours with me. They were obliged to serve themselves, since the servant Juliette did not show herself at all while they were here.[9] This morning I therefore sent her back to town, where Saturnin can deal with her as he sees fit.

[Mme Saturnin's imperious ways during a short stay at the Caféière bring Dessalles once again to the realization that he must separate himself from Saturnin and his family.]

9. Juliette, alias Cécé, lived at the Caféière as a *friend*. She had adopted Mme Saturnin's attitude and did not want to be used as a *servant* to strangers.

11 February 1855

Mme Saturnin returned to town only last night. She gave orders here as if she alone were in charge, deciding what to do about food, charcoal, etc. as if all of this belonged to her; and Saturnin, like a fool, approved of everything she did. I must admit that I am far from satisfied.

12 February 1855

Mlle Cécé came back last night, and it looks as if she will stay here at 10 francs a month. I have told Saturnin that since his wife does not want to go along with my views, I will have to separate from them. I said that once his affairs were straightened out I would take care of part of his debts and that what he owed me would eventually go to Théodorine and Théodore, but that I wanted to receive the interest until I die. Beginning on the first of March, I said, I would pay all my household expenses and would keep his two children at my expense if he were to leave them with me. If he did not want to do this he could take them; I would make that sacrifice without complaining. The poor devil did not know what to say to all this. I feel sorry for him, but I cannot put myself under the domination of a young woman of 22.

[After the departure of Saturnin and his wife, Dessalles is at loose ends.]

23 February 1855

On the 18th, after my morning coffee, I went down to town; I heard the high mass there and then went to Numa Littée's and played a hand of *brelan*. Monday and Tuesday after the seven-o'clock mass I went back to Numa's where we played *brelan* until very late. So I slept at this relative's house three nights. I had my dinner brought there, but I do wonder if he enjoyed this visit. On Ash Wednesday after mass I dined at Saturnin's house, then I stopped by at Numa's, and at four o'clock arrived at Ferbeaux's, where I spent the night. On Thursday Dr. Chauvet came by for me, and we went to Roland Dégat's house, where I spent the day. At six I was back in town, where I had a good night. Mme Saturnin is still dreadfully thin and in a foul mood.

3 March 1855

Madame de Valmenier sent me a private contract signed by my children, by which they are giving me a food pension of 3,600 francs per year, but on condition that I leave the Caféière. This is not what I had asked for; I wanted a contract for a pension that would allow me to make immediate confiscations in case I was not paid. I sent this piece back to my daughter with a letter that she can pass on to her brothers and sisters.[10]

Saturnin tells me that his mother-in-law and sister-in-law would like to buy his houses in Gros-Morne. This would be a good deal for him, for it would allow him to pay his debts and recover his peace of mind. Mme Saturnin has begun to send back my things, but they are in sad shape.

[Between March 5 and April 15, Dessalles keeps a record of his household expenses in the margins of his diary. Here, for example, are his expenses for 19 March (in francs).]

Beef shank	.80
Tapioca meal	.30
Butter	.50
Laundry starch	.30
Bananas	.45
Onions	.05
Candle	.20
Laundry bluing and matches	.15
	2.75
Expenses in town [probably gambling]	6.20
3 pairs of shoes for Théodorine	11.50
6 dresses	12.00
4 small kerchiefs	10.00
1 parasol	4.10
3 outfits for Théodore	7.00
1 pair shoes for the same	4.00
Given for candy	.60
Pomade, velvet, comb (Théodorine)	4.25

16 March 1855

Saturnin arrived at eleven. He told me that he has bought all of M. Pra's land, including the forge, for 6,000 francs (2,000 in cash, as much a year from now, and 1,000 a year interest-free). This is not a bad bargain, but it aggravates his shortage of money. He believed that I was going to help him, but I made it

10. We do not know if Dessalles received such a contract.

clear to him that I did not want to become involved in this affair in any way. He went back to town this evening with his little Théodorine.[11] I intend to go to town tomorrow so that I can be present for the celebration on Sunday of the Church's new dogma of the Immaculate Conception.

10 April 1855

I am having some bad nights; I am being devoured by ants and terribly fatigued from the Lenten food.

Yesterday I had the honor of being insulted in my own home by Mme Saturnin, who came to treat me to a thousand impertinences: "We are living in a different age," she told me. "You do not have the right to lord it over anybody." And then she wanted to defend all the people who have wronged me. Unable to restrain myself, I told her to go and have herself f——ed. I am determined never to set foot in her house again unless she repairs her insolence by making a public apology. Saturnin is a fool who is setting himself up for terrible trouble.

12 April 1855

Last night little Théodorine said to me, "Godfather, you have insulted my mommy." "Who told you that?" I asked. "Mommy did, and she was crying."[12]

I confess that I was thunderstruck. How can a mother reveal such things to a child of three? I must get away from all these people and even sacrifice these little children whose hearts I had hoped to shape. It will hurt me very much, but it would not be right to insist on staying close to the children of a woman who has wronged me in so many ways.

21 April 1855

Little Théodorine had not been well for a few days; when she developed a fever, I asked Saturnin to take her to her mother. So he wrote to his wife, telling her that his daughter had a slight fever and that he would bring her to her house this evening. At noon—we are at table—the mother bursts into the room like a fury. I get up from the table to go tell Saturnin, who then loudly scolds her and tells her to behave herself. All upset at losing the little girl, I throw myself on my bed where I have a fit of nerves. Saturnin and his wife bring the child to me; I take her into my arms and, in order to avoid speaking to the

11. Saturnin's children are constantly shuttled back and forth between the town and the Caféière.

12. This little dialogue is in Creole in the text.

mother, I turn to Saturnin, asking him to leave with his child. I will never again speak to this woman as long as she does not make up for her wrongs. Finally they left. I spent an hour at the feet of my Christ, and now I am more calm. . . .

9 May 1855

Mme Saturnin came to the Caféière accompanied by Chéry Magloire,[13] who spoke for her, for she kept her mouth tightly shut. She is back in my good graces, but she will no longer take care of my household, which she neglected too much.

9 June 1855

Saturnin returned Saturday. . . . He sold [to his sister-in-law] the houses at Gros-Morne for 5,000 francs: 1,500 in cash and 1,100 that he owes to Mme Cognet to be paid in his stead, 1,200 in 1856, and the remaining 1,200 francs in 1857.

27 June 1855

I had a visit from Agricole, and his son Eugène is with me right now. Saturnin is very busy readying the house for the party that is to take place here the day after tomorrow, on my name day. Without being really ill, I feel out of sorts. Théodore had a fever all last night.

4 July 1855

On June 29 [Dessalles's name day] I had here M. Degage [de Gage?] and his children's tutor, M. Cardin—a big eater and intrepid card player—Dégat father and son, Harold de la Salle, Jules and Numa Littée, Dr. Chauvet, Michaud, and M. Lalung. We ate a lot and left the dinner table only to sit down at the card table. I lost three doublons and a quarter, M. Chauvet lost five. As usual, nobody kept track of the money.

14 July 1855

Yesterday I received a letter from d'Oysonville [childhood friend in France], who sends me 1,000 francs. What a precious friend! This little sum helps me

---

13. Chéry Magloire intervenes again; one wonders about the origins of his friendship, indeed his influence, with Dessalles [HF and LE].

out a great deal. I am proposing to sell my beautiful table service to Mme de Valmenier for four doublons. Three she would keep for herself as board for the two months I spent at her house, and one is for the hat I gave to Anna to wear when she makes her wedding visits.

4 August 1855

My life is so sad and monotonous that I have nothing to write into this notebook. I will go to town this evening. I have a cold. . . .

23 August 1855

During my absence a batch of coconuts was stolen from the Caféière, but the thieves were caught red-handed. I was about to hand them over to the law when their mothers came to ask for an arrangement. So I indentured these two young men for a term of five years, and they will work with Saturnin. . . .

19 September 1855

Last night we experienced a bloody scene that was quite upsetting to me. Saturnin, who had left with his son at two o'clock, stayed in town. He sent me the young farm worker Galibi with a basket of provisions. At seven o'clock this young negro arrived at the Caféière all covered with blood and explained to us that when he was halfway here he ran into three men, one of whom was the colored man Saint-Prix, an indentured worker of the Caféière [who was working off the theft of some coconuts]. The latter fell on him and beat him with his rod and his machete, so that he was unable to defend himself. He put down his basket; when he was assaulted by three individuals, he realized that he could not possibly stand up to them. So he ran away as fast as he could and arrived at the Caféière dripping with blood. I sent for his father, who took him to town to make his statement [to the police]. This morning they came back here with Saturnin, to whom I dictated an official complaint and a letter to the mayor which Galibi himself, who was given a horse, will take to M. Bonneville. Saint-Prix, who was arrested right after the incident, has been set free. All the evidence about this ambush will be sent to the authorities, which will probably issue an arrest warrant. Saint-Prix's mother came at eight in the evening to take her son home. She was ready to leave him here, but Saturnin said to take him away and bring him back early in the morning. This woman, who clearly gives bad advice to her son, claims that he is not indentured at all and wants him to be free to do as she sees fit. She spouted a great deal of nonsense.[14]

14. The background of this affair is not altogether clear. At the time of slavery, fruit trees

20 October 1855

Inexplicable things are going on in my home. Mme Saturnin and Cécé, after they have quarreled and decried each other, seem to get along quite well, except for occasional little tiffs. Jealousy is the main motive for these discussions. I do not know if Saturnin realized how much trouble he was creating for himself when he took advantage of this girl, but it seems certain that love plays the biggest role in everything that goes on here. On the 16th, as I was before my Christ meditating on his Passion, I was distracted by a conversation between the two women; they were discussing what they had said to the curé in confession, and I understood what they were talking about. Mlle Cécé said that the priest had asked her if she loved Saturnin and that she had replied yes. Tired of their jabbering, I said my prayer and went to bed.

On the evening of the 17th someone said at prayer time that it would be dangerous for Saturnin to leave the house during the night. I asked where this rumor came from and was told that Saint-Prix and his father are roaming about in the prairies [*savanes*] at night, looking for vengeance. Then Mlle Cécé said that "someone" had urged her to warn Saturnin never to be in an open space at night, but she refused to name the person. Saturnin pointed out to her that this matter deserved to be brought to the mayor's attention. Cécé was furious and said that she would deny everything, not name anybody, and in fact not even go to the authorities. So I told her that if she did not go, the gendarmes would come to get her and that the law always has means to make people obey. This made the girl even more furious, and she talked on and on until midnight. . . . This is what I am condemned to hear every day. What a life!

[An added problem arises when Dessalles's widowed daughter Mme de Valmenier has to leave her failing plantation, which is now managed by her brother-in-law. For a time it looks as if she will have to come live with her father.]

22 November 1855

. . . My daughter is to be pitied. Yet in all that is happening now, I recognize the hand of God. I am avenged, although I certainly did not ask for it, for my heart is pure and my feelings for my children are always tender and affectionate. Nonetheless, the memory of all they made me suffer comes back to me in spite of myself, and I cannot help seeing the hand of Heaven at work in the bad

---

planted by slaves were their hereditary property, and they sometimes even sold their fruit to the masters. Trees thus had a special meaning. We should therefore know just who had planted these coconut trees. But surely a better way could have been found to handle this affair [HF and LE].

state of their affairs and all their other troubles. God of kindness, have mercy upon them and deign to make them prosper!

1856

[Early in the year, Dessalles goes to spend some time with Mme de Valmenier at Rivière-Monsieur.]

24 January 1856

. . . My daughter lives very economically. Her brother-in-law's dealings with her are most ungenerous and unfair. Unfortunately I can do nothing about it. We hear that M. Languavant-Cléret [Antoinette's husband] will soon be here; perhaps he can do something for Mme de Valmenier, who is still determined to come to live at the Caféière. But her motives for doing so are absurd, and it is not difficult to see that her real reasons have to do with a lot of gossip and her fear that I am becoming more and more attached to Saturnin and his children. They are offering me 4,000 francs in exchange for giving up all my reserves. If I had a good contract guaranteeing me this pension, I would accept these conditions. When they see that I am giving up the Caféière, perhaps they will decide to rent it to Mme de Valmenier.

In order not to be a burden to my children, I give [my daughter] two francs a day.

13 March 1856

I went to Saint-Pierre on the ninth. When I arrived at Mlle Anaïs's [the boarding house where he usually stays] at six o'clock it was rather dark. Saturnin's two children were not there, which quite upset me. I sat down in such a way as not to be seen right away. Théodorine, who arrived first, was placed on my lap. She looked at me, and when she recognized me, she put her little arms around my neck and broke into tears. She was very very happy, and I could hardly stop her tears. Théodore recognized me right away; he was startled, but he jumped on me, crying, "It's my godfather!"

I must admit that I was deeply moved when I saw these little beings who allowed me to escape from ennui during my long isolation at the Caféière. My children, who rejected me by their ungenerous behavior—which I would like to forget—may be displeased with my affection for these children, but they will never destroy it. My situation no longer permits me to do anything for them, but as long as I live in Martinique I will share with them what I have.

[In April Dessalles's daughters Antoinette, Louise, and Emilie come for a very brief visit to Martinique, apparently at government expense. Clearly their purpose is to straighten out the family's finances. The daughters' suggestion that their father move to France falls on deaf ears: "They already talked to me about going to France. But my mind is made up. As long as I can think for myself, I will remain independent and I will live in my own place (chez moi)."]

13 April 1856

My children spent all week talking business. Languavant went to see Marchet and to Sainte-Marie; there is nothing but secrecy and mystery. Calixte—who used to tell me everything—no longer says anything. Even Léon Pelet [Mme de Valmenier's new son-in-law] is involved in these shenanigans, for which I was prepared. It is a comedy that would make me laugh if I did not know that I am the one they are trying to dupe and to lull to sleep with false caresses. It would be easy to be taken in by my daughters, but I know them only too well. They want to take me along . . . but like a codfish or a ham that is dragged along behind the boat until all its salt has leached out. I will keep silent until the end; I want to see the dénouement of this comedy.

18 April 1856

I spent twenty-four hours at Saint-Pierre. Mme Saturnin is back in my good graces, and I have every reason to believe that she will never lose them again. When I returned to Fort-de-France I found the whole family in tears. Languavant has persuaded Mme de Valmenier to follow her sisters to France. . . . My pension contract for 4,000 francs was given to me; if I am paid punctually I will have no complaints.

[On 20 April the daughters sail for France; Dessalles accompanies them as far as Guadeloupe, where he spends a month visiting old friends and distant relatives whom he has known there as a young man. On his return to Martinique he moves into a rented house at Saint-Pierre, since under the new contract with his children, he has had to move out of the Caféière. He is obviously bored, plays a great deal of cards, and does not feel very well. In June he begins a general confession.]

19 June 1856

Last Monday I began a general confession with Abbé Girardon. Two more sessions, and I hope I will be worthy of preparing to receive the Body of our Lord Jesus Christ. Nothing is more painful and fatiguing than a general confession; it is a dreadful thing to have to go through a long life filled with sins and crimes. This is the last general confession I will make, for God is now in my heart. He sees how frankly I admit my transgressions and how much I suffer for having offended Him. Fully confident in His mercy, I shall serve Him with zeal and courage to my last moment.

[At this point the diary becomes more and more desultory, and seems to stop altogether in August 1856. In a brief epilogue, the French editors note that in late 1856 Dessalles's daughters came for another brief visit and, this time, persuaded him to go to France with them. Arriving at Brest in early 1857, he suffered intensely from the cold weather, did not dress properly, and soon became ill. After a brief illness he died of a "chest congestion" on 5 March 1857. His body was taken to Paris and deposited in the presence of his two sons in the Père Lachaise cemetery in the same vault where he had buried his wife eleven years earlier.]

Index

Library of Congress Cataloging-in-Publication Data

Dessalles, Pierre, 1785–1857.
   [Vie d'un colon à la Martinique au XIXème siècle. English.
Selections]
   Sugar and slavery, family and race : the letters and diary of
Pierre Dessalles, planter in Martinique, 1808–1856 / edited and
translated by Elborg Forster and Robert Forster.
      p.   cm. — (Johns Hopkins studies in Atlantic history and
culture)
   Includes index.
   ISBN 0-8018-5153-X (alk. paper). — ISBN 0-8018-5154-8
(pbk. : alk. paper)
   1. Martinique—Social life and customs.   2. Dessalles, Pierre,
1785–1857.   3. Martinique—Biography.   I. Forster, Elborg,
1931–   .   II. Forster, Robert, 1926–   .   III. Title.   IV. Series.
F2081.D4813   1996
972.98'2—dc20   95-34519
                                                          CIP